CONTENTS

Verses 26–33 show how gifts are to be used in the local church.

Verses 34–40 show how women are to use their gifts in the local church.

Verses 1–4 deal with the resurrection of Christ.

Verses 5–11 present a list of those who witnessed the resurrection of Christ.

Verses 12–19 present the necessity of the resurrection of Christ.

Verses 20–23 give the order of the resurrection of Christ and believers.

Verses 24–28 deal with the millennial reign of Christ on this earth.

Verses 29–34 are about the resurrection of believers.

Verses 35–50 major on the certainty of the resurrection of believers.

Verses 51–53 deal with the marriage supper of the Lamb.

Verses 54–58 show how the rapture of the church shall occur.

Verse 59 emphasizes steadfastness.

Verses 1–12 are about Christians supporting saints in Jerusalem.

Verses 13–18 teach that Christians should do everything with love.

Verses 19–24 present Paul's benediction and farewell.

LAUNCHING

We don't just exist with a temporary life that eventually dies and goes back to dust. We have a Saviour who gives us hope and security of a better life beyond this life. Where does your hope and security lie? Some find hope and security in a job, some in savings, some in material possessions, some in wealth, some in pleasures, and some even find hope and security in relationships with family and friends. I say again, where does your hope and security lie?

King David nailed down his hope and security with the words he spoke in 2 Samuel 22:3,

> The God of my rock; in him will I trust: he is my shield, and the horn of my salvation, my high tower, my refuge, my Saviour; and saves me from violence.

John H. Sommis, writer of the song "Trust and Obey," found his hope and security in obeying the Lord. Notice how his song goes:

> Not a burden we bear, nor a sorrow we share, but our toils he does richly repay; not a grief or a lost, not a frown or a cross, but is blessed if we trust and obey.
>
> Life itself offers no hope or security, but we find it within the Word of God. Surprisingly, however, the Bible itself does not bring hope and security. Most people have a Bible lying on a shelf or coffee tables, but they never open them nor read them. A Bible lying on a shelf or a coffee

table will never bring hope and security. They must be read. Therefore the words within the Bible does bring hope and security. Within the pages of the Bible we can find God's plan of salvation and how we should live after we receive Him as our personal Saviour. That is what 1 Corinthians is all about. There we find hope and security by knowing why Jesus suffered and died on the cross, by knowing we are born again, by knowing how God wants us to live after we are saved.

This book is a verse-by-verse commentary on 1 Corinthians. So the theme of this book is about finding God's plan of salvation and how to please God in our daily walk with Him. So let's examine 1 Corinthians from God's perspective. But before we do that, we must consider two issues.

This covers two important issues: the method of interpreting Scriptures and fundamentalism. These issues are the foundation upon which this book is written. If you don't understand these two issues, you may not understand this book. So it is of the utmost importance you read and remember these two issues.

First, we must settle the issue of what method to use in interpreting Scriptures. There are only two methods that is used in interpreting Scriptures: the literal method and the allegorical, symbolic method.

Let's consider the literal method first. The literal method of interpreting Scriptures is that Scriptures have a literal meaning. The Scriptures say what they mean and mean what they say. Interpreting Scriptures literally means they do not have an allegorical symbolic meaning. If there is any symbolism implied in Scriptures, the Scriptures themselves explains the symbolism and gives the literal meaning. So by using the literal method in interpreting Scripture, this book stays as close to the original manuscript as possible. This book treats Scriptures as literal. The writer of this book is a literalist!

Next, let's consider the allegorical/symbolic method of interpreting Scripture. This method of interpreting Scriptures is that Scriptures mean something other than what is written, and it is left up to the reader to find that hidden meaning. In other words, Scriptures have an alternate meaning. It says one thing but means another.

Some allegorical symbolic interpreters believe a few Scriptures are literal, but most are symbolic. If that is true, then what part is literal and what part is symbolic? The answer, of course, is, the reader decides, not the Scriptures themselves. By interpreting Scriptures allegorically, people can make it say anything they want them to say. For example, if you say the six days of creation (as recorded in Genesis 1) is six twenty-four-hour days, the allegorical interpreter will say the six days of creation means six long periods of time—like millions of years. Many religions hold that view because they believe science has proven evolution to be true. So they change the Scriptures to fit their theory.

Symbolic allegorical interpreters also hold the theist evolutionary theory. *Theist* means God, and *evolution* means everything came into existence through natural processers—thus, God evolution. By treating Scripture that way, theistic evolutionist gives credibility to evolution. God and evolution do not fit together by any stretch of the imagination.

It's interesting to note if evolution is true, there is no room for Adam. In fact, allegorical interpreters believe there was no such person as Adam. They believe he never existed. They believe Adam and Eve represents good and evil and embrace the idea that good and evil are just two sides of the same reality.

If Adam did not exist, who is to say we exist? Who is to say Christ exists? We are not just a figment of own imagination. If you don't think you exist, just hit your finger with a hammer.

I can understand why the allegorical interpreters deny the existence of Adam. They believe God created a world in the beginning but stepped away from it and let evolution take its course over billions of years. During that time, everything came into existence. So a person named Adam would not fit into their scheme of things.

Furthermore, they believe Adam did not exist because he is not part of the Gospel. They embrace that theory because they believe everyone is born innately good. We are not born good. We are born with a sinful nature. Therefore, Adam has to be a fundamental part of the Gospel. We inherit a sinful nature from him. We are born sinners because Adam sinned. Romans 5:12 says,

> Wherefore as by one man (Adam), sin entered into the world, and death (comes) by sin; so, death passed upon all men, for all have sinned.

First Corinthians 15:22 says this:

> For as in Adam all die, even so in Christ all shall be made alive.

The effect of Adam's sin is placed upon all God's creation. It is written in Romans 8:21–22.

> Because the creation itself will also be delivered from the bondage of corruption. For we know the whole creation groans and labors with birth pains until now [to be delivered from corruption].

So I write this book from a literal perspective. Any other method would be senseless and stupid. I'm not saying people are stupid, but the method some people use in interpreting Scripture is stupid. I have settled this issue in my own heart, and I am not about to change.

There is another important issue we need to consider that is related to the method of interpreting Scripture. That issue is fundamentalism. Some things are fundamental to salvation as well as being fundamental to rightly interpreting Scriptures.

Allow me to explain fundamentalism. *Fundamentalism*, according to the dictionary, is "a religious movement characterized by a strict belief in the literal interpretation of Scriptures." I plead guilty to believing that. Furthermore, allow me to give an illustration of what fundamentalism is to drive home the importance of fundamentalism. I will use an automobile for this illustration. An automobile has some fundamentals that are absolutely essential to make it run. Things such as a gas tank with gas in it, a motor, a battery, wheels, a transmission, a steering wheel, and some other necessary items. Those things are fundamental for the automobile to run. However, some other items are not fundamental for a car to run, such as a radio, windshield wipers, headlights, rearview mirror, a spare tire, and many other items.

Similarly, the Bible has some absolute fundamentals that you must believe, and embrace, before you can be born again. You must believe the fundamentals such as the literal interpretation of the Bible, the virgin birth of Christ, the sinless life of Christ, the atoning blood of Christ, the death, the burial, the resurrection of Christ, the coming again of Christ, the fall of Adam, the sinfulness of mankind, the new birth, the inspiration of Scripture, and some others in order to be born again.

Introduction to Corinth

The following introduction gives insight into the city of Corinth, the people of Corinth, the church of Corinth, and why Paul wrote 1 and 2 Corinthians.

If you could see what Paul saw when he walked into Corinth, it would open your eyes to things you have never seen before. Just imagine taking a tour of Corinth with Paul.

In the following pages, I will introduce you to the city of Corinth, to the attractions, the people, and to the things Paul and his entourage encountered when they walked into Corinth. Furthermore, you will see why Corinth was such a poplar city in Paul's day. You will learn about their religion, their culture, and their beliefs. You will learn about the Corinthian people's night life and exotic places. You will look in on one of their perverted temple worship services and see what went on there. You will also visit a synagogue worship service and listen to Paul preach." Stay with me because you will learn a lot. Consider the following nine points.

First, consider the people and the city of Corinth. The people of Corinth were very wealthy. Corinth was a thriving commercial city, and many ships frequently visited their ports with the purpose of buying and selling goods. Ships consistently traveled to and from Corinth. The city of Corinth had a population of about five hundred thousand and was a growing city. It was no small city in Paul's day. The people of Corinth were mostly immigrants from all over the knowing world. Many people made Corinth their home after visiting the city. Over time the ancient city of Corinth dwindled down to just a few inhabitants and eventually died and turned to rubble. A new city was built about three miles from the ancient city. It, too, ceased to exist after being destroyed by an earthquake.

Second, consider Paul's arrival in Corinth. Paul's first visit to Corinth was around AD 51, about twenty to thirty years after the death, burial, and resurrection of Christ. Acts 18:1 said,

> After these days Paul departed from Athens and
> came to Corinth.

If you would follow the missionary journeys of Paul, from the day of his conversion until the time he entered Corinth, you will find he visited Corinth about twenty to thirty years after the resurrection of Christ. Remember that time period because it is very important. Paul's letters to the church of Corinth was closer to the time of Christ's death and resurrection than any other portion of Scripture in the New Testament. You would think Matthew, Mark, Luke, and John would be closer to the time of Christ's death, but they weren't. Paul's epistles were. We will look at that in deeper detail later.

When Paul arrived in Corinth, he went to a Jewish synagogue and preached that Jesus Christ was the way of salvation. The Jews and the synagogue members had never heard the name Jesus before. That caused an uproar when Paul preached that Jesus was the way of salvation.

Allow me to sidetrack here and add something that needs to be said. I think members of all churches, regardless of their denominations, need to hear the Gospel of Jesus Christ like the religious people in the synagogues where Paul preached. God's preachers should not confine their messages to their group only. The world needs to hear the Gospel. In fact, John 3:16 states,

> God so loved the world, that He gave his only begotten Son, that whosoever believeth in Him should not perish, but have everlasting life.

How can the world believe in Him if they do not have someone to preach the Gospel to them? Preachers whom God calls are to take the Gospel to the world in every way possible. When preachers restrict their messages to their group only, they hinder God from using their ministry to accomplish more. Acts 1:8 states,

> You shall receive power, after that the Holy Ghost is come upon you: and ye shall be witnesses unto me both in Jerusalem, and in Judaea, and in Samaria, and unto the uttermost parts of the earth.

Think about this: If Paul had confined his messages to the Jews at Jerusalem only, we would not have the writings of Paul. We are to take the message of salvation to the world, and that portion of the world begins with our communities.

Third, notice how Paul started the church in Corinth. He preached in a synagogue when he arrived in Corinth, and he preached that Jesus Christ was the way of salvation. His preaching didn't set so well with some of the synagogue leaders and members. Many did not like Paul's preaching, but others did and accepted it. For example,

Crispus, the chief ruler of the synagogue, his family, and many others believed on Jesus Christ and were born again. Acts 18:8 said,

> Crispus, the chief ruler of the synagogue, believed on the Lord with all in his house; and many of the Corinthians hearing believed, and were baptized.

That is, they were baptized into the family of God by the Holy Spirit. They were born again. Paul, Crispus, his family, and several other members, including Aquila and Priscilla, were asked to leave the synagogue.

By the way, Aquila and Pricilla had arrived in Corinth from Rome. Acts 18:1–3 said,

> Paul departed from Athens and came to Corinth and found a certain Jew named Aquila, born in Pontus, lately came from Italy, with his wife Priscilla; because Claudius had commanded all Jews to depart from Rome, and [they] came unto them. And because he [Paul] was of the same craft [a tent maker], he made his abode with them.

Evidently, when Aquila and Pricilla moved to Corinth, they joined the synagogue where they met Paul and were converted to Christianity by hearing him preach. Aquila and Pricilla had a close relationship with Paul from that day onward.

Fourth, notice Paul's reaction as recorded in Acts 18:6 when he was dismissed from the synagogue.

> [He] shook his raiment [clothes] and said unto them [those who dismissed him from the synagogue], your blood be upon your own heads; I am clean; from henceforth I will go unto the gentiles.

Paul and his followers moved to a Gentile's house beside the synagogue. A man by the name of Justus owned the house. Justus was Paul's first Gentile convert. Acts 18:7 said,

> And he [Paul] departed thence, and entered into a certain man's house, named Justus, one who worshiped God, whose house joined hard [was connected] to the synagogue.

Paul evidently introduced him to Christ. So Paul started the church in his house with Aquila and Pricilla and those who were dismissed from the synagogue.

Fifth, consider the location of Corinth. Your Bible probably has maps that shows Paul's missionary journeys. With these maps you can trace Paul's second missionary journey that took him through Corinth. This was his first visit to Corinth. By the way, Paul made three visits to Corinth.

You can see from your maps Corinth was located between Northern Greece and Southern Greece. There was a four-mile strip of land near Corinth that separated the Mediterranean Sea from the Aegean Sea. It's interesting to note that Nero started digging a channel to connect these two seas, but it was not completed until the nineteenth century.

Corinth was the capital city of Achaia of Southern Greece and the crossroad to the ancient world. There were several seaports located on the Mediterranean seaside and several seaports on the Aegean seaside. Ships brought cargo into these ports on a daily bases, and their crews carried most of the cargo across the four-mile strip of land to other vessels to be transported to other parts of the world. It was more convenient to move cargo across the land than to sail the long distance down the coast and back up to the other ports. So this gives some insight into Corinth's location.

Sixth, consider the problems Paul faced when he went to Corinth. When ships visited Corinth, they brought cargo for the purpose of selling or trading. In addition to that, sailors brought vice of all kinds to Corinth. Paul had to face that. They brought their idol gods. One was named Apollo, the male goddess of the sun, art, and music. Another idol was Aphrodite, the female goddess of beauty, love, sex, and fertility. As a result of that, Corinth established many pagan temples that were manned by prostitute women and prostitute men. These leaders worshipped these idol gods and invited others to worship them too. Most worshippers were men who worshipped Aphrodite, the goddess of beauty, love, sex, and fertility. Men joined their worship because prostitutes were used in their religious rituals, and most men participated. You can imagine how wicked they were.

Corinth was considered the most wicked city in the Roman empire. The Romans didn't object to that so long as they made them money. Corinth was favored by sailors and visitors alike because of the pagan temples. Many Bible teachers refer to Corinth as the city of sin, and rightly so because of their wicked lifestyle. Corinth was more wicked than Pampa. In fact, Pampa pales into insignificance when it comes to comparing their wickedness to that of Corinth. We can't overstate the sexual perversion and wickedness of Corinth. Paul had to face that when he arrived in Corinth. That is why he said in 1 Corinthians 2:3,

> I was with you in weakness, and in fear, and in
> much trembling.

Paul feared for his life. It didn't take him long to figure out how wicked they were. He preached the Gospel nonetheless, which highly disturbed them. It threatened their way of life. Paul faced a tremendous problem preaching to the Corinthian people.

Seventh, Paul wrote a personal letter from Southern Greece to the church of Corinthian following his first visit there. We don't have that letter because it was specifically designed for the Corinthian church only. However, we have an idea of what the letter was about, because Paul covered many problems in his other two epistles. First and Second Corinthians perhaps covered what the personal letter was about.

Eighth, Paul's first visit to Corinth lasted about eighteen months. When he left Corinth, he took Aquila and Pricilla with him and went to Southern Greece where he met Sosthenes. I will say more about Sosthenes later when I begin the verse-by-verse study of 1 Corinthians.

After Paul departed from Corinth, some church members slid back into their old ways. Around AD 54 Paul heard disturbing news about the Corinthian church. Notice 1 Corinthians 1:11,

> For it hath been declared unto me of you, my brethren, by the house of Chloe that there are contentions among you.

The word *contentions* means "disagreements, disputes, and divisions." Immorality had crept into the church. Their contentious acts polluted their church doctrine and new life in Christ. They moved away from their original commitment and tolerated sexual perversion in the church like the pagan temples did. First Corinthians 5:1 said,

> It is reported commonly that there are fornications among you, and such fornication is not so much as named among the gentiles that one should have his father's wife.

What a despicable wicked sin. A man was living with and committing immoral sexual acts with his father's wife—probably his stepmother. That is exactly what the church of Corinth got involved in. The church left Jesus (their first love) and got involved in immoral acts.

Paul received the letter (which is now lost) from their church asking him to settle a specific problem they were having. Paul said in 1 Corinthians 7:1,

> Now concerning the things whereof you wrote to me.

After Paul left, some moved in and took over the church and proclaimed themselves to be apostles. They wanted to be the leaders and rulers of the church. The church congregation was mainly made up of Gentiles who had been converted to Christianity; therefore, they had very little prior experience in Jewish teaching of the Old Testament and nothing in writings from New Testament writers. The direction in which the Corinthian church would go depended on whose leadership they would follow—Paul's leadership or of the ones who claimed to be apostles.

Paul knew true doctrine was essential to the survival of the church. Notice the statement about true doctrine in 2 Timothy 3:16,

> All Scripture is given by inspiration of God, and is profitable for DOCTRINE, for REPROOF, for CORRECTION, and for INSTRUCTION in righteousness.

This Scripture verse is simply saying a good leader must preach doctrine, reprove and correct, and instruct in righteousness. After all, it is preaching God's Word that leads people to faith in Jesus Christ. Romans 10:17 said,

> Faith cometh by hearing and hearing by the Word of God.

Paul wrote what we call 1 and 2 Corinthians to address the problems they had in the church and about things that were destroying their faith in Christ.

First Corinthians was written from Ephesus around AD 58 at the close of Paul's three-year residence in Corinth. First Corinthians is the letter we hold in our hands. Just think: We hold in our hands a letter written to the Corinthian church two thousand years ago. Of course, we don't have the original manuscript, but we do have an accurate and reliable translation in the KJV.

Ninth, consider the theme of 1 Corinthians. First, the theme of 1 Corinthians shows that salvation is found in Jesus Christ and Jesus

Christ alone. Secondly, it shows us how to live after we are converted. Both 1 and 2 Corinthians emphasize that salvation is found in Jesus Christ. That is why God's plan of salvation is presented at the beginning of 1 Corinthians.

It takes the Holy Spirit to rightly interpret 1 Corinthians, or any other book of the Bible for that matter. Only Christians have the Holy Spirit dwelling in them. Without the aid of the Holy Spirit, the Bible is just another book. It doesn't make sense at all without the interpreter—the Holy Spirit. None of the Bible makes sense without the Holy Spirit interpreting it. The Holy Spirit is the interpreter of Scripture.

Chapter 1

Has Four Subjects

Verse 1 introduces Paul as an apostle and author of 1 Corinthians.
Verse 2 presents God's plan of salvation.
Verse 3 presents God's grace and God's peace.
Verse 4 covers the subject of Thanksgiving.
Verses 5–9 present the way to be enriched in Christ.
Verses 10–17 show how splits in the local church occur.
First Corinthians 1:14–17 deals with Baptism.
Verses 18–31 deal with those who call preaching foolishness.

The first subject in the outline is found in 1 Corinthians 1:1, and it deals with Paul as an apostle and author of 1 Corinthians.

Verse 1 introduces Paul.

Paul called to be an apostle by Jesus Christ through the will of God, and Sosthenes our brother.

Both 1 and 2 Corinthians open with words about Paul being an apostle. Paul was called to be an apostle by Jesus Christ through the will of God. Jesus called Paul and gave him a special job. Acts 9:6 and

21

15 state that Paul's call to be an apostle happened immediately after his conversion. Paul said to Jesus,

> Lord what wilt thou have me to do? And the Lord said unto him [you are], a chosen vessel unto Me to bear My name before the Gentiles, and kings, and the children of Israel.

Notice the three groups Paul was called to evangelize: Gentiles, kings, and Israel. He accomplished that over his lifetime. His voice lives on.

Paul reminded the Corinthian church of the source of his calling. Romans 11:13 said,

> I speak to you Gentiles in-as-much as I am the apostle of the Gentiles, I magnify mine office.

Paul was an apostle to the Gentiles, but he often preached to the Jews and to those in the upper echelon of life—even kings.

Many believe Paul was the twelfth apostle that took the place of Judas, who hanged himself. The following information about Paul being the twelfth apostle is not fundamental to salvation; nevertheless many believe Paul was the twelfth apostle to take the place of Judas. This is a fascinating thought to consider.

The eleven remaining apostles chose Matthias to take the place of Judas. However, there are several reasons that some believe Paul was chosen by God to be the twelfth apostle.

First, apostles had a unique calling and title. Man cannot assign this calling to himself or to others. Only God through Jesus Christ can call a person to be an apostle. Since that is true, did Peter overstep his authority when he suggested they choose Matthias to take the place of Judas? Many Bible teachers suggest he did.

Second, they assembled with Peter to "cast lots" (a form of chance) to determine who should take the place of Judas. Acts 1:23 states,

> They appointed two, Joseph, called Barsabas, who was surnamed Justus, and Matthias.

Acts 1:26 states,

> And they gave forth their lots, and the lots fell on Matthias; and he was numbered with the eleven apostles.

Each candidate had a 50 percent chance of winning. It happened that Matthias won.

Third, perhaps it occurred to the remaining eleven apostles that Jesus had called twelve and it was their duty to choose someone to take the place of Judas. The Scriptures do not explain why they chose to do it the way they did. Even though they prayed and sought God's advice, God nor Christ was not mentioned in influencing them in their decision.

Fourth, Matthias was never heard of again. Signs and wonders always followed apostles to authenticate their appointment. Nowhere does the Bible record Matthias performing signs to authenticate his apostleship. Perhaps he did, but it's not recorded in the Bible.

No one knows for sure whether Paul or Matthias was chosen to take the place of Judas. To be frank, it doesn't make that much difference. Only God knows for sure, and if you want to know, you will have to wait until you get to heaven and ask Matthias or Paul. Bible scholars can make a case for either, but it doesn't matter because neither belief is essential to salvation. This was just an intriguing thought. However, we do know from Scripture Paul was called to be an apostle to the Gentiles.

God gave signs to authenticate Paul's calling to be an apostle. Second Corinthians 12:12 said,

> Truly the signs of an apostle were wrought among you in all patience, in signs, and wonders, and mighty deeds.

Acts 16:16–23 tells about one sign Paul performed to authenticate his apostleship. He was cast into prison for it. Acts 16:16–23 says,

> And it came to pass, as we [Paul and Silas] went to prayer, that a certain damsel possessed with a spirit of divination [fortune-telling] met us, which brought her masters much gain by soothsaying. The same followed Paul and us and cried, saying: These men are the servants of the Most-High God, which show unto us the way of salvation. And this she did for many days. But Paul, being grieved, turned and said to the spirit, I command thee, in the name of Jesus Christ come out of her. And he came out the same hour.

On the surface this woman looked as though she was doing a great deed, but keep in mind, she was possessed with a demon and was a fortune-teller. Demons and fortune-tellers don't promote the cause of Christ. She had a hidden motive in mind. The demon in her was working to silence Paul's ministry in Philippi.

An illustration may explain this better. Let's say you were in an Islamic country secretly leading Muslims to Christ. As you walked through the streets looking for opportunities to tell Muslims about Jesus, a woman followed you day after day saying, "This person is a servant of the Most High God who proclaims to us the way of salvation." Don't you agree the Islamic government would silence you? That was what concerned Paul when he traveled through the streets of Philippi. I personally believe the woman had a sneered lip, and her comment sounded like she was asking a question. That is why Paul, through Jesus Christ, cast the demon out of her. However, it was too late. The woman accomplished what she had set out to accomplish—silence Paul. Let's pick up the story in Acts 16:19 and read through verse 24,

> And when her masters saw that the hope of their gain was gone, they caught Paul and Silas, and drew them into the marketplace unto the rulers, and brought them to the magistrates, saying, these men, being Jews do exceedingly trouble our city, and teach customs, which are not lawful for us to receive, neither to observe, being Romans. And the multitude rose up together against them, and the magistrates rent of their [Paul's and Silas's] clothes and commanded to beat them. And when they laid many stripes on them, they cast them in prison.

Let's go back to verse 1 where we introduced Paul.

> Paul called to be an apostle by Jesus Christ through the will of God, and Sosthenes our brother.

Notice the name Sosthenes. Who was Sosthenes, and what did he have to do with Paul's calling? Notice how Sosthenes was introduced...

> AND Sosthenes our brother.

That implies he had something to do with Paul's calling to be an apostle, but I must say that could not be true. Allow me to explain. After Paul's eighteen months stay in Corinth, he left the city and took Aquila and Pricilla with him to Achaia—Southern Greece. After they arrived in Achaia, they joined the synagogue. Sosthenes was the ruler of the synagogue. He was converted to Jesus after hearing Paul preach that Jesus was the way of salvation. What happened to Sosthenes after his conversion to Christ is found in Acts 18:17,

> Then all the Greeks took Sosthenes, the chief ruler of the synagogue, and beat him before the judgment seat.

That gives us an idea of who Sosthenes was, where he lived, and what he did for a living, but it does not tell us what he had to do with Paul's calling to be an apostle. The truth is, Sosthenes had nothing to do with Paul's calling to be an apostle.

The reason 1 Corinthians 1:1 included Sosthenes was that Sosthenes became Paul's secretary and recorded the Scriptures that God gave to Paul. Evidently, Paul relayed those messages to Sosthenes, and he recorded them. By the way, it's interesting to note that Timothy recorded the second half of 1 Corinthians, not Sosthenes.

The reason Paul did not pen his own letters was probably because he had an eye problem. Paul said in Galatians 6:11,

> You see what a large letter I have written to you.

Galatians is not a large letter, per se, compared to some other letters Paul wrote. The Scripture above implies that the book of Galatians was the only Scripture Paul recorded himself because he could not see very well and had to use large letters. That explains why Paul needed Sosthenes to be his secretary.

There are no apostles today. Paul was "called to be an apostle by Jesus Christ through the will of God" (1:1), and he was the last apostle. First Corinthians 1:1 state that apostles were called personally by Jesus Christ. It was not through some fuzzy feeling or a revelation but through Jesus Christ in person. The purpose of apostles was to authenticate Christ as the Messiah. The purposes of apostles were fulfilled, so there is no need for apostles any longer.

First Corinthians 1:2 is the second subject in the outline, and it presents God's plan of salvation.

First, this section could be the most important section in this book because it explains God's plan of salvation in plain and easy-understood language. I will spend the next few pages presenting proof about God's plan of salvation. I sincerely encourage you to read all of them. I will show how salvation can be found in none other than Jesus Christ.

Notice 1 Corinthians 1:2,

> Unto the church of God which is at Corinth, to them that are SANCTIFIED [the sanctified are those who are born again and are set apart for a sacred use] IN CHRIST JESUS [the born again are] called to be saints, with all that in every place [who] CALLS UPON THE NAME OF JESUS CHRIST our Lord [for salvation]. [And Jesus can be] both their Lord and our Lord.

This verse is saying, whoever calls upon the name of the Lord shall be saved.

> Grace [God's favor of salvation] be to you, and peace from God our Father, and from the Lord Jesus Christ. (2 Corinthians 1:2)

> Who [Jesus Christ] hath also sealed us, and given us the earnest [or payment] of the Spirit in our hearts. (1 Corinthians 1:22)

Notice Acts 2:21 below.

> And it shall come to pass, that whosoever shall call on the Lord shall be saved. (Acts 2:21)

God's plan of salvation, which is in Jesus, is so important that your eternal souls depend on it.

> Not by works of righteousness which we have done, but according to His mercy He [Jesus] saved us. (Titus 3:5)

> The Father sent the Son to be the Saviour of the world. (1 John 4:14)

> For we [the apostles] have heard Him [Jesus] ourselves and know this indeed that He is the Saviour of the world. (John 4:42)

> Whosoever shall call upon the name of the Lord [Jesus Christ] shall be saved. (Romans 10:13)

> Who [Jesus] gave Himself a ransom for all, to be testified in due time. (1 Timothy 2:6)

> The Son of Man has come to seek and save that which was lost. (Luke 19:10)

It is very clear these verses are urging all to call upon Jesus for salvation. Therefore, 1 Corinthians 1:2 emphasizes that salvation is for all who calls upon the name of the Lord Jesus Christ for salvation.

Second, you must believe salvation is found in Jesus Christ and Jesus Christ alone. You must not add anything to it or take anything away from it. God's salvation plan is made clear that a person is saved when he or she calls upon the name of the Lord Jesus Christ for salvation. Salvation is totally, completely, one-hundred-percent of Jesus Christ—nothing more and nothing less. Psalms 3:8 said,

> Salvation belongeth unto the Lord.

Since salvation belongs to the Lord, it is His salvation to freely give without requiring anything in return. There are no strings attached to those who call upon Jesus for salvation. Therefore, there is nothing we can do to save ourselves, nor anything we can do to keep ourselves saved. The only thing necessary to become a member of God's family is to believe, repent, and receive Jesus Christ into our hearts. To believe is to be willing to turn from sin and receive Jesus into our heart.

God has only one plan of salvation, and it is found in Jesus Christ alone. God does not have a backup plan in case the first one does not work. Ephesians 2:8 tells us salvation is a "GIFT" from God.

> For by grace are you saved through faith, and that
> not of yourself, it is a gift of God. (Ephesians 2:8)

If it is a gift, there is no good works required to get it. It's not Jesus and good works that gets you to heaven. Having faith in something or someone other than Jesus Christ for salvation is a tragic mistake. Those who put their faith in religions, in religious leaders, in cult religions, in denominations, in good works, in baptism, in keeping the Sabbath, or in anything else other than Jesus Christ is making a horrible mistake. That will guarantee them eternal separation from God. Salvation is a gift from God.

Even the IRS (Internal Revenue Service) knows the difference between a gift and something you get by working for it. Let me explain. Let's say I give you a million-dollar gift with no strings attached. The IRS says that money is not taxable because it is a gift. However, let's say I give you a million dollars, but I say, I require only one thing, and that is, you go down to the river and be baptized. The IRS will say that money is taxable because you worked to get that million dollars. Baptism is work.

If you add something that you must do to obtain salvation, like being baptized in water, then salvation is no longer a gift. It becomes a gift plus work. Jesus either paid the total price for your salvation when He died on the cross or He did not. If He did not pay the total price for your salvation, you do not need Him because you can save yourself. But we do need Him because we cannot save ourselves. If I say I must do something to save myself or to keep myself saved, that is a slap in the face of God. It is saying, "Jesus, You do not have enough power to save me, You need my help." That is like spitting in the face of God. It's not wise to minimize Jesus as being incapable of providing salvation in its entirety.

Salvation is all of Jesus or it is nothing at all. If Jesus needs help in saving you, then He made a mistake in coming into this world to suffer the cruel treatment to save you. Jesus does not make mistakes. He had a purpose for coming into the world, and that was to save you because you cannot save yourself. There are no strings attached, not any works required to receive God's gift of salvation. The only thing you must do to become a member of God's family is to believe on Jesus, turn from your sins, and receive Him as your Saviour.

Third, you cannot believe in good works for salvation. Someone might say, what about Philippians 2:13 that says,

> Work out your own salvation with fear and trembling.

This verse is saying, you need to work out your salvation you already have by living day by day as Christians should live. Every day we face a powerful evil opponent (Satan) who seeks to destroy our faith in Christ. That is why we need to work out our salvation with fear and trembling.

> We are his workmanship created in Christ Jesus
> unto good works. (Ephesians 2:10)

We are not called to work to get salvation but work out the salvation we already have. We are to work to defeat the world, the flesh, and the devil. We don't work to bring salvation to ourselves. We already have salvation if we have received Jesus as our Saviour.

Fourth, salvation does not come to us by what we do or don't do. Someone might say, what about Romans 13:11 that says,

> For now is our salvation nearer than when we first believed.

This verse explains itself. It is saying our salvation we already have brings us closer to heaven every day we live. We are closer to heaven today than we were yesterday. We are much closer to heaven today than when we first got saved, and we will be closer tomorrow than we are today.

We as fallen sinners cannot save ourselves, so we cry out to Jesus to save us. Jesus gave His life on the cross to save us, and He saves us the very moment we believe and receive Him as our Saviour. He saves us by baptizing us into the family of God by the Holy Spirit.

> For by one Spirit are we all baptized into one body, whether we be Jews or Gentiles, whether we be bond or free. (1 Corinthians 12:13)

It is not that we deserve to be saved, but it is out of the goodness, mercy, and love of Jesus Christ that He saves us.

> For God so loved the world that He gave His only begotten Son, that whosoever believeth in Him should not perish, but have everlasting life. (John 3:16)

It's important to know salvation is found in Jesus Christ and Jesus Christ alone.

Fifth, many people totally miss the way to salvation. False religions teach that there are many ways to heaven. However, people who believe that totally miss the way to heaven. There is only one way to heaven, and that is by believing, and receiving, Jesus as Saviour. Salvation is in Jesus. Jesus said in John 14:6,

> I AM THE WAY, the truth, and the life: no man
> cometh unto the Father but by me.

The way to heaven is the most important lesson you can ever learn in your life. After all, your eternal soul depends on it. Therefore, its ultimately important you understand what the Bible has to say about the way to salvation. You must understand God's plan of salvation is in Jesus. Notice what Romans 10:13 says,

> Whosoever shall call upon the name of the Lord
> shall be saved.

That simply means to become a member of God's family, you must call upon Jesus Christ for salvation and receive His shed blood as the atonement for your sins.

Sixth, you must believe the blood of Jesus Christ washes away your sins. First John 1:7 says,

> The blood of Jesus Christ, His [God's] Son
> washes away our sins.

The blood of Christ has everything to do with salvation. Without Jesus shedding His blood to pay the price for our sins, there is no salvation. Acts 4:12 said,

> Neither is there salvation in any other: For there
> is none other name under heaven given among
> man, whereby we must be saved.

People who want to go to heaven when they die must believe Jesus paid their sin debt by dying on the cross of Calvary. Therefore, whoever calls upon Jesus Christ for salvation while here on earth will be saved. To cry out for salvation after death is too late.

Seventh, following are four fundamental truths that will lead you to salvation. These four fundamental truths, if accepted, will get you into the family of God. Knowing these truths are extremely important. Although there are four truths that lead to salvation, there is but one door into God's family, and that door is Jesus Christ.

Number 1. This truth is to believe on God. Not just believe about God but believe on God. What is the difference between believing about God and believing on God? An illustration may help. An individual may believe an airplane can take him to his desired destination, but if he never gets *on* the airplane he only believes about the airplane. It takes a deeper trust when he boards the airplane. He must believe the airplane is capable of taking him to his destination. That is believing *on* the airplane. That is also true with God. It's not enough just to believe about God; we must believe *on* God. Hebrews 11:6 said,

> He who cometh to God must believe that He is...

To just believe about God is not enough. You must believe on God. Believing *on* God is step one toward salvation, but that is not enough. Someone asked a man if he was a Christian. He said, "Oh, I believe in God." James 2:19 said,

> Thou believeth there is one God; thou doest well: the devils also believes, and trembles.

Demons believe in God, but they do not believe on God; they cannot believe on God. There is a great deal of difference between believing about God and believing *on* God. To believe on God is to commit your soul, body, and spirit to Him. Following is another fundamental truth one must accept other than just believing on God.

Number 2. This truth is to believe on Jesus Christ the way you believe on God. Jesus Christ was God manifested in the flesh. Matthew 1:23 said,

> Behold a virgin shall be with child, and shall bring forth a son, and they shall call His name Emmanuel, which being interpreted is, GOD WITH US.

Jesus was God with us in the body of Jesus. Jesus was born of Mary, but it was God in Jesus she delivered. Therefore, we must believe Jesus Christ was God in the flesh. God manifested Himself in the body of Jesus Christ. Some believe on God but will have nothing to do with Jesus Christ. Jesus said in John 14:1,

> Let not your hearts be troubled: ye believe in God believe also in Me.

God reveals His plan of salvation to those who really believe on Jesus Christ. If a man does not believe on Jesus Christ, he really does not believe on God, for Jesus is God. We must believe on God and believe on Jesus Christ to find God's plan of salvation. To believe on Jesus Christ is to surrender your body, soul, and spirit to Him. Therefore, the first truth to salvation is to believe on God. The second truth to salvation is to believe on Jesus Christ.

Number 3. This truth is to believe Jesus Christ paid your sin debt you owed and could not pay. Every time you sin you make your sin debt large. In fact, your sin debt is so large it demands eternal separation from God forever in hell to pay it. Romans 6:23 said,

> For the wages of sin is death.

That means the sentence of death is eternal separation from God, always dying but never consumed. The good news is, Jesus paid your sin debt by taking your sins upon Himself and shedding His blood on the cross to pay your sin debt. You owed a sin debt too large to pay. You accumulated that debt by sinning against God. If you die as a sinner who has not been forgiven of your sins, you must spend eternity in hell paying that sin debt. God knows your sin debt is too large for you to pay; therefore Jesus paid it for you by taking your sins upon himself and dying in your place.

> For He [God] hath made him [Jesus] to be sin for us, who knew no sin; that we might be made the righteousness of God in Him. (2 Corinthians 5:21)

> Who [Jesus] His own self bore our sins in His own body on the tree, that we who are dead to sin, should live unto righteousness: by whose stripes we are healed. (1 Peter 2:24)

> All we like sheep have gone astray; we have turned everyone to his own ways; and the Lord hath laid on Him (Jesus) the iniquity of us all. (Isaiah 53:6)

People who want to become members of God's family must firstly believe on God, secondly believe on Jesus Christ, thirdly believe Jesus died on the cross to pay their sin debt. The following is the most important point of the four points.

Number 4. This truth is that you must repent of your sins and receive Jesus Christ into your life to become a member of God's family. John 1:11–12 states,

> He [Jesus] came to His own, and His own received Him not, but as many as receive Him to them gave He the power [power of the Holy Spirit] to become the sons of God, even to them that believe on His name.

Many people reject Christ as the only way to heaven because they don't like Jesus. However, the Bible teaches that there is only one way to heaven, and that is through Jesus. We must believe, confess our sins, and receive Jesus Christ as our Saviour to become a member of God's family. There is no other way to get into God's family but through Jesus Christ. Romans 10:9 says,

> If thou shall confess with thy mouth the Lord Jesus and shall believe in thine heart that God hath raised Him from the dead, thou shalt be saved.

The four truths mentioned above are absolutely of the greatest importance to becoming a born-again Christian and a member of God's family. You must believe on God, believe on Jesus, believe Jesus paid your sin debt, and then confess your sins and receive Jesus as your Saviour. God's plan of salvation is as plain as can be.

Following are four reasons people miss out on God's plan of salvation.

Number 1. People miss out on God's plan of salvation because they will not accept the fact that God has only one plan of salvation. God is the one who invented His plan of salvation. It is His plan of salvation, not ours. Our plan of salvation will not get us to heaven but send our souls to hell. God's plan of salvation is the only plan of salvation there is. People come up with different plans, but it will not get them to heaven. They must go to heaven through God's plan of salvation which is in Jesus Christ, or they don't go to heaven at all. God does not have a backup plan in case His first plan does not work. Someone said God has many roads that leads to heaven. God does not have plan 1, plan 2, plan 3, and so on. He has only one plan of salvation, and that one plan of salvation is in Jesus Christ.

Even before God created the world, He created His plan of salvation, and His plan of salvation is in Jesus Christ. Writers of the Bible relentlessly, consistently, strongly, vigorously, and perpetually insists that God made Jesus to be His plan of salvation. That is brought to light in the following Scripture verses:

> We are justified freely by the grace through the redemption that is in Jesus Christ. (Romans 3:24)

> Sin hath reigned unto death, even so might grace reign through righteousness into eternal life by Jesus Christ our Lord. (Romans 5:21)

> The wages [that is, the wages one earns for being a sinner] of sin is death: but the gift of God is eternal life through Jesus Christ our Lord. (Romans 6:23)

There are hundreds of Scripture verses that show Jesus Christ is God's plan of salvation. In fact, Jesus was foreordained to be God's plan of salvation before the world was made.

> He [God] hath chosen us in Him [Jesus] BEFORE THE FOUNDATION OF THE WORLD. (Ephesians 1:4)

> [Jesus] "was foreordained BEFORE THE FOUNDATION OF THE WORLD [to die for sinners]. (1 Peter 1:20)

These verses show that God chose Jesus to be the Saviour of the world before He created the world. Before God made the world, He knew Jesus would be slain for sinners.

> For we who have believed do enter the rest…although the works [God planned of salvation] were finished [by Jesus] BEFORE THE FOUNDATION OF THE WORLD. (Hebrews 4:3)

> [God] is not willing that any should perish, but that all come to repentance. (2 Peter 3:9)

> Who hath saved us, and called us with a Holy calling, not according to our works, but according to His own purpose and grace, which was given us in Jesus Christ BEFORE THE WORLD BEGAN. (2 Timothy 1:9)

Did you get that? God invented His plan of salvation in Jesus Christ before He created the world. He provided salvation for all who would receive Him. Even before the world was made, He knew who would receive Him. So it's important we embrace Him and witness to others about God's plan of salvation.

Number 2. Many miss out on God's plan of salvation because they don't want to accept the fact that Jesus is the only way to obtain salvation. They will not allow the thought to enter their minds that Jesus is the only way to salvation. There is a reason they can't get it. Second Corinthians 4:4 says,

> The god of this world (the devil) hath blinded the minds of them that believe not.

It's not God's fault they are blind but their fault. They choose to believe Jesus cannot be the only way to get into God's family. Nicodemus, spoken of in John 3, had the problem of not believing Jesus was God's plan of salvation. The reason he did not believe was that he did not understand God's plan of salvation that is found in Jesus Christ. John 3 records the conversation between Jesus and Nicodemus. John 3:1 said,

> There was a man of the Pharisees named Nicodemus a ruler of the Jews.

Most Pharisees were people who adhered to strict religious and moral standards, thinking it would get them into the family of God.

Most Pharisees were committed to their religion. Nicodemus was one of them. I must caution you: Strict adherence to religious and moral standards will not get you into the family of God.

Nicodemus was a ruler of the Jews. He was probably a member of the Sanhedrin, a group of judiciary officials much like our Supreme Court, yet he realized he needed something more than religion. That is why he went to Jesus. John 3:2 said, "The same [Nicodemus] came to Jesus by night." He said,

> Rabbi, we know that thou art a teacher come from God, for no man can do these miracles that thou doest, except God be with him.

Jesus did not respond and elaborate on his question. Nicodemus wanted to know how He performed those miracles. Jesus did not engage in a dialog about how He did His miracles. Jesus did not attempt to answer the question. The response Jesus gave is recorded in John 3:3,

> Except a man be born again, he cannot see the kingdom of God.

Nicodemus did not understand the born-again issue. It did not make sense to him, and it left him in a confused state of mind. He wanted to talk about miracles, yet Jesus changed the subject to "you must be born again."

Notice how Nicodemus responded to that statement in John 3:4.

> Nicodemus sayeth unto Him, how can a man be born again when he is old? Can he enter his mother's womb and be born again?

What a ridiculous question. Jesus explained the difference between a natural birth and a spiritual birth. Notice John 3:6,

> That which is born of flesh is flesh, and that which is born of the Spirit is spirit.

Keep in mind, there are two different births here: the fleshly birth and the spiritual birth.

From verses 3 John 7–19, Jesus explained the difference between the physical and spiritual birth. Nicodemus finally got it and received Jesus as his Saviour. You may want to read the whole story. It is found in John 3:1–19.

Yes, some miss out of God's plan of salvation because they will not accept the fact that Jesus is the only way to salvation. Some miss out on God's plan of salvation because they do not believe God has only one plan of salvation.

Number 3. Some miss out on God's plan of salvation because they do not want to accept the fact that they are sinners in need of salvation. Individuals and religious organizations are confused about the sin issue in God's plan of salvation. So they develop a plan that does not include repenting of sins. They say what matters most is living a good life. They are saying, "God, you give me salvation and I will reciprocate with my good works." Therefore, they don't want to accept God's plan of salvation of repenting of sin but develop a plan of good deeds. They don't want to admit they are sinners in need of forgiveness. They will never figure out God's plan of salvation on their own, because they will not accept the fact that they are sinners. People must accept the fact they are sinners.

The Bible tells us that every person born on this earth is born in sin. Romans 3:23 states,

For all have sinned...

There are no exceptions. All have sinned. Everyone was born in sin, thereby making them sinners. People are born with an innate nature to do wrong things—to sin.

I must add this about children. Although they are born sinners, they are safe from eternal damnation until they come to realize they are sinners. Then they must repent and receive Jesus as their Saviour. Until they reach the age of accountability (that age varies), they are safe in God through Jesus Christ.

All people have sinned. Someone may say, occasionally I do something bad, but overall I'm a good person. To be sure, no one is good. Romans 3:10–12 says,

> It is written, there is none righteous, no not one: there is none who understands; there is none that seeks after God…there is none that doeth good, no not one.

Good people don't go to heaven because they are good. Good people are sinners like rapist, murders, thieves, and so on. They were born sinners because their father Adam passed sin down to them. Therefore, they are sinners by birth, sinners by nature, sinners by choice, and sinners by practice. Jesus said in Matthew 19:17,

> There is none good, but one, that is God.

According to the Bible, I'm not good, you're not good, your mother and dad are not good, your spouse is not good, your children are not good, your friends are not good, your relatives are not good. No one is good. The Bible states that "there is none good."

Trying to be good to get to heaven is the problem. Sin keeps us from being good.

> There is none that doeth good, no not one.
> (Romans 3:12)

> All have sinned and come short of the glory God.
> (Romans 3:23)

That means we have come short of God's demands to be good enough to go to heaven. To glorify God, we must measure up to God's standard of perfection. God's standard of perfection is to keep the law as it is written in the Old Testament and never sin. However, we do not keep the law; in fact, we cannot keep the law. It's impossible to keep the law. God's law was not given so we could be saved by keeping it; it was given to show us we are sinners. Actually, it shows us we cannot live good enough to be saved.

God's standards are to keep the law, be perfect, and be good. Jesus said in Matthew 5:48,

> Be ye therefore perfect, even as you Father which is in heaven is perfect.
>
> But as He who hath called you is holy, so be ye holy in all manner of conversation; because it is written: Be ye holy; for I am holy. (1 Peter 1:15–16)

In other words, God is saying, "You are to be holy like Me." God demands perfect holiness, yet God knows we cannot be perfectly holy. It is impossible to be perfectly holy and measure up to God's standard of perfection. God's standard of perfection is to keep the whole law, be good, be holy, and be perfect, yet God knows it is impossible for us to be perfect enough to be like Him. That leaves us in a frightening and confused state of mind, knowing God demands perfection when He knows we cannot be perfect. We can't live a perfect, sinless life. We cannot keep the law in its totality.

If a person could live perfect, he would have to be sinless from birth to death. If he isn't, he will die and go to hell because he would be classified as a sinner, and God said no sin will enter into His heaven. That is being blunt, but that is just the way it is. I'm shooting straight with you. God expects us to be perfect. The truth is, it's impossible to live a perfect sinless life all of our lives. All have come short of God's demands of perfection, and that includes you and me. We cannot reach God's standards. We come short of His standards. Unbelieving sinners cannot go to heaven, because sin is not allowed into God's heaven. Revelation 21:27 declares,

> There shall in no wise enter anything that defileth, either whatsoever worketh abomination, or maketh a lie; but they that are written in the Lamb's book of life.

If unrepented sinners could enter heaven, it would cease to be heaven. Therefore, because we were born in sin, we inherited Adam's sinful nature. That makes us sinners.

We will always be sinners while we are here on earth. That means we cannot go to heaven by being good. Romans 5:12 said,

> Wherefore, by one-man (Adam) sin entered into the world, and death by sin; and death passed upon all men, for all have sinned.

That means we are sinners because we inherit Adam's sinful nature. Every person on earth was born in sin. Since that is true, we cannot go to heaven simply because we are sinners. No sin shall enter heaven.

Here is an illustration of what it means to come short of God's standards. Let's say you and I had a contest to see which one of us could throw a rock to the moon. Your rock may come closer to the moon than my rock, but neither of us can throw a rock to the moon. It is impossible to throw a rock to the moon! That is what it means to come short of God's demands of perfection. God's demands are so high we cannot reach them. It's impossible to live up to God's demands of perfection.

If we could live a perfect sinless life from birth to death, we would still die and go to hell. We must be born without sin if we are depending on our goodness to get us to heaven. What I'm about to say is important! To be born without sin, you must have an earthly mother but no earthly father. You see, we inherit our sinful nature from our father Adam, not our mother. We all have both earthly mothers and earthly fathers, so we inherit a sinful nature from our father. Adam, our first father, sinned and passed that sinful nature down to our fathers, and our fathers passed it down to us. That was done through our fathers, not through our mothers. Therefore, to be born without an earthly father and never sin once in our life will qualify us for heaven.

How many of us can say we have never sinned? None of us. First John 1:10 says,

> If we say we have not sinned, we make God (out to be) a liar...

God said you have all sinned. Notice Romans 3:23 again,

> For all have sinned.

That leaves us in a terrible predicament because we all have earthly fathers, and that makes us sinners because we inherit our sinful nature from our fathers, not from our mothers. When we were conceived in our mother's womb, we receive a sinful nature from our earthly father. Therefore, we cannot meet the qualification God demands because we were born with a sinful nature. We are sinners by birth, sinners by nature, sinners by choice, and sinners by practice. Since that is true, we are destined to be separated from God forever.

Jesus did not have an earthly father. Jesus was not born a sinner. He was born without sin and lived a perfect life all His life. Mankind is born a sinner and cannot measure up to God's standards of perfection. Therefore, we must pay for being a sinner. We will be eternally separated from God with all other sinners. Romans 6:23 said,

> The wages of sin, is death.

That means the wages we earn for being a sinner is eternal separation from God forever, always dying but never consumed. That means every person on earth will be separated from God because they are not perfect. They have not met the qualifications God demands.

But wait! There is good news! Sinners who cannot meet God's demands don't have to worry about meeting God demands, because God came down to this earth and met His own demands through

Jesus Christ, His Son. Jesus was placed on the cross and died in our place to save us. Romans 5:7–8 states,

> For scarcely for a righteous man will one die: yet peradventure for a good man some would even dare to die. God commendeth His love toward us, in that, while we were yet sinners, Christ died for us.

In other words, Jesus paid the sin debt that separated us from God. He was perfect and never sinned, yet He became our substitute, our replacement, our propitiatory sacrifice, our sin bearer so we could go to heaven by putting our faith in Him. All that is required of us is to repent and receive Jesus as our Saviour.

Jesus met God's requirements of perfection for us. He had an earthly mother but no earthly father; therefore, He was not born in sin. He was born without sin, and He never sinned one time throughout His life on this earth. He never had an evil thought, never did anyone wrong, and never committed any of the other millions of sins we have committed. He was perfect. Jesus met God's requirements and made it possible for us to be reconciled to God. He became sinful that we might become sinless.

> For He [God] hath made Him [Jesus] to be sin for us, who knew no sin, that we might be made the righteousness of God in Him. (2 Corinthians 5:21)

Jesus was perfect yet became imperfect so we could become perfect. He did no sin but took our sins on himself and paid our sin debt by being punished and dying on the cross for us. First Peter 2:24 states that Jesus Christ...

> Himself bore our sins in His own body on the tree that we, having died to sin [we who died to

sin by accepting Jesus as our Saviour] should live
unto righteousness.

This verse tells us, if we put our faith and trust in Jesus Christ
as the one who paid our sin debt, we can be saved and go to heaven
when we die.

God's Word leaves no room for doubt or confusion as to when
and how salvation is obtained. John gives us a clear, concise record.

And this is the record, God hath GIVEN to us
eternal life, and this life is IN HIS SON, and he
that hath NOT THE SON OF GOD HATH
NOT LIFE. (John 15: 11–12)

Some miss out on God's plan of salvation because they will not
accept the fact that God has only one plan of salvation. Some miss
out on God's plan of salvation because they will not accept the fact
that Jesus is the only way to salvation. Some miss out on God's plan
of salvation because they do not accept the fact that they are sinners
in need of salvation.

The *fourth* reason people miss out on God's plan of salvation is
that they have established a good-works salvation plan. I call that a
concoction by man because it was invented by Satan. A good-works
salvation is not taught in the Bible. It denies Christ and replaces him
with good works. Those who believe and embrace that belief have
fallen for one of the biggest lies Satan has ever concocted. First John
2:22 says,

Who is a liar but he that denies that Jesus is the
Christ? He is antichrist that denies the Father
and the Son.

Some who believe good works will save them trust God to forgive their past sins, but not their future sins. They believe they must
do good works to keep themselves saved. They feel they must reciprocate God for their salvation. One said, "If Christians commit sin

after they are saved, they lose their salvation until they repent and 'start living right again.'"

If Jesus forgives past sins only, then He only makes a down payment on our salvation, and we must keep up the installments to stay saved. Salvation then is like buying a piece of furniture. Let's say I went to a furniture store to buy a piece of furniture. The furniture store owner agrees to sell me the furniture and even make the initial down payments. But we both sign a contract that states I must pay a monthly payment to keep the furniture. Does that mean the owner of the furniture store bought me a piece of furniture by making the initial down payment? Of course not! Neither can I say Jesus paid for my salvation if He only made the initial down payment. If Jesus did not pay for my salvation in full, then I must do something to keep myself saved. Furthermore, if I must do something to keep myself saved, I can give myself credit for my salvation, and then I can say I don't need Jesus because I can get myself to heaven by my good works. If I must keep myself saved, I can boast about how good I lived to get myself to heaven. However, the Bible says salvation is...

Not of works, lest any man should boast. (Ephesians 2:9)

We have no room for boasting because we did not, and could not, pay for our salvation. Furthermore, it's a sin to boast about our goodness to get ourselves to heaven. A person than brags about his goodness is no better that Satan. Satan fell because his heart was full of pride. He believed he was better than God. A person who boasts about his goodness is full of pride.

Jesus either paid the total price for our salvation or He did not. If he did not, then we don't need Him because we can save ourselves. But we do need Him, because we cannot save ourselves by being good. Without Jesus Christ there is no salvation. Salvation is a gift from God, not by the good works we have done or will do. Ephesians 2:8–9 states,

> For by grace are you saved through faith; and that not of yourself: it is the gift of God: not of works, lest any man should boast.

Salvation is a gift. When God gives us a gift, He does not take it back. Who then is made righteous in God's eyes? The answer is found in Romans 4:5,

> But to him that WORKETH NOT [works not for his salvation], but believeth on Him that justifieth the ungodly, his faith is counted for righteousness.

Accumulating a large amount of good work for salvation does not save you. Sinners are not made righteous by placing their faith in their good works but saved by placing their faith in Jesus Christ. A person must receive Jesus as his or her Saviour to be made righteous and become a member of God's family.

Jesus was crucified, buried, and rose again to justify us. The Bible said in Romans 4:25 that the Lord Jesus Christ "was delivered for our offenses."

You and I offended God because we sinned against Him and did not meet His requirements. Therefore, we accumulated a large debt of sin. Jesus Christ paid that sin debt for us. In fact, He paid the sin debt for every person in the world and paid it in full. That does not mean every person in the world will go to heaven, just those who confess their sins and put their faith and trust in Jesus for salvation.

We go to heaven by the goodness of Christ, not our goodness. His goodness was transported to us when we believed, confessed our sins, and put our faith and trust in Him. Therefore, when God looks at us, He sees the righteousness of Jesus in us, not our own righteousness. There is a requirement for God to see the righteousness of

Jesus in us. We must believe, confess our sins, and receive Jesus as our substitute—our Saviour. It is written in John 1:12,

> As many as receive Him, to them gave He the
> power (the power of the Holy Spirit) to become
> the sons of God.

It's important we know it was God who created His plan of salvation. Only God could come up with a plan like that. It was God who became Jesus here on earth. Yes! Matthew 1:23 states,

> Behold a virgin [Mary] shall be with child, and
> shall bring forth a Son, and they shall call His name
> Emmanuel, WHICH BEING INTERPRETED
> IS, GOD WITH US.

God and Jesus are one and the same in one body. God took up residence in the body of Jesus and stayed there until they went through the cruelty that led up to the crucifixion.

The Father and Son hung on the cross until they neared death, but God left Jesus so He could die alone. Notice what Jesus said as recorded in Matthew 27:46,

> About the ninth hour Jesus cried with a loud voice,
> saying, Eli, Eli, Lama sabachthani? That is to say:
> My God, my God why hast thou forsaken Me?

That was one of the most traumatic events in the life of Jesus. God left Jesus to die alone to pay our sin debt. Jesus was forsaken by God because Jesus became sin for us.

> For He [God] hath made Him to become sin for
> us, who knew no sin. (2 Corinthians 5:21)

God could not look upon sin, so He turned His face from His Son so His Son could die alone. All through the Old Testament animals were sacrificed for God's people, but God did not desire an animal sacrifice to pay your sin debt. God sacrificed the body of Jesus for your salvation. Jesus took our sins upon Himself and became our substitute and died in our place. It's of utmost importance that you believe and accept that because that is what the Bible teaches, and if you don't accept it, there is only one place you can go after death, and that certainly is not heaven.

Notice John 1:14,

> And the Word [meaning God] was made flesh and dwelt among us.

Jesus was God manifested in the flesh. *John* 1:1–2 and 14 says,

> In the beginning was the Word, and the Word was with God, and the Word WAS GOD. The same was in the beginning with God…And the Word was made flesh and dwelt among us…

Who was made flesh and dwelt among us? Jesus was made flesh and dwelt among us. John 1:2 states,

> Jesus was God.

Salvation was made possible by Jesus Christ, who was God manifested in the flesh that came to dwell among us.

God has a purpose in allowing His Son to be crucified. That purpose was to demonstrate His love and provide a way for fallen men to come back to Him. God came into this world in the body of His Son, Jesus. Jesus took our sins on Himself and paid our sin debt in full. Now we can be saved by confessing our sins and putting our faith and trust in Jesus as our Redeemer. Our sins separated us from God, but God reconciled us to Himself through Jesus Christ.

Did it ever occur to you that God made the body of Jesus Christ for Himself? Man had absolutely nothing to do with it, nor contributed anything to the making of the body of Jesus. God made Himself a perfect body to dwell in. Hebrews 10:4–5 states,

> It is not possible that the blood of bulls and goats should take away sin. Wherefore when He [Jesus] cometh into the world, He sayeth, Sacrifice and offering thou wouldest not [God did not desire animal sacrifices].
>
> But [Jesus said] A BODY [for a sacrifice] THOU HAST PREPARED FOR ME. (Hebrews 10:5)

The Bible is saying God made the body of Jesus for a sacrifice.

> Then sayeth He [Jesus] Lo, I come to do thy will O, God. (Hebrews 10:9)

Matthew 1:23 said,

> Behold a virgin shall be with child, and shall bring forth a son, and they shall call his name Emmanuel, which being interpreted is, GOD WITH US.

We are correct by saying God made Himself a body. John 1:3 said,

> All things were made by Him, and without Him was not anything made that was made.

God not only made the earthly body of Jesus but made the body of Mary for a gestation place for Jesus to be born. In fact, He made the sperm that fertilized the egg in Mary's womb. Isaiah 7:14 said,

> The Lord Himself shall give you a sign; Behold, a virgin shall conceive, and bear a Son, and shall call His name Immanuel, which means God with us.

Luke 1:25–39 gives the account of Mary's pregnancy.

> In the sixth month the angel Gabriel was sent
> from God unto a city in Galilee, named Nazareth,
> to a virgin espoused [engaged] to a man whose
> name was Joseph, of the house of David, and the
> virgin's name was Mary. And the angel came in
> unto her and said, Hail [Mary], thou art highly
> favored, the Lord is with thee: blessed art thou
> among women. And when she saw him, she
> was troubled at his saying, and cast in her mind
> what manner of greeting this should be. And the
> angel said unto her, Fear not, Mary: for thou hast
> found favor with God. And, behold thou shalt
> conceive in thy womb, and bear a Son, and shall
> call His name JESUS… Then said Mary unto the
> angel, how can this be, seeing I know not a man?
> And the angel answered and said unto her, The
> Holy Spirit shall come upon thee, and the power
> of the Highest shall overshadow thee: therefore,
> also that holy thing which shall be born of thee
> shall be called the Son of God.

Allow me to sidetrack and add a note here. Mary was a highly favored young lady chosen by God to bear His Son, but as far as being an intercessor between God and man, she did not have that power, nor does she have that power now. That means, we cannot go to heaven through Mary interceding for us. It must be through her Son Jesus. Oliver Green in his book on Acts put it this way:

> Mary was highly blessed of God in that the Holy
> Spirit overshadowed her, and she brought forth
> God's only begotten Son. But in so far as inter-
> ceding to God on our behalf there is NO SUCH
> SCRIPTURE, nor any such doctrine taught in

the Bible. And anyone who seeks to reach God through Mary will be sadly disappointed.

Mary was a sinner like you and me in need of salvation. There is no denying she was a virgin and committed Christian. She was a wonderful dedicated young lady used by God for a special purpose of bringing His Son into the world. God chose her and protected her, yet she needed Jesus herself as her Saviour. Mary was impregnated by the Holy Spirit, and she carried her baby nine months just like any other woman.

Mary was nearing her ninth month of pregnancy when the degree went out that she and Joseph should go to Bethlehem to register for taxing purposes. Did you ever think about Mary making that long tedious trip from Nazareth to Bethlehem right before she gave birth to Jesus? That was a ninety-mile trip. Think about a pregnant woman traveling many of those miles on foot, and at other times riding on a donkey. That occurred just days before her delivery.

The following is a story my wife Carolyn put together. She organized the story for a preschool Christmas program at Tri-Cities Christian school when she was director there. The story is about what might have happened as Mary and Joseph made their way to Bethlehem.

There were no buses, nor cars, and no trains on which to travel from Nazareth to Bethlehem, where Jesus was to be born. But Joseph did have a donkey for Mary to ride on. The donkey was slow, and the roads were very rough and rocky. Mary undoubtedly got tired, stiff, and sore from being out on the rough rocky road so long. Joseph's feet must have hurt from walking on the rocky road. Perhaps many times Joseph said to Mary, "Mary, are you all right, can we go a little further before making camp for the night?" Of course, the answer was always yes.

It took many days for them to make that ninety-mile trip from Nazareth to Bethlehem. They probably thought they would never reach Bethlehem. Finally, late one evening as darkness was falling, they saw a little light in the distance. Joseph must have said, "Look, Mary, there is Bethlehem!" Mary responded with, "Oh, I'm so glad,

Joseph. We will have a soft warm bed to sleep on tonight instead of the rocky ground, and we can get some good food to eat."

They finally reached Bethlehem, their destination. Joseph said, "Look, Mary, how crowded it is! Where will we ever find a place to sleep?"

Mary replied, "We had better try, Joseph, because the time for the baby's arrival is drawing near."

And so they did try. They made the rounds, but everywhere it was the same: "We're sorry, we don't have any room!" Perhaps someone suggested they try the village inn. Joseph wearily led the donkey with Mary down the rough cobblestone street to the Inn. The innkeeper said in a rough voice, "I'm sorry, there's not one tiny bit of space left!"

If the innkeeper had only known that the Messiah, the Saviour, God Himself would take upon Himself a body that night, surely he would have found a place somewhere for Mary and Joseph. But he didn't. He turned them away.

Maybe it happened that as Joseph turned to leave, the innkeeper saw Mary's condition and suggested they go out in the back to the stable. He probably said, "There are mules, sheep, and calves in the stable, but at least you can find room in there for the night, and if it rains you will have a roof over your heads."

That night as all of Bethlehem slept in their snug warm beds, the King of Kings and Lord of Lords was born. God left heaven's glory where all the angels bowed down to Him and came down to this world to be born as Jesus in a stable.

Jesus had to be born in a stable. That event of Him being born in a stable was God's plan down through the ages. It finally happened. The Christ, the Messiah was born. God became man. There was no beautiful little crib, or bed, for King Jesus to sleep on. So Joseph cleaned out the crib and put some fresh hay in it. Mary wrapped Jesus in swaddling clothes and laid Him in a manger.

It's sad there was no room for Jesus in Bethlehem, no room for Him in the inn, no room for Him in the homes of the people, and saddest of all, no room for Him in the hearts of most people upon earth today. The Bible said,

> He came to His own, and His own revived Him
> not.

I wonder if there is room in your heart and in your home for Jesus. Have you invited Him in to be your Saviour? Have you crowned Him King of Kings and Lord of Lords of your life? Jesus said in Revelation 3:20,

> Behold I stand at the door and knock, if anyone
> hears my voice and opens the door I will come in
> and sup [dine] with him, and he with me.

Just bow your knees before Him, and confess your sins, and ask His forgiveness, then open your heart and invite Him in. End of story.

Mary never knew a man in an intimate way until after she gave birth to Jesus. Matthew 1:24–25 was put in the Bible to dispel all doubt about man having a part in her pregnancy.

> Joseph...took to himself his wife [Mary], and
> knew her not [that is, in an intimate way] till she
> brought forth her firstborn, and he called His
> name Jesus.

Make no mistake about it; this verse makes it clear that Mary did not get pregnant any other way, but by the Holy Spirit.

God created the body of Jesus for a place for Him to dwell in. But not only did He create Jesus, He created us as well. That means God owns us. In fact, the book of Acts, 17:28, states,

> In Him we live, and move, and have our being.

Daniel 5:23 said,

> In whose hand [God's hand] thy breath is.

In other words, God holds our breath in His hands. So it's God who gives life, it's God who sustains life, it's God who owns life, and it's God who gives us everlasting life. God made us and gave us a choice to accept Jesus as our Saviour or reject Him. To be sure, if we choose not to choose Him, our choice is made for us already. John 3:18 said,

> He that believeth in Him is not condemned, but
> he who believeth not is condemned ALREADY,
> because he does not believe in the name of the
> only begotten Son of God.

God made us with a free will to receive Him or reject Him. Have you received Him? It's your choice!

Another point about salvation is found in Ephesians 2:8–10.

> For by grace are you saved through faith; and that
> not of yourself: it is the gift of God: not of works,
> lest any man should boast.

Notice the following four observations.

Number 1, we are saved by "grace"—but what is grace? Grace is an underserved and unmerited favor from God. He freely given us that favor without expecting anything in return. To be sure, salvation is a free gift from God that we did not deserve nor worked to get. We did not earn it, thus an unmerited favor.

Number 2, we are saved *"through faith"*—that is, faith in Jesus who freely paid our sin debt on the cross; faith that His death, burial, and resurrection was sufficient to save us if we would only believe in Him, confess our sins to Him, and receive Him as our Saviour.

Number 3, you cannot save yourself because salvation is "not of yourself"; it is by Jesus Christ. Salvation is not by your own efforts, or something you do or don't do, but by the grace of Jesus Christ.

Number 4, we are not saved by good works because Ephesians 2:10 says, salvation is "not of works lest, any man should boast."

We are not saved by depending on our good works to outweigh our bad works. Think about the thief on the cross? Did he have enough good works to balance the scales in his favor? First John 5:13 states,

> These things I have written unto you that believe on the name of the Son of God; that YOU MAY KNOW [present tense, know right now] you have eternal life.

You cannot know you have eternal life if you are depending on your good works to outweigh your bad works. There is no security in good works. Ephesians 2:10 tells us we should have good works because we are saved, not to be saved.

> For we are his workmanship CREATED in Christ Jesus unto good works.

That means, God saved us to do good works. Don't get the cart before the horse however. Ephesians 2:10 goes on to say,

> God has before ordained [decreed] that we should walk in them.

That is, walk in good works because we are saved, not to be saved.

First Corinthians 1:2 is to show Jesus came into this world to bring salvation to all who put their faith and trust in Him. He gave His life on the cross as a total payment for our sins, so we would not have to spend eternity in hell to pay our sin dept. By believing in

Jesus, confessing our sins to Him, and putting our faith in Him for salvation, we can be saved and assured a home in heaven.

Let me remind you once again, it was God who made the rules on how to obtain salvation. It was God who invented His plan of salvation. It's up to us to embrace those rules and act upon them or reject them and be separated from God forever. We must be born again by God's plan of salvation, or else we will never enter heaven.

It's not surprising that 1 Corinthians 1:2 starts with God's plan of salvation, because Paul wanted to settle that issue up front. That should be the goal of every one of us. We should settle God's plan of salvation up front for ourselves and for others. Let's read 1 Corinthians 1:2 again,

> Unto the church of God which is at Corinth, to them that are sanctified in Christ Jesus, called to be saints, with all that are in every place call upon the name of Jesus Christ our Lord, both theirs and ours.

I have spent a considerable amount of time explaining 1 Corinthians 1:2. I hope you will head it and act upon it.

The third section of the outline is found in 1 Corinthians 1:3–9, and it deals with God's grace and God's peace.

Notice verse 3,

> Grace be unto you, and peace, from God our Father, and from the Lord Jesus Christ.

Following are 2 things we need to understand about God's grace, and God's peace.

First, to understand how a person is blessed with God's grace, we must understand what grace is. God's grace is a gift we don't deserve or work for. We don't earn it. It is free. God gives us the gift of salvation without expecting anything in return. There is not enough righteousness or goodness in us that could merit God's grace. God doesn't look at us and consider us good enough for His grace. No! God's grace is a gift regardless of our worthiness. We receive God's gift of grace when we repent of sins and receive Jesus Christ as our own personal Saviour. Jesus Christ is God's gift of grace to us. That means grace is the gift of salvation through Jesus Christ that God gives us when we believe in Jesus, confess our sins to Him, and put our faith and trust in Him for salvation. There is nothing we can do or ever will do to merit God's gift of grace.

Second, we are not only blessed with God's grace, but we are also blessed with God's peace. Notice again 1 Corinthians 1:3,

> Peace from our Father, and from the Lord Jesus
> Christ.

In what ways are we blessed with God's peace? We must understand there are two kinds of peace that comes from God through Jesus Christ. There is a great deal of difference between the two. There is peace *with* God, and then there is the peace *of* God. We must possess peace *with* God before we can possess the peace *of* God. Ephesians 2:14 said,

> For He [Jesus] is our peace...

We must confess we are on the outs with God—separated from God, enemies of God, sinned against God, and have no peace with God. Then we must repent and put our faith in Jesus Christ for salvation. If we have no desire to do that, Matthew 12:30 describes our condition:

> He that is not for me is against me.

We must confess our belief in Jesus, come to God to confess our sins, and ask Jesus into our life as our personal Saviour. He is a loving God who will forgive us, save us, and welcome us into His family.

Back before I came to know Jesus as my Saviour, I realized I had to make peace with God. I knew I was on the outs with God and needed to confess my sins and make things right with God. I wanted with all my heart to possess God's salvation. Therefore, when I made peace with God, I knew I was born again. I knew I would go to be with Jesus when I die.

Peace with God is to know Jesus accepts us and gives us eternal life. When I put my faith and trust in Jesus for salvation, God's peace entered my life. The Holy Spirit moved in and took up residence in my heart. I was given the assurance of eternal life. John stated in First John 5:11–13,

> And this is the record that God hath given to us eternal life, and this life is in His Son. He that hath not the Son of God hath not life. These things have I written unto you that believe on the name of the Son of God; that ye may know ye have eternal life...

Knowing you are saved and knowing you have eternal life brings peace with God. You have peace with God by receiving Jesus as your Saviour.

There is another kind of peace, and that is the peace *of* God. We make peace *with* God when we receive Jesus as our Saviour, but we can only have the peace *of* God by totally committing ourselves to Him. Peace *with* God is available only to those who put their faith and trust in Jesus for salvation. You cannot have the peace *of* God without first making peace *with* God. In John 14:27, Jesus said,

> Peace I leave with you, my peace I give you: not as the world giveth, give I unto you. Let not you heart be troubled, nether let it be afraid.

The reason people and nations don't have peace is because they don't have Jesus, the Prince of Peace. Philippians 4:7 said,

> The peace of God, which passeth all understanding, shall keep your hearts and minds through Christ Jesus.

That is the only peace that brings everlasting peace.

Paul is saying to the church of Corinth and us, not only can we have peace with God, but we can also have the peace of God. Many in the Corinthian church didn't realize what they had in Jesus, and frankly, many Christians today don't realize what they have in Jesus. They struggle because of their many adversities, but really, all they need to know to overcome life's difficulties is to receive the peace God has to offer. How do we find peace in the midst of adversities? We are to take our troubles to Jesus and leave them there. That is a trite saying, but it's true, and it works. First Peter 5:7 said,

> Casting all your cares [troubles] on Him, for He careth for you.
>
> The peace of God which passeth all understanding shall keep your hearts and minds through Christ Jesus. (Philippians 4:7)

We can only experience peace with God, and the peace of God, when we believe in Jesus, confess our sins to Him, and commit ourselves totally to Him.

First Corinthians 1:3 assures us we can have peace *with* God which can never be severed. That peace is the assurance that we have eternal life in Jesus. That peace gives us the assurance to know we will go to be with Jesus when this life is over. Once we confess our sins and open our heart's door and ask Jesus to come in and be our

Saviour, He will come in and abide with us forever. He adopts us into His family, and we will never be disowned. Jesus said,

> I give unto them eternal life and they shall never perish, neither shall any man pluck them out of my hands (John 10:28).

So when you make peace *with* God, that peace will never be severed, broken, or lost. However, the peace *of* God can be severed. We separate ourselves from the peace *of* God when we get out of His will. God does not break that peace. Christians break that peace. Christians can move away from God. That is called "backsliding." When a Christian backslides, he does not lose his salvation or his peace *with* God, but he does lose the peace *of* God. He must repent and come back to God to enjoy the peace *of* God. The peace *of* God is given to us for daily living. You cannot live a successful Christian life without the peace *of* God.

First Corinthians 1:4 is the fourth point in the outline, and it covers the subject of Thanksgiving.

Paul's now writes about being thankful to God for His grace, which is given to those who are in Jesus Christ. Notice verse 4,

> I thank my God always on your behalf, for the grace of God which is given you by Jesus Christ.

Paul gave thanks for God's grace on the Corinthian church. He made it a practice to thank God for his fellow Christians. We too should give thanks for our fellow believers. That leads me to the subject of Thanksgiving.

We set aside one day every year to give thanks, and that day is called Thanksgiving Day. Thanksgiving Day is observed every year in November. Our first Thanksgiving Day was held near Cape Cod in Massachusetts in the fall of 1621, by Pilgrims and Wampanoag Indians. They celebrated their first harvest. They gathered together to thank God for His blessing on them. That is how Thanksgiving started. Thanksgiving Day, however, is far removed from what it was intended to be. People have a feast meal now to celebrate what they have accomplished instead of thanking God for what He has accomplished through them.

Thank God, we have someone to give thanks to. Every day we should give God thanks for His grace and mercy on us and for all His blessings. Praying for and giving thanks for our fellow believers would help us through tough times. Furthermore, it would take care of a lot of problems, especially problems in our personal lives and our churches.

First Corinthians 1: 5–9 is the fifth point in the outline, and it presents the way to be enriched in Christ.

Paul now turns to the subject of enrichment in Christ. Notice verses 5–6:

> That in everything you are enriched by Him, in all utterance, and in all knowledge; even as the testimony of Christ was confirmed in you.

This Scripture is saying we are enriched by Jesus in utterance and knowledge—which means, we can be made better in knowledge of the Word of God. Furthermore, that is confirmed in the testimony of Peter, who gave us a pattern to go by. Notice 2 Peter 1:5–8,

> Giving all diligence, add to your faith virtue; and to virtue knowledge; and to knowledge temperance; and to temperance patience; and to patience Godliness; and to Godliness brotherly kindness, and to brotherly kindness love. For if these things, be in you, you should never be barren nor unfruitful...

You will be an enriched productive Christians who will never be "barren or unfruitful."

If you are not being made better, you are being made bitter. No one remains neutral. If we are not going forward, we are going backward. If we are not making progress, we are digressing. If we are not advancing, we are still babes in Christ that need to grow up. Paul said in 1 Corinthians 13:11,

> When I was a child, I spoke as a child, I under-
> stood as a child, I thought as a child: but when I
> became a man, I put away childish things.

Second Peter 1:5–8 are good Scriptures to memorize and put in practice. It will help you grow in Christ like no other method, sermon, or lesson I know of. You will never want to remain a babe in Christ and stop your spiritual enrichment in Him.

To be enriched in Christ is to be made better in Christ. The goal God sets for believers is to be made better, and believers can be made better by totally committing themselves to Christ in studying His Word. Let me expand on some ways a believer can be made better.

First, believers can be made better in "utterance." The word *utterance* is the gift of witnessing to people about God's salvation. When we were born again, God gave us the gift of utterance. Many don't use it, but they were given that gift nevertheless. To utilize your gift of utterance, just tell others about your salvation experience. That should not be hard to do. Do you remember when you came to Christ for salvation? Just tell them what brought you to that decision.

You can be made better if you speak openly about what you have become in Christ. Once you receive Jesus Christ as your Saviour, you are commissioned to tell others about the salvation God offers unbelievers. First Peter 3:15 said,

> Sanctify the Lord God in your hearts: and be
> ready always to give an answer [testimony] to
> every man that asketh you a reason for the hope
> that is in you, with meekness and fear.

Those who have trusted Jesus Christ as Saviour understand God's plan of salvation and can tell others. After all, one must understand God's plan of salvation to be saved. Therefore, God gives us the ability to carry that truth to the world. Acts 1:8 tells us to do just that:

> You shall receive power after the Holy Ghost is
> come upon you, and you shall be witnesses...
> unto the uttermost parts of the world.

Witnessing is not something we have to do but something we want to do. It's a desire God places in our hearts after we are born again.

Second, believers can be made better in "knowledge." God gives us the gift of knowledge of His Word. God did not save us and leave us without the ability to understand the Bible. We knew what it takes to become a Christians; therefore, it is easy to understand the Bible because the Holy Spirit dwells in us, and He interprets the Scriptures for us. I encourage you to spend at least one hour a day in God's Word.

Third, believers can be made better by using the gifts God gives them. First Corinthians 1:7 says,

> So that you come behind in no spiritual gift,
> waiting for the coming of the Lord Jesus Christ.

The Corinthian church could have been made better by utilizing the gifts God gave them, but they showed evidence they did not fully understand what gifts they had in Jesus. Most of us understand what gifts we have in Jesus, but frankly, we don't always utilize those gifts. God gives us spiritual gifts to be used in His service; therefore we should utilize those gifts in the light of His Second Coming. If we intend to do anything for the Lord, we had better do it now, because time is running out. From all indications, the Lord is coming soon.

When God gives us gifts, He equips us to use those gifts. So let's use our gifts: preaching, singing, serving, working with young people, witnessing, and many other things are gifts from God. You may feel inadequate, but just remember, it's God who does the equipping. We should always use the gifts God gives us to further His cause. It's not very wise to ignore what the Lord called us to do. Please don't misunderstand. I'm not saying get involved in some ministry just because you are afraid not to get involved. I'm simply saying it's not very wise to put off what God calls you to do because after death you will never get another chance to "do your first works over."

If you are not sure what your gifts are, just keep doing what you know to do, and the Lord will make it clear what He wants you to do. God does not call you to do something you cannot do, but you can do what He calls you to do, and He calls all of us to do something specific for Him. I know what my calling is, and so can you. If you will just open your senses to His desire, He will reveal to you what He wants you to do. I have found it to be true that if you have a burning desire to get involved in a specific ministry that is your gift God is calling you to do. For example, if you have a burning desire to preach, that is your calling. Let God lead you to do what He wants you to do, and then do it.

Paul's heartbeat was to totally commit himself to God's work in preaching the Gospel of Jesus Christ. If anything could motivate us to get involved in God's work, it is Paul's example. Furthermore, our Lord Jesus urges us to mimic Him. He said in John 12:26,

> If anyone serves me, let him follow me; and where I am, there my servant shall also be. If any Man serves me, him will my Father honor.

First Corinthians 1:8–9 encourages the church to use their gifts because the coming of Jesus is near. Notice verses 8–9,

> Who shall confirm you unto the end, that you may be blameless in the day of our Lord Jesus Christ [when He comes again]: God is faithful, by whom you were called unto the fellowship of His Son Jesus Christ our Lord.

We know Jesus is coming soon, because 2 Timothy 3:1 says,

> This know also, that in the LAST DAYS perilous
> [dangerous] time shall come…

We have never lived in a more dangerous time than today. I can remember a time when church was the safest place you could be, but not anymore. In fact, it's dangerous to go anywhere now, or even stay in your home. That clearly points to the coming of Jesus. Notice the Scripture says, "IN THE LAST DAYS." We are in the last days.

We can trust Jesus that all will be well at His coming. Psalms 20:7 said,

> Some trust in chariots, and some in horses; but
> we will remember the Lord our God.

I encourage you to keep the Lord before you and trust Him to lead you and give you strength to face each day. Notice Proverbs 3:5–6,

> Trust in the Lord with all thine heart, and lean
> not unto your own understanding. In all your
> way acknowledge Him and He will direct thy
> paths.

Allow me to sidetrack here and say something about "*direct your paths.*"

Some modern Bible translations interpret Proverbs 3:6 this way: "In all your ways acknowledge him and he will make your paths straight." There is a world of difference between "directing your path" and "making your path straight." God does not always make your paths straight, but He has promised to always direct you on the path He wants you to take. Whether your path is straight, crooked, twisted, or uncertain, God directs you as to which path you should take. Trusting the Lord to make your path straight leads to a misunderstanding of God's plan and purpose for your life. If you believe

God always makes your paths straight, then when your road gets crooked and full of confusing curves, you become disillusioned and, in most cases, quit serving Him. When you encounter bumps and bends in the road, God helps you navigate through those times. He always directs your paths. He has promised,

> I will never leave thee, not forsake thee. (Matthew 13:5)

Many Christians are like those who put their trust in wealth, in careers, in popularity, and so on, but Matthew 6:33 tells us to…

> Seek ye first the kingdom of God, and His righteousness, and all these things shall be added unto you.

That is, put Christ first, and trust Him to direct your path, and He will supply your needs and work things out for good. I think the song Edward Mote wrote pretty well sums it up:

> My hope is built on nothing less than Jesus's blood and righteousness. I dare not trust the sweetest frame, but wholly lean on Jesus's name.

Just trust Jesus, and He will direct your paths! Verses 8–9 above are saying, if you do what God calls you to do, you will be approved by God when Jesus comes. You will be blameless in the day of the Lord.

There is nothing that pleases the Lord more than leading others to Him for salvation. After all, 2 Peter 3:9 states,

> The Lord is not slack concerning His promises, as some men count slackness: but is longsuffering toward us-ward. Not willing that any should perish, but that all should come to repentance.

Someday in the future, God will call us into the fellowship of His dear Son. Christians who have been faithful will receive a reward and will experience the enrichment of God in person in its fullness.

First Corinthians 1:10–17 is the sixth subject in the outline, and it shows how to prevent splits in the local church.

There was a four-way split in the church at Corinth, and Paul sought to correct the problem. The method he used should be used to prevent church splits today. Following is the method Paul used.

First, Paul stated we must speak the right things. Speaking the right things will solve problems in the church quicker than anything. Notice 1 Corinthians 1:10,

> Now I beseech [beg] you brethren, by the name of our Lord Jesus Christ that you all speak the same thing, that there be no divisions among you, but that you be perfectly joined together in the same mind and in the same judgment.

This Scripture encourages us to speak the right thing by working together. Have you ever been in a church where members differ on everything instead of speaking the right thing? Paul is not saying compromise your stand for Christ. Some church members will compromise to bring unity in their church. One pastor was interviewed by the news media. The reporter asked the pastor, "Why do you never say anything about hell, or sin, or God's judgment?" His response was, "I never say anything that will make people feel bad when they leave. I keep my messages positive, so they will come back." That is the wrong method to use. That is compromising on Christian principles. We are to speak the right things from the Bible whether it is encouraging or rebuking. We are to speak the right thing regardless of how church members receive it.

Churches that are joined together in the same mind and speak the right things from God's Word will not divide the church. So the first thing we are to do to help the church solve divisions is to speak the right things.

Second, the church is to expose the problem. Notice 1 Corinthians 1:11.

> For it hath been declared unto me, of you my brethren by them which are of the household of Chloe, that there are contentions among you.

The word *contentions* means "disruptions, disputes, problems, or disagreements." The household of Chloe exposed the problem to Paul and asked for his advice. Romans 16:17 says,

> Now I beseech you brethren, mark them which cause division and offences contrary to the doctrine which you have learned, and avoid them.

That means, expose them to the church. Paul responded with the second thing they should do, and that was to expose the problem to the church.

Dr. Curtis Hudson once said to his congregation, "Some of you are stirring up trouble that could split this church. I know who you are, you know who you are, and God knows who you are. If you don't stop it, I'm going to get a big black marker pen and put a big *X* on your forehead so the rest of us can recognize you and avoid you, because the Bible says, 'Mark them which cause divisions contrary to the doctrine which you have learned and avoid them.'"

I'm sure that Scripture verse is not instructing us to use that method. However, problems should be named and exposed to the church so they can be resolved.

Some in the Corinthian church believed their group was the right way. They separated themselves from the main body of believers. That is the way it is with many churches today. They separate themselves from those who do not agree with them. They form another church to promote their cause. The question arises: Is there any one group of people or church or denomination the right way to heaven? Of course not! Jesus is the way!

There was a four-way split in the Corinthian church because members wanted to follow different people and start different churches. First Corinthians 1:12 said,

> Now this I say, that every one of you sayeth I am
> of Paul; and I of Apollos; and I of Cephas; and I
> of Christ.

In other words, many in the church joined a group and insisted it was the right group to belong to.

The problem with the Corinthian church was with people aligning themselves with Paul, Apollos, Cephas (Peter), and another Christ (not the Christ of the Bible) and with another Gospel. They were aligning themselves with a false Jesus, who they claimed was the right Jesus to follow. Second Corinthians 11:4 said,

> For if he that cometh to you preaching another
> Jesus, whom you have not preached, or received
> another spirit you have not received, or preaches
> another Gospel you have not accepted, bear with
> him.

The phrase "bear with him" means to be patient with him, but don't believe and accept his false Jesus. It also means tolerate him if there is a possibility of winning him over to the real Jesus. Paul is not saying run those off who cause problems but seek to bring them back into fellowship with Jesus and the church. But one thing we must keep in mind; if he does not repent, avoid him.

Paul, Apollos, and Cephas were important men in the work of Christ, but the Corinthian church was not to exalt them to a higher degree than Jesus. The problem makers had created and preach another Jesus, by another spirit, and by another Gospel. Do not accept a false teacher's deceptive doctrine, nor condone his actions in the church, but make every possible effort to win him over to Christ, but if that does not work, avoid him. That's what Paul is saying.

Paul was the founder of the church in Corinth. Apollos was an evangelist who visited the church. Cephas (Peter) had also visited the church, but they were not to be exalted above Jesus Christ. Christ is the head of the church, and we must exalt Him and follow Him.

All the members in the church at Corinth should have been followers of Jesus Christ of the Bible; however, they were not. They believed their salvation depended on their affiliation with Paul, Apollos, Cephas, or another Christ—another religion. It's sad but true; many people trust some cult, some religion, some person, or some denomination to lead them on the path to salvation. Some trust Buddha, the founder of Buddhism. Some trust Mohammed, the founder of Islam. Some trust Charles Russell, the founder of Jehovah's Witness. Some trust Joseph Smith, the founder of Mormonism. Some trust the founders of baptismal regeneration. Some even trusted in Jim Jones, who led nine hundred people to commit suicide. People are guilty of trusting other forms of weird religions that gives them credit for their salvation. We are to put our faith and trust in Jesus because He is the only way to heaven.

> Neither is there salvation in any other: for there is none other name given among man whereby we must be saved. (Acts 4:12)

Jesus is the way to salvation.

Notice what Paul said in 1 Corinthians 1:13 about Christ being the way to salvation:

> Is Christ divided? Was Paul crucified for you? Are you baptized in the name of Paul?

Paul is not just making statements but asking questions. By applying this same principle in our churches today, we can say, Christ did not divide His church into parts, nor are you to be baptized in of anyone's name other than the Father, the Son, and the Holy Spirit.

However, the church of Corinth did divide their church into parts and sought to baptize them in the name of Paul, Apollos, Peter, or another Christ. The real true church is one in Christ and cannot be divided into parts. However, Satan's people will infiltrate the church ranks and try to destroy it. I'm convinced the devil has his cohorts planted in every church that is trying to follow Jesus. Matthew 7:15 said,

> Beware of false prophets that come to you in sheep clothing, but inward they are ravenous [predator] wolves.

A good example is "Shi'ite" or "Sunni" Islamic radicals. They claim Allah and God are one and the same just to infiltrate your church, but their main objective is to destroy your church. Some churches accept them in the spirit of love, but that is the wrong thing to do. Read Matthew 7:15 again.

There are no less than eleven sections in the New Testament that deals with divisions in the church. First Corinthians is one of them. Paul is saying, "Come together agreeing on one thing, and that one thing should be to follow Jesus Christ and work together. We are not to trust in any other way, but Jesus alone." The Corinthian church was not to give their allegiance to Paul or Apollos or Cephas or to another Christ, but to the Christ of God alone.

Third, Paul offered a solution similar to the one Jesus recommended. Paul suggested they used the method he recommended. He firstly encouraged them to do the right thing; secondly, he urged the church to expose the problem; and thirdly, he offered a solution to the problems similar to the one Jesus gave.

It's interesting to note how Jesus Himself gave a solution to church problems. The solution Jesus gave was to correct people who cause church problems.

First, Jesus said, "You should confront those who are causing problems and splits in the church." He said in Matthew 18:15,

> Moreover if thy brother shall trespass against thee, go and tell him his fault between thee and

him alone: if he shall hear thee, you have gained
thy brother."

Second, if he does not hear you, then you should take two or three witnesses and confront him about the problem. Jesus said in Matthew 18:16,

> But if he will not hear thee, then take with thee
> one or two more, that in the mouth of two or
> three witnesses every word may be established.

Third, if he neglects to hear the witnesses then tell the church. Jesus said in Matthew 18:17,

> If he neglects to hear them tell it to the church.

Fourth, if he refuses to hear the church then classify him as a heathen (a heathen is one who adheres to a religion that does not acknowledge God, Christ, or Christianity). Jesus said in Matthew 18:17,

> But if he neglects to hear the church, let him be
> unto thee as a heathen man and a publican.

This is the advice Jesus gave to solving church problems.

The solution to any church problem is always the same—the Word of God. Many churches split because some disgruntled or deceptive member want the church to embrace his religion. That's what happened to the Corinthian church. The leaders of the divisions wanted the church members to follow them. Paul feared they would trust in them for their salvation rather than trust in Jesus. No pastor, evangelist, teacher, member, or church leader should set themselves up as the guru to follow to find the way to salvation. The only place to find salvation is in Jesus Christ of the Bible, and that should be preached and emphasized above everything else. Therefore, you should not follow someone to find the way to salvation, but follow Jesus.

Paul was concerned that people might place him, Apollos, Cephas, or another Jesus, on the same level as Jesus of the Bible. He encouraged them to keep their sights on Jesus, not on people. A person is born into the family of God, not by following someone's leadership, but by receiving Jesus Christ as their Redeemer. Jesus said,

> I am the way... (John 14:6)

If it were possible to obtain salvation any other way than through the sacrificial death of Jesus Christ on the cross, then why didn't God use it? It would have saved God the Father, God the Son, and God the Holy Spirit from all the agony and pain they suffered. One of the reasons God used Jesus (the innocent for the guilty) was to demonstrate His love.

> For God so loved the world that He gave His only begotten Son, that whosoever believeth in Him should not perish, but have eternal life. (John 3:16)

Therefore, we are not saved by joining the right church, hearing the right preacher, belonging to the right denomination, doing good works, being baptized in water, or following the "right" religion; we are saved by believing in Jesus Christ, confessing our sins to Him, and accepting Him as our personal Saviour. After all, the Bible emphasizes over and over that Christ came to give his life on the cross to provide salvation for us.

Paul now turns to a specific problem—the problem of baptismal regeneration. He did that to show that a person is not saved by choosing some other way instead of Jesus the author of salvation. There has been nothing more controversial than salvation by baptism in water as appose to salvation by grace.

75

First Corinthians 1:14–17 deals with baptism.

What did Paul teach about baptismal regeneration? Paul said in 1 Corinthians 1:14–16,

> I thank God that I baptize none of you, but Crispus and Gaius. Lest any should say I baptized in my own name. And I also baptized the household of Stephanas: besides, I know not whether I baptized any other.

Allow me to say this up-front. God has only one plan of salvation, and that plan of salvation is by believing on Jesus, confessing our sins to Him, and receiving Him as our own personal Saviour. Salvation is not by what you do or don't do; it's by what Jesus did.

Paul said he did not baptize very many. It is obvious he is referring to water baptism. He did not emphasize being baptized in water for salvation but emphasized receiving Jesus Christ for salvation. Paul did not want any to put their confidence in water baptism, nor did he want anyone to place their hope in him, in Apollos, in Cephas, or in another Christ for salvation. He emphasized putting confidence in Jesus Christ of the Bible for salvation. Notice 1 Corinthians 1:17.

> For CHRIST SENT ME NOT TO BAPTIZE, but to preach the gospel, not with wisdom of words, lest the cross of Christ be of none effect.

Water baptism is not part of the Gospel. Let me say that again. Water baptism is not part of the Gospel.

If Paul was called to baptize people in water for salvation, that would have been his main emphasis throughout his epistles, but it's not. His main emphasis is to receive Jesus Christ for salvation. Therefore, salvation is totally separate from water baptism.

A good rule in interpreting God's plan of salvation is to interpret it in the light of what the Bible teaches about salvation. Those who use certain Scriptures to teach that baptism in water is necessary for salvation commit a serious error called the negative influence fallacy. That means two statements (or Scriptures) that contradict each other cannot be true. May I put it this way: Two statements about salvation that contradict each other cannot be true. One is totally true, and the other is not totally true.

If I say, salvation is by grace through faith absent baptism in water, it is totally true. However, if I say salvation is by grace through faith plus baptism in water, it is not true. Why? Anything you add to grace for salvation such as water baptism is wrong. Salvation must be by grace or by grace plus water baptism. It cannot be by both. Ephesians 2:8 says we are saved "by grace through faith, and that not of yourself."

Furthermore, if you are saved by water baptism, then the person baptizing you becomes your Saviour. Baptism is something you do to obtain salvation; therefore it is a work you must perform just like other religions that teach you must perform good works to obtain salvation. You can't add works to grace. If you do, it is no longer grace.

To settle this issue, we must decide what the Bible teaches about salvation. Ephesians 2:8–9 says,

> For by GRACE are you saved through faith, and that not of yourself, it is a gift of God, NOT OF WORKS lest any man should boast.

Allow me to list two other Scriptures that show salvation is by grace alone, not by works. Titus 3:5 says,

> Not by works of righteousness which we have done, but according to His murcy he saved us…

John 6:47 reads like this,

> Verily, verily, I [Jesus] say unto you, he that believeth on Me hath everlasting life.

Keep in mind that water baptism is a work. The Bible never contradicts itself. It does not say salvation is by grace in some Scriptures verses but by works in other Scripture verses.

The Bible teaches that salvation comes by believing on Jesus, confessing sins, and receiving Jesus Christ as Saviour. Baptism in water is important but not necessary for salvation. If I say, he that believes on the Lord Jesus Christ shall be saved, and then baptized in water to show he has been saved, it is a true statement. But if I say, he who believes and is baptized in water will be saved, it is not a true statement. Some churches, denominations, and ministers place their emphases on water baptism for salvation. Their message is, believe, repent, and then be baptized in water for salvation. The Bible's message, and God's plan of salvation, is, believe on Jesus and you will be saved.

Please don't put Christ down by saying He does not have the power or the ability to completely save you without your help—your work of baptism. Baptism is a work. Salvation is "not of works, lest any man should boast" (Ephesians 2:9). Adding water baptism to your salvation is something you physically do, thus a work. You must realize that Jesus does not need your help to save you.

God has only one plan of salvation, not two. He does not have a backup plan. Salvation is either by believing, confessing your sins, and receiving Jesus as your personal Saviour, or it is by believing, repenting, and being baptized in water. It cannot be by both.

First Corinthians 1:14–16 above is not saying water baptism is not important. It is important because it is a picture that shows Jesus died, was buried, and rose again to provide salvation for the lost. It shows the world that the death, burial, and resurrection of Christ is essential to salvation. Salvation must come before water baptism. Water baptism comes after salvation, and it is confessing that you are identifying with Jesus Christ in His death, burial, and resurrection. After we turned to Jesus for salvation, we are born again, and water baptism is a testimony we are born again and have become members of God's family by believing in the Gospel of Christ. We do not become members of God's family by being baptized in water but by believing in the death, burial, and resurrection of Christ.

We receive Jesus as our Saviour, and at that moment we are baptized into the family of God by the Holy Spirit. First Corinthians 12:13 said,

> For by ONE SPIRIT are WE ALL baptized into one body, whether we be Jews or gentile, whether we be bond or free, and have been all made to drink into one Spirit.

If a person is born again by being baptized in water, it is not the Holy Spirit doing the baptizing but some man; thereby he becomes the Saviour. Galatians 3:27 said,

> For as many of you as have been baptized into Christ (this is referring to baptism by the Holy Spirit) have put on Christ.

In John 1:33 John the Baptist said,

> He [Jesus] sent me to baptize with water, the same said unto me, upon whom thou shall see the Spirit descending, and remaining on him, the same is he which BAPTIZES WITH THE HOLY SPIRIT.

John the Baptist was sent to baptize with water, which showed repentance by the people that responded to his message, but Jesus came to baptize with the Holy Spirit that brought salvation to the repentant sinner. The disciples of Christ led people to Christ for salvation by presenting the Gospel, and once they repent and receive Jesus as their Saviour, the Holy Spirit baptized them into the family of God. Therefore, we are baptized into the family of God by the Holy Spirit, not by water. God's plan of salvation is also Paul's emphasis throughout his epistles.

Below Are Some Scriptures That Seem to Contradict God's Plan of Salvation

When two Scriptures seem to contradict each other, there must be an explanation. The Bible has several Scriptures that do just that. I will attempt to answer a few of those Scriptures that seem to contradict God's plan of salvation.

First, consider Mark 16:16.

He that believeth and is baptized shall be saved?

It is obvious this verse is referring to baptism by the Holy Spirit. It is saying, he that believeth and is baptized into the body of Christ by the Holy Spirit shall be saved.

Second, consider 1 Peter 3:21.

> The like figure whereunto even baptism doeth also now save us [not putting away the filth of the flesh, but the answer of a good conscience toward God], by the resurrection of Jesus Christ.

We are not saved by "putting away the filth of the flesh...but by the resurrection of Jesus Christ."

Is a person baptized into the family of God by water, or by the resurrection of Jesus Christ? The Scripture above answers that. The previous verse, 1 Peter 3:20 does mention water, "eight souls [meaning Noah and his family] were saved by water."

That means eight people were saved by building an ark to save themselves from the worldwide flood. The ark saved them. Water is mentioned because if there were no water, there would be no need for an ark. Jesus saves us by His sacrificial death on the cross, not by water.

Water baptism is a work. If 1 Peter 3:21 is teaching one is saved by being baptized in water to wash away his/her sins, then it means repentance has nothing to do with salvation. If "the like figure whereunto even baptism saves us" means water baptism saves us, then it means Jesus had to experience salvation for Himself, because He was baptized in water. The reason Jesus was baptized in water was to present a picture of His coming death, burial, and resurrection, which is essential to salvation. Those who believe, repent, and receive Jesus as Saviour are saved and then baptized in water to show they are saved. We are placed into the body of Christ by the Holy Spirit when we believe on Jesus, confess our sins, and receive Jesus as our Saviour, not when we are baptized in water. Water baptism has nothing to do with salvation. It has everything to do with our belief in Jesus, because it is an outward testimony of an inward change.

Third, notice Acts 22:16.

> And now why tarriest thou? Arise, and be baptized, and wash away thy sins, calling on the name of the Lord.

The key to understanding this verse is to settle the issue by asking whether a person's sins are washed away by water or by the blood of Christ. "Wash away your sins" is not a command to Paul that he must repent of sins and let water wash his sins away. Paul was saved when he met Jesus on the road to Damascus. A person's sins are washed away by the blood of Jesus Christ. Someone explained it this way: "Calling on the name of the Lord" is not a present participle, but must be translated as "having called on" or "since you called upon," thus having previously called upon the name of the Lord. Your sins are washed away by calling upon the Lord, not by water baptism, but by the blood of Jesus Christ.

Does Acts 22:16 teach that Paul was saved by Jesus Christ on the Damascus road, or at Juda's house with the help of Ananias? That can be answered by the Scriptures. Ananias called Paul "Brother Saul" in Acts 9:17. That meant he had already been saved. The Gospel was presented directly to Paul by Jesus Christ on the Damascus road. Galatians 1:11–12 says,

> But I certify [confirm] to you, brethren, that the gospel which was preached to me is not of

man [Ananias]. For I neither received it by man
[Ananias], neither was I taught it [by Ananias],
but by the revelation of Jesus Christ.

The name Ananias was added for clarification and to show Paul
was not saved by man such as Ananias commanding him to be baptized in water, but he was saved by personally seeing Jesus and receiving Jesus Christ as his Saviour on the Damascus road.

So according to Galatians 1:11–12, it is obvious that Paul
received salvation when Jesus preached to him, not when Ananias
talked with him. In fact, after Paul was saved, he called Jesus "Lord"
as recorded in Acts 22:10 and 9:6. First Corinthians 12:3 goes on to
say,

No man can call Jesus Lord, but by the Holy
Ghost.

Paul was saved by the Holy Spirit, baptizing him into the family
of God then he called Jesus Lord.

Acts 9:17–18 states,

And Ananias went his way, and entered the
house: and putting his hand on him [Paul], and
said, BROTHER Saul, the Lord, even Jesus that
appeared unto you in the way as thou comest,
hath sent me that you might receive thy sight,
and filled with the Holy Spirit [be controlled by
the Holy Spirit].

Do you know you can receive the Holy Spirit but not be controlled by the Holy Spirit? Acts 9:17–18 goes on to say,

And immediately there fell from his eyes as it had
been scales, and he received his sight, forthwith,
arose, and was baptized.

He was baptized in water because he was already saved. Notice this verse does not say he received the Holy Ghost, but says he was given back his eyesight. From that day forward, the Holy Spirit took complete control of him. Paul was not concerned about being filled with the Holy Spirit; He was already filled with the Holy Spirit. He was concerned about getting his eyesight back and being controlled by the Holy Spirit. From that moment on the Holy Spirit took control of him, that was the moment he received his eyesight. He was saved and filled with the Holy Spirit before he was baptized in water. In fact, a person is washed and saved by the blood of Jesus Christ, *not* by being baptized in water. Notice Revelations 1:5,

> Unto Him [Jesus] that loved us and washed us from our sins in His own blood.

Notice 1 Corinthians 6:11,

> And such were some of you [wicked sinners] but you are washed, but you are sanctified, but you are justified in the name of the Lord Jesus, and BY THE SPIRIT OF GOD.

People are washed, sanctified, and justified by Jesus and the Spirit of God, not by water baptism. In other words, people are baptized into the family of God by the Holy Spirit because they believe on Jesus, confess to God they are sinners, and then receive Jesus who died for them on the cross to take away their sins.

Fourth, another Scripture is found in John 3:5. This verse states that Nicodemus asked Jesus about being born all over again by a fleshly birth. He said,

> How can a man be born when he is old? Can he enter the second time into his mother's womb and be born? Jesus answered, "Verily, verily, I say unto you except a man is born of water [that is

a fleshly birth] and of the Spirit [that is a Spirit birth], he cannot enter the kingdom of God.

If you read the rest of John 3, you will find Jesus explaining the difference between a water birth (which is a fleshly birth) and a spiritual birth (which is a birth by the Holy Spirit). The first thing that happens to a woman when she is about to give birth is that her water breaks. That results in a water birth. Jesus goes on to say in John 3:6,

> That which is born of flesh is flesh. And that which is born of the Spirit [the Holy Spirit] it is Spirit.

Two births—one by water and one by the Holy Spirit. A person is saved by being baptized into the family of God by the Holy Spirit, not by being baptized in water.

Fifth, Acts 8:36 is another verse I need to explain. When the Ethiopian eunuch asked Phillip to baptize him, he was already saved. You must understand, the Ethiopian eunuch accepted Jesus Christ as his Saviour before he was baptized in water. He was reading Isaiah 53 about the prophecy of Jesus. Notice Isaiah 53:4,

> Surely He hath borne our grief.

That's talking about Jesus bearing our sins. Notice Isaiah 53:5,

> For he was wounded for our transgressions: He was bruised for our iniquities: the chastisement of our peace was upon Him; and with His stripes we are healed."

That describes the price Jesus paid for our sins. Notice Isaiah 53:7,

> He was oppressed, and He was afflicted…

That describes the crucifixion of Christ. Phillip used these Scriptures to preach unto the eunuch that Jesus Christ was the way to salvation. After the eunuch believed on Jesus, confessed his sins, and received Jesus as his personal Saviour, he then asked Phillip to baptize him in water to show he believed in the death, burial, and resurrection of Christ for salvation. He wanted to be baptized in water to identify himself with the death, burial, and resurrection of Jesus for salvation. Jesus made it possible for him to be saved by His death, burial, and resurrection. The Ethiopian eunuch identified himself with Jesus by being baptized in water.

Sixth, the next Scriptures are Ephesians 5:25–26.

> Christ loved the church and gave himself for it; that He might sanctify and cleanse it by the washing of water by the word.

The question arises: Is the church sanctified and cleansed by the word or by water? The answer, of course, is obvious—the word. Notice how it reads:

> By the washing of water BY THE WORD.

In that Scripture, water is a type or symbol of the Word of God. For instance, in John 15:3 Jesus said to his disciples,

> Now you are clean through the Word I have spoken to you.

In James 1:18 we read,

> Of his own will begat he us through the Word.

First Peter 1:23 tells us that we are "born again, not of corruptible seed, but of incorruptible, by the word of God."

Water represents the word, and we are washed and cleansed by the Word, not by water.

Seventh, consider Mark 16:16.

> He that believeth and is baptized shall be saved,
> but he that believeth not shall be damned.

Notice it said, "he that BELIEVETH, and is baptized shall be saved."

This Scripture refers to baptism by the Holy Spirit. A person is saved when he believes Jesus paid his sins debt on the cross, and he confesses his sin and then receives Jesus as His Saviour. A person is saved by being baptized into the family of God by the Holy Spirit, not by being washed in the water. Furthermore, notice something else this Scripture verse says:

> He that believeth not, shall be damned.

It does not say "He that believeth not and is not baptized in water shall be damned." Therefore, a person is saved by putting his faith and trust in the resurrected Christ, not by being baptized in water. To be sure, water is not mentioned in Mark 16:16. First Corinthians 12:13 says,

> For by one SPIRIT are we all baptized into one
> body, whether we be Jew or gentile, whether we
> be bond or free; and all have been made to drink
> into one Spirit.

If a man is saved by being baptized in water, then that means the cross of Christ was not necessary. Paul believed and preached everywhere he went that the cross was not only necessary but essential to salvation. First Corinthians 1:17–18 makes that clear.

> For Christ sent me not to baptize, but to preach
> the gospel…but unto us which are saved it is the
> power of God.

Paul said in Romans 1:16,

> For I am not ashamed of the gospel of Christ: for
> it is the power of God unto salvation to everyone
> that believeth; to the Jew first, and also to the
> Greek.

Baptism by water is not part of the Gospel. Paul would have added the words "and baptized in water" after *"believeth"* if water baptism was essential to salvation. Romans 1:16 teaches that a person is not saved by water baptism. It was Paul's burning desire to present Christ, and Christ alone as the way to salvation, not by believing, repenting, and being baptized in water.

Eighth, look Acts 2:38.

> Then Peter said unto them REPENT, and be
> baptized every one of you, in the name of Jesus
> Christ for the remission (forgiveness) of sin, and
> you shall receive the gift of the Holy Ghost.

Water is not mentioned in this verse of Scripture. To allow the Holy Ghost to control one's life, he must first be baptized into the family of God by the Holy Ghost. A person has not received remission of sins until he is baptized into the family of God by the Holy Spirit. At that time, he receives the gift of the Holy Spirit. Acts 2:38 is emphasizing repentance as the main thought, not water baptism.

In Paul's day, people wanted the gift of the Holy Spirit. They said,

> Men and brethren, what shall we do? (Acts 2:37)

In other words, they wanted the Holy Spirit in their lives, not remission of sins by being baptized in water. However, after they repented, and were baptized into the family of God by the Holy Ghost, about five hundred were added to the church. Five hundred were not baptized in water until they received Jesus as their Saviour.

They probably were baptized later because they were already born again and desired to identify themselves with Christ in His death, burial, and resurrection.

By the way, Peter said they were to be baptized in the name of Jesus. They believed in God and believed in the Holy Spirit. There are no less than forty times the Spirit, Holy Spirit, Holy Ghost are mentioned in the Old Testament. The Jews believed in God and the Holy Spirit, but they did not believe in Jesus Christ. Peter is saying, "You must not only be baptized in the name of the Father and of the Holy Spirit, but you must be baptized in the name of the Father, the Son, and the Holy Spirit." A person *does not* receive the Holy Spirit by being baptized in water in the name of Jesus only. When some of the apostles came to Samaria, they found the people had been baptized in the name of Jesus, yet they had not received the Holy Spirit. Acts 8:15 and 16 said,

> Who, when they were come down, prayed for them, THAT THEY MAY RECEIVE THE HOLY GHOST. For yet He [the Holy Ghost] was fallen upon none of them: that they were baptized in the name of the Lord Jesus.

To receive the Holy Spirit, they had to be baptized into the family of God by the Holy Spirit. They were baptized in the name of the Father, the Son, and the Holy Spirit after they were saved.

Those who believe in baptismal regeneration base their religious belief on the word *for*. They say Acts 2:38 teaches to get remission (forgiveness) of sins one must be baptized in water *for* (in order to get) the forgiveness of sins. However, the emphasis is placed on "repentance" to receive forgiveness and the gift of the Holy Ghost. It does not mean be baptized in water to receive remission of sins. Acts 2:38 is based on the word *repent*. To be sure, water is not even mentioned in Acts 2:38.

There are two Greek words—one pronounced *eis* and the other *hina*—that are translated *for* in the Bible. Both mean *for* but must be translated to fit the Bible's teaching about God's plan of salvation.

The Greek preposition *hina* is used over five hundred times in the New Testament, and it means "because," "so that," "that," and "to the intent." And the word *eis* is also used many times and means the same as *hina*. If one receives remission of sins when he/she is baptized in water, either of these Greek words could be used because they both mean the same thing. However, in the case of being born again, they must be interpreted to fit the overall subject of God's plan of salvation. The Bible emphasizes over and over that salvation is obtained by believing, repenting, and receiving Jesus Christ as Saviour. So the word *eis* and/or *hina* must be used to rightly interpret Acts 2:38. Translators should have used the words *because of* instead of *for* in Acts 2:38.

Ninth, Galatians 3:27 is another Scripture.

> For as many of you that have been baptized into
> Christ have put on Christ.

The previous verse (verse 26) states that we are saved by faith in Jesus Christ.

> For you are all children of God by faith in Jesus
> Christ.

God does not contradict Himself. God would not say we are children of God by faith in Jesus Christ, then in the very next Scripture verse say we must be baptized to be saved. God does not work that way. First Corinthians 10:2 says,

> And all were baptized unto Moses and in the
> cloud and in the sea.

If baptism did not put them into Moses, neither would being baptized in water put us in Christ. Verse 26 is saying, "Those who were baptized into Christ were baptized by the Holy Spirit into Christ." By the way, water is not mentioned in verse 27.

Allow me to say one other thing about baptism that emphasizes the truth that a person is baptized into the family of God by the Holy Spirit, not by water. When Jesus came to John the Baptist to be baptized in water, He did it for one of two reasons. He presented a living demonstration of His coming death, burial, and resurrection for salvation, or He was a sinner that needed to be saved by being baptized in water to wash away His sins. It would take a demon-possessed moron (the devil himself) to say Jesus was a sinner in need of salvation. The baptism of Jesus was to present a message, a picture of His death, burial, and resurrection to show mankind God's plan of salvation is found in Jesus and Jesus alone.

The Lord has never used any other way to bring people to Himself but through faith in the Gospel, and the Gospel is the death, burial, and resurrection of Jesus Christ.

> For if they which are of the Law [those who keep
> the Law and are baptized in water for salvation]
> be heirs, faith is made void, and the promise is
> made of none effect. (Romans 4:14)

It takes preaching the death, burial, and resurrection of Jesus Christ to bring a person to salvation. When we get God's plan of salvation backward (that is, baptism by water before salvation), we make the cross of Christ void. The word *void* means to "nullify, empty, delete, invalidate, or make useless." In other words, Christ made a mistake by dying on the cross to provide salvation for us if we can be saved by being baptized in water to wash our sins away. It's a sin, a wicked sin, to make the cross of Christ void. Those who make a law that water baptism is essential to salvation are making faith void. Curtis Hudson said, "The very fact that one is trusting water baptism in any degree shows he is not fully trusting in Jesus Christ." Dr. Hudson goes on to say, "If placing someone under water and bringing him up again actually remits sins, then it would be the preacher who remits sin, and not Christ Himself."

The world doesn't accept the Gospel of Christ, so they major on something else. Many major on water baptism for salvation. Many major on works for salvation, and I could go on and on, but Paul presented Christ crucified, buried, and raised again as the way to salvation. Nothing more and nothing less will get a person to heaven.

You must decide for yourself whether salvation is by water or by the cross of Christ. It cannot be by both. God has only one plan of salvation, and that plan of salvation is in Jesus Christ. Jesus said in John 5:39,

> Search the Scriptures, for in them you think you
> have eternal life: and they are they that testify of
> me.

Eternal life is found in Jesus Christ, or else John 5:39 would not be in the Bible. John 3:36 says,

> He that believeth on the Son of God hath eternal
> life, and he that believeth not in the Son shall not
> see life; but the wrath of God abideth on him.

You must interpret the Scriptures in the light of God's plan of salvation, which is to believe that Jesus paid your sin debt on the cross, confess your sins to Jesus, and receive Jesus as your own personal Saviour. Please try to understand, water baptism is not part of salvation. God has only one plan of salvation, and that plan was set in force before time began. Acts 2:23 says,

> Him [Jesus] being delivered by the determinate
> counsel [the determinate counsel was God the
> Father, God the Son, and God the Holy Spirit)
> and foreknowledge of God, ye have taken, and by
> wicked hands have crucified and slain.

In Luke 22:22 Jesus said,

> Truly the Son of man goeth, as it was determined.

In the beginning, before the dawning of creation, God designed His perfect plan of salvation. Therefore, God has only one plan of salvation, and that is in Jesus Christ. If you have a few Scriptures that seem (notice I said *seem*) to contradict God on His plan of salvation, you must interpret them in accordance to God's plan of salvation. Salvation is all about Jesus, not about water baptism.

I conclude this section on baptismal regeneration by calling your attention once again to 1 Corinthians 1:17 where Paul said,

> For Christ sent me not to baptize, but to preach
> the Gospel: not with wisdom of words, lest the
> cross of Christ should be made of non-effect.

The question I want to ask is this: If baptism in water is essential to salvation, then why did God not call Paul to baptize people in water for salvation? After all, it was Paul's burning desire to lead people into the family of God.

If baptism in water washes away sins then Paul would *not* have said, "Christ sent me not to baptize," but the fact is, Paul boldly stated,

CHRIST SENT ME NOT TO BAPTIZE, BUT TO PREACH THE GOSPEL.

People are saved by believing the Gospel, repenting of sins, and receiving Jesus Christ as Saviour, not by being baptized in water.

If baptism is not part of God's salvation plan, then why does all these Scriptures above indicate it is? The answer is, these Scriptures are placed in the Bible to show that people are baptized into the family of God by the Holy Spirit and to show that people invent many ways just to bypass the sacrificial death of Christ for salvation. That is of the devil.

First Corinthians 1:18–31 is the fifth subject in the outline, and it deals with those who call preaching foolishness.

Notice 1:18,

> For the preaching of the cross is to them that per-
> ish foolishness but unto us that are saved it is the
> power of God.

Unbelievers call preaching the death, burial, and resurrection for salvation foolish. But unto those who are saved, it is the power of God unto salvation. After all, it is the Gospel that brings us to salvation. Does that sound foolish? Absolutely not!

The above Scripture tells us why preaching the cross of Christ is necessary. It is the door to salvation because it leads us to Christ. Romans 10:13 says,

> Faith cometh by hearing, and hearing by the
> word of God.

Preaching the Word of God produces faith that brings salvation.

Some say the message of the cross is *not* necessary because the cross was not necessary. It's not that they don't believe in the existence of God. They say preaching the cross is only about a Jewish man who lived about two thousand years ago, and that man went about doing good deeds but was crucified for crimes He did not commit. They say by Jesus doing good deeds and dying for what He believed, it leaves us a good example to follow, even if we must die for what we believe. Therefore, they say, if we do good deeds as Jesus did, we can make it to heaven. No, a thousand times no! Salvation is "not of yourself" (Ephesians 2:8). Jesus had a purpose for being crucified. It cost Him His life.

First, salvation was costly. To understand God's plan of salvation and why it was so costly, we must know the reason Jesus came into this world. We must know why He died on the cross, why He was

buried, and why He rose from the grave. Right before Jesus was crucified, He said to His Father as recorded in John 12:27,

> Now is my soul troubled, and what shall I say?
> Father save me from this hour: but for this cause
> came I into this hour.

What was the cause Jesus came into that hour? He came to take
our place on the cross and died to pay our sin debt. Jesus said,

> I am the living bread which came down from
> heaven…the bread that I give is my flesh, which
> I will give for the life of the world. (John 6:51)

Without Jesus dying on the cross to pay our sin debt, there is
no salvation.

> [Christ] gave Himself for us, that He might
> redeem us from all iniquity, and purify unto
> Himself a peculiar people zealous, of good works.
> (Psalms 104:4)

The salvation Jesus Christ has to offer is the greatest revelation
this world has ever known. That is wisdom beyond man's compre-
hension. Therefore, they call it foolishness. But Hebrews 2:3 says,

> How shall we escape, if we neglect so great salva-
> tion; which at the first began to be spoken of by the
> Lord, and was confirmed by them that heard him?

The greatest words in the Bible are about salvation. Salvation
has everything to do with Jesus coming into this world. After all,
Jesus said in John 5:39,

> Search the Scriptures, for in them you think you
> have eternal life; and they are they that testify of Me.

We could elaborate on that single Scripture forever and never exhaust its meaning. That is wisdom beyond the grasp of mankind.

Second, salvation is eternal. Hebrews 5:8 says,

> And [Jesus] being made perfect. He became the author of ETERNAL salvation to all them that obey him.

That means all who obey the Gospel by putting their faith and trust in Jesus for salvation. Notice what Hebrews 10:10 and 17–18 has to say,

> By [Jesus] we are sanctified [saved, and set apart for a sacred use] through the offering of the body of Jesus Christ ONCE FOR ALL....and their sins and iniquities I will remember no more... THERE IS NO MORE OFFER ING FOR SIN.

Jesus died to take away our sin *once*, and He will never repeat that process again. Notice Hebrews 6:4 and 6,

> For it is impossible for those who were once enlightened [saved] and tasted the heavenly gift [gift of salvation] and were made partakers of the Holy Ghost...if they should fall away. To renew it unto repentance, seeing they have crucified to themselves the Son of God afresh, and put Him to an open shame.

These two verses are saying, if you could become unsaved after you were saved, then Jesus would have to die for you again to save you again. That will never happen. Furthermore, if you could become unsaved, and then repent and be saved again, you would be responsible for your salvation, but more than that you would put Christ to an open shame.

Not only is our salvation costly, it is eternal, and third, it is common.

Third, our salvation is common. *Common* means it is widely known. No one can say they did not know. Jude said in Jude 3,

> I gave all diligence to write unto you of the common salvation.

Our salvation is common and simple, but so complicated unbelievers cannot understand, nor want to understand it. They call it foolishness. Salvation is not wrapped up in some great mystery that only a select few can find but is common and easily understood by those who yield to the calling of the Holy Spirit. One can have it by coming to Jesus by faith. God's plan of salvation is so simple I am mystified how people miss it, but they do because the devil blinds their minds to it. Second Corinthians 4:4 states,

> In whom the god [Satan] of this world hath blinded the minds of them that believe not, lest the light of the glorious gospel of Christ, who is the image of God, should shine unto them.

Salvation is simple to those who exercise faith in Jesus Christ. Acts 2:21 said,

> Whoever calls on the name of the Lord Jesus shall be saved.

That is a simple message and easily understood, yet unbelievers don't get it, and cannot get it because they let Satan blind their minds.

People who miss God's plan of salvation will have an eternity to pay for their deliberate self-imposed ignorance. First Corinthians 1:19 said,

> For it is written, I will destroy the wisdom of the wise, and bring to nothing the understanding of the prudent.

People cannot come to Christ any other way but by the cross. It must be the convicting power of the Holy Spirit that reveals to them the need to come to Christ for salvation. You would think people could understand God's simple plan of salvation, but they don't. They believe it is foolish.

Most unbelievers have the belief that if you want something, you must do something to get something. Have you noticed almost all religions base their beliefs on that? They feel they must do something to get salvation. That's not the way to get salvation. God freely gives us salvation without works or anything we do or don't do. As far as works are concerned, we have the privilege of producing good works after we are saved, not producing good works to be saved.

In the following Scripture, Paul uses rhetorical questions to chide the Corinthians people into believing the truth. What is a rhetorical question? It is a question requiring no response. It's the art of persuasive language, figure of speech, or a statement that sounds like a question but only a statement. Paul is not asking questions, per se, that demands answers, but he makes statements in the form of questions. The answers are obvious according to the way the questions are phrased. For example, someone who is looking at a beautiful sunset might say, "What a beautiful sunset?" He is not asking a question about the beauty of the sunset but making a statement that sounds like a question. Someone might say, "What suffering, what pain, what agony that person is going through?" These comments sound like questions, but they are only statements that sound like questions. It is obvious what the statements are all about. That is called rhetorical questions. That is the method Paul used here.

Paul asked several rhetorical questions in 1 Corinthians 1:20. Notice how he phrased them.

> Where is the wise? Where is the scribe? Where is the disputer of this world? Hath not God made foolish the wisdom of this world.

Both Paul and Jesus knew how to use rhetorical questions in a way that would have the greatest impact on their readers and listeners.

Where is the wise?

Paul is not trying to find someone wise but making a statement about those who think they are wise.

Where is the scribe?

Paul is not searching for a teacher who is wise but is making a statement about those who think they are wise teachers.

Where are the disputers of this world?

Paul is not searching for someone who questions God's creation. He is saying those who argue against God's creation are already here and they think they are wise.

Allow me to further comment on "where are the disputers of this world."

There is a dangerous and destructive doctrine that has risen recently that is called "the new evolution." It is invading churches at an alarming rate. It is even infiltrating fundamental churches. The New Evolution is a belief that evolution has been proven to be true. Therefore, the new evolution believers say churches need to interpret the Bible to accommodate that belief.

It's imperative we recognize who the disputers of this world are. They are theistic and atheistic evolutionists. They call themselves "the new evolutionists." They argue against God's instant creation and even call it "a myth."

The word *theist* means God, and the word *evolution* means all things evolved by natural processes. Putting those two words together means God-evolutionist. Those two words do not fit together and could not fit together. God did not use evolution to bring about everything. Theistic evolutionists teach that God made the earth in the beginning but stepped away from it and let evolution take its course over billions of years until things came to be what they are now. The fact is, God spoke, and everything came into existence, not over billions of years, but instantly. God was very careful to define days of creation as twenty-four-hour days, not long periods of time. Genesis 1:1 says,

> In the beginning God created the heaven and the earth.

Genesis 1:3–5 stated,

> God said, let there be light: and there was light… and God divided the light from darkness. And God called the light day, and He called the darkness night, and the evening and morning [twenty-four hours] were the first day.

Anyone with common sense knows a day consists of twenty-four hours. A day has a few hours of darkness and a few hours of light that makes up twenty-four hours. How can you make long periods of time out of that? Someone may say, when that statement was made, God had not created the sun yet. If God can create a universe, He sure can create a twelve-hour day and a twelve-hour night whether there is a sun or not.

The above passage of Scripture can be understood no other way than twenty-four-hour days. The allegorical symbolical interpreters of Scripture see twenty-four-hour days as long period of time—that is, they make Scriptures say something they do not say. The literal, or fundamental, method, on the other hand, translate Scriptures the way the Bible teaches: twenty-four-hour-day pattern.

So when Paul said, "Where is the disputers of this world?" he is using a rhetorical question. He already knew who the disputers of this world were—those that believed in evolution.

Notice the last question in 1 Corinthians 1:20. This is the only legitimate question in the group of question. Notice what Paul said,

> Hath not God made foolishness the wisdom of
> this world? (1 Corinthians 1:20)

Worldly wisdom is foolish wisdom when it is compared to God's wisdom. People cannot understand the Bible, nor come to know Jesus through their own wisdom. They depend on their wisdom, that is why they call preaching the Gospel foolishness. First Corinthians 1:21 said,

> For after that in the wisdom of God the world by
> wisdom knew not God, its pleasing to God by
> the foolishness [what unbelievers call foolishness]
> of preaching to save them that believe.

The truth of the Gospel is before their eyes, yet they miss it. They keep seeking it through their intellectual reasoning but never finding it. Through wisdom people cannot understand God's wisdom. It is pleasing to God to save some through what people call foolishness—that is, preaching the Gospel.

> For the Jews require a sign, and the Greeks seek
> after wisdom: but we preach Christ crucified,
> unto the Jews a stumbling block, and to the
> Greeks foolishness; but unto them which are
> called, both Jews and Greeks, Christ the power
> of God, and wisdom of God. (1 Corinthians
> 1:22–24)

The Jews require a sign, the Greeks seek after wisdom, but preaching the Gospel is a stumbling block to the Jews and foolishness to the Greeks.

God's Word contains more wisdom than all the books in the world. Most books deal with things unbelievers can relate to, but God's Word deals with supernatural things of eternity that unbelievers cannot relate to, nor understand. Jesus said in John 12:32,

> And I, if I be lifted up from the earth, will draw
> all men unto Me.

Unbelievers cannot understand that Scripture verse, but to the believer, profound wisdom is found there. God draws unbelievers to Himself through the preaching of the cross of Christ. To the Jews that does not make sense, and to the Greeks that is foolishness.

Once we understand what preaching the cross means to the unbelievers, we can understand why they would call preaching foolishness. To be sure, unbelievers are fools themselves for not accepting it. They do not know they are fools, but they are self-imposed fools. Psalms 14:1 says,

> The fool hath said in his heart, there is no God.

Every person on earth has an equal opportunity to know Jesus as Saviour, but that does not mean every person on earth will come to Christ for salvation. God chose to reveal Himself through the preaching of the cross of Christ. Paul said in Romans 1:16,

> For I am not ashamed of the gospel of Christ: for
> it is the power of God unto salvation to everyone
> that believeth; to the Jew first and then to the
> Greeks.

The reason God does not call men to Himself through intellectual reasoning is the same reason God does not save people through their good works; it's just not what the Bible teaches about finding salvation. We cannot brag about our good works or intellectual reasoning to bring us to salvation, because that is not the way to obtain salvation. First Corinthians 1:25 states,

> Because the foolishness of God [what unbelievers call the gospel of God] is wiser than men; and the weakness of God [what man calls weakness] is stronger than men.

Notice how God calls mankind to Himself. First Corinthians 1:26 said,

> For you see your calling, brethren, how that not many wise men after the flesh, not many mighty, not many noble, are called: but God hath chosen the foolish thing of the world [what man calls foolish] to confound the wise [the worldly wise].

Why does God call simple people to Himself instead of the notable, wise, and intellectuals? The wise, the mighty, the intellect, and the noble will not come to God by faith but seek answers to complicated questions through their own intelligence. A person does not, and cannot, reason his way to salvation. Don't misunderstand me. I'm not saying God does not call the wise, the intelligent, and the noble to the truth that Christ is the Saviour of the world. I'm saying the absence of faith and depending on one's intelligence to find salvation is senseless and futile. One must hear and receive the Gospel as the truth of God. A person's journey to the truth that Jesus Christ is the Messiah must be by faith in Jesus alone. Jesus said,

> I am the way, the TRUTH, and the light. (John 14:6)

When a person comes to Jesus by faith, Jesus sets him free from all the confusion of trying to find his way to salvation. Jesus said in John 8:32,

> You shall know the truth, and the truth shall set you free.

First Corinthians 1:27–30 states,

> God hath chosen the weak [what unbelievers classify as weak] things of the world to confound things which are mighty; and base things [fundamental principles] of the world, and things which are despised, hath God chosen, yea, and things which are not, to bring to naught [bring to nothing[things that are: that no flesh should glory in His presence. But of Him are you in Christ Jesus, who of God, is made unto us wisdom, and righteousness, and sanctification, and redemption.

The death, burial, and resurrection of Jesus is the wisdom of God. It is righteousness, sanctification, and redemption. Jesus met God's requirements to redeem us. Now we can say we have been made wise, righteous, sanctified, and redeemed in Jesus. Ephesians 3:27 said,

> In whom we have redemption through His blood, the forgiveness of sins, according to the riches of His [God's] grace.

There is nothing we have done that we can glory in, but if we glory, we must glory in the Lord. First Corinthians 1:31 said,

> That, according as it is written, he that glorieth let him glory in the Lord.

CHAPTER 2
HAS FOUR SUBJECTS

Verses 1–5 present reasons for preaching God's Word.
Verses 6–8 show Bible revelation is not discovered by man's wisdom.
Verses 9–13 show Bible revelation is given by the Holy Spirit.
Verses 14–16 show God's special people are given the right to judge.

First Corinthians 2:1–5 is the first subject, and it presents reasons for preaching God's Word.

God has a purpose in preaching His Word, and that purpose is to lead unbelievers to Christ. Paul knew God's purpose for him was to preach His Word. Notice verse 1,

> And, I brethren, when I come to you, came not with excellency of speech or of wisdom, declaring unto you the testimony of God. That your faith should not stand in the wisdom of man, but in the power of God.

Paul did not come to them with excellent speeches nor with wise words but came preaching the simple Gospel.

True preaching is not majoring on speeches with flamboyant words, nor is true preaching done to demonstrate one's intellectual wisdom. But true preaching is to be done with simple understandable words. That is what Paul sought to do, and that is what we should do. We should not mimic other preachers but preach the way God wants us to preach. Make it simple. Make it simple!

Notice what Paul said in verse 2,

> For I determined not to know anything among
> you, save Jesus Christ, and Him crucified.

Paul was not interested in intellectualism, but only about Jesus Christ and His crucifixion. He was interested in getting the truth across to them. Should not that be our goal? After all, it is getting the message of the death, burial, and resurrection of Jesus to people so that it will lead them to Christ.

Notice what Paul said in verse 3, "And I was with you in weakness, and in fear, and in much trembling."

What caused Paul to be weak, fearful, and tremble? He was recently challenged by atheistic Athenians in Athens, a city of hostile people toward the Gospel. Paul faced vicious hate toward the Gospel, and since he preached the Gospel, they took their hostility out on him. He was afraid the Corinthian people would treat him the same way. He feared for his own life; nevertheless, he preached anyway. Notice what he said in verse 4,

> And my speech and my preaching were not with
> enticing words of man's wisdom, but in demon-
> stration of the Spirit and power.

Paul repeated his intention in verse 4 by saying he did not come to them with impressive speeches nor human wisdom, but through the power of the Spirit. Evidently, Paul was motivated to preach by God's power, God's wisdom, and the Holy Spirit. If Paul could come back right now, he wouldn't change his message. He would stress the fact that God used him to glorify Jesus and lead others to Christ. Paul devoted His entire life telling others about the saving grace of Jesus Christ. He has a place in history as the greatest man who ever lived apart from Jesus Christ. God wants you and me to leave a legacy like that, and we can if we spend our time in studying God's Word and preaching it.

Although we have unique opportunities to preach to unbelievers, our accomplishments come far short of what Paul accomplished. However, our objective should be to preach the Gospel and point the lost to Christ. For example, preaching God's Word at a funeral offers tremendous opportunity to glorify God and reach unbelievers for Christ. Funerals are sad times for some but encouraging times for others.

I will never forget a funeral I went to while pastoring on Lookout Mountain above Chattanooga. I met a missionary couple who lived in Africa for over forty years. Their mission was leading people to Christ. They came back to Chattanooga because of health problems and rented a little house near the church I pastored. The little house was below the road. The top of the house was about level with the road. I stopped by one day to invite them to church. I introduced myself as the pastor of the Baptist church. An elderly man eagerly invited me in. He spoke a few moments about the mission work he and his wife had been involved in for the past forty years. Then he said, "Pastor, my wife has leukemia and only has a few days to live. I want you to meet her." He stepped into the little bedroom to help her. It took him twenty minutes or more to get her up and come into the living room. She looked pale and sickly, but she had gotten out of bed, dressed, and put on makeup just to meet the pastor. I talked with them for a few minutes. Their eyes brightened with joy as they talked about their mission work in Africa.

A day or so later, I stopped by again. No one was home. I asked a neighbor lady if she knew where they were. She said, "The lady passed away last night.

I called several funeral homes to find where the funeral was going to be. On the day of the funeral I went to the little church where they were having the funeral. There was perhaps fifteen or twenty people at the funeral. I watched as the minister spoke a few kind words, and then they carried her body to the little cemetery beside the church. I watched as her husband stood alone at the grave site, and I watched as the grave was being covered. He had lost his best friend, his wife, his companion, and the love of his life; now he was alone.

Driving back up Lookout Mountain, I began to talk with the Lord. I said, "Lord, it's just not fair, when they came back to Chattanooga, half of Chattanooga should have been at the airport to welcome them home and honor them for their missionary work." I said, "Half of Chattanooga should have been at that funeral to pay their respects for such a wonderful couple." The Lord seemed to whisper to me, saying, "You're forgetting, Walter, Chattanooga was not her home. You should have seen the reception she received when she arrived home." An old song came to my mind, and I began to sing as I drove up the mountain:

> This world is not my home, I'm just passing through.
> My treasures are laid up somewhere beyond the blue.
> The angels beckoning me from heavens open door, and I can't feel at home in this world anymore.

This missionary lady and her husband were a witness in her death just like they were those forty years on the mission field. Oh! What a story she could tell if she could come back for a few moments!

Oh! What a story Paul could tell if he could come back a few moments! Wherever Paul went, he preached the Gospel. He made no exception when he came to Corinth. His preaching was motivated by God's power, God's strength, and God's wisdom. Paul was noted for preaching the Gospel. His life consisted of preaching the Gospel. Paul was convinced that preaching the Gospel was God's call on him. He made it very clear that it was not his purpose to engage in intellectual debate to arrive at a better way to approach religion. He stuck with the fundamentals. Paul determined to preach Christ, His death, His burial, and His resurrection, which is the Gospel. After all, what else is there to preach?

David Brainerd, a missionary to the American Indians, died of TB at the age of 27 because of his travels across America in the cold and snowy weather preaching the Gospel. He said, "I have never gotten away from Jesus and His crucifixion." He preached that salvation was in Jesus and Jesus alone. He made the following statement: "Once a person is saved, God's Word will change his life forever." God's Word is the only thing that will genuinely change a person's life. When people fall in love with Jesus and His Word, they are changed. Second Corinthians 5:17 said,

> Therefore if anyone be in Christ, he is a new creature, old things have passed away; behold all things are become new.

When a person becomes a believer in Christ, he falls in love with Him. The more he knows Him, the more he loves Him. The more he loves Him, the more he serves Him. The more he serves Him, the more he wants to be like Him.

> O to be like Thee, Blessed Redeemer, this is my constant longing and prayer. (A song by Thomas O. Chisholm)

Paul made the statement that he would preach nothing but Jesus Christ and Him alone for salvation. Read again 1 Corinthians 2:2

> For I determined not to know anything among you save [except] Jesus Christ and Him crucified.

Paul's preaching was not with impressive words; it was by the power of the Holy Spirit that was in him. Notice again 1 Corinthians 2:4,

> My speech and my preaching were not with enticing words of man's wisdom, but in demonstration of the Spirit and power.

It's better to speak one word that is understandable than to speak ten thousand words that cannot be understood. Notice what Paul said in 1 Corinthians 2:5,

> That your faith should not stand in the wisdom
> of men, but in the power of God.

Paul was emotional about his service to Jesus. He never boasted about his accomplishments. He did not depend on his intelligence to get things done. Paul was intelligent, but he did not put his intelligence before the power of God. Frankly, being proud of one's intelligence will bring a person down quicker than anything.

I heard a story about a young man that just graduated from a theological seminary. He was asked to preach at a somewhat large church. When introduced he ran to the platform, strutted over to the podium, but made a mess of his sermon. Realizing he had failed, he bowed his head and walked slowly back to his seat. The pastor met him later and said, "Son, if you had walked up to the podium like you came down from the podium, you could have come down from the podium the way you went up to the podium." Proverbs 16:18 states,

> Pride goeth before destruction and a haughty
> spirit before a fall.

Paul had an inner sense of weakness that drove him to totally depend on Jesus. Is it not true we need that too? Paul said,

> I can do all things through Christ who strengthen
> me. (Philippians 4:13)

We can accomplish things too, but it must be through the power of Jesus Christ that strengthens us.

The second subject of the outline in found in 1 Corinthians 2:6–8, and it shows Bible revelation is not discovered by man's wisdom.

Allow me to emphasize an important point at the very outset of this section. I am not putting those down who have a high degree of intelligence. Unless a preacher has a good education from a fundamental, reputable college or seminary, he is more likely to get his biblical doctrine screwed up and lead people astray. By the way, I'm not putting a premium on ignorance. Someone may say, I don't need an education to preach. No, you don't, but if you don't have an education, you are more likely to misinterpret Scriptures. You need the right kind of education.

The standard on which the world values wisdom is certainly not God's standard for wisdom. Comparing God's wisdom with worldly wisdom is like comparing the vastness of space to a grain of sand. God's wisdom is so great that nothing can compare to it. Isaiah 55:8–9 records a statement from God,

> For My thoughts are not your thoughts, neither are your ways my ways, sayeth the Lord. For as the heavens are higher than the earth, so are my ways higher than your ways, and my thoughts than your thoughts.

Romans 11:33 states,

> Oh, the depths of the riches both of the wisdom and knowledge of God! How unsearchable are His judgments and His ways past finding out?

God is an awesome God!

Someone said, "The more I know about God, the smaller I become, and sometimes I feel I am no bigger than a blip on the radar of existence." That applies to me too because God is so great; we cannot possibly come near to understanding His greatness. Psalms 94:8–9 said,

> Understand, ye brutish among the people: and ye fool, when will you be wise? He who planted [made] the ear [for mankind], shall he not hear? He that formed the eye [for mankind] can he not see?

The concept of evolution according to this verse above is nothing more than bruit-like foolishness. If a car demands a carmaker, and a computer demands a computer maker, surely the infinitely more intricate and complex eyes and ears of living creatures demand an eye maker and ear maker! The law of cause and effect means the effect cannot be greater than the cause. It becomes nonsense when fools say the chaos is the cause of the cosmos. That is, the universe evolved by chance from chaos. The only evidence for evolution is the fact of leaders of intelligence believe it, and the only reason they believe it is their frantic desire to escape God.

When one thinks he has accomplished something through his own intelligence, he tends to give himself glory instead of glorifying our creator God. When I see God as He really is, I stand in awe. People cannot grasp the greatness of God through their intellectual pursuit of knowledge. However, we as Christians get a glimpse of His greatness and wisdom from the Word of God.

Notice what Paul said about wisdom. First Corinthians 2:6,

> Howbeit, we speak wisdom among them that are perfect: yet not the wisdom of the world, nor the prince of this world, that comes to naught.

In other words, Paul is saying, "I speak God's wisdom that is from above." God's wisdom is not gained from worldly wisdom, nor is God's wisdom found in the prince of this world—Satan. God's wisdom is not a flagrant performance of one's intelligence, but a demonstration of the power and wisdom of Jesus Christ. The more we know about Jesus, the more we understand the greatness of God's wisdom.

Paul said in 1 Corinthians 2:7,

> We speak the wisdom of God in a mystery, even
> the hidden wisdom, which God ordained before
> the world unto His glory.

God's wisdom is a mystery that lies beyond the grasp of man's understanding. God does not transfer His wisdom to unbelievers, because they cannot get it. However, He transfers a limited portion of His wisdom to us when we come under conviction to receive Him as our Redeemer. He reveals to us why He paid our sin debt. Then after we confess our sins and receive Him as our Saviour, we read and study His Word and gain more wisdom.

Notice the word *ordained* in the above Scripture verse. It means God predetermined before the world was created that He would send Jesus to this earth to provide salvation to anyone who would receive Him. His proclamation was that anyone could be saved if they would repent of their sins and receive Jesus as their Saviour. That is profound wisdom.

God's wisdom cannot be found through man's intellectual pursuits because it is hidden from him. Jesus said in Matthew 11:25,

> I thank thee, O Father, Lord of heaven and earth,
> because thou hast hid these things from the wise
> and prudent and hast revealed them unto babes.

Unbelievers cannot understand the truth of God's wisdom, but it is revealed to the simple who receives Jesus as their Saviour.

People say, "I'm searching for the truth." The fact is they will never find truth. In John 14:6 Jesus said,

> I am the Way, the TRUTH, and the Light. No
> man cometh unto the Father but by me.

It's impossible for the natural man to understand truth apart from God reveling it to him. Man will never know the real truth until he is willing to know Jesus as his Saviour.

When an unbelieving Hollywood producer makes a movie about Jesus, he/she always get it wrong. They cannot do any better. They are like a child trying to explain Albert Einstein's theory of relativity. It is impossible for any unbeliever Hollywood producer to get anything right without knowing Jesus as Saviour. Simply stated—the death, burial, and resurrection of Jesus Christ to pay the price for our redemption is pure nonsense to the unbelievers in Hollywood.

Paul now brings up the subject of God's hidden wisdom. Notice what he said in 1 Corinthians 2:7,

> But we speak the wisdom of God in a mystery
> even the hidden wisdom, which God ordained
> before the world for His glory.

People who have not received Jesus as their Saviour are like the prince of this world (Satan) who cannot understand God's wisdom. Only the redeemed can understand God's wisdom. Job asked a question,

> Can you find God by searching for Him? (Job
> 11:17)

No, you can't because God's wisdom is hidden from the unredeemed. The deep things of God cannot be known apart from God revealing it to His redeemed ones. Notice verse 8,

> None of the princes of the world knew: for had
> they known it, they would not have crucified the
> Lord of glory.

First Corinthians 2:9–13 is the third subject in the outline, and it shows that Bible revelation is given by the Holy Spirit.

These Scriptures show that spiritual truths are not discovered by human wisdom but revealed by the Holy Spirit. Notice verses 9–10,

> But as it is written, eye hath not seen, nor ear heard, neither hath entered into the heart of man, the things God hath prepared for them that love Him.
> But God hath revealed them unto us by his Spirit; for the Spirit searches all things, yea the deep things of God.

Eye has not seen, ear has not heard, nor has God's truth entered the hearts of unbelievers, because it can only be revealed by the Holy Spirit to the born-gain Christian. Born-again Christians can understand God's wisdom. They can make sense of God's Word through the Holy Spirit revealing the secret things of God to them. The Holy Spirit must be involved in the revelation of God's hidden truths. We who are born again have the Holy Spirit in us; therefore we can understand Bible truths from God's perspective. We do not understand all of what God has prepared for us, but we will, and what a glorious day that will be.

The unbeliever cannot understand because he does not have the Holy Spirit in him. Notice verse 11,

> What man knoweth the things of man save [except] the spirit of man which is in him? Even so the things of God knoweth no man but the Spirit of God.

Unbelievers cannot understand things of God because they have an unredeemed spirit in them. Spiritual things of God can be so clear that even a babe in Christ can understand them, yet the greatest intellects who has an unredeemed spirit just can't get it. God's redeemed ones have no problem in understanding the "deep things" of God because they have the Holy Spirit abiding in them. Notice 1 Corinthians 2:12,

> Now we have received, not the spirit of the world,
> but the Spirit which is of God; that we may know
> the things freely given to us of God.

There is a great deal of difference between the spirit of the world and the Spirit of God. When I became a Christian, I lost most of my "friends" because I had a different Spirit in me. I can no longer relate to the spirit of the world because the Holy Spirit moved in and I was changed. Those who have been born again know for certain they have been changed. Furthermore, those who have been changed speak a different language and live by a different Spirit—a differ standard. Notice verse 13,

> Which thing we also speak, not in words which
> man's wisdom teaches, but which the Holy Spirit
> teaches, comparing spiritual thing with spiritual.

Paul is saying that God reveals Bible secrets to us through the Holy Spirit. It doesn't take a college graduate or someone with a PhD to know and understand God's Word. In fact, unbelievers cannot understand God's Word regardless of how many degrees they may have. But even the simpleminded who are born again can understand the Scriptures. It is the Holy Spirit that enlightens their minds to God's holy truths. Don't get me wrong—I am all for a seminary education or a PhD, but in the last analysis it's the Holy Spirit that gives understanding to God's secrets that are tucked away in His Word. We can understand God's Word by comparing spiritual things with spiritual things. Unbeliever cannot find God's secrets through their intellectual ability.

I heard an intelligent man preach on "What the wall cannot do," or else that's what I thought he was preaching on until I realized he had an impediment in his speech and could not pronounce the word *law*. He was saying *wall* instead of *law*. God used that impediment for his glory, and that morning I and several other people experienced a profound impact on our lives because of the hidden thing of God's Word revealed to us. God got the glory, not the preacher. It was all because of the Gospel of Jesus Christ and the Holy Spirit that enlightens his mind to the secret things of God.

Being effective in preaching is not by man's articulate ability or oratorical delivery, but by the working of the Holy Spirit. I am not saying you must have an impediment in your speech or some kind of defect to be effective in ministry. I'm simply saying we can be effective in the ministry if we depend totally on God's Holy Spirit to enlighten our mind to the secret things that are in His Word. Notice 1 Corinthians 2:14,

> The natural man receives not the things of the Spirit of God: for they are foolishness to him: neither can he know them, because they are spiritually discerned.

It is the Holy Spirit that makes the Bible come alive. The Holy Spirit gives understanding into the deep things of God that intelligent unbelievers cannot understand. For unbelievers to hear a person preach with an impediment in his speech, it makes them call such preaching foolish. The natural man—the unbelieving man—cannot receive the things of the Spirit of God but sees them as foolishness. However, God's special people can understand spiritual truths.

First Corinthians 2:14–16 is the fourth subject in the outline, and it shows God's special people are given the right to judge.

All born-again Christians are God's special people. They must never forget who they are, what they do, what they say, and the life they lived for Christ is special. That is not being proud but leaving an example so others can see that Jesus made us God's special people. We should never forget out victories and accomplishment in God's work, and we should leave a good legacy for people to remember us by. We should never forget what God has done for us.

Speaking of forgetting, it reminds me of a humorous story I heard about a man who had a problem of forgetting. He, like most men, had a problem in forgetting special events. Men tend to forget such things as birthdays, anniversaries, Valentine's Day, and so on. Don't you agree?

A wife said to her husband one morning as he was leaving for work, "Honey, do you know what day this is?" "Sure do," he replied, but he didn't know what day it was. All day long he tried to recall why this day was so special to his wife. He thought, "Maybe it's the first day we met." "Maybe it's the first day we went on a date." And on and on he thought. To save his life, he could not think of why the day was so special to his wife. On his way home from work, he stopped at a flower shop and bought her a dozen roses, but he thought, "Since this day is so important to her, I need to buy her more than just a dozen roses. So he stopped by a jewelry store and bought her a beautiful expensive diamond ring." When he arrived home, he presented her with the roses and the diamond ring and said, "See, honey, I didn't forget what day this is." She began to cry. He said, "What's wrong? I didn't forget." Between her sobs she said, "This is the best Groundhog Day I have ever had."

Have you ever forgotten where you parked your car or about an important appointment or event? Someone said, "There are three things I can't remember. I can't remember names, I can't remember faces, and I can't remember the other one."

We must never forget what God has done for us. Paul judged people as being saved or unsaved, spiritual or carnal. Paul knew he was very special to God. Notice verse 15,

> But he that is spiritual judging all things, yet he
> himself is judged of no man.

This verse is simply saying God's special people can judge things from a spiritual perspective. Unbelievers cannot judge spiritual matters or spiritual people, because unbelievers do not have the Holy Spirit to give them insight into spiritual matters. Notice 2:14 again,

> But the natural man receives not the things of the
> Spirit of God, for they are foolishness unto him:
> because they are spiritually discerned.

Those who are filled with the Holy Spirit can make right judgments simply because they have the Holy Spirit dwelling in them and He gives them understanding. God's special people are not judged by human standards because unregenerate people do not have the ability to make the right judgment in spiritual matters. First Corinthians 2:15 above is saying born-again Christians can make right judgments because they can relate to the Bible and what the Bible teaches about Bible truths. We have the mind of Christ because we have the Holy Spirit dwelling in us. Therefore, we can judge correctly.

Someone might say, "You are not supposed to judge others." I agree, but when it comes to a believer as opposed to an unbeliever, we can judge and make right judgments. Notice 1 Corinthians 2:16 that states we have the mind of Christ. Therefore, we can judge from Christ's perspective.

> For who hath known the mind of the Lord, that
> he may instruct him? But we have the mind of
> Christ.

When we preach God's Word, we preach the mind of Christ. That is our limit on judging. We can only go as far as God's Word allows us to go. We are to stay within the perimeter of the Word of God. To be sure, it's the Word of God that does the judging. Anything beyond that will trip us up. We must be careful not to lambast, nor be sharply critical of someone or something, and pass it off as preaching God's Word.

I encourage you to preach God's Word and let it do the judging. After all, Hebrews 4:12 says,

> [God's Word is] sharper than any two-edged sword, piercing even to the dividing asunder of soul and spirit, and of the joints and marrow, and is a discerner of the thoughts and intents of the heart.

CHAPTER 3
HAS FOUR SUBJECTS

Verses 1–5 show carnality prevents spiritual growth.
Verses 6–17 present Christians as builders for Christ.
Verses 18–23 show the difference between God's wisdom and man's wisdom.

First Corinthians 3:1–5 is the first subject in the outline, and it shows that carnality prevents spiritual growth.

What is carnality? A better question would be, what is it to be a carnal Christian? The answer is desiring the satisfaction of the flesh instead of seeking to satisfy God. To be more specific, carnality is the erotic desires of the body. Notice 1 Corinthians 3:1,

> And I brethren, could not speak unto you as unto
> spiritual, but as unto carnal, even as unto babes
> in Christ.

Carnality characterizes the unbeliever's life, but some Christians are characterized as babes in Christ. Babes in Christ do not grow spiritually as they should. They profess Christ as Saviour but live to satisfy the flesh. Therefore, they are carnal Christians, and carnality prevents spiritual growth.

Immature Christians live their lives as though they have never been born again. It's not that they are not born again; it's the fact that they have never grown in Christ as they could and should have. They stay as "babes in Christ" for years because they never study and apply the Word of God to their lives. To be sure, knowing God's Word, and applying it to one's life, is the only way a babe in Christ can grow to be a mature Christian. The way new Christians grow to be mature Christians is to read, study, and apply God's Word to their lives.

You and I know people who are babes in Christ. In fact, in some churches, carnal Christians rule in decision-making, and that creates problems. Carnality is the main culprit in church divisions. Babes in Christ are believers in Christ, yet they cause problems. We must never profile troublemakers as having never been born again. The fact is, if they have repented and received Jesus as their Saviour, they have the Holy Spirit in their lives but do not allow the Holy Spirit to control their lives. That is why Paul called them "babes in Christ."

In other places some are called "natural men," meaning they are unbelievers, not babes in Christ—not born again. Keep in mind carnal Christians are not called "natural men." There is a difference between believers and unbelievers. The "natural man" does not have the Spirit of God in his life, but the "babe in Christ" has accepted Christ as his/her Saviour but does not allow the Spirit to control their lives. The believing "babe in Christ" and unbelieving "natural man" cause trouble in the church. Believe it or not, there are natural men in every church. The devil has planted them there.

The "natural man" cannot understand spiritual matters. First Corinthians 2:14 said,

> The natural man receives not the things of the Spirit of God: for they are foolishness to him, neither can he know them, because they are spiritually discerned.

The "natural man" may be a good person, a church member, a deacon, a preacher, and have moral standards, but if he has not been born again and totally committed to Christ, he will be used by the devil to create problems in the church. The natural man cannot relate to the preaching of the cross. Whether the "natural man" is a pastor, deacon, teacher, or a lay member, he cannot understand the spiritual things of God if he has not committed himself to Christ. He is oblivious to the leadership of the Holy Spirit. Jesus Christ dying on a cross doesn't make sense to him. Natural men cannot relate to Jesus Christ shedding his blood on the cross. Their minds are blind to the reality of the Gospel. Second Corinthians 4:3 said,

> The god [Satan] of this world hath blinded the minds of them who believe not, lest the light of the glorious gospel of Jesus Christ, who is the image of God, should shine unto them.

It's true—babes in Christ are much like natural men. They never study their Bibles, never witness, never give to the church, and never show any sign of being a Christian. Wait! Let me remind you that doing these things does not make you a born-again Christian, but these things will continually characterize your life if you are born again. Ephesians 2:10 says,

> We are created in Christ Jesus unto good works.

Sad to say, the number of years a person has been saved does not determine the level of his spirituality. Notice again what Paul said in 3:1,

> I, brethren, could not speak unto you as unto spiritual, but as unto carnal, even as unto babes in Christ.

Notice 1 Corinthian 3:2. These verses gives an example of carnal Christians or babes in Christ. Paul said,

> I have fed you with milk, and not with meat: for hitherto you were not able to bear it, neither yet now are you able.

Hebrews 5:12 said,

> For when for the time ye ought to be teachers,
> you have a need that one teaches you again which
> be the first principles of the oracles of God: and
> are become such as have need of milk, and not
> strong meat.

Consider seven things that characterize carnal Christians or babes in Christ.

1. They crave recognition.
2. They live like those who are not born again.
3. They are troublemakers.
4. They want to control the church.
5. They are like wolves in sheep clothing.
6. They cause divisions in the church.
7. They are carnal.
8. They are envious.
9. They cause strife.
10. They walk as unsaved natural men.

First Corinthians 3:3 calls such people carnal.

> For ye are yet carnal, for whereas there is among
> you envying, and strife, and division, are you not
> yet carnal, and walk as men [natural men]?

They cause envying, strife, and divisions. In other words, Paul is saying you walk as unbelievers walk.

Verse 4 shows the destructive effects a carnal Christian can cause in the church,

> For while one sayeth, I am of Paul; and another,
> I am of Apollos; are ye not carnal.

Both unbelievers and carnal Christian are characterized by carnality, and they cause divisions in the church. You cannot recognize the difference between them because both act alike. They both create problems in the church and sometimes splits in the church.

To avoid carnality, Christians must follow Jesus and pattern his/her life after Him. Churches should strive for unity in following Christ. Paul is saying to the Corinthian church, you are to direct your priority on following Jesus. Paul cautioned them to neither follow him, nor Apollos, nor Peter, nor another Christ, but to follow Christ of the Bible. Notice 1 Corinthians 3:5,

> Who then is Paul, and who is Apollos, but ministers by whom you believed, even as the Lord gave to every man.

God, the preeminent one, gave Paul, Apollos, and Peter a ministry to help them to grow in Christ, but Paul is saying carnal Christians miss the point when they exalt themselves over Christ's leadership. So we are to commit ourselves totally to Christ as our Saviour, not to someone else. Then we must do what He, and He alone, asks us to do.

Paul was totally committed to Jesus and His Word. He said,

> For me to live is Christ, and do die is gain.
> (Philippians 1:21)

Committing yourself to Christ is the second-best choice you can make in life. The first is to receive Jesus as your Saviour. Paul is saying, "If I live, it's all right, if I die it's alright. Whether I live or die, the important thing is to know I committed my life to serving Christ and preaching the Gospel." He worked at building God's church. Notice what Paul said in 1 Corinthians 4:16:

> Wherefore, I beseech you be ye followers of me.

Paul followed Christ, and he wanted the Corinthian Christians to follow him, not as their Saviour, but as a servant who followed Christ. He encouraged them to develop the traits of Christ. We need to develop the traits of Christ and follow Him as Paul did.

The second subject of the outline is found in verses 3:6–17, and it shows Christians are builders for Christ.

Notice what Paul said in verses 6 and 7,

> I have planted, Apollos watered, but God gave the increase. So, then neither is he that planteth anything, neither he that watereth; but God who giveth the increase.

Paul is talking about God's universal church in this Scripture verse. He is talking about all local churches working together to build His universal church. Some plant, some water, but the most important one in the building process is God who gives the increase. When we follow Jesus, we work together with God in building His church. God is the all-powerful one who blesses our ministry in allowing us to build on the foundation He laid, which is Himself. Your commitment of planting the seed of the Gospel in the hearts of those whom God brings before you is most definitely an honorable work indeed. Thank God for you that practices Acts 1:8.

> But you shall receive power, after that the Holy Ghost is come upon you, and you shall be witnesses unto me.

Witnessing should be high on our priority list, because that is the way God chose to build His church. Paul stressed the importance of working together promoting the cause of Christ and letting God use us in building His church.

The following verse not only tells us we are working with God in building His church but that we are His church. Notice verse 8,

> Now he that plants and he that waters are one,
> and every man shall receive his reward according
> to his labor.

We are God's family. We are members of God's church working together to build up each other and bring the unsaved into His church. We will receive a reward for that. Someone called it the soul winner's crown.

Notice verse 9,

> For we are labors together with God: ye are God's
> husbandry, ye are God's building.

The word *husbandry* means "a property manager." Isn't that great! We who are born-again Christians are working in God's vineyard as managers of His property. We are not only working to build God's church; we are God's church working together to bring more into His church.

Verse 11 shows us there is only one church, and Jesus Christ is the foundational stone on which the church stands.

> For other foundations can no man lay than that
> is laid, which is Jesus Christ.

Acts 4:11 states,

> This is the stone, which was set at naught of
> ye builders, which has become the head of the
> corner.

Jesus Christ is not only the foundational stone but the headstone of the church. Sometimes we refer to the church as a building. Someone may say, "I go to the Baptist church," "I go to the

Methodist church," "I go to the Catholic church," and so on. God's real church is neither a building nor a denomination, but consists of all who have put their faith and trust in Jesus Christ for salvation.

We must be careful what local church we support though. We must *not* go to a church that does not acknowledge Jesus Christ as the foundational head stone. We are to make sure we are building on Jesus Christ. It's ultimately important we build on the right foundation. Jesus talks about that in Luke 6:47–49,

> Whosoever cometh to me, and hearth my sayings, and doeth them, I will show you whom he is like. He is like a man who buildeth his house, and dug deep, and laid the foundation on a rock… But he which hearth, and doeth not, is like a man that without a foundation built a house upon the earth; against which did the storms beat vehemently, and immediately it fell, and the ruin of that house was great.

Someday we will give an account of what foundation we built on. In that day the Lord will also reveal our motive in building. Many of us work hard to build our local churches, but what motivates us? Is it for recognition, applause, money (many do it for money), or do we build our local church for bragging purposes? If we work to build a church for any other reason than to glorify God, we are building for the wrong reason. Our purpose for building a church should be to glorify God. People that build their local church for the wrong reason means they are building their hopes on sinking sand like the person Jesus mentioned in Luke 6:46–49.

There is only one cornerstone and one church which is Jesus Christ and His body of believers. Christians must build on that church. Yet there are six symbolic structures people build on. All six are mentioned in 1 Corinthians 3:12,

> Now if a man builds upon this foundation gold, silver, precious stone, wood, hay, stubble…

The six symbolic structures are gold, silver, precious stone, wood, hay, and stubble. The first three are symbolic of God, Jesus Christ, and the Holy Spirit. If we build on gold, silver, and precious stone we are building on something that will last, something of worth, something of importance, and that something is the Trinity. If we serve Jesus to glorify Him, we are building on the right foundation. We are building on Jesus. That kind of service will last forever. Let's make sure we are building on the right foundation. Let's make sure we are building on gold, silver, and precious stone.

On the other hand, wood, hay, and stubble is symbolic of the world, the flesh, and the devil. These are worthless materials. Just think of building a house with wood, hay, and stubble. If we build upon anything other than Jesus Christ, we are building on wood, hay, and stubble. At the very first adversity the house will fall. Serving the Lord for any reason other than to glorify Him is building on wood, hay, and stubble, and it will fall when the storm comes. It will not satisfy God in the Day of Judgment. It will not stand the test.

People either build upon gold, silver, and precious stone, or wood, hay, and stubble. Notice 1 Corinthians 3:13,

> Every man's work shall be made manifest: for the day shall declare it, because it shall be revealed by fire, and the fire shall try every man's works of what sort it is.

Gold, silver, and precious stone will come through the fire unharmed; yet wood, hay, and stubble will be consumed by the fire. But what does Paul mean when he said a man's works shall be revealed by fire? The word *fire* means the eyes of Jesus that appear as a flame of fire. Jesus can see the facade of a man's heart and know why he is doing what he is doing. In Revelation 1:14–15, John describes Jesus in His glorified body and the way He will appear in the Day of Judgment. In verse 14 of Revelations 19, John said, "His eyes were as a flame of fire."

Notice it says, "His eyes WERE AS a flame of fire," not a flame of fire, *but as a flame of fire*. In that day Jesus will see through the pretense of a person's heart. Jesus knows everything about us, even the hidden things in our hearts. If our works pass the test of His flaming eyes, we will receive a reward. Notice 3:14,

> If any man's works abide which he hath build thereupon, he shall receive a reward.

Matthew 16:27 said,

> The son of man shall come in the glory of His Father, with His angels, and then He shall reward every man according to his works.

Paul said in 2 Timothy 4:8,

> Henceforth, there is laid up for me a crown of righteousness, which the Lord, the righteous judge, shall give me at that day: and not to me only, but unto all them also that love his appearing.

In Revelation 22:12 Jesus said,

> Behold, I come quickly, and my reward is with me to give to everyone according as his works shall be.

What a wonderful day that will be for some, but not so pleasant for others. Some will not receive a reward. However, those who have been faithful in building on the right foundation will be rewarded. That will be shouting time in glory for some but weeping time for others. Their weeping will not last long, because Revelation 7:17 says,

> God shall wipe away all tears from their eyes.

Matthew 19:27 records a statement Peter made to Jesus about rewards.

> We have forsaken all, and followed thee, what shall we have therefore?

The answer is given by Jesus in Mark 10:29–30,

> I say unto you, there is no man that hath left houses, or brethren, or sister, or mother, or wife, or children, or land, for My sake, and the gospels, but he shall receive a hundredfold now in this life time, houses, and brethren, and sisters, and mothers, and children, with persecution, and in the world to come, eternal life.

There are two important things we need to understand about the above Scripture. First, Jesus is not saying if you do these things you will gain eternal life. Living a good moral life will not get you into heaven. You must be born again. It takes believing, repenting, and receiving Jesus as Saviour. Secondly, promising hundred-percent increases to all those who give up everything to follow Jesus does not mean material gain. God's promise of hundred-percent increase in wealth is taught by those who want you to believe God exists just to make you wealthy. That is health, wealth, and prosperity preaching. That kind of preaching does not work. It does not make people rich but leaves them disillusioned and without hope in our wonderful Saviour. Health, wealth, and prosperity preaching does not work. It's not God's fault it does not work, but deceivers who lie about it working, they do it to make money.

What Mark is really saying in the Scriptures above is that the things we receive in this life that we can give to the Lord to promote His cause is a hundred-percent more valuable than the things we keep. Our most valuable material possessions will pass away, but things we give to Jesus in building His church will last forever. That makes it hundred-percent more valuable. Jesus advised His followers in Matthew 6:19–20 to

> Lay not up for yourselves treasures on earth, where moth and rust doeth corrupt, and where thieves break through and steal, but lay up for yourself treasures in heaven.

How do you lay up treasures in heaven? You do it by turning everything over to Jesus, including yourself, and letting Him use it to build His church. I'm not saying give everything away. God knows you need things to survive. I'm saying instead of laying up a large amount of wealth in a bank somewhere, give some to Jesus, and you can draw eternal dividends in heaven. Actually, the treasures you lay up in a bank belongs to the Lord anyway. So save some for yourself and give the rest to the Lord to build His church. The things you give to Jesus become hundred-percent more valuable than the treasures you lay up on earth for yourself. The good news is, our faithfulness and service to the Lord is not in vain when we work with Jesus in building His church.

Do you know the Bible teaches that having just a few treasures are better than having great wealth? Proverbs 15:16 says,

> Better is little with the fear of the Lord than great treasures with trouble therewith.

Almost always having wealth hinders our commitment to Christ. If we dedicate our all to the Lord in building His church on the right foundation, we will receive a reward for our dedication and service that is hundred-percent more valuable than money we can make here on earth. Giving up everything to serve Jesus is worth it. After all, our treasures on earth will he burned up one day, but the things we give to the Lord will last forever. We think we cannot make it if we give up everything to follow Jesus, but we can make it because Ephesians 3:20 says,

> Now to Him who is able to do exceedingly abundantly above all that we think according to the power that worketh in us.

God will take care of His own.

Quite often we give gifts to church members to motivate them to bring someone to church, motivate them to be at church for a certain number of Sundays, and we give something to motivate them to be faithful in God's service. We give them something for being faithful in doing what they should do anyway, but they do not always do it anyway. Therefore, the church gives them something to motivate them to do it. Think about this! Why does the Lord give crowns to His faithful servants? He gives crowns to show His love and appreciation for their faithfulness, and to motivate them to lead others to Him for salvation. He motivates them to be faithful in building His church.

So if our work of building His church is done for God's glory, we shall receive a reward—a crown. Just remember, crowns are earned for doing something for the Lord; salvation is not earned, but a gift. Salvation was earned for us by Jesus dying on the cross. Crowns are given for our faithfulness. Salvation is given because of Christ's faithfulness. Those who serve the Lord for any other reason than to glorify Him will receive no crown at all. Notice 1 Corinthians 3:15–17 says,

> If any man's works shall be burned, he shall suffer loss: but he himself shall be saved; yet so as by fire. Know you not that you are the temple of God, and the Spirit of God dwelleth in you? If any man defiles the temple of God, him shall God destroy. For the temple of God is holy, which temple you are.

The Holy Spirit dwells in the Christian's body, thereby making him the temple of God. The word *defile* means "to make filthy." When Christians defile (make filthy) their bodies, they are defiling God's temple. It's not wise to allow our bodies to become a filthy place for the Holy Spirit to dwell in. Oh, I know we can't be perfect so long as we are in our earthly bodies, but we can live like Christians the best we know how. We need to be careful, because if we "defile [make filthy] the temple of God. Him shall God destroy."

That means if we decide to embrace a sinful lifestyle, God will take us prematurely.

There are many ways Christians defile their bodies. First, Christians use their bodies for questionable practices rather than using it to build God's church. Romans 8:9 said,

> Ye are not in the flesh, but in the Spirit, if the
> Spirit of God dwells in you. Now if any man hath
> not the Spirit of Christ, he is none of His.

In other words, you belong to God if you have put your faith and trust in Jesus Christ for salvation. You have the Holy Spirit dwelling in you. You are not your own. God owns you. You have been bought with the sacrificial death of Christ. Therefore, using your body for questionable practices is not the right thing to do. We must glorify God in our spirits and in our bodies. Notice what 1 Corinthians 6:19–20 had to say about your body belonging to God,

> What? Know ye not that your body is the tem-
> ple of the Holy Ghost, which is in ye, and ye are
> not your own? For ye are bought with a price:
> therefore, glorify God in your spirits, and in your
> bodies, which are Gods.

In 2 Corinthians 6:16 God said,

> I will dwell in them, and walk in them; and I will
> be their God, and they will be my people.

If the Holy Spirit dwells in your body, then you must please God by walking as a Christian.

Second Corinthians 6:16 above is teaching that God is building a church that consists of people who are indwelled by the Holy Spirit. Ephesians 2:19–22 said,

> Now therefore you are no more strangers and foreigners, but fellow citizens with the saints, and of the household of God. And are built upon the foundation of the apostles and prophets, Jesus Christ himself being the corner stone; in which all the building fitly framed together growth into one holy temple in the Lord.

These verses are not talking about building a church made with wood and stone but referring to people who are indwelled by the Holy Spirit and are building upon an exclusive foundation which is Jesus Christ. Any other Christian service we may do will not stand the test at the judgment if it is not built upon Jesus Christ and done for His glory. We are to do all we do for God's glory and to promote His cause.

First Corinthians 3:18–23 is the third subject in the outline, and it shows the difference between God's wisdom and man's wisdom.

In most cases you can arrive at God's wisdom by reversing man's wisdom. God's wisdom is the very apposite of worldly wisdom. The Athenians, of the ancient city of Athens, prided themselves in gaining worldly wisdom, yet had no godly wisdom at all. Acts 17:21 said,

> They spent their time in nothing else but to tell or hear of some new thing.

They proudly sought wisdom through their own intellect, but failed to realize the futility of such. Proverbs 16:18 says,

> Pride goeth before destruction, and a haughty spirit before a fall.

When worldly wisdom prides itself in the things it has accomplished, God's wisdom says pride is a sin. When worldly wisdom says there is no such thing as truth, God's wisdom shows Jesus is truth. God's wisdom is the very opposite of worldly wisdom. When a person embraces worldly wisdom over God's wisdom, he deceives himself into thinking he is wiser than God. Notice Proverbs 12:15,

> The way of a fool is right in his own eyes: but he that hearkeneth to counsel [God's counsel] is wise.

Proverbs 3:7 said,

> Do not be wise in your own eyes: fear the Lord and depart from evil.

Evil is at its highest when one embraces worldly wisdom over God's wisdom. The world calls God's wisdom foolish, but the worldly wise who deny God are the ones who are fools. Psalms 14:1 says,

> The fool hath said in his heart, there is no God.

Read 1 Corinthians 3:19,

> The wisdom of this world is foolishness with God. For it is written, 'He taketh the wise in their own craftiness.

God is omniscient, which means God has total knowledge of all things. There is nothing God does not know. Has it ever dawned upon you that nothing has ever dawned upon God? God never learns anything new because He has knowledge of all things. Just think of man, with his little, finite brain, claiming to be smarter than God. That is foolishness in its ultimate stage.

We are not to glory in man's wisdom, but glory only in God's wisdom. Notice what 1 Corinthians 3:18 says,

> Let no man deceive himself. If any man among you seemeth to be wise, let him become a fool [what the world calls a fool], that he may be wise.

When a man claims he is wise, he is deceiving himself. The devil has used intellectualism on him to keep him from Christ. So in reality, he is the fool. When a man finds himself in that predicament, he must become what the world calls a fool—a believer in Christ. Then he will become wise in God's eyes. Notice what God said in verse 19–20,

> For the wisdom of this world is foolishness with God, for it is written, He taketh the wise in their own craftiness. And again, the Lord knoweth the thoughts of the wise, that they are vain.

When intellects brag about their intelligence—and there are plenty of them out there—God will judge them by their own craftiness: deception. Don't kid yourself, unbelievers; the Lord knows your thoughts are vain. The definition of *vain* is "showing or having an excessive high opinion of oneself—appearance, abilities, or looks." There is a solution however. Notice verses 21–22.

> Therefore, let no man glory in man. For all things are yours; whether Paul, or Apollos, or Cephas, or the world, or life, or death, or things present, or things to come; all are yours.

Paul is saying, don't let the unbeliever persuade you to be vain like he is. Don't glory in man, because if you do, you will miss heaven and spend eternity regretting it.

Paul goes on to say, there is nothing we need but Christ. In Christ we have everything we need. Satan has control of this world now, but God owns this world and everything and everybody in it. Whatever belongs to God belongs to us, for God has given it to us. We will take possession of this world during the thousand-year reign of Christ on earth. After the millennium, the new earth and New Jerusalem will be ours to enjoy forever.

By the way, just because God made everybody does not mean everybody is going to heaven, only those who put their faith in Jesus Christ for salvation. Notice 1 Corinthians 3:23,

And ye are Christ's, and Christ's is God's.

In other words, you belong to Christ, and whatever belongs to Christ belongs to God, and one day God will give it to you to enjoy forever. You will inherit it when we get to heaven. Is God good to you? He certainly is. There is nothing more you need, but Jesus— just rest in Him!

CHAPTER 4
HAS FOUR SUBJECTS

Verses 1–10 deal with judging God's servants.
Verses 11–14 deal with being persecuted for Christ.
Verses 15–17 deal with being a father to the church.
Verses 18–21 deal with pride ("being puffed up").

First Corinthians 4:1–10 is the first subject in the outline, and it deals with judging God's servants.

God's servants should not be judged wrongly because they have been given special jobs that unbelievers cannot understand.

First, God calls each of us to serve as ministers and stewards in revealing His mysteries to others. God's primary mystery is the reason for the death, burial, and the resurrection of Christ. We need to explain the purpose of His mysteries. First Corinthians 4:1 says,

> Let a man so account us, as the ministers of Christ, and stewards of the mysteries of God.

Stewards are ministers who takes care of God's property. Paul was a minister. He did not want people to misjudge him in matters of spiritual service to God. God's servants are often judged as having an ulterior motive for being in the ministry. To be sure, many ministers do have an ulterior motive for being in the ministry, such as making money, having an easy life, or being popular. If ministers do not measure up to God's requirements for being a minister as taught in God's Word, they most certainly do have an ulterior motive for being in the ministry.

Paul wanted people to see him and his followers as being capable of making right judgments in relation to the ministry. Mankind is not qualified to judge the motives of pastors and churches based on their own preconceived opinions. Some may have had a bad experience with a minister or a church; therefore they have the tendency to put all ministers and churches in the same category. That is wrong. People may feel ministers are out for money only, and they are right about some ministers, but not right about all ministers. We are not to profile people on our past experiences. Paul wanted people to see him and his followers as ministers truly sent from God. He wanted people to see him as God's steward, God's minister, revealing God secrets.

The qualifications for stewards are to be faithful. Notice 1 Corinthians 4:2,

> Moreover it is required in stewards that a man be found faithful.

Paul was a faithful steward of God. He was a minister and manager of God's property. Paul was totally committed to the ministry and stewardship of God's possessions. His life was totally given over to serving his Lord in an honest and trustworthy manner. An unfaithful steward cannot be trusted.

Allow me to give an illustration of what it means to be an unfaithful steward. There were two men applying for a job that required honesty and integrity. Only one would be selected. The one selected would be responsible for handling large amounts of money. Both were qualified, but one was more qualified than the other. The CEO interviewed the two candidates. After the interviews he invited them to join him at a restaurant for lunch. He watched them closely as they walked through the line to get their lunch. Each one got a slice of butter along with other things. They both opened their biscuits and slid the butter inside. When they checked out with the cashier, one did not mention his slice of butter and went to his table without paying for it. The other one paid for his butter. When they arrived back at the company's corporate office, the CEO announced that he had decided which one to hire for the job. The more qualified man was sure the CEO would choose him; but to his surprise, he was not chosen. The CEO chose the lesser qualified candidate. The other one protested, pointing out his superior qualifications.

The CEO said, "Yes, I realize you are more qualified, but I made my decision on the way you paid for your butter at the restaurant. You did not pay for your slice of butter, but the other candidate did. If a man would steal a ten-cent slice of butter, he would still a million dollars." This illustration shows how an unfaithful steward cannot be trusted. It's required in stewardship that a man be found faithful.

Second, rightly judging others comes only from Jesus. We are not capable of judging impartial in the flesh. Our ability to judge fairly is limited. Rather than make a judgment on which religious leader we should follow, as the Corinthian church was doing, we should follow Jesus Christ who is qualified to judge.

Did you know judging is the favorite indoor sport of many Christians? Paul is saying, don't be a critical judge out of God's will, because one day you will be judged by Jesus himself. Romans 14:10 says,

> Why dost thou judge thy brother? Or why dost
> thou set at naught thy brother? For we shall all
> stand before the judgment seat of Christ

The word *naught* means "classifying others inferior to self." That is what we call a bigot. A bigot sees his brother or sister in Christ as inferior to himself. The Bible is saying, if we judge our brother as being inferior to us, we are hypocrites and bigots. Notice Romans 14:12–13,

> Each of us shall give account of himself to God.
> Let us not therefore judge one another anymore:
> judge this rather, that no man put a stumbling
> block, or an occasion to fall in his brother's way.

There have been many ministers destroyed because someone falsely judged them.

The problem we have in judging someone is that we don't really have the facts. God has all the facts, and that makes Him a capable judge. Romans 2:16 says,

> God shall judge the secrets of man by Jesus Christ.

Let God do the judging through Christ. We should judge ourselves instead of judging others.

Notice what 1 Corinthians 4:3–4 says,

> With me it is a very small thing that I should be judged by you, I judge not my own self. I know nothing by (against) myself, yet am I not hereby justified, but He that judges me is the Lord.

Paul is not saying he does not make decisions about himself. He is saying he is not conscious of neglecting any of his duties. Paul did not find anything that he was doing he should not do, nor did he find anything he was not doing that he should do. That made him a good candidate for stewardship. Yet Paul said, "The one who has the right to judge me is the Lord."

God through Jesus is the one who has the right to judge us. Paul was not aware of any secret sin in his life but acknowledged that his understanding of the depths of sin was limited. Therefore, he stated that he could not render the final verdict because of his inability to judge himself fairly. He is saying only God has all the facts to render the final verdict.

God judges us by what is written in our hearts and what is written in His Word. Hebrews 4:12 said,

> The word of God...is a discerner [judge] of the thoughts and intents of the heart.

That is why it's so important we know God's Word because we will be judged by it.

Many Christians boasts of living a sinless life, yet they cannot see the depths of sin, or who is guilty or not guilty. They judge from their perspective, not from God's perspective. God has all the facts; we don't. Therefore God can make the right judgment; we can't.

Third, God shall judge the inner motives of man's heart. First Corinthians 4:5 states,

> Judge nothing before the time, until the Lord comes, who both will bring to light the hidden things of darkness, and will make manifest the counsels of the heart, and then shall every man have praise of God.

The "hidden things of darkness" means man's inner motives and thoughts. People do things against other people, but do not understand the inner hidden motives of the heart. They pretend they are concerned about other people's welfare, but they are only concerned about satisfying their inner motives. Romans 2:16 says,

> God shall judge the secrets of man by Jesus Christ.

Notice again how 1 Corinthians 4:5 above puts it, God *"will bring to light the hidden things of darkness."*

God will reveal the hidden things of the heart. Since God knows the hearts of man, He will judge by what is in man's heart. There is nothing hidden that God does not know. God knows that man's "heart is deceitful above all things, and desperately wicked" (Jeremiah 17:9).

A Christian's outward work and inner motives may differ, but since his outward work and inward motives determine his rewards in heaven, it is ultimately important man measure up to God's requirements. First Corinthians 10:31 said,

> Whether you eat, or drink, or whatever you do,
> do all to the glory of God.

Man will be rewarded according to the motives of his heart, not according to his outward acts.

Fourth, people are responsible for judging themselves. First Corinthians 4:6 says,

> And these things, brethren, I have in a figure
> transferred to myself and to Apollos for your
> sakes.

In other words, Paul is saying, "Apollos and I present ourselves as an example of judging and present ourselves as examples to others on how they should judge themselves." Notice the rest of 1 Corinthians 4:6,

> That you might learn in us not to think of men
> above that which is written, that no one of you be
> puffed up one against another.

Paul is saying, "When you judge those who appear to you to be higher than Christ, you become puffed up." *Puffed up* means "proud." Paul and Apollos are saying, "We want to be examples for you to follow, not as proud leaders making demand of you, but as having your best interest in mind." Some church members at Corinth were proud they had chosen those whom they considered higher than Christ. They chose Paul, Apollos, Peter, and another Christ over the Christ Paul preached about.

We should be good examples like Paul and Apollo. Others who judge us should see a good example in us and find a reason to follow us. What kind of example am I? What kind of example are you? Do others see Christ in us and want what we have? I hope so!

First Corinthians 4:7 encourages church members to stop saying they have no sin when they judge themselves.

> Who maketh thee to different from another?
> And what hast thou that thou didst not receive?
> Now if thou didst receive it, why dost thou glory
> as if thou didst not receive it?

Paul is saying that you are no different from other people. He is saying don't be proud as though you got everything you have by your own ability; and yes, you did receive it, but why do you glory in yourself as though you did not receive it from by your own ability? It's worthy to note that everything you have or ever will have comes from God.

Notice the phrase in 1 Corinthians 4:7, "what maketh thee to differ from another."

Judging ourselves to be better than others is a natural tendency for mankind to do, but it's a sin of pride. Pride was the root cause for the problems in the Corinthian church. Pride is prevalent and very common in our churches today. Let's face it—some people feel they are better Christians than others, but are they? A Christian may say, "I go to every church service"; "I give more than anyone else"; "I witness more often than others"; "I read my Bible regularly"; "I sing in the choir"; and so on. Notice again 1 Corinthians 4:7,

> What hast thou that thou didst not receive?

It is a sin if we are using what God gives for our own purpose. If we esteem ourselves spiritually superior to others, we are "puffed up." Things we have are not our own but a gift from God. Therefore, we have nothing to gloat over. We have nothing to be proud of in ourselves. We are servants of God and stewards of His property. We should brag on Jesus, not on ourselves.

Fifth, 1 Corinthians 4:8 brings to light how foolish it is to play the role of a bigot and use the wrong judgment. A bigot exalts himself above other people. A bigot feels he is bigger, better, brighter, and

144

worth more than others. A bigot is a person who is totally intolerant of anyone who has a different opinion or has accomplished more than he has accomplished. Bigots think of themselves as being more capable than anyone else. To be sure, those who exalt themselves above others are committing the sin of pride, and that makes them bigots. They have a "better than thou" attitude. Paul chides them for that. Notice 1 Corinthians 4:8,

> Now ye are full, now ye are rich, ye have reigned as kings without us: and I would to God you did reign, that we also might reign with you.

Paul is saying, "You think you are full and rich and think that you could reign as kings without us." That is nothing more than pride and self-exaltation above Paul, and that made them bigots. Paul said, "I wish you did let Christ reign in your hearts that we might reign with you."

Some members in the Corinthian church had a bad case of bigotry. Paul was troubled with their prideful, arrogant, disgruntled, bigot attitudes, so he reverts to sarcasm in hopes of getting them on the right track. It's okay to be sarcastic, but only on rarest occasions. Sarcasm is used to rebuke or insult a person. Let me explain sarcasm by giving you an example of what happened to me some years ago.

I was saved at a tent meeting at the age of fourteen. Two preachers set up a big tent in our community to preach the Gospel and lead the unsaved to Christ. I was one of many who gave their hearts and life to Christ during that tent revival. When the revival was over, they pulled up stakes and moved to another community. I had no church to go to, so I joined a church that was not biblical sound at all. I didn't know that. In fact, they were legalist. They believed in "holding on and holding out" until the end to be saved. Over many months I started believing some of their false teaching that a man had to work his way to heaven.

At work one Monday morning I said to a preacher friend, "Yesterday our pastor got two deacons and a preacher resaved." My preacher friend responded, "When I preached yesterday, I got two preachers and ten deacons resaved. I said, "That's great, have you baptized them yet?" He said, "No! I pulled out my pistol and shot all twelve of them right there on the spot. I was afraid they would get unsaved again and go to hell." To say the least, I was shocked. Of course, he was being sarcastic. That confrontation opened my eyes to search for the truth. Thank God, I found the truth by reading the Bible and listening to preachers that believed in the fundamentals of God's Word.

I would not recommend you make it a habit of using sarcasm, but if it turns someone to Christ, go for it. It worked for Paul. It worked by the preacher who used it on me. It may work for you. Decide for yourself, but be careful.

Paul chided them for thinking they were greater than anyone else. They were ignoring Paul's motives for bringing them to salvation. They were exalting themselves above him. Yet Paul mocked them by drawing the obvious conclusion that they were infected with a bad case of self-exaltation that resulted in their becoming bigots. Paul is saying, "If you are so great worth to God, then what about me and my fellow ministers who suffered so great hardship in the ministry?"

Notice what Paul said at the end of 1 Corinthians 4:8,

> I would to God you did reign that we might also
> reign with you.

Paul did not want to be sarcastic but wished they really did excel in the ministry that he might excel with them. However, Paul used himself and Apollos as examples of the way Christians should live as opposed to the way the Corinthian Christians were living. They were puffed up with pride. Paul used sarcasm to warn against pride that so often rule lives.

Pride will bring a church, or individual, down quicker than anything. Pride is one of the worst sins a person can commit. God hates the sin of pride because it separates Him from His created angel

Lucifer. Pride was the sin that brought Lucifer and a third of God's angels down. Proverbs 16:18 said,

> Pride goeth before destruction and a haughty spirit before a fall.

Proverbs 29:23 states,

> A man's pride will bring him low.

James 4:6 adds,

> God resisteth the proud, but giveth grace to the humble.

Some of the Christians in Corinth were haughty, arrogant, and preoccupied with their own importance to the extent it made them proud.

A phrase people sometimes use goes like this: "Who died and made you king?" This is the approach Paul used. He said, "Who made you different from others?"

God doesn't have favorites. Thank God, we who are born again are precious favorites of God. What do we have that we did not receive from God? If God gave us what we have, then why glory in ourselves as though we obtained it? James 1:17 says,

> Every good and perfect gift cometh from above.

Everything we have or ever will have are gifts from God.

Paul continues his approach with sarcasm to point them to the right way of judging. Notice how he chides them in 1 Corinthians 4:9–10.

> For I think that God hath set forth us the apostles last, as it were appointed to death: for we are made a spectacle unto the world, and unto angels,

and to man. We are fools for Christ's sake, but
you are wise in Christ, we are weak, but you are
strong, you are honorable, but we are despised.

These verses deal with those who exalted themselves above Paul
and others. Notice what Paul had to say about himself and those who
were his disciples.

We are made as a spectacle [exhibit] unto the
world, and unto angels, and unto man.

That means we are exhibits to the world, to man, and even to
angels. We are being watched by angels to see if we are doing what
God calls us to do. Notice Paul's sarcasm.

We are fools for Christ's sake, but you are wise in
Christ. We are weak, but you are strong. You are
honorable, but we are despised.

Paul chides them for being so indifferent to the Gospel. Those
who are occupied with themselves at the exclusion of others are
self-centered and bigots. They are always the heroes in their imagi-
nary stories. They are always the ones that set everything right. They
are always the "good guys" that wear the white hats.

It was God who inspired Paul to be sarcastic. If God is in it, use
it, but you had better make dead sure God is in it, because if God is
not in it, you could drive someone away from Christ.

*First Corinthians 4:11–14 is the second subject in the outline, and it
deals with being persecuted for Christ's sake.*

Notice how Paul used words of warning in 1 Corinthians 4:11.
These words should make us run to God for protection and security.

Even unto this present hour we both hunger, and
thirst, and are naked [deprived of proper cloth-

ing], and are buffed [beaten], and have no certain dwelling place.

Paul is referring to himself here. If it happened to Paul it can certainly happen to us. If you try to do what is right, don't expect the world to love you. Someone said, "If you try to do what is right, your friends will become your enemies." When I first heard that, I thought he was being overly dramatic, but now I know better. I know what it is to be rejected by people I thought were my friends. Perhaps you have experienced that too. Jesus said in John 15:18–19,

> If the world [people] hates you, ye know it hated me before it hated you. If ye were of the world, the world would love its own: but because ye are not of the world, but I have chosen you out of the world, therefore the world hates you.

Jesus did not have Paul write this to frighten you, but warn you. Many give up on God when adversities come, but don't quit now friend because Jesus is coming soon.

It is obvious the world hates you because you do not love the things that worldly people love. You have been chosen out of the world. You cannot relate to this world because you do not have the same philosophy this world has. God chose to separate you from the world. Mark it down: the world will no longer be your friend if you receive Jesus Christ as your Saviour. The world hates you, but they will not hate you very much longer. I believe the Lord is coming soon.

Paul continues his defense against those that misunderstood his purpose in the ministry. He even goes so far as to say in 1 Corinthians 4:12–13,

> Being defamed, we entreat [persuade unbelievers to come to Christ]: we are made as filth of the world, and off scouring of all things unto this day.

Christians are not to seek the approval and favor of the world, but seek the approval and favor of Jesus Christ. Serving Jesus was Paul's most urgent priority. Can we say the same? Are you willing to become what the world calls off scouring and filth for Christ? Paul knew why the world thought of him as filth, but that didn't matter to him because he sought to win them to Christ. Paul esteemed his relationship with Christ and the influence he could have on others so important that he would not use his ministry as a means of retaliation. Paul allowed nothing to come between him and his Lord.

Perhaps someone is saying, "I'm not being persecuted." If professed Christians are not being persecuted, it is an indication they are not fully dedicated to Christ, or they may be unbelievers pretending to be Christians. We will all be persecuted and abused if we take a stand for Jesus. Abuse comes to all Christians who seek to share their faith. First Peter 4:12 says,

> Beloved, think it not strange concerning the fiery
> trials which is to try you, as though some strange
> thing happened unto you.

Notice again what Paul said in 1 Corinthians 4:13. We are "made as off scouring [scum] of all things."

Let me inform you Christian, that is how the world sees you. It will get worse as the day of the Lord draws near. In 2 Timothy 3:1 Paul said this about the end-times,

> This know also, that in the last days, perilous
> [dangerous] times shall come.

Paul is saying in his letter to Timothy, "Dangerous times will come, you will be blasphemed, despised, falsely accused, and looked down on as scum, but take heart, Jesus is with you."

I'm not trying to discourage you but trying to get you to see what it is really like to be a dedicated Christian. I'm just telling you what is happening. Persecution of Christians is accruing worldwide, and it's getting worse. The devil is fighting viciously to introduce other religions to the world who hate Christianity. He rejoices in promoting his cause. He is even deceiving preachers to embrace another religion—a religion that is violent. John 16:2 says,

> Yes, the time will come, that whosoever kills you will think he is doing God a service.

That is happening on a worldwide scale right now. All religions believe in a god, but not the God of the Bible. Religions are being promoted as superior to Christianity. I pray every day that God would intervene in the affairs of our nation and bring people back to Himself.

Let's face it—if you are a witness for Christ, those who believe in another god will persecute you, even kill you in the name of their god.

Paul said in 1 Corinthians 4:14,

> I write not these things [being called filth and scum] to shame you, but as my beloved son I warn you.

Paul is saying, "I write these things not to frighten you away from living the Christian life, but to urge you to stick with Jesus and witness for Him."

Just because the world sees you as filth and scum doesn't mean you are. We are not to look down on ourselves as filth and scum, but servants of Almighty God—the God who created everything. To serve Him is the greatest honor that can be bestowed upon any individual. Paul said in Romans 6:17–18,

> Ye were servants of sin, but you have obeyed from the heart that form of doctrine [the Gospel] which was delivered to you. Being made free from sin you became servants of righteousness [that is, servants of our righteous God].

What an honor that God has chosen us to serve Him and witness for Him. Serving God is the highest honor one can attain. After all, when we stand before Him at the judgment it will be a blessing indeed to hear him say, "Well done, thy good and faithful servant."

In the face of persecution and cruelty, we learn patience and humility. Therefore, we have the assurance we shall see Jesus face-to-face and be rewarded for the stand we took for Him.

First Corinthians 4:15–17 is the third subject in the outline, and it deals with being a father figure to the church.

First Corinthians 4:15 states,

> Though [although] you [may] have ten thousand instructors in Christ yet have not many fathers: for in Christ Jesus have I begotten you through the Gospel.

Paul tells them it was he who brought them to salvation through preaching the Gospel of Jesus Christ. No one cared for the Corinthian people like Paul did. He felt a close connection with them because he introduced them to Christ. Very few pastors care for their church like Paul cared for the Corinthian church. A preacher once said, "Pastoring would be a good job if it wasn't for people." I know people can be ornery, cantankerous, and irritable, but pastors are to love and care for them. After all, they are God's gift to the pastor. God sets pastors over His local congregations to love them, guide them, and care for them. The only way a pastor can do that is to be totally committed to Jesus Himself and totally committed to helping people whom God gave him to pastor.

Pastors must set an example of dedication and love for Jesus and the church. Members will see that in their pastor and have a desire to follow Him. Pastors, don't center your attention on people that irritate you, but on those who love you, and support you. All too often pastors preach to those who irritate him when the rest of the church sits there longing for something that will help them on their journey toward heaven. My advice is to do what you should do and, if possible, ignore those irritating you.

How can a pastor expect the church members to be totally committed to Christ if he is not totally committed to Christ himself? I have heard of pastors being asked to resign their church because of their lack of dedication to Christ and the church, but I have never heard of a pastor being asked to resign for being overly dedicated to Christ and his church. I'm sure it happens, but I have never personally heard of one.

In the final analysis, spiritual leaders must set an example of Christ likeness for others to follow. There is an old saying that goes like this: "Actions speak louder than words." That is a very true statement. A pastor must be a father figure to his church. He is to serve God and love people like Paul served Christ and loved the church at Corinth. If a pastor doesn't love his people, it will come through loud and clear.

In 1 Corinthians 4:16 Paul said,

Wherefore I beseech you, be ye followers of me.

Paul has a deep loving relationship with Christ and the church, which meant everything to him. Therefore he encouraged the Corinthian church to follow him as he followed Christ. Allow me to put it this way: Encourage the church to follow you as you follow Christ. Pastor, if you want the church to follow you, follow Christ. That is a guaranteed method for success in your pastorate. Don't change your message to gain followers, but stay with God's Word. Oh yes, you may lose some if you do, but the ones who stay with you will be good, dedicated Christians. Paul said in 1 Corinthians 11:1,

Be ye followers of me, even as I am of Christ.

On Paul's behalf that was the only thing he had to offer.

Paul not only stated that he was a follower of Christ, but he also proved it. It is one thing to say you are a follower of Christ but another thing to prove it. Paul proved it by his dedication to Christ and the church, and his dedication came through loud and clear. He urged the church to follow him as he followed Christ. You can be successful by urging the church to follow you as you follow Christ.

Paul's desire for the church of Corinth was to continually walk in the ways of Christ. In 1 Corinthians 4:17 Paul states,

> For this cause have I sent unto you Timothy who is my beloved son [in Christ], and faithful in the Lord, who shall bring you into remembrance of my ways which be in Christ, as I teach everywhere in every church.

The Corinthian church was slowly drifting from the standard Paul left for them to keep. They had slipped back into their pernicious ways. So Paul sent his friend Timothy to help get them back on track. Timothy was led to Christ by Paul and Paul considered him his son in the faith. In fact, in 1 Timothy Paul called him,

> My son in the faith.

Timothy was entrusted to promote the faith Paul held. Paul knew Timothy and trusted him to promote the Gospel—promote the fundamentals of the faith, reinforce the Gospel upon which the church was established.

We should thank God for church members who can be trusted to keep the church on the right track. If you have a position of leadership in your church, be trustworthy and help it to stay focused on the Lord.

First Corinthians 4:18–21 is the fourth subject in the outline, and it deals with being "puffed up" (being proud).

Paul now comes to the subject of being characterized by pride, or as the KJV puts it, "being puffed up." First Corinthians 4:18 said,

> Now some are puffed up as though I would not come to you.

Some in the Corinthian church were proud or glad that Paul could not come to them. They were "puffed up" (proud) about it. They believed they could handle things themselves. However, Paul said in 1 Corinthian 4:19,

> I will come to you shortly, if the Lord wills, and will know, not the speech of them that are puffed up, but the power.

Paul is saying, "It's just a matter of time I will come to you, not to know why you are arrogant, proud, and boastful, but to see if the Holy Spirit is in control of your lives."

Evidently, Paul has already thought about their problem and concluded that a big percentage of them were "natural men," worldly men, unbelievers. Notice 1 Corinthians 2:14 again.

> The natural man receives not the things of the Spirit of God, for they are foolishness unto him.

The truth is that the above Scripture implies that some in the Corinthian church were not Christians, or at their very best backslidden Christians without the Holy Spirit controlling their lives. In fact, 1 Corinthians 4:20 said,

> The kingdom of God is not in word, but in power.

God's church here on the earth is the kingdom of God that is controlled and promoted by the Holy Spirit. The kingdom of heaven is where God dwells. The kingdom of God (the universal church) is not a church in word only but empowered by the Holy Spirit.

Evidently, some Corinthian church members were majoring on impressive speeches and calling themselves the church. Rather than following the Holy Spirit, they were being controlled by their sanctified pride. A person's work in the ministry cannot be measured by impressive words but by the power of the Holy Spirit that dwells in him. God's Holy work is not reserved for those who use impressive words but to those who are totally committed to the cause of Christ. By the way, when you are studying your Bible, you may want to remember the kingdom of heaven is the place where God dwells but the kingdom of God is God's church here upon earth.

Paul said in 1 Corinthians 4:21,

> What will you? [What is your desire?] Shall I come to you with a rod, or in love, and in the spirit of meekness?

The phrase *a rod* is referring to strong rebuke that comes through preaching God's Word. Spiritual leaders must use God's "rod" to correct people. Paul did! Pastors don't like to use the "rod," but it must be done when circumstances demand it. A spiritual leader would much rather come to his members with love and gentleness (and I am sure Paul wanted it that way too), but sometimes it takes a harsh rebuke to get people on the right track. Paul knew they were puffed up, arrogant, and boastful, and needed to be reprimanded.

CHAPTER 5
HAS THREE SUBJECTS

Verse 1 deal with immorality in the church.
Verses 2–8 deal with indifference to immorality in the church.
Verses 9–13 instruct believers to be friendly with unbelievers but not participate with them in their sins.

I must issue a caution before I start. This chapter may not be suitable for teaching children. It deals with sex and sex activities throughout the chapter. In fact, that is what this chapter is all about. In the world in which we live today, most children know what perverts and sex predators are. Since I am teaching 1 Corinthians verse by verse, I should not skip over chapter 5. Some children may not understand it, so use your own discretion whether or not to let them in on your teaching of this chapter. If you teach it to children, my opinion it should be children over twelve.

Readers let me remind you, *sex* is not a dirty word. God invented sex for husbands and wives to enjoy in the confines of marriage and to rear children. The tragedy is, sinful people changed sex from what God made it for to something dirty. There are more sex perverts and child predators today than at any time in American history, and perhaps the world. Rape and molestation of children is a common occurrence nowadays.

Corinth was a city like that, and Paul wrote about the wickedness that has infiltrated the church. The church adopted some of the evil practices of the pagan temples. Therefore, this chapter tells us about immoral sex activities in the Corinthian church.

The wicked activity of the church of Corinth is about a young man living with his mother and committed incest with her. His father had divorced her, and his son took up with her. That is a reprehensible, wicked sin! It's incomprehensible that anything like that could happen, especially in the church!

Do you believe incest happens today? You would be surprised if you only knew how much of that goes on in our society, and even in churches. Today's sins that are committed by church members are as bad and wicked as the young couple in the Corinthians church. I could tell you story after story of what I have seen in my many years of ministry. Some are so atrocious it would outrage you.

The Corinthian church was not only a church involved in incest as many are today. Churches that are involved in the wicked sin of incest are evil indeed.

By way of introduction, allow me to give the following story. This story is not true. I made up this story to introduce 1 Corinthians chapter 5. But it describes our society and churches in general and what is going on today. Many Christians are sickened by the things that are going on in our society and our churches.

If this story was played out in a movie theater, it would certainly be X-rated. The perverted details are not unusual because we are living in an X-rated society. I don't use explicit language, but you will get the message.

This story has only four characters. I chose these names randomly, and they certainly do not reflect the lifestyle of anyone I know personally. I have given them the names Eric, Samantha, Joel, and Alisha. Let's raise the curtains on the first scene of this story and see what is happening in the lives of these four people, and their church.

Right off we see a clean suburban neighborhood. Their neighborhood is an upper-class neighborhood and well maintained. There is a church nearby that adds to the serenity and peacefulness of the community.

Eric, Samantha, and their son, Joel, lives at the end of the street in an older, but modernized and well-maintained house. Alisha lives down the street in a smaller, but modern home. Alisha's husband left her for another woman, and she lives alone in a house that was once filled with laughter and love, but not any longer.

Eric and Samantha were married only ten months when their son Joel was born. That was twenty years ago. They decided not to have any more children, but to dedicate their lives to their jobs, traveling, and working in their church. They were very active in church. In fact, Samantha sang in the choir and Eric taught a Sunday school class. Alisha was a member of Eric's class. Joel had just turned twenty and was working on his engineering degree at the university nearby. On weekends he took a very active part in the church youth program.

The church highly respected these four people. They were considered good examples to follow. But the truth was, things weren't going so well at home with Eric and Samantha. They would usually begin their conversations with mild disagreements, but they always escalated into screaming at each other. Finally, one morning Eric and Joel awoke to find Samantha had moved out. A note on the kitchen table read, "Eric, don't look for me. I'm fed up with your abuse, and I'm filing for divorce."

A few weeks later their divorce was finalized, but during that time, Eric became very friendly with Alisha. Eric was much older than Alisha, but they felt they were right for each other. After all, they both felt they deserved a life of love and happiness since both of their spouses had left them. Their courtship was short. Eric and Alisha were married. Alisha's age was closer to Joel's age than to Eric's age. Nevertheless, Alisha accepted her role as a tender, caring stepmother to Joel.

It wasn't long, however, after the marriage of Eric and Alisha that they began to have marital problems. Alisha felt Eric wasn't meeting her needs. Therefore, she told Eric one morning he wasn't the man she thought he was, and she asked for a divorce. A few weeks later, their marriage ended in divorce. Eric moved out and rented an apartment near the church, but Joel and Alisha remained at home.

Eric, Alisha, and Joel went to the same church. Joel and Alisha sat on one side of the church, and Eric sat on the other side. The church supported Joel and Alisha. They felt sorry for them for having to go through with such an experience as Joel's mother, Samantha, leaving, and his dad, Eric, divorcing Alisha. However, some felt Joel and Alisha should not be living in the same house since they were not biologically kin to each other and they were about the same age. Others suspected there would be accusations if they continued living together in the same house. Others went so far as to say something more was going on than just a stepmother and stepson living in the same house.

Joel had dropped out of school to spend more time with Alisha. Someone was heard to say, "They are too affectionate toward each other." Their suspicion was realized when someone caught them caressing and kissing.

Their hidden immoral behavior went on for some time, but some insisted the church leaders should solve the problem. After all, it was the church leader's responsibility to handle problems in the church.

So in the second scene, we see the church leaders with a church committee selected by the church discussing the problem. They talked of several ways to settle the issue between Joel and Alisha. After long debates and much discussion, some community members insisted the lifestyle of church members should be of no concern to the church leaders. Others suggested they tolerate Joel and Alisha in the spirit of Christian love and unity and let them solve their own problems. When the curtain falls on the last scene, we see the problem still exists, and the church is doing nothing about it.

Of course, this story didn't happen. It is a story I made up to introduce 1 Corinthians 5. Nonetheless, it describes the Corinthian church and churches in our nation that are involved in incest. Evil such as that should not be happening in our churches, or in our society, but it is.

First Corinthians 5:1–2 is the first subject in the outline, and they deals with immorality in the church.

Notice 1 Corinthians 5:1–2.

> It is reported commonly that there is fornication
> among you, and such fornication is not so much

as named among the Gentiles, that one should have his father's wife.

And you are puffed up [proud], and have not rather mourned, that he that has done this deed be taken away from you.

What I am about to say is desperately needed, not only in this book, but in churches in America and around the world. Paul received a letter from members of the Corinthian church who told him about the problem of incest. We don't have that letter, but we can say it was about incest because Paul dealt with that in this chapter, along with many other issues in other chapters. Chances are the information Paul received was about the young man living with his mother (probably his stepmother) as his sex companion.

First, notice the word *commonly* from verse 1 above. This word means something that was common knowledge. Allow me to give a hypothetical story of what the town of Corinth might have known about the Corinthian church. Two friends meet on the street near the church. One said to the other, "Come visit with us at church next Sunday." His friend responded, "Where do you go to church?" He replied, "I go to the church Apostle Paul started." His friend said, "You mean you go to the church where a young man commits fornication with his mother?" His friend said, "Do you know about that?" "Sure." He added, "Everyone in Corinth knows about that. It's common knowledge all over town that the young man in your church not only commits fornication with his father's wife, and lives with his father's wife in his father's house, but goes to church where his father goes and where you go."

It was common knowledge that everyone knew about the young man living with and committing fornication with his father's wife. Can you think of anything more despicably evil than this incest? This verse describes what kind of wickedness existed in the Corinthian church.

Second, notice the phrase *"is NOT so much as mentioned among the gentiles that one should have his father's wife."*

That kind of shenanigan was so reprehensible it was not even named among the Gentiles. Paul is not saying the Gentiles did not embrace and practice that lifestyle. He is saying they did not brag about it or advertise it like the Corinthian church members and the couple doing it did.

Perhaps you know a church that is described as a permissive immortal church, tolerating perverted sins? I have been propositioned many times in my years of ministry. Thank God, I can say I have never succumbed to sexual temptation in my many years of marriage. Oh, I have been tempted to, but have never fallen into that sin. I take my wife with me when I do not feel safe going alone. I am not bragging, just stating a fact. The Lord has kept me from that type of sin. There are numerous churches, pastors, church staff, and church members who are carrying on secret affairs with each other in the church and outside the church. Even this week as I wrote this section, the news media mention a great number of priests who are involved in rape and molestation of children.

In a town near where I live, a pastor dressed in women's clothing was arrested for soliciting homosexual affairs. The tragedy and despicable evil of this occurrence is that he is still pastoring the same church.

Living an immoral life with someone outside the church is bad, but a man living an immoral life with his mother in the church is reprehensible.

Third, notice the phrase in verse 1, *"fornication among you."* *Fornication* means "sexual relationships between two people that are not married." The young man's father in chapter 5 divorced his wife, and his son took up with her and lived together as man and wife, yet not married. Can you imagine anything more disgusting to God than that? You can expect that from animals, but humans? It's hard to imagine that about human beings, but it is a common occurrence in our society. Incest is common in churches, and it is certainly common in our society. Immorality has become an epidemic in our nation, in our churches, and in all other countries as well. It's not uncommon for couples to live together but not married. Every day we hear of some church member, priest, pastor, or church leader getting involved in immoral acts. Jude, the one-chapter book, said in verse 4,

> Ungodly men have crept in unawares and turned
> the grace of God into lasciviousness.

Lasciviousness means "having a right to sin." That is, they turned God's grace, which is a good thing, into an evil thing and said it permits one to sin without any repercussions.

The pathetic thing about the Corinthians' lifestyle was that they accepted incest as a normal way of life and made no effort to correct the problem.

Third, notice the first part of verse 2.

> You are puffed up [proud] and have not rather
> mourned.

They did not weep and mourn over their wicked sin of incest, but lived as though they had a right to live that way. Paul's solution was to weep and morn over sin. The point of this verse is for us to weep and mourn over sins in the church. That is the solution in any church.

Notice the last part of verse 2. "That he that hath done this deed might be taken away from among you." Paul is not saying throw him out of the church, but rather mark his name out of the church membership roll. He is saying the church is to cease praying for him. Paul is not talking about delivering him over to Satan. However, Paul had something further to say about this in verse 3–5.

> For I verily, as absent in the body, but present in
> spirit, have judged already as though I were pres-
> ent concerning him that hath done this deed, in
> the name of the Lord Jesus Christ when you are
> gathered together, and my spirit, with the power
> of our Lord Jesus Christ, to deliver such a one
> over to Satan for the destruction of the flesh, that

the spirit may be saved in the day of the Lord
Jesus.

What does "deliver such a one over to Satan" mean? It does
not mean deliver him over to Satan so Satan can take him to hell.
It means remove him from the church's prayer list, the membership
list, and from the church's protection. It means turn him over to
the world where Satan dwells. It means excommunicate him from
the church. By the way, do you pray for God's protection on your
Christian brothers and sisters?

Those who are born again cannot survive long in Satan's
domain. If this couple were born again, it was dangerous for them to
be delivered over to Satan. God demanded they repent or He would
withdraw His protection and allow Satan to deal with them. Neither
the church nor the couple doing it were mourning over it. They did
nothing about it. They were not weeping over it. They did not cry
out to God over it. The church sinned also because they tolerated it
for a long time and did nothing about it. This young man and his
stepmother were not married, which made the sin more atrociously
evil. I'm not implying we should put our stamp of approval on marriage between a man and his stepmother. My opinion is, nothing
good could come out of a marriage such as that.

Before I proceed, I must clear up something about this young
man and his stepmother's salvation, or lack of salvation. Some say
this couple doing this wicked sin were not Christians.

There are three views concerning this young man and his stepmother's salvation.

First, some say this young man was a Christian, but lost his salvation. They use Matthew 10:22 to support that argument,

He that endureth to the end shall be saved.

The answer to that is Matthew 10:22 does not apply to Gentiles.
Gentiles are those who are not Jews. What Jesus said applied to the
twelve disciples only. In Matthew 10:1 Jesus instructs His twelve dis-

ciples to go to the "house of Israel" and preach the Gospel to Jews, not to Gentiles like you and me. Jesus said in Matthew 10:5–6,

> Go not into the way of the Gentiles, and unto the house of the Samaritans [half Jews and half Gentiles] enter you not: But go rather to the house of Israel.

The twelve disciples went forth to preach to authenticate Christ as the Messiah. We don't need to authenticate Christ today because Christ has already been proven to be the Messiah. Notice what Matthew 10:22 says,

> You [disciples] shall be hated by all for my name's sake: but he that endureth to the end shall be saved.

Jesus is saying, "Some of you may be killed, but if you make it through to the end of this assignment, you will be saved from being killed." Matthew 10:22 had nothing to do with our salvation; it applies only to the Jews.

Those who believe a person must endure unto the end to be saved take Matthew 10:22 out of context to make it fit their belief. In studying the Bible, you must keep a verse in its context to rightly interpret Scriptures. God does not contradict Himself. He does not say salvation is without works (Ephesians 2:8–9) and then turn around and say, "You must do good works until the end to be saved." Salvation is either by God's Grace or by your good works. It cannot be by both. In fact, to believe salvation is by grace plus good works is to question the honesty of Christ. It is as though you are rebuking Christ for saying,

> For by grace are you saved through faith; and that not of yourself: but it is the gift of God. NOT OF WORKS, lest any man should boast. (Ephesians 2:8–9)

To deny that Salvation is not by Jesus alone is like saying, "Christ, you are not capable of saving me without my help."

You don't lose your salvation when you get out of God's will. You will repent, but if you have no desire to repent, it is an indication you were not saved to begin with. Dr. Robert Jeffers, pastor of First Baptist Dallas, Texas, put it this way, "If there is no sanctification, there was no justification." Romans 8:29 states,

> For whom he did foreknow, He also did predesti-
> nate to be conformed to His Son.

Second, there is a view that the young man and his stepmother were not saved to start with. They explain it this way: "If the young man is excommunicated from the church, he is more likely to be saved under the domain of Satan than if he was left in the church." If that be true, then Satan is instrumental in pushing people toward Jesus for salvation. That cannot be true. Satan's objective is to lead people away from Jesus and send them to hell, not push them toward Jesus.

Third, there is the view that this young man and his stepmother were Christians—out of God's will, but needed to repent. The Bible teaches, whatever a person does after he is born again, he can never be unborn and lose his salvation. Notice John 10:28,

> I give unto them eternal life and they shall never
> perish.

Romans 6:23 says,

> For the wages of sin is death; BUT THE GIFT
> OF GOD IS ETERNAL LIFE THROUGH
> JESUS CHRIST OUR LORD.

That leads me to the following thought: Can Christians lose their salvation if they sin after they are born again? The answer is *no*! When a person receives Christ as his Saviour, he is born again. If he loses his salvation, he would have to become unborn. The facts are, when a person is born again, he becomes a member of God's family; he cannot get unsaved, unborn, or lose his salvation. The following Scripture verse proves that. In John 10:28 Jesus said,

> I give unto them eternal life: and they shall never perish, neither shall any man pluck them out of my hand.

I didn't say that; God said it. A heard a preacher use John 10:28 to promote his belief that a man can lose his salvation. He said, "No one can pluck you out of God's hand, but you can pluck yourself out." Someone said, "Are you a man? The Bible said, neither shall any man pluck them out of my hand."

When God gives a gift, He does not take it back. Ephesians 2:9 states that a gift is not given for what we do or don't do, but what Jesus did. Notice Ephesians 2:9 says, Salvation, "is not of works lest any man should boast."

So I can confidently say the Scriptures imply that this couple in chapter five were saved, but out of God's will. You can make a case each way. Just make sure you understand God's plan of salvation.

They could have become Christians before they got involved in incest, and instead of renouncing it, they embraced it by backsliding on God. To me it appears they were Christians out of God's will. They were not acting like Christians, but do we always act like Christians? If acting like Christians makes us Christians, then hypocrites are Christians, because in church they act like Christians, but in the world they act like the world.

Facts from the Bible show that Christians can commit any kind of wicked sin. There is no man or woman who can truthfully say they have never sinned after they have come to know Jesus as their Saviour. A man may be a born-again Christian, but if he is living in sin, he sure isn't a good, dedicated Christian. Being a Christian but not living like a Christian reminds me of the church of Thyatira.

After the Lord commended the Thyatira church for their good deeds, He turned to what their problem was. He said,

> Notwithstanding I have a few things against thee, because thou suffer [allows] that woman Jezebel, which calls herself a prophetess, to teach and seduce my servants to commit fornication, and to eat things offered to idols. (Revelation 2:20)

Notice the phrase "to teach and seduce my servants."

That most certainly shows Jezebel was seducing Christians. The problem is that many are judged by their outward appearance, but Jesus knows what is in the heart.

First Corinthians 5:3–8 is the second subject in the outline, and it deals with indifference to immorality in the church.

Verses 3–5 inform us that immorality is a subject the Bible deals with, and if we are indifferent to it, we avoid the Word of God. The Bible most definitely warns us to be concerned about it.

A survey of all church denominations in America revealed that 30 percent of ministers were involved in watching pornography on the web, in movies, and magazines. That is only the ministers who admit it. Not many will admit it, but if the real factual truth was known, perhaps as much as 60 percent or more church members, and pastors, are involved in watching pornography. Pornography promotes an incestuous lifestyle. It's not just a pastime sport for men any longer; women are involved in it too. There is a rapid rise in child abductions and molestation of children by men and women. They are what we call sex predators. Sex predators are in every community. You know that, I know that, and God knows that. Sex crimes against children are happening at an alarming rate. Pornography inflames the passion of men and women to satisfy their sexual drives.

What can be done about indifference to immorality in the church? We can take a stand against pornography and incest that is destroying our families, our young people, and especially children.

Taking a stand against pornography and incest will not make you popular, but it will make you popular with God. I would rather be popular with God than popular with the devil and sinful compromising churches.

Pornography is a sin that characterizes the lives of those who are indifferent to immorality in the church. Pornography is a multibillion (not *million*, but *billion*) dollar business. Who pays that much to watch pornography? The answer, of course, is unbelievers, church people, pastors, priests, religious people, and so-called Christians.

When Paul sat down to write this letter to correct their problem, he was heartbroken. He said in 2 Corinthians 2:4,

> Out of much affliction (grief) and anguish of heart I wrote unto you with many tears.

Paul is saying, "I wept when I heard you had departed from the faith and practice perverted sexual acts of sin." The Corinthian church should have approached the problem like a deadly plague that swept through the church, but they didn't. They tolerated it just like many "Christians" tolerate it today.

Second Corinthians 7:12 implies that the father of this young man was still living while this shenanigan was going on between his son and his previous wife. Notice 2 Corinthians 7:12,

> I did not write this for his cause [the young man who was living with his father's wife] that had done this wrong, nor for his cause [the father of this young man] that suffered the wrong, but that our care for you in the sight of God might appear unto you.

Instead of the church having an influence on this young couple, the young couple were having an influence on the church. Furthermore, instead of the church having an influence on the city of

Corinth, the city of Corinth was having an influence on the church. It should not have been that way because First John 4:4 says,

> You are of God, little children, and have over-come them [sins]: because greater is He [Holy Spirit] that is in you than he [Satan] that is in the world.

I understand a woman and a man needs and wants internment sexual gratification, but that should be between wife and husband only. If you do not have a husband/wife, you must exercise moral restraint. I know that is easier said than done, but there is no other alternative. Christian men/women want spouses with integrity, moral character, faithfulness, and Christian convictions. They should exercise moral restraint to get the right spouse.

God saved us to manifest Christ, not promote the devil's cause. When God saves us, we are not free to do our own thing. We are not to live a life of sin and promote the devil's cause. God changes a person when he/she becomes a Christian. Read 2 Corinthians 5:17,

> If a man [or woman] be in Christ, he/[she] is a new creation: old things are passed away, behold, all things are become new.

If we are truly born again, we can no longer live in sin and enjoy it. The Bible teaches if we get out of God's will and embrace a sinful lifestyle, God will discipline us.

Paul is stressing the fact that God will not tolerate a sinful life-style but will discipline His own. God expects Christian faithfulness out of us, and if we don't perform, He will discipline us. Second Corinthians 6:16–17 says,

> Ye are the temple of the living God…wherefore come out from among them [those that are of the world] and be ye separate sayeth the Lord, and

touch not the unclean things; and I will receive
you.

These Scriptures teach that our bodies are houses in which the
Holy Spirit dwells. Therefore, we are not to pattern our lives after the
world. Don't live like the world. Don't get caught up in the world's
system. The Lord's message to us is to be separate and touch not
the unclean things. God chastens those who get involved in worldly
pursuits. The Bible allows far liberties, but not liberties to live a life
of sin. We must not allow room for selfish pride and perverted sin in
our lives or our churches.

Notice again what Paul said about disciplining in 1 Corinthians
5:5,

Deliver such a one unto Satan for the destruction
of the flesh.

If disciplining does not work on the unrepentant sinner, the
church is to deliver him/her over to Satan's domain. That will force
him to repent, or he will be taken over by Satan and destroyed. Paul's
suggested harsh treatment. God approves of that type treatment for
unrepentant Christians who will not get right with Him.

There are two statements in 1 Corinthians chapter 5 that say
the same thing. These statements speak of having someone removed
from the church. First, notice 1 Corinthians 5:2,

You are puffed up, and have not mourned, that
he that has done such a deed might be taken
away from you.

Secondly, 1 Corinthians 5:13 states that the wicked one should
be driven out.

Therefore, put away from among yourselves that
wicked person.

If a person has been confronted over and over again and refuse to repent, dismiss him/her from the church. That sounds harsh, but it must be done if we follow God's advice on disciplining.

The Corinthian church was not only tolerating their sin of incest and adultery, but applauding it. Can you imagine a church doing that? That kind of wickedness broke the heart of Paul. He knew what would happen to the church if they stayed on that path. He knew it would destroy the church. Paul said in 1 Corinthians 5:6,

> Your glorying is not good. Know you not that
> a little leaven [yeast that makes bread rise] leav-
> eneth the whole lump?

Paul is saying a little yeast (a little sin) affects the whole lump (church). Sin promotes sin, and it will become a big sin. Sin left in the church will entice others to sin. It will destroy the church. Paul did not want that to happen.

Church discipline is a thing of the past nowadays. The reason is that people are saying, 'You have no right to judge others," and they used Matthew 7:1 to defend their position.

> Judge not that ye be not judged.

Matthew 7:1 is teaching it is wrong to judge others when you are guilty of committing the same sins yourself. Jesus strongly condemned those who had sin in their life yet were judging others for the same sin. In Matthew 7:5 Jesus said,

> Thy hypocrite, first cast out the beam [sin] out of
> thine own eye; and then shalt thou see clearly to
> cast out the mote [sin] of thy brother's eye.

We do not have the right to judge when we are not right with God ourselves.

There were some in the Corinthian church totally committed to Christ and were highly disturbed over incest and adultery in the church. They had a right to judge the wayward sinner, and they had the right to excommunicate him from the church if he refused to repent. It's the right thing to do if a church member is involved in a sin that is detrimental to the cause of Christ. Sin left lingering in the church is like cancer left untreated. It will destroy the whole body. Sin left in the church will spread throughout the church and eventually take life out of it. Do you not know it is more damaging to let a sin linger in the church than to correct it? Yes, the church may lose a few members when it disciplines someone, but it is better to lose a few members than to lose the whole church, or lose fellowship with God.

It is very rare to see a church today that is willing to use church discipline on a wayward church member. A church is not very popular that disciplines its members. They get a lot of criticism, but it is better to be criticized by the public than to be criticized by God. Paul's advice is to get rid of the sin of incest even if the person doing it has to be dismissed from the church.

Notice what Paul said in 1 Corinthians 5:7,

> Purge out therefore the old leaven [sin], that there may be a new lump [a renewed righteousness in the church], as you are unleavened. For even Christ our Passover is sacrificed for us.

At the Passover, unleavened bread symbolized being free from Egyptian bondage. In the case of the Corinthian church, they needed to be absent from the sin of incest, adultery, and other sins because they had been set free in Christ.

Allow me to point out five reasons our bodies should be absent of sin. I'm not saying born-again Christians can reach the state of perfection. We cannot be totally free from sin as long as we are in this earthly body. We all sin, even after we are saved. I'm simply saying, our bodies must strive to be free from sin

First, our bodies must strive to be free from sin because we are members of the body of Christ. That involves dismissing sinful Christians from the church who hinder the church from doing what the Lord wants them to do. That was God's advice in 1 Corinthians 5:7 above.

I'm not talking about Christians that sin occasionally. We all sin occasionally. First John 1:8 states,

> If we say we have no sin, we deceive ourselves,
> and the truth is not in us.

First John 1:8 is written to Christians, so it means Christians sin. John even includes himself as one who committed sin. Read 1 John 1:8 again and notice the word *we* found three times, *ourselves* found once, and the word *us* is found once. John includes himself in that verse. Yes, we all sin. I know we sin. You know we sin, and God knows we sin after we are saved. First John 2:1 says,

> My little children [it's obvious John is writing to Christians] these things write I unto you, that you sin not, but if any man sin we [notice John said we, meaning himself] have an advocate [someone to plead our case] with the Father [and it is] Jesus Christ the righteous.

Christians need to repent every day because that is what Jesus taught us and His disciples to do in His model prayer. Notice Matthew 6:12 where Jesus taught them what to say,

> Forgive us of our debts [sins] as we forgive our debtors [those who have sin against us].

Even the apostle Paul had a problem with his body that wanted him to sin. Read Romans chapter 7 verses 15–25. Paul said he wanted to do right, but sin kept him from doing it. We all have sinned. That applies not only to the unbeliever, but to Christians as well. We sin with our bodies, but we are not allowed to continually entertain sin. Those who stay in sin and refuse to repent are the ones who need to be disciplined. The emphasis is to repent of persistent sins or suffer the consequences.

Some people dogmatically teach Christians who sin lose their salvation. They say a real born-again Christian will not sin. I can understand why they would say that. They depend on their good works and their so-called perfect lives to get them to heaven. Yes, we must strive to be free from sin because we are part of the body of Christ, but we can never be totally free in our earthly bodies from sinning.

Second, we must strive to be free from sin so we can be a consistent testimony for Christ. The Holy Spirit in us wants us to testify for Christ, but our sinful body keeps us from doing that. We need to understand our bodies are of this world and are subject to commit sin which will hinder our testimony. The body has nothing to do with getting us to heaven or keeping us out of heaven. We don't have a perfect body. Our bodies are capable of sinning. However, our souls never sin. God would never allow sin to occupy a place where the Holy Spirit dwells. Our saved souls abide with the Holy Spirit. First John 3:9 says,

> Whosoever is born of God doeth not commit sin; for His (God's) seed remains in him: and he cannot sin, because he is born of God.

In other words, the Holy Spirit keeps the soul from sinning. Remember the soul is the place of love and hate for the unbeliever, but when the Holy spirit moves in at the new birth, hate moves out and the love of the Holy Spirit takes control.

Someone may say, this is referring to the Holy Spirit that does not sin. That cannot mean the Holy Spirit because the Holy Spirit was not "born of God," says 1 John 3:9. The Holy Spirit is God. John 4:24 says,

> God is a Spirit.

Only sinners are born of God. This verse is referring to the soul of a person who has accepted Jesus as his Saviour. The saved *soul* never sins, but the body does sin. Once the Holy Spirit moves into our lives, He keeps our souls from sin that occurs in the body. The fact is, a person's body is just as wicked as it was before the Holy Spirit moved in. The difference is when we sin as Christians, we are condemned and disciplined for it; whereas when we sin as a lost person, it does not bother us.

Thank God, one day we will get a new body—a perfect body, a sinless body, an incorruptible body—a body that will never have a desire to sin. Until then we must contend with this sinful body we have.

We Christians get frustrated when our saved souls and the Holy Spirit want us to do right but our bodies want us to do wrong. No matter how much we want to serve God in our minds, our bodies lead us to sin. Even though we sin, we must not be controlled by sin. First John 4:4 says,

> Greater is He [the Holy Spirit] that is in you than
> he that is in the world.

Then again, 1 Peter 1:23 says we are "born again, not of corruptible seed, but of incorruptible [seed], by the word of God, which liveth and abideth forever."

You must understand when you are born again, you become part of the body of Christ—member of God's family and kept by the Holy Spirit. Therefore, you are not controlled by sin but your sinful flesh entices you to sin. Sin will harm your testimony as long as you are in your body. What one does in this earthly body has nothing to do with his/her salvation. Notice 1 John 3:9 once again,

> Whosoever is born of God doeth not sin; for
> His seed remaineth in him: and he cannot sin,
> because he is born of God?

Our *souls* are saved forever from the moment we put our faith and trust in Jesus Christ, and it will never sin again. But our bodies are not saved, and our bodies sin. It's ludicrous to think a person's body is saved. To live forever in a decaying body such as ours would be hell in itself. At the resurrection we will get a new body—a perfect, saved body. Paul said in 1 Corinthians 9:27,

> I keep under [control] my body, and bring it into subjection lest by any means, when I preach to others I myself should be a castaway.

Paul did not mean he would be cast into hell but be cast away from serving God in the ministry. He is saying if he allowed his body to run rampant with sin, he would lose his opportunity to serve in the ministry. He would be disqualifying himself from God's service if he did not bring his body under control.

How many have been set aside from being a productive Christian because they did not control their bodies? Our bodies cause us problems, but thank God, one day we will get a new body—a perfect body—a glorified body that will never decay and give us trouble or lead us to sin. We will never know sin in our glorified bodies. We can serve the Lord forever in perfect holiness of soul and body.

First, our bodies must strive to be free from sin because we are members of the body of Christ.

Second, our bodies must strive to be free from sin so we can be a consistent testimony for Christ.

Third, our bodies must strive to be free from sin because it will keep us from sinning like the young man and his stepmother in this chapter.

Why would some suggest that this couple were born-again Christians even though they lived in sin? You could fall into grievous sin even though you are a born-again Christian. This scenario that this young couple were involved in shows that living a good life to be saved will not work, because the flesh will not allow you to be good. Living good and doing good has never saved anyone and never will.

It's good to do good works because the law demands that, but doing good and keeping the law will not save you. In fact, ever truly born-again Christian will do good works not to be saved but because they are already saved. Ephesians 2:10 states that we are "created in Christ Jesus unto good works."

But a belief that one must do good works to be saved will separate him from God forever.

Oh, I personally know some people that are saved, but they ignorantly embrace the belief that they can work their way to heaven. Once I believed that too, but it's not taught in the Bible. The flesh has nothing to do with our salvation, nor does it have anything to do with keeping us saved. If we are honest with ourselves and honest with God, we will admit we sin every day. We must admit there are little rooms in our bodies that are not always clean. We try to keep them clean but fail. Sometimes it gets cluttered up with worldly things, and we have to repent and clean house. We sin and even try to hide our sins, but it is necessary to clean house occasionally. We want to do right, but we come short because sin dwells in our bodies. God reprimands and disciplines us when we sin, but we do not lose our salvation when we sin.

God wants us to keep our bodies under control, and we can do that by letting the Holy Spirit control our bodies. If we persist in sin, God will severely discipline us. God would have done that to the young man who was living with his father's wife if he had not repented. After all, if we are no longer on God's side, we are doing a disservice to God, and He might as well take us out. Paul said in Romans 7:25,

> With the mind I serve the law of God; but with
> the flesh the law of sin.

Did you get that? Paul is saying, "It's not the Holy Spirit who lives in me that leads me to sin, but the sinful flesh leads me to sin." Paul inherited a sinful nature from Adam just like you and me. So when he wanted to do good, sin was in his body. Paul had a war going on in his body, so do we.

First, we must strive to be free from sin because we are members of the body of Christ. Second, we must strive to be free from sin so we can be a consistent witness for Jesus. Third, we must strive to be free from sin so we can keep our bodies from committing the sin of incest like the young man and his stepmother in chapter 5 of 1 Corinthians.

Fourth, we must strive to be free from sin to avoid the discipline hand of God. The goal of every church member should be to discipline their bodies when they fall into sin. If they discipline their body, they could avoid being disciplined by God. The couple in the Corinthian church needed to discipline their bodies and repent so they could be restored to full fellowship in the church.

God's disciplinary process is to excommunicate a wayward member but not avoid him or her but keep in touch and seek to win them back to the Lord. We should make every effort to restore a wayward brother or sister to the fellowship of the church. After all, they are our Christian brothers and sisters. We are to consider them because we also could fall into sin. Galatians 6:1 says,

> Brethren, if a man be overtaken in a fault, ye which are spiritual restore such a one lest thou also be tempted.

If it wasn't for God's grace and mercy, we could fall into sin—disgusting sin, sin as bad as the young man and woman in 1 Corinthians 5. We should never condone or permit sin to continue in our churches and in our lives. We are to deal with it, considering ourselves less we fall into temptation and sin.

We must understand what the Corinthian church's problem was and what our church's problems are. We must discipline ourselves and other members in the church who have fallen into sin. That is the way God handles it. That was Paul's advice to the Corinthian church. I think we should consider Paul and God's advice and do it.

Some people feel disciplining the fallen brother or sister should be done to hurt them for their disobedience to God. No! God does not do that; neither should we do that. Discipline should not be done to hurt the fallen brother or sister but done to help them spiritually and to lead them back into fellowship of the church. Disciplining our wayward brother or sister in Christ should cause us to weep and leave us with a broken heart. We should feel the same way when we discipline our child/children.

Allow me to depart for a moment and say something about disciplining our children. It should not be done to hurt them but to restore them to a right relationship in the home. Our whole duty before God is to love our children and let them know we love them and lovingly let them know why we put restrictions on them. Let them know disciplining is for their benefit. The world wants to take advantage of our sons and daughters. Teach them that restrictions are for showing the world they are not one to play around with. It is to send a message to others that they have moral Christian principles and will not compromise. If your children break those rules, you are to discipline them.

I heard of a boy who was adopted into a wealthy home. The boy wore dirty ragged clothes and dirty shoes with holes in them when he was adopted. The family who took him in never threw his old shoes and ragged clothes away. When the boy got out of line, they would pull out his old shoes from the closet and say, "This is where we brought you from, and we can sure send you back." Don't be guilty of pulling out old shoes on your child who falls into sin. That is the wrong thing to do. Lead him/her to repentance and come back into the fellowship of the home. Read Galatians 6:1 again,

> Brethren, if a man be overtaken in a fault, ye
> which are spiritual restore such a one in the spirit
> of meekness; considering thyself lest thou also be
> tempted.

We must strive to be free from sin because we are members of the body of Christ. Second, we must strive to be free from sin because sin hinders our Christian testimony. Third, we must strive to be free from sin to keep ourselves from incest like the young man and his stepmother in this chapter. Fourth, we must strive to be free from sin to avoid the chasing hand of God.

Fifth and last, we must strive to be free from sin because sin is like a cancer that destroys the body if left untreated. Sin left in the local church will destroy the church. Therefore, we need to be totally committed to Christ and strive to be without sin.

Paul gave an illustration about total commitment to Christ. Notice what he said in 1 Corinthians 5:8,

> Therefore let us keep the feast, not with old leaven, neither with the leaven of malice and wickedness; but with the unleaven bread of sincerity and truth.

What "feast" is Paul referring to here? It's about the Jewish feast they performed the night before they were delivered from Egypt's bondage which came to be called the Passover. Pharaoh refused to release God's people from slavery, and God sent a plague of death upon every first born in Egypt. God told the Jewish people to prepare a lamb for the feast and put the blood on the side posts and above the door, and when the death angel passed through, no one would be harmed. God told the Jews to commemorate this feast every year. The lamb's blood represented the blood Christ shed for us.

Paul said,

> Let us keep the feast.

Paul is not saying to us who are under the grace dispensation to celebrate the Jewish Passover but celebrate the New Passover— Jesus Christ. Every time we observe the Communion service, we are observing the New Passover—Jesus Christ.

The Jews kept the Passover without leavened bread—that is, without sin. Leaven represents sin. We must celebrate Jesus, our New Passover, with a life free from deliberate sins. We should never again get involved in things we repented of. We must totally dedicate our lives to the Lord before taking part in the Communion service.

We are to keep the New Passover without malice and wickedness and with sincerity and truth. Our lives must be totally committed to Christ without leaven (sin). We are to celebrate Jesus. Anything short of that is displeasing to God. Those who are permitted to remain as members of local churches that are living in sin are adding extra leaven to bread. Leaven keeps growing and growing until the whole loaf becomes corrupt. Notice again what 5:7 had to say about sin,

> Purge out therefore the old leaven, that you may
> be a new lump, as you are unleaven for even
> Christ our Passover is sacrificed [set apart by God
> for a sacred use] for us.

We are to let God set us apart for a sacred use like God set Christ apart for a sacred use.

By using Israel as an illustration, Paul is saying, if sin is left in the local church, it keeps growing and growing until it will eventually take life out of the church. Sin left in the church is a sin in itself. Paul reminded us Jesus was sacrificed to take away our sins. The Jewish people were to celebrate the Passover without leaven—without sin. So Paul is saying we are to celebrate our Passover—Jesus—without sin. Jesus Christ is our Passover. The lamb represented Christ who was slain for Israel, so they would not have to die when the death angel passed over. Jesus Christ was slain for us so we would not have to suffer eternity in hell, but have eternal life with Him in heaven. First John 5:13 states,

> These things I have written unto you that believe
> on the name of the Son of God; that you may
> know you have eternal life.

Notice it is saying, "You may know [presentence] you have eternal life."

The phrase *old leaven...leaven of malice and wickedness* means "leaven of sin." Did you know some have committed themselves to a life of sin, even some Christians?

> Therefore, let us keep the feast, not with old leaven, neither with the leaven of malice and wickedness; but with the unleavened of sincerity and truth.

First Corinthians 5:9–13 is the third subject in the outline, and it instructs believers to be friendly with unbelievers, but not participate in their sins.

Notice verse 9,

> I wrote unto you in an epistle not to company with fornicators.

Evidently, some Corinthian church members misunderstood Paul's advice and stopped associating with immoral people altogether. Many people outside of Christ and outside of the church are unsaved and immoral, but we should not totally disconnect ourselves from them. We are to seek to win them to Christ. We are not to judge those outside the church. God will judge them at the Great White Throne Judgment. Those are they who died without repenting and receive Jesus as their personal Saviour. We are to be friendly to unbelievers, but not participate in their sinful lifestyles. You can't join them and do what they do to win them to Christ. That does not work. Our friendship should be to witness to them about the salvation Jesus has to offer, but we are to separate ourselves from their sinful deeds.

Where judging is concerned, our most important duty is to judge those inside the church who are involved in sin, not those outside of the church. The young couple in the Corinthian church were sinning; the church was sinning by allowing them to continue in their sin. They were not judging them about their sinfulness. That was wrong.

Paul mentioned several sins Christians are to separate themselves from, but he is not referring to separation from sinners. First Corinthians 5:9–11 names some specific sins Christians are to separate themselves from: "fornicators, converters, extortioners, and idolaters." This is not an exhaustive list of sins we are to separate ourselves from, but we are to separate ourselves from all sins we know to be sins.

Notice Paul's admonition in 1 Corinthians 5:9–11,

> I wrote to you in an epistle not to company with fornicators, yet not covetous, or extortionist, or with idolaters, for then must you go out of the world.

Paul added an additional rule in verse 11.

> But now I have written unto you not to keep company, if any man that is called a brother [a Christian brother] be a fornicator, or covetous, or idolaters; or a drunkard, or an extortioner; with such a one no not to eat.

Evidently, the phrase "no not to eat" is referring to the Communion service. We are not to participate in the Communion service with someone that does not live a righteous life. If someone is a fornicator, covetous, idolater, drunker, or extortioner or have other sins in his/her life we know about, we should not allow them to participate in the Communion service.

Some churches use this phrase to promote their belief on the "closed Communion service." That is, they believe and teach that their denomination is the only one that is right, so they will not allow anyone else to participate in their Communion service, thus "closed Communion service." Do they not know they might have fornicators, coveters, idolaters, drunks, or extortioners in their own church?

In many churches the leadership will say nothing about sin lingering in *their* church. Are churches naive enough to deny sin in *their* church? If they are, it will show their ignorance of God's Word and hinder the lost from coming to Jesus for salvation. A local church is commanded to correct its members when they get out of God's will and live an open life of sin and rebalance. The unsaved can see the church is no better than they are if their sinful members are not corrected. A church with a good testimony is where the unsaved wants to come to learn about Jesus and the way of salvation. So the church must correct its members, not so much over trivial matters, but major perpetual sins that projects a bad image of the church. Do it for God's sake, for the church's sake and for the sake of the lost.

Paul concludes this section by saying in verses 12–13,

> For what have I to do to Judge them also that
> are without? Do not ye judge them that are
> within. But them that are without, God judges.
> Therefore, put away from among yourselves that
> wicked person.

Paul is saying you should not have anything to do with judging those outside of the church. He goes on to say,

> Them that are without, God judges.

He means, when all is said and done, God is the ultimate Judge. Paul wanted the Corinthian church members and us to know we both are obligated to judge those that are within the church.

> Do you not judge those within?

Notice what he says in verse 13:

> Therefore, put away from among yourselves that
> wicked person.

Of course, Paul is talking about the young man and his stepmother living together and committing adultery.

The question arises: What happened to the church in relation to the young man and his stepmother? Did the church judge them, or did they remain in the church living in sin? Paul's friend Titus visited the Corinthian church. Sometime after that Titus met Paul in Macedonia and reported to him what happened. Notice what Paul said in 2 Corinthians 7:6–9,

> God comforted us…by the coming of Titus. And not by his coming only but by the consolation whereby he was comforted in you, when he told us of your earnest desire, your morning…so I rejoice the more.

Second Corinthian 7:9 states,

> For though I made you sorry with a letter, I do not repent… Now I rejoice, not that you were made sorry, but that you sorrowed to repentance: for you were made sorry after a godly manner.

These verses not only say the church repented for allowing sin to continue in the church, but indicated the young man and his stepmother repented too. These verses above presents not only that the roll the church played in the lives of the young couple who were living in sin, but also shows they disciplined themselves.

Chapter 6
Has Four Subjects

Verses 1–5 deal with Christians going to court with each other.
Verses 6–9 deal with the insincerity of Christians.
Verses 10–12 deal with the holiness of the body of Christ.
Verses 6:13–20 deal with the Christian's body that belongs to the Lord.

First Corinthians chapter 6 is so desperately needed. It tells us how to settle church issues from God's perspective. The Bible will keep us from making wrong decisions. Therefore, those who do not understand nor study the Bible cause problems in the church. So it is ultimately important that church members have a personal time of prayer, Bible study, and lessons on how to solve problems from God's perspective.

Can you recall any church that is, or has been, involved in a court case over issues that could be settled in the church? Having served in the ministry many years, I have seen some dirty, underhand dealings in churches that personified Satan's power.

Allow me to give a story that is based on a true story. This story could have happened in a church you belonged to, or it could have happened to a church you know. The details of this story have been changed, but a problem of this magnitude did happen in a church I am familiar with. My purpose in telling this story is to show that going to court before unbelieving judges to settle a spiritual issue does not work. This story will also show you that we are not far removed from the Corinthian church. In fact, we are much like them.

I will not give the name of the church, nor its members, nor the location of the church, but I will give a few details that characterized the church. The incident is about a little town I call Oaktown (not the real name, nor a real location).

Oaktown was located on the east side of Shad County near Oak Mountain (not a real mountain, nor a real county). It was secluded from most of the world until Interstate 99 snakes its way up the valley. Since the interstate ran right by Oaktown, many strangers visited this little quaint town. The folks in Oaktown were not accustomed to seeing outsiders so often, and to add to their problems, they only had a part-time mayor, a chief of police, and one patrol officer.

Oaktown seldom saw court cases. When a case of any major magnitude occurred, it was moved to a larger city some fifty miles away. There might have been one or two court cases a year that consisted of minor issues in Oaktown, but nothing large. To have a court case over church problems was never heard of in Oaktown, nor even occurred to them it might happen. However, things changed since strangers moved in.

There were only two churches in Oaktown: Oaktown Baptist and Shad County Methodist. Most local folks made Oaktown Baptist their home church. They had a good number on Sunday morning and a thriving Sunday night and Wednesday night Bible study service. Strangers moved in and joined the church which added to that number. The church welcomed them because they believed it was the right thing to do. However, as you may guess, not all that joined the church were born-again Christians, nor did they hold the same beliefs that Oaktown Baptist held.

It wasn't long until problems arose in the church. Some new members wanted to incorporate activities and beliefs their former churches held. The local church folks strongly disagreed. Nevertheless, the newcomers pushed ahead. The problem escalated to the point that the new members threaten to take the church to court before an unbelieving judge. The older members opposed it, of course. They were convinced that unbelieving judges did not have the same moral and spiritual values they had. Nonetheless, the new members pressed ahead and went to court.

Nothing was accomplished. The issue wasn't even settled, but the church lost its testimony, destroyed its influence in the community, and split over an issue that could have been settled in church. Now the church is struggling to survive. They have just a few on Sunday morning and no service Sunday night or Wednesday night. End of story.

That is why God commanded Paul to write about the issue of churches going to court before unbelieving judges.

First Corinthians 6:1–4 is the first subject, and it deals with believers going to court before unbelieving judges.

Notice 1 Corinthians 6:1,

> Dare any of you, having a matter against another,
> go to law before the unjust [unbelieving judge],
> and not before the saints?

Paul had been in Corinth eighteen months, but when he left some church members slipped back into their old ways. They replaced their spiritual values for their own values. Instead of following the Spirit of God, they were taking each other to court before unbelieving judges.

I must first say, it is necessary sometimes to go to court before an unbelieving judge. Paul himself once appealed to an unbelieving court system for justice. Acts 25:9–11 states,

> Festus, willing to do the Jews a pleasure, answered
> Paul, and said: Will thou go up to Jerusalem, and
> there be judged of these things before me? Then
> Paul said I stand at Caesar's judgment seat, where
> I ought to be judged: to the Jews I have done no
> wrong, as you very well know.

Paul appealed to the civil court under the authority of the unbelieving monarch, Caesar, of the Roman empire to be judged.

Allow me to give an example of a judiciary court case I was involved in. A church I once pastored had bus routes that brought people to church each Sunday morning that could not otherwise come to church. On one Sunday a lady rode one of our busses. She had never come to church before, and we welcomed her in. We thought everything went great—that is, until we were served a summons to appear in court on a certain day. The lady claimed she was injured on the bus and sued us for several thousands of dollars. We did go to court, but someone testified she had injured herself a week before coming to church. The case was thrown out, and the lady never came to church again.

Could we have settled that case in church? Not very likely. Sometimes it's necessary to go to a civil court to settle an issue that cannot be settled in church. However, many church people have a mind-set to rebel against all Bible teaching when it comes to their so-called rights. They say, "I have a right to get even. I have the right to sue someone. I have a right to get what belongs to me." They want to lash out, or at least get revenge. That rarely ever accomplishes anything good but creates more problems. The Bible's mandate is the very opposite of that. Jesus said in Luke 6:29,

> He that taketh away your cloak, forbid [him] not
> to take away thy coat also.

Christian, instead of destroying your testimony, it is better to surrender your rights. That is what Jesus is saying here in Luke 6:29. When you go down fighting for your rights, it's displeasing to God. Scriptures clearly states that Christians should settle their issues in the church if possible, not through a civil court of unbelievers.

It's wrong to take your Christian brothers or sisters to court before unbelieving judges if you can settle the issue in the church. Paul suggests three reasons why going to court before unbelieving judges is wrong.

First, it is wrong for Christians to take their issues before unbelieving judges if it can be settled in the church.

Paul is not condemning civil courts or unbelieving judges. We are fortunate to have civil courts and judges to defend us in civil cases that are not church related. It's understandable that our judiciary system is flawed simply because fallen men and women cannot always reach the right verdict all the time. Let's not put unbelieving judges down because of their inability to render right verdicts in spiritual matters. Paul is simply saying it is wrong for a Christian to take another Christian to court before an unbelieving judge about an issue that could be settled in church.

By the way, the word *matter* in verse 1 means "something that is related to the operating of the church, or some spiritual matter." It's okay to take your case before an unbelieving judge when your civil rights have been violated, but not where spiritual matters are concerned. Suing for restitution in a civil case is okay if it is a ligament claim and not a frivolous lawsuit. A Christian should never go to court over some frivolous matter.

I know a lady that was crossing the street to go to a furniture store on the other side of the street. She was wearing open toe shoes, and when she lifted her foot to step over the curb, she hit her toe on the curb and stumbled, resulting in the loss of her toenail. She sued the furniture store and was awarded over $2,000. That was a frivolous lawsuit as far as I am concerned. That should never have happened. Don't you know there are people out there that will sue you over anything? A Christian has the right to go to court before an unbelieving judge, but a case that could be settled in the church is not one of them. So it's wrong to take a case before an unbelieving judge if it can be settled in the church.

Second, Paul is saying, it is senseless and foolish to take your issues before an unbelieving judge if they could have settled them in the church. First Corinthians 6:2–3 says,

> Do you not know that the saints shall judge the world, and if the world shall be judged by you, are you not worthy [do you not have the ability] to judge the smallest mater? Know ye not that we

shall judge angels? How much more things that
pertain to this life.

Saints of God are very qualified to judge. In fact, verses 2–3 are
referring to the coming thousand-year reign of Christ on this earth.
Christ will allow saints to judge the world, and angels—fallen angels.

Believers who lived in the past that went to be with Jesus and
those who are raptured will come back to this earth with Jesus and be
judged over the world and angels for a thousand years. God's kingdom will exist on this earth much like the one we have now, except
Jesus will be the supreme judge and ruler. Therefore, Paul is saying,
"Are you not capable of judging the smallest matter?

By the way, Revelation 20:1–4 said this about the millennial
reign of Christ on this earth,

> And I saw an angel come down from heaven, hav-
> ing the key to the bottomless pit and a great chain
> in his hand. And he laid hold of the dragon, that
> old serpent, which is the Devil, and Satan, and
> bound him a thousand years, and cast him into
> the bottomless pit, and shut him up, and set a
> seal upon him that he should deceive the nations
> no more, till the thousand years be fulfilled: and
> after that he must be loosed a little season. And
> I saw thrones, and they that set upon them, and
> judgment was given unto them.

In other words, judgment will be given to the saints to judge here
on this earth during the thousand-year reign of Christ. Revelation
5:10 states,

> Thou hast made us [Christians] unto our God
> kings and priests: and we shall reign on the earth.

The Scriptures tell us we will reign with Him and judge the world *and judge angels.* Let's read again what 1 Corinthians 6:3 has to say,

> Know you not that we shall judge angels, how
> much more things pertaining to this life?

Paul is saying to the Corinthian church, and us, "If you're going to reign with Christ and judge this world and angels, are you not capable of judging in the smallest matters in the church? If the Lord considers you capable of judging angels in His thousand-year reign on earth, can't you handle small matters in the church?" The truth Paul was getting across was that the Corinthian church was acting in ignorance by taking each other to court before unbelieving judges. It is wrong, absurd, senseless, and foolish to take a case before an unbelieving judge if it can be settled in the church.

Third, it is ludicrous, absurd, and ridiculous for Christians to take an issue before an unbelieving judge that could be settled in the church. Do they not understanding what the Bible teaches about going to court before unbelieving judges? The Corinthian church, and we as well, have been taught that even the least esteemed member of the church is more capable of making a right judgment in spiritual matters than the highest esteemed unbeliever. Notice 1 Corinthians 6:4,

> If then you have judgment pertaining to this life,
> set them to judge who are least esteemed in the
> church.

The least qualified born-again Christian in the church can settle spiritual issues because they have the Holy Spirit living in them. They have more spiritual discernment than the best among unbelieving judges.

If you are not spiritual enough to understand how to settle minor issues in the church, how can you understand biblical doctrine that shows you how to live a productive Christian life and tell others how to become a believer in Christ? Ignorance in understanding the Bible leads to all kinds of weird beliefs. That is how cults (false religions) get started. Cults just understand enough of the Bible to form their own religion. They do not believe in the atoning death, burial, and resurrection of Jesus Christ who paid the supreme sacrifice for their salvation. All cult religions are built on works salvation. Their belief is, if you want something, you must do something to get something. That makes sense by the world's standards, but not for salvation that Jesus provides through His death, burial, and resurrection. They carry their works theory over to their religion. But salvation does not come that way Romans 3:20 states,

> By the deeds of the law [that is, by doing good deeds and keeping the law] no flesh shall be justified.

All those depending on good works to get them to heaven will be turned away at the great White Throne Judgment. Revelation 20:12 said,

> I saw the dead [unsaved], small and great, stand before God, and the books were open: and another book was open, which was the book of life: and the dead were judged out of those things which were written in the books, according to their works.

Unbelievers will be judged by their works they thought would save them.

Paul admired you who are least esteemed and least qualified in the church as having the ability to judge in the most pressing issues, so don't take your case before an unbelieving judge. First, it is wrong to take a case before an unbelieving judge if it can be settled in the church. Second, it is absurd, senseless, and foolish to take a case before an unbelieving judge if it can be settled in the church. Third, it is ludicrous and ridiculous that the Corinthian church, and many in our day, do not understand what the Bible teaches about going to court before unbelieving judges

First Corinthians 6:5–8 is the second subject, and it deals with inconsistency of Christians.

Inconsistency means "not staying the same—changing back and forth." Someone used the following expression to describe inconsistency: "wishy-washy." Paul confronts the Corinthian church, and us, about inconsistency. He said in 1 Corinthians 6:5–6,

> I speak to your shame. Is it so, that there is not a wise man among you; no, not one that shall be able to judge between his brothers? But brothers goeth to law with brothers and that before the unbeliever.

Joe and Sam were friends all their lives. In fact, they went to high school and college together. They both played on their high school and college basketball teams. They were closer than brothers. They both married their high school sweethearts. And they both joined the same church, eventually chosen as deacons.

There was a twenty-acre plot of ground on the country road near the church. So Joe and Sam decided to buy ten acres each and build homes for themselves. They lived side by side many years. Their children grew up together and were like brothers and sisters. However, something happened to sever their friendship.

Joe liked shade trees around his house and planted plenty when he first built his house. Over the years the little trees grew to be large trees.

Sam, on the other hand, disliked trees and said they were a nuance. He kept his property mowed and clean like a golf course. The problem was that wind blew leaves from Joe's property over on Sam's property. Sam confronted Joe about that, but all his suggestions went unanswered. One day Sam called Joe and told him if he didn't do something about his leaves blowing over on his property, he was going to see a lawyer. Joe ignored his threats, but eventually had to appear before a judge for desecrating Sam's property.

Their case was taken before a civil court of unbelievers, and it was settled in Sam's favor. But the tragedy made headlines in the local newspaper that read, "DEACONS SUE OVER LEAVES."

Joe and Sam's many years of friendship were over, and their testimony, and their churches' testimony, was dragged through the mud.

Sam and Joe are good examples of inconsistent Christians. They had been close friends all their lives, but one little issue changed that. They could have settled their issue in the church but chose to go before an unbelieving judge to settle it.

Paul is saying to the Corinthian church, "Shame on you for not stepping up and doing what God expects of you." Notice 1 Corinthians 3:1,

> I could not speak unto you as unto spiritual, but
> as unto carnal.

That means the number of years a person has been saved does not determine the level of his spirituality. Evidently, Joe and Sam were "babes in Christ." They had never grown to be mature Christians. First Peter 2:1–2 commands us to

> Lay aside all malice [ill will toward each other],
> and all guile [craftiness, or cunning attitude], and
> hypocrisies, and envy, and evil speaking, as new
> born babes, desire the sincere milk of the word
> that you may grow thereby.

Paul spent eighteen months with the Corinthian church, teaching and preaching every day. That amounted to about 540 sermons. A pastor would have to preach six years, three sermons a week, to preach that many sermons. Paul did it in eighteen months. The Corinthian church was exposed to messages that taught them how to conduct their lives, yet they were taking each other to court before unbelieving judges.

Following are four principles that will change inconsistency into consistency in a Christian's life. We need to get hold of these principles.

First, church leaders must be responsible for settling disputes in their church. Paul emphasized over and over again that church disputes should be settled in the church, yet the first thing many think of is to take their brother or sister in Christ to court before an unbelieving judge. That should never be done.

Second, Christians should never drag their Christian testimony through the mud for the entire world to see. That is exactly what happens when they go before an unbelieving judge to settle issues that could be settled in the church. Our Christian testimony should mean more to us than winning a case in court.

Third, if we don't do the right thing, our witness will be at risk, and the very purpose of the church will be thwarted. It's better to take a loss than stand in the way of someone coming to Jesus Christ for salvation.

Fourth, by settling church issues within the church, we set a good example for our young people to follow. After all, they will be the church leaders of tomorrow, and it's ultimately important we be consistent in training them right.

First Corinthians 6:7–8 exposes the major fault of inconsistency in the church.

> Now therefore there is utterly a fault among you, because you go to law one with another. Why do you not rather take wrong? Why do you not allow yourself to be defrauded? Nay, you do wrong, and that to your brother.

The major fault among the Corinthian church was they went before unbelieving judges to settle their issues rather than taking a loss. Paul is saying, "You would be better off by taking a loss than to do God, your Christian brother and sister, and the church an injustice." The Bible states in Proverbs. 20:22

> Say not thou, I will recompense evil; but wait on
> the Lord, and He shall save [repay] thee.

You should not say "I will pay him back for the wrong he did to me." Wait on God; He will repay. Wait on God because God will save you from an evil intention. Romans 12:17 states,

> Recompense no man evil for evil.

That is, don't pay people back for wrongs they do to you. God will take care of that. Jesus stated in the prayer that He taught His disciples to pray.

> Forgive us of our debts [wrongs], as we forgive
> our debtors [those who have done us wrong].
> (Matthew 6:12)

You are better off if you take a loss and leave it in God's hands rather than pay someone back. Romans 12:19 encourages us to speak thus with our brothers and sisters in Christ,

> Dearly beloved, avenge not yourselves, but rather
> give place unto wrath: for it is written, vengeance
> is mine; I will repay, sayeth the Lord.

If you go to court before an unbelieving judge and win a case that could have been settled in church, you still lose. Christ said the church is brought to an open shame when we go against God's will. Someone may say, "I have been wronged, and I have a right to go to court." Perhaps you do have a right to go to court, but would it not be better to bear the loss than to bring harm to the cause of Christ? We do have a right to take others to court, but our right is not as important as God's right to be glorified. When we do the right thing, it glorifies God. Therefore, we accomplish nothing even if we win when we take another Christian to court.

Christians that go to court before an unbelieving judge to reconcile their differences are driven further apart. It would be better to reconcile the difference within the church and remain in a right relationship with each other and with Christ. When two Christians go to court before an unbelieving judge with an issue that could be settled in church, it makes it impossible to please God and stay in fellowship with each other.

In a civil court case, involving an unbelieving judge spiritual issues are not always settled in favor of God and His people. Christians are doing an injustice to each other when they take each other to court before unbelieving judges. They are doing a dishonor to God, a dishonor to their brother or sister in Christ, and a dishonor to the church. Paul shows us we cannot win apart from using God's method of settling church issues.

First Corinthians 6:9–12 is the third subject, and it deals with holiness of the body of Christ.

Paul starts this section by pointing out the fact that evil characterizes unbelievers. Notice verses 6:9–10,

> Know you not that the unrighteous [those who are not born again] shall not inherit the kingdom of God? Be not deceived: neither fornicators [those who have sex outside of marriage], nor idolaters, nor adulterers, nor effeminate [homosexuals/lesbians], nor abusers [homosexual acts] of themselves with mankind, nor thieves, nor covetous, nor drunks, nor revilers, nor extortionist, shall inherit the Kingdom of God.

These things characterize unbelievers and unbelievers who presently practice the evils mentioned in the above Scriptures will have no part with God in heaven. There is always a chance for anyone to join

God's family, yet some will not come to Jesus because they love their sins more than they love God. These verses refer to those who do not know Jesus as their Saviour and have no desire to come to Christ for salvation. It appears they have no intention of ever changing.

We are to love those who practice the evils mentioned above and seek to win them to Christ but not participate in their sins. We are to separate ourselves from their wicked deeds. For Christians, old things must pass away, and all things must become new. Notice 1 Corinthians 6:11–12,

> And such were some of you: but you are washed, but you are sanctified, but you are justified in the name of the Lord Jesus Christ, and by the Spirit of our God. All things are lawful unto me, but all things are not expedient.

Notice this last sentence, "All things are lawful to me, but all things are not expedient." The word *expedient* means "something that does not achieve a purpose." Paul is not saying, "It is all right to do those things mentioned in 6:11." he is saying, "I could do those things and not lose my salvation," but he knew it would be displeasing to God. Paul is saying, "My body could get involved in those sins, but the Holy Spirit that lives in me is strictly against it." Paul goes on to say,

> All things are lawful for me, but I will not be brought under the power of any.

A Christian's body is not immune to getting involved in sinful acts, but the Holy Spirit urges them not to do it. Furthermore, it would not achieve a purpose that would glorify Christ.

We once lived like unbelievers because we were unbelievers. That was our desire, but God washed us in the blood of Jesus Christ. First John 1:7 states,

> The blood of Jesus his Son cleanseth us from all sins.

Therefore, we don't have to be brought under the power of sin because the Holy Spirit gives us strength to overcome sin.

We are not only washed from our sins, set apart to serve Jesus, but we are justified. Someone said, being justified is like we have never sinned. Justification means our souls are right and pure in the sight of God because we received God's righteousness in Jesus Christ. When God looks at us, He sees Jesus Christ in us. Oh yes, our bodies sin, but our soul never sins. We have the righteousness of Christ imported unto us. That does not mean our bodies never do anything wrong; it means our souls have been cleansed and purified and never sin, but our bodies which are unsaved do sin. First John 3:9 states,

> Whosoever is born of God doeth not commit
> sin; for His seed (Holy Spirit) remaineth in him:
> and he cannot sin, because he is born of God.

You must always keep in mind you are a trinity—soul, spirit, and body. It's the body that sins, not the soul.

Christians should never allow their bodies to live like unbelievers. James 4:8 says,

> Draw nigh to God, and He will draw nigh to you.

If Christians allow their sinful flesh to dictate their life, God will move away from them. First Corinthians 6:9–10 states that Christians should not get involved in fornication, idolatry, homosexual acts, lesbianism, thievery, covetousness, drunkenness, reviling, extortion, or any other sins that characterize an unbeliever. Our bodies will not be brought under control of any of these sins so long as we allow the Holy Spirit to set upon the throne of our hearts and rule our lives.

First Corinthians 6:12 above points out that the Christian's soul is the place where God dwells. Paul himself admitted he could get involved in these sins, but he loved God too much to be unfaithful to Him. The bottom line is, dedicated Christians are set aside and sanctified for God's service.

First Corinthians 6:13–20 is the fourth subject, and it deals with the believer's body that belongs to the Lord.

Notice 1 Corinthians 6:13,

Meats for the belly and the belly for meats.

This verse does not mean gluttony or filling one's self until he/she is sick. Some say it does mean that. This Scripture verse presents the ridiculous excuse some in the Corinthian church used to justify their wicked sexual sins. They were saying sex is for the belly just like eating meat is for the belly. They were saying having sex is as normal as eating meat, and God made the belly for meat and for sex. Of course, sex is right, good, and pure for a married couple, but not for fornication. To participate in a sex act outside of marriage is extremely displeasing to God. Hebrews 13:4 states,

Marriage in honorable in all, and the bed undefiled: but whoremongers [someone who consorts with whores—prostitutes] and adulterers God will judge.

It's not natural. It's a wicked dirty sin to have sex outside of marriage. Perverted men and women are doing the same when they seek to justify their homosexual and lesbian lifestyles. Furthermore, married couples are doing the same when they are unfaithful to their spouses.

Paul condemned them for such sins. Verse 6:13 goes on to say,

God shall destroy both it and them.

This verse is referring to unbelievers as well as Christians. That's strong language, but it is the Word of God. God will destroy the sin and destroy those who habitually commit it. God is not saying He will send Christians to hell for such sins, but if they persist in such sins, they will meet God's judgment. He is saying they will lose their opportunity to serve Him in His kingdom work if they continually persist in those sins. In fact, they will be taken to heaven prematurely if they persist in those sins.

Did you know that lust can characterize a Christian's life? According to Matthew 5:28, just thinking about intimate sexual sins it is as bad as doing it. Notice what Matthew 5:28 said,

> Whosoever looketh upon a woman to lust after her hath committed adultery with her already in his heart.

First Corinthians 6:13 informed the Corinthian church, and us, what the body is for.

> Now the body is not for fornication, but for the Lord, and the Lord for the body.

God made a way for men and women to enjoy sex, and that is through marriage only.

God is the owner of our bodies and has a purpose for our bodies. That purpose is to glorify Him. Romans 12:1 says,

> I beseech you therefore brethren by the mercies of God that you present your bodies a living sacrifice, holy and acceptable unto God, which is your reasonable service.

Our bodies are not to be used for fornication but to glorify God, which is our reasonable service.

First Corinthians 6:14 seems to be out of place, but it's not. It is very much in place, and so desperately needed.

> God hath both raised up the Lord and will also raise us up by His power.

Verse 14 is talking about the resurrection, but verse 13 is talking about overcoming sin. It looks as though the resurrection and overcoming sin do not fit together. It looks as if it does not fit with the flow of Paul's teaching. Many commentators and Bible translators avoid this verse. That is a terrible mistake. It's dangerous to avoid Scripture verses. We are not given permission to avoid Scripture verses. To avoid them is the same as removing them from the Bible, and it's dangerous to remove Scripture verses from the Bible. Revelation 22:19 shows how dangerous it is.

> If any man shall take away from the words of the book of this prophecy, God shall take away his part out of the book of life.

That means removing Scripture verses from the Bible is an act that characterizes unbelievers, and those who do it will be judged by God. So how do we make the connection between verse 13 and 14?

Allow me to say this first. Have you ever been talking with someone when he/she makes a remark that has nothing to do with the subject at hand? That's what verse 14 seems to do, right? *Wrong!* What does the resurrection have to do with overcoming sin and living a good moral productive Christian life? We must keep in mind that God does not put words in the Bible just to fill up space. Yet how do we make the connection between overcoming sin and the resurrection? The verse explains itself.

Paul had just given a stern warning against the foolish belief that adultery is as normal as eating meat. He informed them in 1 Corinthians 6:13 what the body is for.

> Now the body is not for fornication, but for the Lord, and the Lord for the body.

Then Paul makes a comment in verse 13 about the resurrection. The connection is that Jesus had power to raise Himself from the dead, and He gives us the same power to overcome temptation and sin. Notice how verse 14 reads,

> God hath also raised up the Lord and will also raise us up by His own power.

Jesus said to the Laodicea church in Revelation 3:21,

> He that overcometh [a person needs God's power to overcome] will I grant to set with Me in my throne, even as I also overcome [Jesus overcame temptation and never sinned], and am set down with my Father in His throne.

Jesus said God's power will raise you up from the dead, and you must have the same power to overcome temptation and evil. It is not in our power to resist temptation, nor is in our power to deliver ourselves from temptation and evil. It's God's power we need and must have. First Corinthians 2:5 tells us,

> Your faith [that is, faith to overcome temptation and sin] should not stand in the wisdom of man, but in the power of God.

Paul simply stated in 1 Corinthians 6:14 that we need resurrection power to overcome temptation and sin. We cannot go up against Satan in our own strength and win. Satan is like a hacker that slips into your computer and destroys your hard drive. That is the way Satan works. He has worked that way from the beginning. We need the resurrection power of Jesus Christ to overcome Satan's strategies. God's resurrection power will keep us from being hacked by the devil. We must have God's power to overcome temptation and evil.

Satan has had years of experience in deceiving people, but thank God, he is no match for Jesus. If we have God's power in us, we have nothing to worry about because God is with us and will help us.

We can overcome sin and live moral Christian lives through God's power. That is what Paul is getting across to us in verses 13 and 14.

First Corinthians 6:15 shows us our bodies are members of Christ's body. We are part of God's family. Our bodies belong to God. Therefore, we are not to use our bodies for something that displeases God. Notice 6:15,

> Know you not that your bodies are the members of Christ? Shall I then take the members of Christ and make them the members of a harlot [prostitute], God forbid.

Paul is saying we are not to use our bodies for prostitution. This admonition leads us back to the subject Paul covered in 6:13,

> Meats for the belly and the belly for meats...

Paul is saying your body was not designed for fornication but for glorifying God. Men and women glorify God when they marry and live in a sexual relationship that God designed. In Mark 10:8 Jesus said,

> A man shall leave his father and mother and cleave to his wife, and they twain [two] shall become one flesh: so, they are no more twain but one flesh.

God's plan of intimacy is between a man and his wife only. Sexual intimacy was designed by God for a wife and husband to enjoy in the confines of marriage. Sex outside of marriage for a Christian is an evil sin God hates and will chasten those who do it.

Some of the Corinthian church members were saying sex between couples was as normal as eating meat. Can you imagine such despicable reasoning? First Corinthians 6:16–18 tells us,

> What? Know ye not that he that is joined to a harlot is one body [same as a husband and wife]

for two, sayeth He, shall be one flesh. But he that is joined unto the Lord is one spirit. Flee fornication [run from it like Joseph ran from Potiphar's wife]. Every sin that a man does is without the body, but he that commits fornication sins against his own body.

That means he sins against his body when he takes his body that belongs to God and his spouse and uses it to fulfill his fleshly sexual desires outside of marriage. That kind of sin will bring God's judgment upon his body.

I heard a story that I don't know whether it is true or not. Even if it is not true, it gets across a truth that God judges Christians who sin against their own bodies by having sex outside of marriage.

A man had a job that required he travel to distain cities and sometimes had to stay overnight. One night he found himself in a lonely city far from home. As he settled in for the night, suddenly he realized he had not eaten his dinner. So he made his way down to the bar to get something to eat. While he sat eating, a young lady came over and asked if she could sit with him. "Sure," he answered. After all he was lonely and welcomed someone to talk with. He didn't leave her after he finished eating, but they talked on. To make a long story short, he invited her up to his room, and they slept together that night. The next morning when he awoke, she was gone. That was okay with him. He had enjoyed the night, and his wife and two children would never know about it. He was feeling good about himself until he walked into the bathroom. What he saw shocked him. His hands began to shake, and his legs began to shake. He felt like he was going to faint. Written on the bathroom mirror were these words: "WELCOME TO THE WORLD OF AIDS."

We are part of the body of Christ. Therefore, we are not to use God's body for fornication. That will bring God's judgment on us and sever us from God's protection. Believe me, sex outside of marriage is a serious sin. In fact, notice what God says in 1 Corinthians 3:17 about defiling your body by having sex outside of marriage,

> If any man defiles the temple of God, him shall God destroy, for the temple of God is holy, which temple you are.

That kind of sin is so serious it could bring death. The only remedy is confession and repentance.

Notice what 1 Corinthians 6:19–20 says,

> What? Know you not that your body is the temple of the Holy Ghost which is in you, which you have of God, and you are not your own. For you are bought with a price: therefore, glorify God in your body, and in your spirit, which are God's.

If we take God's temple, our body in which the Holy Spirit dwells, and use it for our own selfish purposes, we are displeasing God. In fact, our bodies are to be reserved for God's glory and God's glory only. Notice again what 6:20 is telling us,

> You are bought with a price [bought with the blood of Christ]: therefore, glorify God in your body and in your spirits, which are God's.

While I'm on this subject of using our bodies for God's glory let me say something more about pornography. Preachers should condemn pornography in any form or fashion. It will not and cannot glorify God. Pornography is a sin that should be exposed in every church as a wicked and destructive sin. Church members as well as unbelievers are involved in pornography. Preaching against pornography may anger church members who are involved in it, but the deadly effects can destroy a person's life. It can destroy children and women by inflaming sex perverts to stalk and molest them. For what reason would a person want to watch pornography if it is not to satisfy his/her sexual drives?

Nothing good can come out of pornography. It is like "rotgut" whisky that destroys your intestines, and eventually your life. Paul told Timothy to "flee youthful lust" (2 Timothy 2:22). That means to run away from it. Pornography is like a venomous serpent that injects its poison into your veins and paralyzes your body to its deadly effects. To watch pornography is like a raging fire in one's body. Solomon said in Proverbs 6:27,

> Can a man take fire into his bosom and his clothes not be burned?

Solomon also gave a story in Proverbs 7:6–27 about a young man with his flaming desire for sex, He yielded to the lustful pull of a prostitute and as a result lost his life. Bible scholars says this story in Proverbs 7:6–27 is that the young man caught a venereal disease that affected his liver that eventually took his life. Tragic story, isn't it? That is what pornography will do for you.

Be careful what you read or watch. It's dangerous as a cobra snake. Once it sinks its venomous teeth in you, there is no hope. Pornography will bite you and leave you to die alone. Anyone can fall for pornography, even you or me, and just like the young man mentioned in Proverbs 7:6–27 who yielded to the pull of prostitution. But we don't have to yield to its power because the Holy Spirit is in us and helps us to overcome the pull of pornography.

Be on guard, Christian friend, because the devil is lurking in the shadows to grab you and destroy you. Take heed, and know your body is your enemy and will lead you into sin—sin as bad as the young couple in 1 Corinthians 5.

What should we do to avoid being caught up in the web of pornography? Have you ever watched a spider weave its web? They do it to capture their victims. There are predators seeking to capture an innocent prey. That is the way pornography works. It will draw you into its web and destroy you. Run away from it! Flee from it! Paul told Timothy to "flee youthful lust" (2 Timothy 2:22). That is good advice, and it works. You must see pornography for what it is—a strong pull toward death and God's judgment. God is not going to stand by and let you defile the body He made for you and Himself. First Corinthians 11:30 says,

> For this cause [desecrating the Communion ser-
> vice] many are sickly, and many are asleep [dead].

If God will do that for desecrating His Communion service, how much more will He do it for using your body to indulge yourself in pornography. Don't use your body God made for Himself to watch pornography on the web or TV, and don't read phonography magazines.

There are many illustrations in the Bible of people being tempted to do wrong. Some fled and some yield. Joseph gives us an example of one that fled. When Potiphar's wife propositioned him to go to bed with her, he left his robe and fled. Joseph believed it was better to lose his coat than to lose his character. You can read that story in Genesis 39.

David gives us an example of one who yields to temptation. He didn't flee from Bathsheba's temptation. He invited her into his palace for the night, and she became pregnant. Because of that, David lost his family, lost his character, and eventually lost his kingdom. You can read about that in 2 Samuel chapter 11.

The warning is to not get caught up in pornographic sins, or any other sin for that matter. Sin will destroy your life. Use your body to glorify God, not to satisfy your lustful desires. Read again 1 Corinthians 6:20,

> For you are bought with a price: therefore, glorify
> God in your bodies, and in your spirit, which are
> God's.

Chapter 7
Has Five Subjects

Verse 1 deals with celibacy, singleness, marriage, and sex.
Verses 2–9 deal with avoiding fornication.
Verses 10–17 deal with marriage and divorce.
Verses 18–24 deal with God's call to ministry.
Verses 25–40 deal with singleness, marriage, remarriage, and sex.

First Corinthians 7:1 is the first subject, and it deals with celibacy, singleness, marriage, and sex.

To be sure, this entire chapter deals with celibacy, singleness, marriage, and sex in one way or the other; however, I divided it up into five important subjects. I will say a lot about sex. After all, that is what this chapter is all about.

May I say this up front. Sex in a marital relationship is not dirty. However, men and women who have sex outside of marriage made it dirty, and that is because of their permissive sexual lifestyles. In the confines of marriage sex is morally right, decent, good, and approved by God. God made humans with a desire for sex, and He approves of sex within the confines of marriage. In fact, sex is so right that God spent much of His time talking about it. We should do no less, but not from a perverted perspective, but from God's perspective.

Allow me to give a fictitious story on the subjects of celibacy, singleness, marriage, and sex to introduce chapter seven. This is a fictitious story I created to help you understand what some Christians are up against.

Abigail and Thomas often dreamed of the day they could embark on a full-time ministry. They also realized they needed to be married to each other to do that. They loved each other very deeply and longed for the day they could be man and wife. They often thought about marriage and ministry and felt it would be the most wonderful life they could live. They had talked about marriage many times. Abigail brought up the subject more often than Thomas, but that was about as far as it went, just talking. Thomas tried to avoid the subject.

Abby and Tom, as they were called, grew up together. Both were dedicated Christians, and both had never had an intimate relationship with the opposite sex. They were both virgins. Abby felt Tom was the love of her life and looked forward to the day they could get married. Wherever you saw one, you saw the other. They enjoyed each other's company immensely. They traveled a little but always stayed in separate motel rooms when traveling. Abby dreamed of the time they could spend their nights together as husband and wife, but she knew her Christian convictions would not allow them to sleep together until they were married. She often dreamed how wonderful their marriage would be.

Over the next few months, they traveled more often. Dating was wonderful, but Abby wanted more than just dating. She wanted to get married. Finally, she talked Tom into setting a date to be married. Following the engagement, every time she talked about marriage, Tom seemed to be troubled about something. Something was eating Tom, but he would never talk about it, and she was reluctant to ask. They didn't feel it was necessary to have premarital counseling, because they thought love would save them from problems.

One day Tom called Abby and said, "Abby, I need to talk with you, it's very important." Abby thought that was strange since Tom had never done that before. She wondered what was on his mind. They met at their local park at the bench they often went to feed the ducks. Tom was silent for a while, just looking into space, and that made Abby uncomfortable. Tom finally spoke, barely whispering, "Abby, I don't know any other way to say this, so I'm just going to come right out and say it, I can't marry you because I am a celibate, and I could not meet your intimate sexual needs." Abby was surprised; shocked was more like it. She didn't even know what the word *celibate* meant.

Tom went on to explain celibacy as someone that has no desire for sexual intimacy, nor could perform a sexual act. He told Abby he was not capable of having an intimate sexual relationship with her to meet her needs, because God made him without the ability to desire sex.

There was a moment of silence; then they both began to weep. When they realized they could not solve their problem, and both being Christians, they did the right thing and went to God's Word for answers. For the next few months, they spent hours studying the Bible for answers. Finally, they came to chapter 7 of 1 Corinthians that deals with the problem of celibacy, singleness, marriage, and sex. What did they find? Well, let's look at 1 Corinthians 7 and see what the Bible has to say about this subject of celibacy, singleness, marriage, and sex. I will tell you the rest of the story at the end of this chapter.

In chapter 7 Paul turns his attention to questions asked by Chloe and his family, members of the Corinthian church. This family is mentioned in 1 Corinthians 1:11. Paul said,

> It hath been declared unto to me of you my breathern, by them which are of the house of Chloe.

Chloe was much like a Christian counselor. One problem that concerned Chloe's family evidently was about some Christian friend who did not have an answer to celibacy, singleness, marriage, and sex. So one question along with many other questions were about celibacy, singleness, marriage, and sex.

We don't know for sure what all the problems Chloe wrote about. We don't have that letter. We only have Paul's response to that letter in 1 and 2 Corinthians. From Paul's response, there is an indication that Chloe's family wrote to him about many things, including celibacy, singleness, marriage, and sex.

Many problems can surface in a couple's life that should be addressed before marriage. That is why a couple should see a Christian marriage counselor before marriage. But more importunely, they should study the Bible on marital problems, because the Bible gives answers to any marital problem Christians may face.

Allow me to clear up one point before proceeding. A celibate is a person God created without a desire to have an intimate sexual relationship with the opposite sex. And that could cause problems. For example, if a husband or wife did not have a desire to have sex, it would cause a conflict in marriage that could never be resolved. To be denied sex from one's spouse could create a feeling of not being attractive, not being desired, or it could create a feeling of being punished for something the spouse did not do. Think about a couple faced with that condition trying to make their marriage work. It's better to get the issue out in the open before marriage than to wait.

The difference between celibacy and singleness is that a celibate has no desire for sexual intimacy, but singles, in most cases, have a desire for sexual intimacy. Notice 1 Corinthians 7:1,

> Now concerning the things [plural] you wrote unto me, it's good for a man not to touch a woman.

Right off, we can understand what the Bible is referring to in 7:1 where it says,

> It's good for a man not to touch a woman.

It's not talking about a casual touch, a handshake, or a hug by a sister, brother, or friend. It is informing couples that their marriage will not work if one is a celibate and the other is not. It's saying if a person is a celibate living as a single, then celibacy is better than marriage. Paul is saying, it's good to be a celibate and not touch a woman in an intimate way. Celibates can devote their time to serving the Lord rather than caring for their spouse. They have no desire for a spouse; therefore they can devote all their time in serving the Lord.

There were singles, celibates, and married couple in the church at Corinth. Each wanted to know their place in the church and in Christian ministry. God has a place for celibates, singles, and married couples in every local church. Each have a specific place of service.

Celibates are often profiled as homosexuals or lesbians. A celibate is not a celibate because he/she desires a relationship with the same sex, but he/she is a celibate because God made them to not desire any kind of sex at all. God does not condone nor approve of a union between the same sex. Such unions are built on passion, and any union outside of God's approval is condemned, doomed, and is a recipe for failure, and ultimately destruction. If you want to know what God thinks of homosexuality and lesbianism, read Genesis 19. It's about a place called Sodom and Gomorrah that God destroyed with fire because of their perverted sexual lifestyles. You don't agree with that? Well, you have the right to be wrong if you choose.

A single may be a celibate or just single, but singles who have no desire for intimate sexual relationships have a better opportunity in ministry. The Bible allows for a celibate life, and it also allows for a single life.

There are three words that mean the same in Scripture: *celibate*, *eunuch*, and of course, *singles*. In the Old Testament, celibates who had no desire for marriage or sexual intimacy were called "eunuchs." Matthew 19:12 says,

> There are some eunuchs who were so born from their mother's womb, and there are some eunuchs, which were made eunuchs by men [surgery]: and there are eunuchs who have made themselves eunuchs for the kingdom of heaven's sake. He that is able to receive it let him receive it.

There are several people mentioned in the Old Testament who were eunuchs. For example, the book of Daniel states that Shadrach, Meshach, Abednego, and Daniel himself were eunuchs. They were not born eunuchs but made eunuchs by Nebuchadnezzar's physicians. They had surgery to remove all desire for sex. Nebuchadnezzar wanted total commitment from them. He wanted them to forget about their heritage, their desires, their wants and serve him only.

First Corinthians 7:7–8 tells us Paul was a celibate/eunuch.

> I would that all men were even as I myself; but every man hath his proper gift of God, one after this manner, and another after that. I say therefore to the unmarried and widows: It is good for them if they abide even as I. But if they cannot contain, let them marry, it is better to marry than to burn [burn with passion for sex].

Paul had no desire for intimate sexual relationships with a woman. He encouraged others to follow his lead if they had that gift. However, he encouraged others to marry if they could not keep from burning with passion for sex.

Celibates/eunuchs receive their gifts from God. They have no desire for a wife/husband. It must be noted that every Christian does not have that gift. Most people I know, which include both men and women, have a desire to marry and have children. I have known only a few celibates/eunuchs in my lifetime. There are cases in the Bible where celibate couples married, and their marriage worked just fine. Actually, but not advisable, two celibates could live together and not be married; their relationship could be like a brother-and-sister relationship. If a celibate man has a desire to live with a woman that is celibate, they should be married. There is nothing wrong with being celibate and single, nor is there anything wrong with being a celibate and marrying another celibate.

If a person does not have the gift of celibacy and marries a non-celibate, he/she is in for big trouble. Paul is saying if a man or woman has the gift of celibacy, it's good not to marry, but if both are celibates, it's okay to marry. I will deal with that in deeper details in 7:32–35.

First Corinthians 7:2–9 is the second subject in the outline, and it deals with avoiding fornication.

The Greek word for fornication is *zanah*. It means intentional sexual intercourse with a married person other than one's spouse. First Corinthians 7:2 tells us one of the purposes of marriage is to avoid fornication. Notice 7:2,

> Nevertheless, to avoid fornication, let every man have his own wife, and let every woman have her own husband.

We are to make sure our spouse's intimate needs are met. It's a fact—both women and men have a desire for intimate relationships if they are not celibates. No society can survive by avoiding God's intimate plan in marriage. A one-night stand or a homosexual relationship does not meet men or women sexual needs as God designed it. Husbands' and wives' intimate needs must be met by their spouse only, not by someone else. Notice what 7:3 has to say about that.

> Let the husband render unto the wife due benevolence [benevolence means a desire to do something good for your spouse]; and likewise, the wife unto the husband.

That means as far as sex is concerned, the husband must give what is due to his wife, and the wife must give what is due to her husband. Having an affair outside of marriage diminishes a man's or woman's desire to meet his/her spouse's need.

First Corinthians 7:4 deals with the exclusiveness of what is due the husband and wife.

> The wife hath no power [no right] of her own body, but the husband [does]; and likewise, also the husband hath no power [no right] of his own body, but the wife [does].

That means a husband and wife has exclusive rights over each other's body in sexual relationships. Notice, I said "exclusive rights." That means the husband and wife excludes everyone else from their sexual life. It's strictly forbidden by God to include someone else into your sexual relationship other than your husband or wife. To avoid a marital disaster, your marriage must include intimate relationship between you and your spouse only.

I am aware that there are times a husband or wife cannot satisfy the sexual needs of each other because of accidents, sickness, age, medical condition, or something else. For fear of getting overly explicit, let me just say, there are other ways to meet your spouse's sexual need other than the traditional way and still be in God's will for intimate relationships. Take that statement for what you think it is worth.

First Corinthians 7:4 above is saying a wife does not have the authority or right to give her body to another man, nor does a husband have the authority or right to give his body to another woman. The husband and wife have exclusive authority over each other's body. Thank God when a man can say, "That's my wife," meaning, she is not available to any other man. Thank God when a woman can say, "That's my husband," meaning, he is not available to any other woman.

The part of the marriage vows that says "forsaking all others and cleave only to each other" has been removed from most marriage vows. However, exclusiveness in marriage is God's plan for marriage, and it's the only way to avoid fornication. When married couples remove themselves from God's martial plan, they are walking on a slippery slope that leads to a fall and, ultimately divorce, or worse. God's plan for marriage is one man for one woman and one woman for one man for life and intimacy only between each other.

Paul gives some additional thoughts on avoiding fornication in 1 Corinthians 7:5–6.

> Defraud ye not one the other [that phrase is saying do not withhold your bodies from each other], except it be with consent for a time, that

you may give yourself to fasting and prayer; and
come together again [in an intimate way], that
Satan tempt you not for your incontinency [lack
of self-control]. But I speak this by permission,
and not of commandment.

Allow me to explain the phrase "I speak this by permission and
not of commandment." Paul is not saying his words are not inspired,
but he is saying Jesus did not leave a commandment on defrauding
one another. However, He gave Paul permission to include additional inspired words on this subject. Notice, it says, "I speak this by
permission." That means Jesus gave Paul permission to speak on this
subject that brought with it a commandment.

The only reason God allows temporary separation in marriage
is for prayer and fasting. Then once that is accomplished the husband
and wife are to come together again so they will not be tempted to
fulfill their sexual desires with someone else.

A husband or wife cannot use the flimsy excuses: "I'm not satisfied with him/her any longer" or "I don't love him/her any longer."
The only excuse married couples have for momentary separation is
for prayer and fasting.

Paul returns to the subject of celibacy and marriage in 1
Corinthians 7:7–9. I have already mentioned that above, but just
remember, Paul was a celibate himself. Notice verse 7 again,

I would that all men were even as I myself. But
every man has his proper gift of God, one after
this manner, and another after that.

Paul goes on to encourage those who are unmarried and those
who are widows to be like him—a celibate. However, he knew most
unmarried could not do that. He knew they would desire a mate.
Therefore, he said in verse verses 8–9,

I say therefore to the unmarried, and widows,
it is good for them if they abide even as I; but

219

if they cannot contain [control themselves], let them marry, for it is better to marry than to burn [that is, burn with passion for sex].

First Corinthian 7:10–16 is the third subject in the outline, and it deals with marriage and divorce.

Marriage is for life in God's plan for marriage. Anything short of that is not God's original plan for you. Most believers and some unbelievers want their marriages to last all their lives, but sad to say, marriage is not the ruling factor in most unbelievers' marriages, and even sadder is the fact that marriage is not the ruling factor in many Christian marriages. In the United States, and I suspect it is true all over the world, many marriages end in divorce although they are Christians. It does not have to be that way, and it should not be that way, but it is that way. Paul gives the formula for a happy marriage that can only be found in a marriage between one man and one woman that have the same sexual desires and are joined together by God for life. That does not mean Christians will not divorce. They do. It means divorce is not in God's options for marriage, except for one reason, and that is a believer marrying an unbeliever.

Married couples often have disputes and conflicts. Marriages are not always perfect, but that is no reason for divorce except for one reason and that is a Christian being married to an unbeliever. Notice 1 Corinthians 7:10–11,

And unto the married, I commend you, yet not I but the Lord. Let not the wife depart from her husband. But and if she departs let her remain unmarried or be reconciled to her husband.

Being unequally yoked together in marriage with an unbeliever is not in the best interest of a couple. After a couple divorces, there are restrictions on how to live after divorce.

First Corinthians 7:12 says,

> But to the rest speak I not the Lord.

Paul taught that the Lord did not go this far in His teaching on this subject, but permitted him to do so. Notice what Paul said in verse 12,

> If any brother hath a wife that believeth not, and she be pleased to dwell with him, let him not put her away [divorce her]. And the woman who hath a husband that believeth not, and he is pleased to dwell with her, let her not leave him.

It is not mandatory that a Christian who is married to an unbeliever get a divorce. They have an option to divorce or remain married. In most cases, it's best if they stay together. Notice 7:14–16,

> For the unbelieving husband is sanctified by the wife, and the unbelieving wife is sanctified by the husband: else were your children unclean, but now are holy. But if the unbelieving husband departs, let him depart, a brother or sister is not under bondage in such cases: but God hath called us unto peace.

Trivial excuses for divorce are not acceptable to God. Thinking about trivial matters in marriage, I'm reminded of a funny story about a man and his wife giving each other the silent treatment over an argument they had. After a week of silence, the man realized he would have to have his wife wake him up at 5:00 AM for a very important business flight to another state. He did not want to break the silence, so he wrote her a note that read, "Please wake me up at 5:00 AM. I have a very important business meeting, and I don't want to miss my flight." He left the note on the bathroom mirror so she could see it. The next morning, he awoke at 9:00 AM. He had missed his flight and his important business meeting. He was furious and started to confront her about it, but then he saw a note on his nightstand that read, "Wake up, it's 5:00 AM."

I don't think that story happened, but it points out that trivial reasons are not viable reasons for divorce. Couples should strive to keep happiness and harmony in marriages. It is better to avoid petty pitfalls that are nothing more than trivial excuses that often lead to divorce. God gives instructions on how to heal a marriage to avoid a divorce, and even after a divorce.

Someone may say, "I divorced my first wife and married again, what shall I do? Should I divorce my second wife and be reconciled to my first wife, or remain married to my second wife?" There are all kinds of problems that could arise from the situation of a second marriage. There could be children involved by the second marriage. Both divorcees could be remarried and have children. It is not God's best for you to remarry after a divorce. However, if the situation of having children should occur, God does allow you to remain married for the children's sake. God prefers singleness after divorce, but if you're married for the second time, and circumstances prevent you from separating, do not get a divorce because if you do, that could escalate your problem. The proper thing to do is to dedicate your life and family to serving the Lord and making the best of your second marriage.

Someone may say, "My wife is not a Christian, shall I divorce her and marry a Christian?" That would not be the best thing to do. Notice again what 1 Corinthians 7:12–13 has to say about that.

> But the rest I speak, not the Lord: If any brother
> hath a wife that believeth not, and she be pleased
> to dwell with him, let him not put her away. And
> if the woman hath a husband that believeth not,
> and if he is pleased to dwell with her, let her not
> leave him.

Allow me to explain the phrase "But to the rest I speak, not the Lord."

Paul is saying, Jesus did not teach in detail on this subject but gave him permission to teach on it in deeper detail. Paul is not adding to the Bible something that God did not give him. He is simply teaching in detail what Christ did not teach. God gave Paul permission to insert further instructions on this. The additional things God gave Paul to teach is that God's best choice is not for a believer to marry an unbeliever; however, if it does occur, and both the husband and wife wish to stay together, let them remain married.

Notice 7:14,

> For the unbelieving husband is sanctified by the wife and the unbelieving wife is sanctified by the husband: Else were your children unclean, but now they are holy.

There is a reason God recommends what 1 Corinthians 7:14 teaches. Let them remain married so the children can be holy. This verse is quite often misunderstood and misapplied. It is not teaching that a believing wife has enough faith to get her unbelieving husband and children into heaven, and likewise, this verse is not saying a believing husband has enough faith to get his unbelieving wife and children into heaven. The words *sanctified* and *holy* mean "being set apart for a sacred use." It has nothing to do with salvation. An unbelieving husband is sanctified by setting himself apart for a sacred use when he supports his wife who is a believer, and likewise, the unbelieving wife is set apart for a sacred use by supporting her husband who is a believer—thus sanctified. Notice the last phrase in 7:14, "Else were your children unclean but now they are holy."

This means they are holy by supporting their father or mother. Verse 7:15 explains 7:12 in deeper detail. First, notice 7:12,

> If any brother hath a wife that believeth not, and she be pleased to dwell with him, let him not put her away.

Notice how 7:15 makes the connection.

> But if the unbeliever departs, let him depart. A
> brother or sister is not under bondage in such
> cases: but God hath called us to peace.

If a Christian spouse cannot cope with his or her unbelieving spouse, they are not under bondage to stay together. The believing spouse can divorce his or her unbelieving spouse. Divorce is permitted here, but the couple should remain together if possible; furthermore, once separation and divorce occur, the believing spouse is to remain single or be reconciled to their spouse.

I'm convinced, in such incidents, God will make something good out of a bad situation if the couple will let Him. Christians who marry unbelievers are out of God's plan for marriage, but if that should occur, you can make something good out of it. Staying together is the best scenario, but sometimes it's not possible to stay together. If one couple insists on separation, the marriage will usually end in divorce. Since divorce is not the best situation, the couple is to stay together if possible.

By staying together, there is a possibility of winning the unbelieving spouse to Christ. God's advice is found in 1 Corinthians 7:16.

> For what knoweth thou, O wife, whether thou
> shalt save thy husband? Or how knoweth thou,
> O man, whether thou shall save thy wife?

This verse is saying, even though you would be justified in separating from your unbelieving spouse, you should remain married, because you may win him or her to Christ. First Peter 3:1 says,

> Wives, be in subjection to your own husband;
> that, if any obey not the word, they also may
> without the word be won by the conversation of
> the wife.

The believing spouse does not have to constantly preach at their unbelieving spouse, but show dedication to Christ and love for their spouse by their conversation. In so doing, the believing spouse may win their unbelieving spouse to Christ.

We all know it's God's will for us to marry if we have a desire for intimate sexual relationship and want to raise a family, and we all know it's not in God's will for us to have sexual relationships outside of marriage. Therefore, it's God's plan for a couple to stay married and not divorce. God's plan for marriage is for life. Divorce for the many things people divorce over nowadays are not an option in God's plan. It never has been, nor ever will be; but couples, even Christian couples, divorce.

The question arises: Is it all right for a Christian to remarry after a divorce? Yes, under certain circumstances. Today traditional marriages are no longer the norm, and marriage vows are meaningless between couples. Divorce increased from 1930 until 2007. Statistics on the reasons divorce escalated those years showed that one or both spouses found someone else they wanted to be with.

An article in *The New York Times* stated that divorce rates occurred more often in the years before 2007. However, divorce rates reached their peak in 2007 with over 50 percent of marriages ending in divorce. But since then divorce rates are on the decline. That sounds like good news until you consider the number of couples living together yet not married. Statistics show that after the 2007 peak in divorce rates, more than twelve million couples (and that increases each year) live together without being married. Marriages and families are rapidly going the way of the dinosaurs. They are becoming extinct. There are less couples marrying today than at any other time in American history. I don't mean to paint a bleak picture, but the truth is, we are at a marital crisis in our country. A nation cannot survive without marriage and family.

A political candidate said, "We are a community." A community absent of the family cannot hold this country together. Chaos follows when the family is torn apart and replaced by a community. If families should ever be replaced for a community union, there would be more orphan homes, more child abuse, more drug addiction, more crimes, more satanic activity, a rapid increase in venereal disease, and widespread child molestation. The nation would be like animals going about doing their own thing.

Since marriage has taken back seat to living together without marriage, our nation has reached a marital crisis. Nothing can replace God's plan for marriage. Marriage for life is God's plan for a man and woman, not only for sexual gratification, but rearing godly children as well. The Lord is against divorce. Yes, I have already said there is a legitimate reason for divorce, but it's a commandment from God that marriage is to last a lifetime. Notice Matthew 19:4–6,

> Jesus said to them, "Have you not read that He which made them at the beginning made them male and female, and said, for this cause shall a man leave his father and mother and shall cleave to his wife and they two shall become one flesh. Wherefore they are no longer twain [two] but one flesh. What therefore God hath joined together, let no man put asunder."

Jesus is saying, let no one instigate a divorce. By the way, years ago, most marriage ceremonies contained the above Scripture verse, but not any longer. I never have nor ever will perform a marriage without including that Scripture. If the couple don't want it, I will not perform the ceremony.

The average man or woman experience two or more marriages in their lifetime. Grant you, sometimes a second marriage works, but according to statistics, a second marriage has a 60 percent less chance of surviving. God's plan for marriage is broken when couples get divorced. If a divorce does occur, the couple should remain unmarried or be reconciled to their spouse if possible. Sometimes reconciliation is not possible.

The following Scripture verse tells us the ultimate solution to any marital problem is to live by the standard God gives in His Word. Notice 7:17,

> But as God has distributed to every man, as the Lord hath called everyone, so let him walk, and so ordained I in all churches.

Paul is saying, "I have given the standard you should follow in your marriage, so don't live as though you don't know how to live, but live as God has called you to live." Paul stated he had preached that message in all the churches he had established, including Corinth.

First Corinthians 7:17–24 is the fourth subject in the outline, and it deals with God's call to ministry.

First Corinthians 7:18 turns to the thought of circumcision versus uncircumcision in relation to God's call to ministry.

> Is any man called being circumcised? Let him not become uncircumcised. Is any called in uncircumcision? Let him not be circumcised.

Circumcision or uncircumcision is not about salvation, but it is about how ministers are to live. Circumcision in the Old Testament was a sign or covenant of dedication between God and man. Circumcision is no longer used as a covenant between God and man in this grace dispensation. However, dedication to Christ is a covenant between God and man to be a dedicated minister.

We are all called to ministry, and there is a certain way Christians are to carry out that ministry. Ephesians 4:12 says,

> For the perfecting of the saints, for the work of the ministry, for the edifying the body of Christ [the church]: till we all come in the unity of the faith, and of the knowledge of the Son of God...

God calls all Christians to a specific service in ministering to Him. Therefore, we need to understand God has no obligation to continue calling anyone into the ministry. I am not saying there is a time God will cease calling people to salvation. There is less chance to be saved if people continually put off salvation, but God will never cease calling them to salvation. However, the call gets weaker each time they reject it. But a person will always have a chance to come to Christ for salvation. There is only one exception, and that is sinning against the Holy Spirit. The person that calls the Holy Spirit an unclean thing sins against the Holy Spirit and cannot be saved. Therefore, when one hears the call of the Holy Spirit to salvation, he or she should respond, because the second, third, and future calls to salvation will not be as intense or urgent. People become more resistant to God's call as they get older. In other words, the call gets less urgent the longer it is ignored.

But I am saying there is a time God will cease calling someone into ministry. God will not cease to call people to salvation, but I am saying there is a time that God will cease calling people into the ministry if they continually put Him off.

Circumcised and uncircumcised in 7:18 has nothing to do with salvation, or proof of salvation. Notice 7:18 again,

> Is any man called being circumcised? Let him not become uncircumcised. Is any called in uncircumcision? Let him not become circumcised.

Judaizers in Paul's day demanded that the Gentile believers be circumcised to finalize their faith and calling into service for Christ. By the way, it may interest you to know the baptismal regeneration believers say much the same. They say you must be baptized in water to finalize your salvation. A person does not have to be circumcised to finalize his faith in Christ for salvation, nor does he have to be baptized in water to finalize his faith in Christ for salvation. Through the inspiration of God Paul was commanded to straighten them out on that subject.

Paul did not change his message and say circumcision is proof of salvation. Circumcision or baptism has nothing to do with salvation. Notice 1 Corinthians 7:19,

> Circumcision is nothing, and uncircumcision is nothing, but keeping the commandments of God.

Circumcision or uncircumcision has nothing to do with salvation, but obeying the commandments of God shows one has trusted Christ as Saviour and is living by God's commandments. A person has a desire to obey God's commandments once he or she has truly been born again.

Notice 1 Corinthians 7:20,

> Let every man abide in the calling wherein he was called.

If a man or woman is called to the ministry, let them respond to that call and remain in that ministry. To ignore God's call is to ignore God. Whatever ministry the Lord calls us to do, we are to respond and continue in that ministry.

Notice 1 Corinthians 7:21,

> Art thou called being a slave, care not for it: but if thou may be made free, use it rather.

This verse is not referring to slavery as it once was in the early days of American history, but it encourages us to be a slave to Christ. Paul even goes on to say a person who is a slave to Christ is free to serve and honor Him. When slavery is mentioned, a chill runs up our spines. However, it is an honor to be a slave to Christ.

Notice the phrase "use it rather."

That phrase is saying, whatever ministry you find yourself in, do it as a slave to Christ to promote His cause. Notice 1 Corinthians 7:22,

> For He that is called in the Lord, being a servant, is the Lord's freeman: likewise, also he that is called, being free, is Christ's servant.

Regardless of what ministry you are called to do, if you are doing it for the Lord as His servant, you are doing it as His slave. There is nothing more blessed than being a slave servant to Christ. Thank God, we will be allowed to love and serve Him forever in heaven.

Paul is not departing from his subject of marriage and divorce. He is saying marriage is a ministry. So if you're in a martial relationship, whether it is with a believing spouse or unbelieving spouse, live as though it is a ministry God has called you into. We are to glorify God in our ministry of marriage as much as any other ministry.

Notice 1 Corinthians 7:23,

> You are bought with a price, be not the servant [slave] of man.

This verse covers two truths. First, it shows the price that was paid for our salvation, which was the blood of Christ. Secondly, it defiantly states that being a slave to someone here on this earth is wrong. Here is something to think about. We know being a slave to someone is wrong, but seldom do we think of being a slave to a job, to drugs, to sex, to pleasure, and to other things are as wrong as being a slave to someone. Being a slave to anything other than God is just as wrong as being a slave to a person. It's true, many consider their spouse as being their slave. That does not make for a good marriage, and it is wrong.

Notice 1 Corinthians 7:24

> Brethren, let every man, wherein he is called, there in abide with God.

Whatever ministry God calls us to do, we are to do it for the glory of God as his servant and remain doing it the rest of our lives. First Corinthians 10:31 tells us,

> Whether therefore you eat, or drink, of whatso-
> ever ye do, do all to the glory of God.

First Corinthians 7:25–40 is the fifth subject in the outline, and it deals with singleness, marriage, remarriage, and sex.

According to the Bible, marriage is recommended, but single-ness is better, if singles have no desire for marriage. Singles must have the gift of singleness to live without a spouse
First Corinthians 7:25 comments on virgins who do not marry.

> Now concerning virgins, I have no command-
> ment of the Lord [that I can refer back to], yet
> I give my judgment, as one that has obtained
> mercy of the Lord to be faithful [to the Lord].

Paul is not saying, "I am giving my own opinion," but simply stating Jesus did not leave a commandment on this subject he could refer back to, but inspired him by the Holy Spirit to write on this subject.
Notice 1 Corinthians 7:26,

> I suppose therefore this is good for the present
> distress, I say, it is good for a man so to be.

This verse is teaching that it is good for a man or woman to remain single if he or she can live without desiring a spouse. Marriage brings stress, and singleness bring stress, but let's face it: stress is min-imized for the single but increased for the married. Marriage brings more responsibility than singleness. It is better for those who have the gift of singleness to remain single. However, those who have a desire for intimate relationships should marry.

Singleness will free people up so they can give the Lord their undivided attention. This is not teaching that one should divorce his spouse to free himself or herself to serve the Lord. That would be wrong, and it would double a person's stress. If a man or woman is married, they are to stay married. That is God's plan, even though marriage brings more stress. Notice 1 Corinthians 7:27,

> Are you bound to a wife? Seek not to be loosed.
> Are you loosed from a wife? then seek not a wife.

Those who are single and have no desire for a spouse can mess up their lives by marrying someone who has a need for marriage. If you are married, stay married; if you are single and have no need for a spouse, stay single.

Verse 28 has something else to say about this. If you have no desire for an intimate relationship but want to marry then marry someone who does not have a desire for intimate relationship, you have not sinned.

> But and if thou marry, thou hast not sinned; and
> if a virgin marries, she hast not sinned, neverthe-
> less she shall have trouble in the flesh: but I spare
> you.

This verse is teaching that it is permissible to marry even though you are a celibate single. You have not sinned if you marry a celibate. But to avoid trouble in the flesh, it is better to remain single.

The phrase "I spare you" means you are spared from trouble if you remain single. If you do not have a desire to have an intimate relationship, it is better not to marry. That will spare you from trouble. If a woman or man is single and have no desire for a spouse, they should remain single to avoid trouble in the flesh such as conflicts, opinions, adjustments, responsibilities, and caring for each other.

First Corinthians 7:29 states that singleness and marriage is meaningless to some. They live a life as though they are not married, and singles live a life as though they are married. Paul is saying that is wrong. Notice 7:29,

> But this I say brethren, the time is short: it remaineth, both they that have wives as though they have none.

What the Bible and God has to say about morals and decency is ignored and scoffed at by unbelievers. Paul is saying, people have no moral restraints at all and are doing their own thing. Notice what 7:30–31 has to say.

> And they that weep, as though they weep not, and they that rejoice, as though they rejoice not, and they that buy as though they possessed not, and they that use this world, as not abusing it: for the fashion of this world passeth away.

These verses are saying, people in the last days will have no moral decency and no sense of reality at all. They try everything, but nothing satisfies. They are like zombies following their father the devil. They have no emotion for anything or anybody.

> They weep as though they weep not. They rejoice as though they rejoice not, and they buy as though they buy not.

Nothing satisfies them. They show the depths of depravity in everyday life. They are numb to reality. It's a fact—you and I know people like that. People are randomly doing things for no reason at all, things that make no sense at all. They are paralyzed to their feeling for God and others.

In the following Scriptures, Paul goes back to teaching on singleness and marriage. Notice 1 Corinthians 7:32–33,

> But I would have you without carefulness [caring]. He that is unmarried cares for the things that belong to the Lord, how he may please the Lord. But he that is married cares for the things of the world, how he may please his wife.

There is nothing wrong with caring for and pleasing your spouse with worldly things, but you will have less stress if you have no need for a spouse and stay single. Singles care for themselves and how they can best serve the Lord, but it will change once they are married, even if they marry someone with the same desires. They care for their mate as well as caring for their self and the Lord.

I must emphasize how short life is and how we, whether married or single, should live our lives to the fullness for our Lord. Life at its best is very short. James 4:14 says,

> Whereas ye know not what shall be on the morrow. For what is your life? It is even a vapor that appeareth for a little time then vanisheth away.

Therefore, do all you can while you can to promote the cause of Christ. Do not ignore your calling. Marriage is a ministry. It is for life, and for the rest of your life, you are to take care of your mate plus take care to fulfill God's call on your life. Singles are free to take care of God's calling on their life only. Notice 1 Corinthians 7:32–33,

> But I would have you without carefulness [stress]. He that is unmarried careth for the things that belong to the Lord, how he may please the Lord but he that is married careth for the things of the world, how he may please his wife.

God is saying, "I don't want you to be stressed out." How many couples do you know that are stressed out with the responsibilities of marriage? Some walk away from marriage because of stress. God wants us to take responsibility in marriage, but He does not want us to be so stressed out that we forget about Him.

People are seeking carefree lives. In fact, the time is coming, and is already here, that marriages will mean nothing. People will be self-centered and care only for themselves. People will have no affection toward anyone, not even their spouse. I caution you, never ignore you spouse, nor get caught up in things that make God second in priority. A person is to be responsible and enter marriage with obligations toward his or her mate, but not to the exclusion of God.

The emphasis is placed on singleness in these verses. It presents singleness as the preferred way in having a carefree life, but it does not rule out marriage. It's not a matter of singleness versus marriage that helps people to have a carefree life; it's a matter of faithfulness to God in singleness and in marriage that helps people have a carefree life. That concept helps both singles and married to have a carefree life.

Notice 1 Corinthians 7:34,

> There is a difference also between a wife and a virgin. The unmarried woman careth for the things of the Lord, that she might be holy both in body and in spirit: but she that is married careth for the things of the world, how she may please her husband.

This verse is saying singles center their thoughts on how they can best serve the Lord. Married couples center on how they can best serve their spouse. A couple should consider marriage very carefully. Both singles and married couples determine where their dedication lies—to their Lord or their spouse. Both are important, but serving the Lord is most important.

In Bible times, a father chose a husband for his daughter. Genesis 24 is about Abraham choosing Rebekah to be Isaac's wife.

I'm not saying that is the way it should be done today, but I am saying if Christian parents could get more involved in their son or daughter's marriage, divorce would not occur so often.

It's very important engaged couples should undergo extensive marital counseling by a qualified Christian counselor before marriage. Young couples contemplating marriage are mesmerized by it and are not capable of making rational decisions. There are many things in courtships that leads to wrong choices. That is why young couples need their parents' help or help from a qualified Christian marriage counselor. They must be sure they choose the right person to marry.

Verse 7:35 states that married couples and singles should not get distracted from serving the Lord.

> And this I speak for your own profit; not that I may cast a snare upon you, but for what is proper, and that you may attend upon the Lord without distraction.

Marital duties are big distractions from serving the Lord. In fact, both married and singles have big distractions from serving the Lord if they are not totally committed to the Lord. The above verse is saying to both singles and married couples: Put the Lord first in your life; serve the Lord with all your heart. Whether you are married or single, nothing should distract you from serving the Lord.

Many married couples who live in a comfortable marital relationship see singles as having something wrong with them because they are not married. They think they are a little strange. We must keep in mind, however, that some singles have no desire for a marital union. Is that strange? Absolutely not! To say it is strange is to say God made a mistake when He made him or her with no desire for intimate relationships.

If you are single and have no desire for a marital union, embrace singleness as a gift from God. Don't let people intimidate you. Paul said in 1 Corinthians 7:7,

> For I would that all men were as I myself [a celibate], but every man hath his proper gift from God, one after this manner, and another after that.

What you have is a gift from God; embrace it as such.

In Bible times, many singles totally dedicated their lives to serving the Lord and never married. Also, many singles in our day totally dedicate their lives to serving the Lord and never marry. Is there anything wrong with that? No! It is a gift from God. But I caution you, never consider singleness as being the best choice if you have feelings toward the opposite sex.

Apparently, some Christian fathers in Corinth had questions about giving their daughters to the Lord to live as singles without a spouse. They were those who held to the Old Testament teaching of fathers giving their virgin daughter to a lifetime of service to the Lord. Judges 11:30–39 give an example of a father dedicating his virgin daughter to a lifetime of service to the Lord to be a celibate. Allow me to paraphrase the story about Jephthah in Judges 11:30–39.

Jephthah made a vow to the Lord that if He would give him victory over the Ammonites, he would offer as a burnt offer of whatever came out to meet him when he returned home. God gave him the victory. However, when he arrived home, he was shocked when his daughter came out to meet him. He told her about his vow. She requested permission to bewail her virginity for two months, then she would live as a celibate the rest of her life.

That story gives us an understanding of the relationship a father and daughter had in Old Testament times. Christian fathers in the Corinthian church had to face up to the fact that some of their daughters did not have the gift of singleness, but had a desire to marry and rear children. They wanted Paul to tell them what to do. Paul gives his answer in 1 Corinthians 7:36.

> But if any man [father] think that he behaves himself uncomely toward his virgin [daughter in not considering her feelings], and if she passes the flower of her age [passes into womanhood] and need so require [wants to get married], let him [her father] do what he will [plan a wedding]. He sinneth not [by not dedicating her to a life of virginity]: let them marry.

A father may realize he has not considered the feelings of his virgin daughter and had been hasty in dedicating her totally to the Lord to live a life of a virginity when she is not a celibate, but if she is mature as a woman capable of bearing children and desires a husband and insists on marriage, her father is to let her marry; he has not sinned in doing that. First Corinthians 7:37 says,

> Nevertheless, he [the father], stands steadfast in his heart, having no necessity, but has power over his own will, and has so decreed in his heart that he will keep his [daughter a] virgin, doeth well.

This verse can be understood by paraphrasing it this way: Nevertheless, the father who has kept his daughter a virgin and is not under constraint by his daughter to change his mind about dedicating her to a life of virginity, he should dedicate his daughter to serve the Lord all her life.

First Corinthians 7:38 summarizes the father's thinking about his virgin daughter by explaining God's will for her.

> So, then he that giveth her in marriage doeth well; but he that gives not her in marriage doeth better.

This verse is not saying the choice is between good and better. It stands to reason that someone who is not married, and is a celibate, has more time to devote to the work of the Lord than one who needs to marry to meet her or his intimate needs. The Scripture says a marriage brings with it a lifetime of responsibilities, but singleness does not bring as much responsibility. Once a virgin marries, it brings forth responsibility and an obligation to stay together so long as her spouse lives. Notice 1 Corinthians 7:39.

> The wife is bound by the law as long as her husband liveth, but if her husband be dead, she is at liberty to be married to whom she will; ONLY IN THE LORD.

In Bible times, marriage was taken very seriously—much more serious than today's marriages. Verse 39 is saying that a man and his wife is bound by God's law to remain married all their life, but if one should die, he or she is permitted to remarry *only* in the Lord's will.

Chapter 7 concludes by saying in verse 40 that a single life is better than a married life as far as serving the Lord is concerned.

> But she is happier if she abides after my judgment: and I think I have the Spirit of God.

I promised at the beginning of this chapter to conclude the story of Abby and Tom. They were deeply in love. After all, they had known and loved each other since they were children. It broke their hearts to think of separation and living the rest of their lives apart from each other. They were both Christians and wanted to do the right thing. They talked about living together without intimate relationships. Abby didn't think that would work. Tom didn't think it would either, but he was willing to try. They made this a matter of intense praying and went to God's Word with a predetermined purpose of following the Lord's leadership and doing what His Word taught. Before they met again, they both had settled the issue by reading and applying 1 Corinthians 7:28.

> But if thou marry, thou hast not sinned...
> Nevertheless such shall have trouble in the flesh.

They both agreed that a marriage such as theirs would bring nothing but trouble. They agreed to separate and go their separate ways, but still be friends.

Tom encouraged Abby to find someone who loved her as much as he loved her and one that could meet her intimate needs. She did find someone and fell in love with him. She married a man that loved her as much as Tom did and one that meet her intimate needs. A few months later, Abby became pregnant and gave birth to a boy. They named him Samuel Thomas after her husband and Tom, her lifelong friend.

Tom never did marry, but spent his days serving as pastor of the local church. Under his leadership the church grew very rapidly, and it became necessary to hire another secretary. Since Abby and her husband Samuel were members of the church, Samuel encouraged her to apply for the position, which she did and was accepted. Abby and Tom's lifelong dreams of serving in a ministry became a reality. They lived their days as good friends and coworkers in the ministry of the Lord, which fulfilled a lifelong dream of serving in the ministry together.

CHAPTER 8
HAS ONE SUBJECT

This chapter deals with offending a weaker brother's or sister's conscience.

To understand this chapter, there are two principles you must learn. *Firstly,* you must learn the difference between legalism and liberalism. *Secondly,* you must learn the law of knowledge and love. Both are clearly taught in this chapter, but sad to say, they are seldom learned by Christians. This chapter has nothing to do with salvation, but everything to do with living the Christian life. Chapter 8 uses the illustration of eating meats offered to idols to teach these two principles. It is important you learn them; otherwise, you cannot understand this chapter.

We might say this is a progressive lesson, so you will learn these principles as we progress through this chapter. When you learn and apply them, you will know what it really is to be a compassionate Christian.

First, consider the difference between legalism and liberalism. A legalist is a person that believes in strict obedience to laws and regulations. A liberal is a person that believes Christ sets us free to do anything the flesh desires.

Allow me to give a fictitious story that might help further your understanding of legalism verses liberalism.

Jeff was a self-confident Christian. He always thought of himself as having the right answer to tough questions, especially when it came to understanding Scriptures. He was quick to give his answers.

After all, he wanted to help others understand their liberty in Christ. It was not that he was arrogant but confident in his ability to explain the Bible. That made Jeff feel good about himself, and he was proud he could help Christians understand what God expected from them, or else that is what he thought he was doing.

Jeff always took the initiative to speak out when it came to what others thought was right or wrong. He believed his liberties were not to be suppressed, but lived out in everyday life. He never thought of his liberties as being offensive to weaker Christians. He never thought of things he approved of might be sinful to others. Yes, he thought he was right, and he thought people would be better off if they followed his advice.

The question arose one day about social drinking. Jeff didn't see any harm in it, because, as he put it, "God has set us free from bondage and rules." He often quoted John 8:36.

> If the Son therefore shall make you free, ye shall
> be free indeed.

He insisted God sets us free to be what we are. He was confident he was right when he insisted that Christians should take advantage of their liberties. It never dawned upon him that he might be offending his Christian brothers and sisters in Christ. Those that disagreed with him were legalists, of course. A legalist is a person that believes in strict laws and regulations.

When it came to the subject of legalism versus liberalism, Jeff always chose the side of liberty. He got a lot of criticism on his opinions, but he didn't mind because he felt he was right.

After much opposition, Jeff began to rethink his position, so he decided to go to 1 Corinthians 8 and do a study on this subject. After spending some time in God's Word, he decided that being so forceful in his opinions could possibly cause his weaker brother or sister to sin. He realized if they saw him doing something questionable that they considered sin, they might be encouraged to mimic him, and their conscience being weak would cause them to sin. That was not what Jeff wanted. He concluded that by being so forcible in his belief would make him a sinner by leading someone else to sin. Jeff admitted, in part, his position might be wrong. Therefore, he toned down his strong opinions and accepted other people's opinions before coming to any conclusion of his own. He encouraged others to never exclusively follow his advice, but go to the Bible and settle the issue in their own minds.

Second, consider the laws of knowledge and love. Knowledge is knowing there is nothing wrong with eating meat offered to idols, or as we shall put it in this lesson, doing something that is questionable about the right or wrong of it. Love is to restrain yourself from doing something that might lead your Christian sister or brother to mimic you and sin. In other words, some things you are doing may not be a sin to you, but if you lead a legalist who has a weak conscience to do it and he feels he has sinned by doing it, you sin by leading him to do it. Love will keep you from doing it.

First Corinthians 8 deals with eating meats offered to idols. However, this book deals with questionable practices that could or could not be sin.

The word *questionable* brings up the thought about how Christians live, or about the things they do or don't do. Is it sinful or not sinful? Notice 8:1,

> Now as touching things offered unto idols, we
> know that we all have knowledge. Knowledge
> puffs up, but love edifies.

Notice there are two principles mentioned in the above Scripture—knowledge and love.

Knowledge is knowing there is nothing morally wrong with eating meat that was offered to idols—or as we shall put it, participating in a questionable practice. When strict legalists got involved in a questionable practice it is wrong to them because they have a weaker conscience. Their conscience is easy defiled. If a legalist has a weak conscience and indulge in a questionable practice, they consider themselves sinners. Furthermore, let's say I am a liberal and I encourage a legalist to do something questionable that he considers sin, even though it may not be a sin to me. I cause him to sin, and I sin by encouraging him to sin. I hope you are following me in what I am saying.

Paul warns us about having a cocky attitude about liberalism versus legalism. Notice 1 Corinthians 8:2.

> If any man thinks he knoweth anything, he knoweth nothing as he ought to know.

This verse instructs us to be cautious about what we believe and practice. Our liberal beliefs could lead our weaker brother or sister to sin. On the other hand, our legal belief could impose burdens on other Christians that are not necessary nor possible to bear.

The legalists in Paul's day felt they could not with a clear conscience eat meat that had been offered to idols. The liberal, on the other hand, felt they were free to eat anything and still have a clear conscience. Therefore, the Scriptures lay down the principles of knowledge and love that should settle this issue. Knowledge is knowing there is nothing wrong with eating meat that has been offered to idols or getting involved in a questionable practice, but love will keep one from doing it for fear of leading a weaker Christian brother or sister to sin. Let me put it this way. Knowledge is knowing; there is nothing wrong with indulging in a questionable practice. However, love will prevent us from doing it and offending our weaker brother or sister in Christ.

We know an idol is nothing and meat offered to idols means nothing, but if the weaker brother is offended by eating meat that has been offered to idols, to him it is a sin. He commits a sin because he does not have the knowledge of what an idol is. If your knowledge should cause you to lead your weaker brother or sister to do what they consider sin, you sin by leading them to do it. If you have knowledge of what an idol is, you must be careful how you react to that knowledge. If you indulge in a questionable practice that causes your weaker brother of sister to sin, you sin by leading them to do it. The bottom line is, don't violate your knowledge by getting involved in questionable practices.

If you have a liberal belief that getting involved in a questionable practice is okay, then don't practice that belief to the extent you lead your legalistic brother or sister to get involved in that questionable practice and sin.

Was the Corinthian church practicing the principle of knowledge and love, or were they living a lifestyle that violated the principle of knowledge and love? They understood the principle of knowledge and love in relation to legalism versus liberalism, but they were living according to their own fleshly desires. The question for us is the same: Are we practicing the principles of knowledge and love, or are we violating the principle of knowledge and love? When we live a life different from what the Bible teaches, we are violating the principles of knowledge and love. Principles from the Bible are to be understood, obeyed, and practiced.

Allow me to bring the point of knowledge and love to a head by giving an example. A man's sexual desires are aroused by looking at a woman. God made him that way. Women are not like that. So why do women dress suggestively to attract a man's attention. Christian women may feel in their hearts they are doing nothing morally wrong. However, the Bible says,

> He that looketh upon a woman to lust after her,
> has already committed adultery with her in his
> heart. (Matthew 5:28)

Christian women may not be doing anything morally wrong by dressing the way some do, yet they are doing something morally wrong by causing a man to lust after them and sin. Knowing the principles of knowledge and love will cause a Christian woman to think twice before she dresses to attract men's attention. I must say, worldly unbelieving women dress to promote their sexual appearance. A Christian woman must restrain herself because she is totally guilty of sinning if she doesn't. Let me add this: Men, you need to restrain yourselves from looking at women because you have no one to blame but yourselves.

By the way, ladies, it's okay to dress any way you want to, or not dress at all in the privacy of your husband to arouse his attention, but not before the public. I hope you understand where I'm coming from.

Verse 3 emphasizes the necessity of loving God and loving others. Notice 1 Corinthians 8:3,

> But if any man loves God, the same is known of
> him.

If Christians love God as they should, it will show in their everyday lifestyle—that is, in the way they live. If Christians do not love God as they should, they may as well forget about the principles of knowledge and love because the first requirement is that one love God first, then they can be taught to love other Christians the way they love God. The Bible teaches us to love God first, then love our neighbor as ourselves (Matthew 22:36–40).

The Corinthian church had knowledge of the way they should live, but they were missing the principles of knowledge and love. They were carnal, proud, and offensive to other believers. Do you know anyone like that? Sure you do, and I do too. If a person's knowledge is offensive to other Christians, he really doesn't practice the principles of knowledge and love. Perhaps he doesn't understand the principles of knowledge and love. In that case, he doesn't love God as much as he says he does. Read 1 Corinthians 8:3 again.

> If a man loves God, the same is known of him.

If we love God, people will know we love God. If our lifestyle does not cause our Christian brother or sister to sin, people will know we love God. John 13:35 says,

> By this shall all men know ye are my disciples if
> you have love one for another.

We should do everything possible to not offend the conscience of our weaker brother or sister, and by doing that, people will know we love God. The principle of love correctly lived out is not being offensive toward our Christian brothers and sisters to wound his/her conscience.

There are three subpoints under the principles of knowledge and love we need to consider. These principles are found in 8:4–6. These verses give us the three principles of knowledge and love and how these principles can have a profound effect on others. First Corinthians 8:4–6 says,

> As concerning therefore the eating of those things that are offered in sacrifice to idols, we know an idol is nothing in the world and that there is none other God but one. For though there be that are called gods, whether in heaven or in earth (as there are gods many and lords many,) but to us there is but one God, the Father of whom are all things, and we in Him; and one Lord Jesus Christ, by whom are all things, and we by Him.

First, it's most important we place God in the highest echelon because "there is but one God," and we are to love God supremely. That is what Jesus taught his disciples to pray:

> Our Father who art in heaven, HALLOWED [holy, sacred, divine] be thy name. (Matthew 6:9).

We will place Him in the highest honor possible if we practice the principle of knowledge and love.

Secondly, eating meat or not eating meat offered to idols doesn't break or make our relationship better or worse with God, with Jesus Christ, or with the Holy Spirit. We break our relationship with them when we allow our liberty to cause our Christian brother of sister to sin, or impose burdens and rules on Christian brothers or sisters that is impossible for them to bear. Not living by the principles of knowledge and love will break our fellowship with God, Jesus, and Holy Spirit.

Third, all things that are made came from God, "by whom are all things." Since God made everything, including us, don't you agree it would be pleasing to Him if we live by His principles of knowledge and love? First Corinthians 8:7 tells us that many Christians that do not have that knowledge; therefore they do not live the principle of knowledge and love.

> Howbeit there is not in every man that knowl-
> edge, for some with conscience of the idol unto
> this hour, eats it as a thing offered unto an idol;
> and their conscience being weak is defiled [they
> sin].

God's Word teaches us that an idol does not live, unless, of course, the idol is someone we admire and esteem above Jesus. An idol is something, or someone, we have a high devotion or admiration for. It's something we place in a higher echelon than God, Jesus Christ, and Holy Spirit. No one should be placed above Christ, God, or Holy Spirit because we are one in Christ and to serve Him should be our first priority. Our devotion should be 100 percent directed toward the Father, the Son, and Holy Spirit.

Eating meat offered to idols or not eating meat offered to idols does not cause us to sin, nor make us better Christians or worse Christians. May I put it this way: Doing questionable things or refraining from questionable things does not make us better Christians or worse Christians. Eating meat offered to an idol is no more than eating meat that has been dedicated to a charitable origination. Meat offered to an idol doesn't change the meat at all. There is only one God, and meat offered to idols is not a god. God loves you and accepts you whether you have a questionable practice or don't have a questionable practice. Since there is only one living God, an idol cannot be a god like our living God. But an idol can be admired more than God.

Some in the Corinthian church who had a weak conscience believed an idol contaminated the meat and they committed a sin by eating it. They did not understand that an idol had no significance in spiritual meaning. They did not understand that eating or not eating meat offered to idols had no effect on the meat or their spiritual standing with God. Notice 1 Corinthians 8:8.

> But meat commendeth us not to God, if we eat,
> are we the better, if we eat not, are we the worse.

Eating meat offered to idols or not eating meat offered to idols didn't make them better Christians or worse Christians.

Many legalist Christians put themselves under heavy burdens trying to keep the rules they imposed on themselves, or the rules some preacher, pastor, or religious leader puts on them. Keep in mind, legalism is putting yourself under rule and regulations that are impossible to keep. As a result, they are miserable Christians! Allow me to give a true story of a deacon that went to a church where they imposed rules and regulations on their members. I must be very careful here, but I want to quote the man word for word. I met the deacon on the street one day, and I realized right off he was drunk. I mean, he was really, really intoxicated. I said, "[Blank], you're a deacon. What do you mean by getting drunk?" Here are the exact words he said: "To hell with that church. I can't live up to all those standards and rules they put on me." He was right by saying he could not live up to their standards and rules; I couldn't either. It's impossible to live up to the standards and rules some churches put on their members. But the man was wrong in giving up on God.

The Pharisees were sticklers at imposing burdens on people, and many did not practice what they preached. Matthew 23:4 said,

> They bind heavy burdens and [that are] grievous
> to be born, and lay them on man's shoulders, but
> they themselves will not move them with one of
> their little fingers.

Isn't that true of many religions that put burdens on their followers? I'm not saying their followers are not born-again Christians. They just get caught up in a legalistic lifestyle.

Some of the Corinthian church members were bearing burdens they didn't need to bear. On the other hand, some were practicing liberties that made them just as bad as carrying heavy burdens that offended their weaker brother or sister's conscience.

Is a person at liberty to do those things that others believe to be a sin? Some respond with, "I'm free to be me." Is the liberated Christians free to do anything the flesh wants them to do? Does a Christian woman or man have the freedom to dress in a way that would causes the opposite sex to look on him/her with lust? The Scriptures are clear that they should not do that, and they will not do that if they are living under the principles of knowledge and love. Notice 1 Corinthians 8:9,

> Take heed lest by any means this liberty of yours
> become a stumbling block to them that are weak.

The key phrase in this verse of Scripture is becoming "a stumbling block to them that are weak."

Paul explained the reason the Corinthian Christians took advantage of their liberty and why it was offensive to other Christians. Notice 1 Corinthians 8:10–12,

> For if any man sees thee which hath knowledge
> setting at meat at the idol's temple, shall not the
> conscience of him which is weak, be embolden
> [encouraged] to eat those things offered to idols;
> and through thy knowledge the weaker brother
> perishes [loses his fellowship with God] for
> whom Christ died, but when ye sin so against
> thy brethren, and wound their weak conscience,
> ye sin against Christ.

These verses could be paraphrased as follows: "If a legalist Christian sees you that have knowledge that there is nothing wrong with having a questionable practice in your life, he will be encouraged to do what you do. After he does, then he is convinced he has sinned. Therefore, through your knowledge, your weaker brother has sinned and lost fellowship with God. But you have sinned too by leading him to do that."

Allow me to give an illustration. Let's say I'm jogging down the street, and I become thirsty. Because of my excessive perspiration I need water. The only place to find water is in a bar. I go in and get a drink of water. Another Christian observes me come out of the bar and confronts me about it. I tell him I went in there to get a drink of water. He is hungry, so he feels if I as a Christian can go into the bar to get a drink of water, he could go into the bar and get something to eat. But when he does, he condemns himself over it and feels he has sinned and lost fellowship with God. It was I who caused him to feel condemned. If this case had really happened, I would have encouraged a fellow believer to sin and lose fellowship with God. I would have been better off if I had waited until I got home to get a drink of water. As far as I am concerned, I did not sin, yet I did sin because I lead a fellow believer to do something he considered sin.

These verses stress how important it is to live by the principles of knowledge and love. The weaker Christian will say to himself, "If that Christian can do that maybe I can too," but once he does his conscience condemns him and he feels he has fallen into sin, and God will bring judgment upon him. The Bible is not saying he will die and go to hell. If that is what verse 11 teaches, then we will all die and go to hell for we have all sinned after we were born again. A better translation of this Scripture would be "lost fellowship with God" instead of "perish."

We must never forget our liberty may lead another Christian astray and encourage them to do something they feel is wrong when it is not wrong. Verse 11 is simply saying, by eating meat offered to idols, a Christian can cause another believer to break fellowship with God if he eats the meat. You may say, "It's his fault." He needs to get his head screwed on right about what the Bible teaches on liberalism and legalism. Well, maybe he should, but what you are saying is just an excuse for you doing what your flesh wants you to do. If you have a questionable practice, you may not be sinning when you do it, but don't do it for the sake of your weaker Christian brother or sister. If you do you cause him/her to sin, then you sin because you led him/her to sin. Some things you are doing may not be a sin to you, but if you lead a Christian who has a weak conscience to do it and he or she feels they have sinned by doing it, you also sin by leading him/her to do it.

We have been thinking on the lines of eating meat offered to idols, but that is not the way we offend our weaker brother or sister's conscience today. Any questionable practice we have has the potential of wounding the conscience of a weaker brother or sister. There is a responsibility that goes with being a Christian. Satan will use this tool to destroy someone's faith in Christ. That's not what we want? Of course not.

Allow me to say, we have the liberty to do things others feel are wrong, but the principle of knowledge and love will prevent us from doing it if it offends our weaker brother's or sister's conscience. If we are sincere in our service to Christ, we will consider how things look to our Christian brothers or sisters. Perhaps it would change our minds about doing those things that offend our weaker brother's or sister's conscience.

One more thing—if we are legalists and impose burdens on people by our rules and regulations that is impossible to keep, we cause our fellow Christians to become disillusioned with Christianity and quit living for the Lord. After all, our Christian brothers and sisters are more important than any liberty or rules we may have. Paul emphasizes in 1 Corinthians 8:13 that loving our Christian brothers and sisters should be our first priority.

> Wherefore, if meat [or, any questionable practice] makes my brother to [be offended] I will eat no flesh [practice no questionable things, impose no rules that is impossible to keep] while the world stands, lest I make my brother to offend.

Wow! Paul's dedication comes through loud and clear, doesn't it? Romans 14:1–3 tells us,

> Him that is weak in the faith receive ye, but not to doubtful disputations [not doubt his faith in Christ]. For one believeth he may eat all things, another, who is weak, eateth herbs [vegetables]. Let not him that eateth, despise him that eateth not; and let not him who eateth not judge him that eateth: for God hath received him.

Paul condemns both those who think it is okay to eat meat offered to idols and those who think it is a sin to eat meat offered to idols.

A person living a questionable life is not leading people to Christ but leading people away from Christ. A person imposing heavy burdens on people that is impossible to bear is not leading people to Christ but leading people away from Christ. They insist on living according their liberty or legalistic views, not considering their Christian brothers or sisters, not considering how detrimental their lifestyle could be to unbelievers, and to the cause of Christ. A good rule to follow is if what you do glorifies God then do it. But for God's sake, and the sake of other Christians, and the unsaved, consider the message you are sending before you do what you want to do.

When a legalist is firm in his belief that he is right and tries to convince other believers to follow him, he is doing an injustice to other Christians and especially to Christ. The legalist puts burdens on people that are impossible to keep and not necessary. The legalist tries to convince others that being a legalist, or as they put it—"living right" (whatever that means) is necessary for salvation they discredit Christ for what He did to provide salvation for them.

CHAPTER 9
HAS THREE SUBJECTS

Verses 1–6 deal with Paul justifying his apostleship.
Verses 7–17 show preachers should make a living by preaching.
Verses 18–27 deal with rewards for true ministry.

First Corinthians 9:1–6 is the first subject in the outline, and it deals with the subject of Paul justifying his apostleship.

Some of the Corinthian church members questioned Paul's right to be an apostle. However, Paul vindicated his apostleship by asking rhetorical questions. What is a rhetorical question, you may ask? Rhetorical questions are hyperbole languages, statements that are not to be taken literal. It is exaggerated language. It is language that does not require an answer to a question because the answer is given in the way the question is phrased. A rhetorical question is the art of making a statement that sounds like a question, but in reality, it's only a statement. For example, someone may say, "What a beautiful sunset." That is not asking a question, but making a statement about the beauty of the sun set.

Notice Paul's rhetorical questions in verse 1,

> Am I not an apostle? Am I not free? Have I not seen Jesus Christ our Lord? Are you not my work in the Lord?

In defending his apostleship, Paul was not bragging about his apostleship, his freedom, his seeing Jesus, his work for the Lord, nor was he asking questions. He was using hyperbole remarks. In other words, he was using exaggerated language that did not require an answer. He wanted the Corinthian church to know God had placed him in a special class called apostles. They knew he was one of the chosen few who was called to be an apostle. They knew he was an apostle to the Gentiles.

Paul is using figures of speech, hyperbolic words, rhetorical questions which are the art of asking question that is not question, but a statement instead. Paul asked four rhetorical questions. He asked his first rhetorical question in 9:1,

Am I not an Apostle?

They knew Paul was an apostle because he had led them to Christ. Notice the unique way Paul presented his proof in verse 2,

If I be not an apostle unto others, yet doubtless I
am to you: for the seal [proof] of my apostleship
are you in the Lord.

Paul wanted them to understand he was not only an apostle, but qualified to be an apostle to them because he won them to Christ. Paul's second rhetorical question is also found in 9:1,

Am I not free?

Paul is saying, "You know what it is to be set free since I led you to Christ." He is saying, "Jesus Christ set me free like you." The Corinthian church knew Paul was free in Christ. Thank God, we too have been set free. John 8:36 says,

If the Son therefore shall make you free, you shall
be free indeed.

We, like Paul, were once in bondage to sin and Satan, but Christ set us free to serve Him.

Allow me to depart for a moment and give a story to show what it means to be set free. The story goes like this. Many years ago, when slavery was legal, plantation owners brought their slaves to town on Saturday mornings to sell them. But on this particular morning, a plantation owner desperately needed money, so he brought the most-prized girl of his group to sell. She was beautiful, slender with long, flowing black hair and dark complexion. He thought perhaps she would bring him the money he needed.

The bidding started with a low bid, but got higher and higher and higher. All the men started bidding for her, but they had to drop out because the biding got higher than what they could pay. Only two men were left to bid. One was a riverboat owner, and the other was a businessman. The biding got so high the riverboat owner was heard to say, "I can't bid any higher because I couldn't make a profit on my riverboat." The girl was sold to the businessman.

The auctioneer, with the sales papers, led the young lady off the stage and presented her to her new owner. She looked at him with contempt and hate in her eyes. He said to the young lady, "I bought you, and I own you," but he looked at her for some time, then he ripped the papers to shreds and said, "Now I set you free." She was surprised and amazed for a moment. After realizing what he had done—realized what an enormous price he had paid for her just to set her free, the hatred and contempt turned to love and appreciation. So she fell down before his feet and said, "Oh, sir, I will love you and serve you the rest of my life."

We were on the auction block of sin, and the devil was bidding for our souls. The bidding got higher and higher until Jesus said, "I will pay the ultimate price," and He did. Therefore, all who receive Him as their Saviour and make Him the Lord of their lives are set free from the consequences of sin, the devil, and hell. Notice again John 8:36,

> If the Son therefore shall make you free, you shall
> be free indeed.

We can now fall before Him and say, "Lord Jesus, I will love you and serve you the rest of our life."

Paul is saying to the Corinthian church, "You have been set free from sin's power, therefore give God thanks." Paul himself won most of the Corinthian church members to Christ. So he proceeded to vindicate his apostleship from those who doubted. Paul's third rhetorical question is once again found in verse 1.

Have I not seen Jesus Christ out Lord?

They knew he had seen Jesus. Personally, seeing Jesus was the supreme highlight of Paul's life. Seeing Jesus changed his life forever. By seeing Jesus in person, Paul met the qualifications for apostleship. Paul was given a special revelation of Jesus on the road to Damascus. He undoubtedly told the Corinthian church about his conversion. He defended his apostolic authority as being from God because he had seen Jesus in person.

Paul's fourth rhetorical question is also found in 1 Corinthians 9:1.

Are you not my work in the Lord?

Paul had personally won the Corinthian people to Christ, and they knew that. Therefore, he was right in making the statement that they were Christians because of Him. Notice verse 2,

> If I be not an apostle to others, yet doubtless I
> am to you: for the seal of my apostleship are ye
> in the Lord.

However, some still questioned Paul's authority as an apostle. Notice his response in 1 Corinthians 9:3–6,

> My answer to them that do examine me is this:
> Have we not the power [right] to eat and drink?
> Have we not power [right] to lead about a sister, a

wife, as well as other apostles, and as the brother of our Lord [James], and Cephas. Or I only and Barnabas, have not the power [right] to forbear working.

Paul defended his rights in these Scriptures.

Sometimes it is necessary to defend our rights in Christ, and it should be done the way Paul defended his apostleship in Christ. Paul used rhetorical questions, so should we if necessary.

First Corinthians 9:7–17 is the second subject in the outline, and it shows that preachers should make a living by preaching the Gospel.

Paul gives several reasons why ministers should be paid for ministering. Although Paul chose not to accept payment for his service, he believed it was the right to do for other ministers. Paul is saying ministers should be paid for their serving in the ministry. First Corinthians 9 verse 7 says,

> Who goeth to war any time at his own charge? And who planteth a vineyard and eateth not of the fruit? Or who feedeth a flock, and eateth [drinks] not of the milk of the flock?

There may be times when people rally for a cause that leads to war, such as the American Revolution, but soldiers don't pay to be a soldier in battle; they get paid for being a soldier in battle. Thus,

> Who goeth to war any time at his own charge?

Paul is not talking about going to war per se but talking about serving in the ministry.

For whatever reasons a person raises fruit or cattle, his main purpose is to eat the fruit and beef and drink the milk. Paul used this illustration to show a man who serves in the ministry should make a living from the ministry. Ministers should not have to serve in the ministry while working on a secular job. This is made clear in 1 Corinthians 9:8–10.

> Say I these things as a man, or sayeth not the law the same also?

For it is written in the Law of Moses,

> Thou shalt not muzzle the ox that treadeth out the corn. Doth God take care of oxen? Or sayeth He it altogether for our sakes? For our sakes, no doubt, this it is written, he that ploweth should plow in hope; and he that thresheth in hope should be partakers of his hope. (Deuteronomy 25:4)

The *first* reason a minister should be paid for ministering is that the law teaches that a person is to eat of his own fruit. Paul is saying, when a man plows and gets a crop ready to harvest, he is hoping the crop will yield enough fruit for him to live on. Notice 1 Corinthians 9:11,

> If we have sown unto your spiritual things, is it a great thing that if we should reap your material things?

Paul had personally led many of the Corinthians to Christ. In fact, he reminds them that it was he who started the church by sowing spiritual seeds among them. Therefore, he is saying, "You owe me a debt, and that debt is your material things." Evidently, others were reaping material things from the church, so Paul thought the right thing for them to do was to be willing to pay him for serving in the ministry.

The *second* reason ministers should be paid is that they have a right to expect a salary from the church. Notice 1 Corinthians 9:12,

> If others be partakers of this power over you, are not we rather? Nevertheless, we have not used

this power; but suffered all things, lest we should hinder the gospel of Christ.

Paul did not take money for his spiritual service, but worked as a tentmaker. Acts 18:3 states,

And because he was of the same craft [a tent-maker] he aboded with [Aquila and Priscilla] for they were tentmakers."

Paul chose not to take money for his services in the ministry because he feared it might hinder the Gospel. Paul is not saying we are to do the same. He is saying we have the right to expect a salary for our services. If we are in the ministry, we should be paid so we can spend more time ministering to our members and studying God's Word. Members expect that of us, but if we work on a secular job, our service to others and studying God's Word is limited.

On the flip side, if we are getting paid as a minister, but not doing our job, we are "dead beats," and our effectiveness will diminish. Anyone who is in the ministry for money only will not receive a reward for that. He is receiving his reward now.

Allow me to give an illustration of a preacher friend who started his ministry in a small church but built a large church. My purpose in giving this story is because I want to show how important it is for ministers to receive a salary for their ministry. Scottie had spent several years in college and seminary training for the ministry. Upon graduation he looked for a church to pastor. A small church, only averaging about fifteen to twenty in attendance, asked him to be their pastor. When Scotty agreed to pastor, they offered him a small salary, just enough to buy his gas. In fact, that was all they could afford at that time.

Under Scottie's skillful leadership, the church grew rapidly until it averaged over three hundred each Sunday. With the increase in attendance, Scottie's responsibilities increased. The church had never offered him an increase in salary. That made it difficult for him to work on a secular job and pastor too. It was not that Scotty wanted their money. He wanted to spend more time working in the church and reaching people for Christ. Therefore, he presented a proposal to the church leaders about an increase in salary. They refused, saying, "We don't feel your contribution to the church made that much difference, the church would have grown anyway because the Lord is blessing it." Instead of getting angry and walking out, Scottie responded, "If there is any man in the church, or from any other church that can do what I do and live on the salary you pay me, I will step down and let him pastor." That surprised them.

After much discussion, the church leaders saw Scottie's point and admitted he was the cause of their church growth. So they asked the church to give him a salary equal to those who pastor churches the size of theirs.

This story shows why a pastor should be paid for pastoring instead of working on a secular job to make a living. It helps the church.

The *third* reason ministers should be paid for ministering is, they are involved in holy things. Notice 1 Corinthians 9:13,

> Do you not know they that minister about holy
> things live of the things of the temple, and they
> that wait at the altar are partakers with the altar?

Old Testament priests were supported by the people. They received tithes, fruits, grains, and animals for their livelihood. They received material things for their spiritual contributions to the people. They did it that way because God ordained it to be that way. God expects his people to do no less for His minister in these days. Notice 1 Corinthians 9:14,

> Even so hath the Lord ordained that they which
> preach the gospel, should live of the gospel.

In other words, they that preach the Gospel should make a living by preaching the Gospel.

Allow me to give a different slant on preaching and pastoring for a living. The Scriptures state that ministers and pastors are to earn a living by preaching the Gospel, but it also means to live what they preach, and that is essential. Notice 1 Corinthians 9:15–16,

> But I have used none of these things: neither have I written these things, that it should be done unto me: for it is better for me to die, than any man should make my glorying void; for though I preach the gospel, I have nothing to glory of: For necessity is laid upon me, yea woe unto me, if I preach not the gospel.

Sad to say, there are many preachers who don't live what they preach. They are not motivated to preach the Gospel for the privilege of preaching and leading people to Christ, but they are motivated to preach for money. They are like the Pharisees our Lord severely condemned. Jesus said in Matthew 23:4,

> They bind heavy burdens and [the burdens are] grievous to be born and lay them on men's shoulders; but they themselves will not move them with one of their fingers.

In other words, they didn't live what they preached, but wanted others to live by what they preached. There is nothing more repugnant than a pastor not living what he preaches. If it wasn't for money, the number of ministers would diminish to half; perhaps as little as a fourth would remain in the ministry. The truth is, ministry is money-motivated. It's an easy way to make a living.

Money did not motivate Paul, neither should it motivate us. Notice 1 Corinthians 9:17,

> For if I do this thing [preach] willingly, I have a reward: but if against my will [or for any other

reason], a dispensation of the gospel is committed unto me.

Paul is saying, if he preached for any reason other than to glorify
God, and lead souls to Him, he was doing it for the wrong reason. Paul
had no other desire other than preaching the gospel. God had called him
and set him aside for that purpose. His burning desire was to preach to
glorify God, not for personal gain. Preaching the Gospel as it should
be preached will anger some, but preaching for money alone disturbs
no one because the preacher avoids controversial subjects. The Word of
God tells us to preach all the Bible the way it should be preached. It's left
up to the members to receive it or reject it. Hebrews 13:17 says,

> Obey them that have the rule over you, and sub-
> mit yourselves for they watch for your souls, as
> they that must give an account, that they may do
> it with joy, and not with grief: for that is unprof-
> itable for you.

We are to preach the entire Bible, because our church congregation needs it. If members do not accept the Gospel, it is unprofitable
for them, but not unprofitable for the one preaching.

If your pastor is called by God to preach, don't make it so miserable for him that he will leave the ministry and lose his rewards.
Notice how the above Scripture puts it,

> That is unprofitable for you.

In other words, it is a bad mistake to do that. So if your pastor is
a God-loving, dedicated pastor, be careful to treat him right; receive
his preaching and pay him well.

If your pastor preaches, but all the while not willing to preach,
God had only entrusted unto him a stewardship. A stewardship is a
duty placed upon pastors and members by the Lord to take care of
His property. If God has called you to preach, you should have no
other desire but to preach. Churches need pastors like Paul.

Paul is not saying pastors should get a secular job like he did and not accept a salary from the church. He is simply saying his ministry was not money-motivated. It was a privilege for him to preach the Gospel, and that without being paid. He decided to reject the right to a salary because his ministerial services pleased him more than making money. It was not that he was forced to refuse a salary, but he chose to refuse a salary to keep others from saying his ministry was money-motivated. He feared anything that might cause other people to see him as abusing the Gospel.

The *fourth* reason a minister should be paid for ministering is the fact he is doing the greatest work that can be done under heaven. He is leading unbelievers to Christ and helping them grow in grace and knowledge of the Lord. Proverbs 11:30 says,

He that winneth souls is wise.

First Corinthians 9:18–27 is the third subject in the outline, and it deals with rewards for true ministry.

A minister can earn rewards for being a true minister in God's vineyard. God's requirement for ministers it to be found faithful. Therefore, God rewards those who are faithful.

Verse 18 tells us a minister earns rewards for being servants for Christ in the ministry.

What is my reward then? Verily that, when
I preach the gospel, I may make the gospel of
Christ without charge, that I abuse not my power
in the gospel.

What is Paul talking about here? Let me explain. Paul did not use the full benefits of preaching, but was concerned about rewards God would give him for leading people to Christ. Paul was looking to the future instead of focusing on the present. He did not want to "abuse" (*abuse* means "to treat in a harmful or offensive way") his power in the Gospel.

Paul was a total committed minister to Christ. He believed preaching was a reward God gave him by allowing him to preach the Gospel and leading the lost to Christ. Oh! I wish more preachers felt that way about preaching!

Notice 1 Corinthians 9:19. This verse tells us what it means to be a true genuine servant of Christ.

> For though I be free from all men, yet have I made myself servants to all, that I might gain the more.

The ministry is a calling from God, and it's not to be a career one chooses. It's not like something you pick and choose from a selection of choices. There are religions out there recruiting candidates for their ministry. However, Jesus made the following statement about those seeking ministry to fill a job. He said in Matthew 23:15,

> Woe unto you, Scribe and Pharisees, hypocrites! For you compass sea and land to make one proselyte, and when he is made, you make him twofold more the child of hell than yourselves.

Anyone can say they are a minister of God, but what is it to be a true minister of God? It means to present your body and soul to God to be his servant and lead others to Him. Romans 12: 1 says,

> I beseech you therefore breathren by the mercies of God that you present your bodies a living sacrifice, holy and acceptable unto God, which is your reasonable service to God.

A servant of God has a 24-7 job, not a nine-to-five schedule. Therefore, a true minister is a servant to Jesus and His church.

If Jesus came to your house, don't you think it would be an honor to serve Him? I am sure you would consider it a high honor! That's the way a true minister of God feels when he serves Christ and serves others. A God called minister's main objective in ministering is to glorify God, serve Him, serve the church congregation, and lead others to Christ. After all, it's God who gets the glory if we serve Him because we love Him, and what better way to glorify and show love to Him than to lead others to Him?

True ministers do not serve Christ for reward, per se, but for the privilege of serving Him and lead others to Him. To lead others to Christ is truly a reward from Christ. Paul became all things to all men that he might win some to Christ. Notice 1 Corinthians 9:20–23,

> TO THE JEWS I became as a Jew that I may gain the Jews; TO THEM THAT ARE UNDER THE LAW [Pharisees put themselves under the law; Paul did too], as under the law, that I may gain them that are under the law; TO THEM WITHOUT LAW, as without law [being not without law to God, but under the law to Christ] that I may gain them without law; TO THE WEAK, I became weak [a legalist], that I might gain the weak. I AM MADE ALL THINGS TO ALL MEN THAT I BY ALL MEANS SAVE SOME. And this I do for the gospel's sake that I may be partakers thereof with you.

We should be willing to go as far as we can to lead people to Christ, but not violate God's principles. Paul did not deny his faith, but was willing to condescend to the level of others if it created an opportunity to lead people to Christ. Notice what he did to win more to Christ.

1. "I have made myself a servant to all, that I might gain the more."
2. "To the Jews I become a Jew that I might gain the Jew." Jews were legalists; therefore Paul pretended to become a legalist to win the legalist to Christ.

3. He said, "To them that are under the Law [Pharisee placed themselves under the law] as under the law that I might gain them that are under the 'Law.'"

4. "To them that are without law [libertarians believe they can do anything the flesh wants them to do and still be right in the sight of God] as without Law [not being without the law of God] that I might gain them without Law." Paul said he would not overstep his commitment to Christ by becoming a libertarian or legalist in practice, but he did say he would become one in theory.

5. "To the weak [evidently, Paul is talking about legalist who are weak in faith] I became as weak, that I might gain the weak." Paul even goes so far as to say…

6. "I am made all things [in theory] to all men that I by all means save some."

He is not saying he was willing to cross the line into sin in order to win sinners to Christ, but go as far as he could in theory to win unbelievers to Christ.

Paul was willing to tolerate other religions that he might lead unbelievers to Christ. After all, isn't leading people to Christ what preaching the Gospel is all about?

There are self-righteous, religious preachers who feel separation is more important than joining other preachers who are leading people to Christ. Allow me to give a true-life story about two different denominational churches that I am affiliated with. They both put emphasis on winning souls to Christ. I prayed hard about including this true story in this book. I debated with myself whether I should include it or not. I concluded that it might benefit ministers and Christians. God seemed to say, If Paul wrote about it, you should too. I do not include personal name, denominations, or churches, so I don't need authorization to include this story. Well, here goes.

In a certain city, an evangelistic preacher along with a decorated war hero joined forces to begin an evangelistic campaign to lead the lost to Christ. The war hero had lost both legs in battle and wanted to give his testimony and encourage people to give their lives to Christ because of the brevity of life. The evangelist wanted to preach the Gospel and give people an opportunity to surrender their lives to Christ. But there was a problem they didn't anticipate. The problem was not with them, but with potential supporters. The war hero belonged to one denomination, and the other one belonged to another denomination. Neither of the denominational churches in that area would support them. The churches would not support them because the war hero belonged to a denomination they did not like, and the other one would not support them because the evangelist belonged to a denomination thy did not like. These two men of God could not get the ministry going. Therefore, God only knows how many people died without Christ because those self-righteous churches who would not support them.

I didn't tell that story to offend anyone. I told it to caution those who are putting others down that are winning people to Christ. Paul would not have done that because he said,

> I become all things to all men that I might by all
> means win some.

Since some preachers major on separation, my question is, How far should separation go? Allow me to give a hypothetical scenario. Let's say I had a friend named Bill. Bill has a relative who had a friend that joined a cult religion. Should I break fellowship with Bill because of his distant connection with a cult religion? I admit this illustration is ridiculous, but you get my point. I say again, to what extent should separation go? How far will you extend your separation? Did it ever occur to you the devil may be using you to hinder people from coming to Christ? No church, no preacher, and no denomination should be put down if they are preaching the Gospel. Many people and churches feel spiritually superior to others. God knows that, I know that, you know that, and we all know they are nothing more than bigots. We should not compromise our Christian convictions or change our message, but be willing to accept other churches, other preachers, and other denominations that preach the Gospel even though they don't do things the way we do. They may not have music like we have. Their method of preaching may not be like ours. The way they dress may not be like us, and they may be different in many respects, but they are still God's servants preaching the Gospel.

Other preachers, other evangelists, and other God called servants preaching the Gospel who do not belong to our group should be accepted and appreciated. They, too, are seeking to lead people to Christ, so accept them as God's servants.

There is something desperately wrong with those who put others down that are seeking to lead others to Christ. Many feel it's more spiritual to exclude them than to join them in an evangelistic campaign to lead the lost to Christ. The fact is, many will not join them because they know they would be ostracized from their little denominational group of bigots. I know that to be true because I was rejected by a denomination that I was affiliated with all my life, simply because I supported a denomination that was not part of theirs, but was leading others to Christ.

A soul winner is a servant of Christ that is willing to condescend to the level of other people to lead them to Christ. Paul did not condone all religious beliefs, but he did condescend to the level of others, so he could win them to Christ. Read again 1 Corinthians 9:22,

> I am made all things to all men, that I by all means may win some.

First Corinthians 10:32–33 says,

> Give non-offence, neither to the Jews, nor to the Gentiles, nor to the church of God. Even as I please all men in all things, not seeking my own profit, but the profit of many, that they may be saved.

The bottom line is to lead the lost to Christ by any means possible. Jesus even went so far as to say,

> For the son of man is come to seek and save that
> which was lost.

He did not say He came to save those who separate themselves from all other religions. Paul also said in 1 Corinthians 11:1,

> Keep the ordinances as I have delivered them
> unto you.

Both Jesus and Paul are saying, "Do as I have done."

I'm not saying you should compromise and change your message. Far be it from that. Paul is not teaching that either. Jesus is not teaching that either. However, within the bounders of God's Word, and with a clear conscience, go as far as God will allow you to go so you can win others to Christ, but don't cross the line into "hobnobbing" with cults.

Paul cared for others so much he was willing to go to the limits to win unbelievers to Christ. He had a heart for God and a love for the lost. Notice Romans 9:2–3,

> I have great heaviness and continual sorrow in
> my heart. For I could wish that I myself were
> accursed from Christ for my brethren, my kins-
> men according to the flesh.

Paul is saying, if it were possible, he would be willing to separate himself from Christ forever if it could bring his Jewish brethren (the ones who sought to kill him) to Christ. However, Paul knew, and we know, it is not possible to separate ourselves from Christ. Nevertheless, Paul was willing if it brought others to Christ. He loved them that much. He had a deep desire to see others saved, especially Israel. Paul said in Romans 10:1,

> Brethren, my heart's desire, and my prayer to
> God for Israel is that they might be saved.

Do we feel that way about leading people to Christ? Are we willing to give up everything to lead people to Christ? Paul was willing. Notice 1 Corinthians 9:23,

> Now this I do for the gospel's sake, that I might
> be partakers thereof with you.

Paul is saying, "I do that because I want to spend eternity in heaven with you." Do we feel that way for unbelievers? They will spend eternity separated from God forever if we don't win them to Christ. Regardless of what denomination they belong to, Jesus died for them.

There will not be a little group of Methodists in one corner of heaven, a little group of Baptists in another corner, a little group of Presbyterians in another corner, and so on. All who put their faith and trust in Jesus Christ for salvation, regardless of their denomination, will live together in heaven. Since that is true, shouldn't we try to live together here on earth?

I say again, we must not compromise our Christians convictions nor our message, but work together to win others to Christ that we may be partaker with them in heaven.

Preachers are called by God to separate themselves from the world's system so they can run the Christian race. Notice 1 Corinthians 9:24–26,

> Do you not know that they which run in a race
> run all, but one receiveth the prize? So, run, that
> you may obtain. And every man that striveth for
> the mastery is temperate in all things.

> Now they do it to obtain a corrupt-
> ible crown; but we [do it for] an incorruptible
> [crown]. I therefore so run, not as uncertainty;
> so, fight I, not as one that beateth the air.

These Scriptures compare those running a race for the purpose of winning a prize and running the Christian race for Christ that they my win a crown. They separate themselves from useless things and practice self-control. We are to do the same in the ministry. Setting ourselves apart to be the best minister we can is crucial in winning the race for Jesus. We are sanctified (set apart for a sacred service) to be used in God's service. The difference in winning in the ministry and winning in a race is that those who win in the ministry receive an incorruptible crown.

When comparing crowns, there is a large difference between corruptible and incorruptible crowns. My daughter won a two-foot-high trophy for scoring more basketball points in one season than anyone else. Now that trophy is sitting in our utility building, gathering dust and fading away. Thank God, our crown for running the race for Jesus will never fade sway. Second Timothy 4:8 says,

> Henceforth there is laid up for me a crown of
> righteousness which the Lord, the righteous
> judge shall give me at that day: and not to me
> only, but unto all them that love His appearing.

You and I will get that crown if we run our race for Jesus.

Paul separated himself from the world's system and kept his body under control. Regardless of his many problems, he lived for Christ for fear he might become a castaway. Notice 1 Corinthians 9:27,

> But I keep under my body, and bring it unto sub-
> jection, lest by any means, when I have preached
> to others, I myself should be a castaway.

Paul had three problems with his body, and so do we. These three problems are the world, the flesh, and the devil. All three seek to separate us from God. Our flesh strives to satisfy our worldly desires. The world's attractions draw us away from God, and the devil is doing all he can to diminish our influence as a Christian. Paul is telling us, we must control our bodies. Notice what he said about himself: "I discipline my body and bring it unto subjection to God." We must keep in mind our flesh is of this world and desires the things of the world. We must control our flesh, or our flesh will control us. We must never think the devil will not tempt us to get involved in worldly pursuits. He puts many temptations in our paths, but we can have the victory by taking Paul's advice he gave in the Scripture above.

Self-discipline is necessary in overcoming temptation. Notice what 1 Corinthians 10:13 says,

> God is faithful who will not suffer [allow] you to be tempted above that you are able to bear; but will with every temptation also make a way of escape.

It's a matter of exercising our wills to overcome temptation. We should not be surprised when temptation knocks at our door, but we should never let it in. Satan is always there, and his purpose is to tempt us to sin.

So to be a good minister, one must be a servant to Christ and his people. If we take the suggestions above, we can be good ministers for Christ.

CHAPTER 10
HAS THREE SUBJECTS

Verses 1–15 are about Israel's wilderness wondering.
Verses 16–22 are about fellowship at the Lord's Supper.
Verses 23–33 are about eating meat offered to idols.

First Corinthians 10:1–15 is the first subject in the outline, and it deals with Israel's wilderness wondering.

Paul used Israel's wilderness wandering as an example that we should not do as they did. Israel wandered through the wilderness forty years because they disobeyed God and refused to follow Moses whom God chose to lead them. They followed God and Moses at times, but for the most part they rebelled against both God and Moses. They disobeyed God and rejected Moses. The Bible gives many examples of Israel not following God and Moses. Numbers 16 gives a classic example. This example is about a person named Korah and his followers who rebelled against God and Moses. God destroyed them by opening the earth and letting it swallow them. Read about this rebellion in Numbers 16.

Israel wanted God's blessings, but chose to serve Satan. In rejecting the leadership of Moses, they rejected God. Israel experienced God's blessing, yet they rebelled against Him. God had promised them the land of Canaan, yet they refused to take it. They also rejected the two messengers—Joshua and Caleb—who said they could take the land. Joshua and Caleb and ten others were sent to spy out the land of Canaan, but only Caleb and Joshua brought back a good report. They had confidence in God's ability to give them victory over the giants. They believed they could take Canaan so long as God was with them.

The other ten spies brought back a bad report. They personified the size of the giant (nine feet, six inches tall) and minimized the power of God. Notice what they said in their report, Numbers 13:33.

> And there we saw the giants, the sons of Anak which came of the giants: and we were in their sight as grasshoppers, and so we were in their sight.

They saw themselves as grasshoppers in the sight of the giants.

Israel was under God's protection. He opened the Red Sea and did many wonderful things for them, yet they failed to put their trust in Him to give them the land of Canaan. Israel wanted to enjoy the things God could give them, but did not want to obey His rules, nor follow His leadership.

How true that is with our flesh. We do the same to a certain extent. Our flesh wants us to rebel against God and not trust Him for the victories we need. We want God's blessings, but at times we don't want any part of His standards. In fact, American people want to live for the devil but be blessed by God. We either love and serve God or live for Satan. We cannot have it both ways. If we live for God, we will be blessed by Him. If we live for Satan, we will be severely chastened by the hand of our Almighty God.

I must confess I am much like the ten spies that brought back a bad report. I fail to trust God at times. I tend to look at the circumstances around me and say it can't be done. We all fail to trust God at times. We have no excuse that will justify us in that. We hesitate to step out when God instructs us to do something for Him. We tend to forget the many victories God gave us. We see the giants of opposition looming before us but fail to see God's power to help us through. We hide in the church congregation and feel safe there. We feel too insecure to get involved.

We need to face our giants with courage, determination, and confidence in God. Someone put it this way, "I'm not afraid to face tomorrow because God is already there." God is always with those who seek to do His will. The safest place on earth is in the center of God's will. It matters not who you are or what circumstances you find yourself in; you can overcome your timidity and fears with confidence in the Lord Jesus Christ.

Paul had a victorious attitude. He said in Philippians 4:12,

> I know both how to be abased [made low], and
> I know how to abound [be prosperous]: every-
> where and in all things, I am instructed to be full
> and to abound...

Paul also said in Philippians 4:13,

> I can do all things through Christ who strength-
> ens me.

God is always with His own. When He calls us to do some-thing, He is always there to provide the strength, courage, and ability to see us through. God will never call us to do something unless He qualifies us to do it and protect us while we do it.

The ten spies who brought back a bad report could not see God as Almighty and more powerful than the giants. They dishonored God and denied His power by not trusting Him. Furthermore, they committed an evil sin by not following God and Moses, and they suffered the consequences which lasted forty years. Joshua 2:20 said this about Israel,

> If you forsake the Lord, and serve strange gods,
> then He will turn, and do you hurt, and consume
> you.

Similarly, how many times do we suffer because we forsake God's desired plans for our lives?

Let me explain 1 Corinthians 10:1–5, and then I will give five examples of Israel's disobedience to God. As we study 10:1–5, notice the number of times the word *all* is used. It simply means all were guilty of going astray and losing sight of what God had done for them.

Notice 1 Corinthians 10:1,

> Moreover, brethren, I would not that ye should
> be ignorant, how that <u>all</u> our fathers were under
> the cloud, and passed through the sea.

Paul is saying to the Corinthian church, don't be ignorant of what God did for your forefathers. God led Israel by a cloud during the day and led them by fire at night. That cloud and fire was Jesus Christ. God opened the Red Sea for them to cross over.

They became one with Moses in the cloud and in the sea. Notice verse 2,

> And were <u>all</u> baptized unto Moses in the cloud
> and in the sea.

In other words, they identified themselves with Moses and with the cloud. Keep in mind, the cloud was Jesus. That did not mean they accepted Jesus into their lives. Evidently, they did not understand the cloud. They only knew the cloud had something to do with protecting them, but it did not occur to them who or what the cloud represented. They did not know whether the cloud was a natural phenomenon or the supernatural power of Jesus Christ. They identified themselves with the cloud and with Moses out of convenience, not out of commitment.

Is it not true many in our day identify themselves as Christians out of convenience rather than out of commitment? It is convenient to identify oneself with Christians in some circumstances. It is profitable at times to be a "Christian." Are you proud to identify yourself with Christ in all circumstances? Do you keep quite when someone asks you if you are a Christian? Are you ashamed to identify yourself with the Bible, with God, with Christ, with the Holy Spirit, and with the church?

First Corinthians 10:3–4 refers to the food and drink God provided for Israel in the wilderness. Notice verses 3–4,

> And did <u>all</u> drink the same spiritual drink: for they drink of that spiritual Rock that followed them: and that Rock was Christ.

That means they had Jesus with them to protect them and supply their needs.

God always supplies the needs of his people. He will supply your needs and my needs, not necessarily our wants, but our needs. Philippians 4:19 said,

> God shall supply all your needs according to His riches in glory, by Christ Jesus.

Whatever needs we have, God supplies. God has amazingly supplied my needs.

Allow me to give a true event that happened to Carolyn and me when we moved to Chattanooga to go to school at Tennessee Temple University.

We had no clue of moving that far from home would be so difficult. First, we took a trip to Chattanooga to find a place to live and to enroll in school. We found a little apartment above a garage on a dead-end street in East Ridge. The following Friday we loaded our furniture in a truck. Carolyn drove our car, and I drove the truck. So we left home and headed out for Chattanooga.

In those days there were no interstates to Chattanooga but two-lane highways that went through many little towns. And it took about seven hours to make the trip. We left home in the late afternoon and didn't arrive in Chattanooga until around eleven at night. When I pulled the truck up to the apartment, I suddenly realized we had no one to help us move the furniture up the winding stairs to our little garage apartment. So we decided to sleep in our car that night and perhaps find someone the next day. During the night, two strong bodied men that looked like Sumo wrestlers appeared by the car window. It's a frightful thing to have someone knock on your car window in the middle of the night. One said, "Do you need help moving your furniture up those stairs?" How did he know we had furniture to move up those stairs? Why would he ask such a question? Why were they on that dead-end street that time of night anyhow? "Sure," I replied.

They moved the furniture up the stairs, set it up, and was through in less than an hour. I said, "How much do I owe you?" They both said, "You don't owe us anything," I insisted they take something. They did and then walked away. Keep in mind, this was a dead-end street. No one should have been walking on that street, especially that late at night. They had suddenly appeared and vanished the same way.

Now, you have a right to believe what you want to believe, but would you allow me to believe God sent two angels to help us in a desperate time of need? If they were not angels from heaven, they were angels to us. I really have a sneaking suspicion they were angels from heaven. Only God knows. God has always supplied our needs.

The above Scriptures (10:3–4) mention the fact that God supplied the needs of his people Israel. Jesus Christ was the one who supplied their needs. First Corinthians 10:5 below shows that Israel was not so much concerned about serving God, but more interested in what they could get from Him. God was not very pleased with them. Notice what 10:5 has to say about that,

> But with many of them God was not well pleased:
> for they were overthrown in the wilderness.

Israel wandered aimlessly through the wilderness forty years because they rejected God and Moses—God's leader. God was so displeased with them that He let all the people over forty die in the wilderness, including Moses and Aaron.

The sin Moses committed was smiting the rock instead of speaking to the rock like God told him to do. The people were thirsty and were on the verge of dehydration. They began to complain. Numbers 20:7–12 says,

> The Lord spoke unto Moses, saying... Speak ye to the rock before their [Israel's] eyes; and it shall give forth His water... And Moses lifted his hand, and with the rod he smote the rock twice: and the water came out abundantly...

Moses did that because he was angry at Israel. That was a direct defiant act of Moses against God's command. God wanted him to speak to the rock so He could get the glory. Because of that, God did not allow Moses to enter the promised land.

The reason Aaron died in the wilderness with the rest of Israel is that he sinned by making a golden calf out of silver and gold and encouraged Israel to worship it. Moses was on Mount Sinai getting the Ten Commandments from God. While he was gone, Aaron took over as leader and made a golden calf for Israel to worship. Notice what excuse Aaron gave to Moses for making the molten calf.

> I said unto them [Israel], whosoever hath any gold, let them break it off. So, they gave it [to] me: then I cast it into the fire, and there came out this calf. (Exodus 32:24)

That was s lie! He melted the gold and made the calf with his own hands. Because of that act God let him die in the wilderness.

Caleb and Joshua were the only two out of the group who came out of Egypt that did not die in the wilderness. The people believed the ten spies that said they could not take the land of Canaan. The people refused to believe Caleb and Joshua, who said they could take the land. So they all died in the wilderness, except Caleb and Joshua, who brought back a good report that they could take the land of Cannon.

Over a period of forty years, Israel committed many wicked sins. Paul said they committed sins that we should not commit. After all, Israel left us an example we should not follow. Keep in mind, the things Israel did was a warning to us not to do as they did. God was displeased with Israel and punished them. If you are not careful, and follow His lead, He might let you wander aimless through life without Him.

The Bible points out five sins Israel committed that we should not commit.

First, they committed the sin of lust. First Corinthians 10:5 says,

> Now these things were our example, to the intent
> that we should not lust after evil things as they
> also lusted.

The word *lust* is mentioned fifty-three times in the Bible and covers many sins. Lust is described as a passionate, overwhelming desire, or craving for things that are sinful.

In 1 John 2:16, lust is summarized into three sins: the lust of the flesh, the lust of the eye, and the pride of life. Notice 1 John 2:16,

> The lust of the flesh, and the lust of the eye, and
> the pride of life, is not of the Father, but is of the
> world.

This was a sin Israel committed many times. Is that not true about our country, our churches, and many Christians?

Lust was the sin Satan enticed Eve to commit. God told Adam to not eat of the tree of knowledge of good and evil located in the mist of the garden. God said, "You will die if you eat of it." Eve was not made when God told Adam to not eat of the tree of good and evil. Evidently, after Eve was made, Adam relayed the message to her. To Adam's dismay, one day Eve was in the garden alone, and Satan in the form of a serpent slid along on the branches and said to her,

> Ye shall not surly die.

Notice Eve was not frightened by the serpent but looked at the fruit with a passionate desire to eat it. Genesis 3:6 said,

> And when the woman [Eve] saw the tree was good for food [lust of the flesh], and was pleasant to the eye [lust of the eye], and a tree to be desired to make one wise [pride of life], she took of the fruit thereof and did eat.

Eve enticed Adam to eat the forbidden fruit, and by his own volition he purposely ate the fruit. Adam knew what the consequences would be but deliberately ate the fruit any way, thus plunging the world into sin. Roman 5:12 states,

> Wherefore, as by one-man [Adam] sin entered into the world, and death [comes] by sin; so, death is passed upon all men, for that all have sinned.

Adam knew what he was doing when he ate the forbidden fruit. Eve was deceived by the devil. God commanded Adam [not Eve] to not eat of the tree of knowledge of good and evil. Genesis 2:17 records God saying to Adam,

> Of the tree of knowledge of good and evil, thou shall not eat of it: for in the day that thou eatest thereof thou shall surely die.

But Adam thought more of Eve than God, so he ate the fruit. He chose the road that led to sorrow, pain, and ultimately death. Adam and Eve chose to do it their way.

People have intense lustful desires for things they do not need, nor can afford, nor good for their spiritual lives. However, they make every effort possible to get them anyway. People are like Israel who committed the sin of lust.

Secondly, Israel committed the sin of idolatry—that is, they committed the sin of worshipping idols. Notice 1 Corinthians 10:7,

> Neither be ye idolaters, as were some of them;
> as it is written: The people set down to eat and
> drink and rose up to play.

This Scripture verse is referring to idol worship of the golden calf that Aaron made, and that is recorded in Exodus 32. They not only committed idolatry in worshiping the golden calf, they committed adultery in their play:

> They rose up to play.

They stripped off their clothes and danced around the golden calf.

The Corinthian pagan temple worshippers in Paul's day worshipped their idol god of beauty, love, sex, and fertility like those who worshipped the golden calf. An idol is anything that takes priority over Jesus Christ, such as home, land, money, job, family, pleasure, positions, sex, and so on.

Do people worship idols today? Yes! I'm sorry to say—they do. They pattern their lives after Hollywood, and Hollywood worships their god of beauty, love, and sex. Whatever Hollywood does, American people do, especially young people.

Third, Israel committed the sin of fornication. Notice 1 Corinthians 10:8,

> Neither let us commit fornication, as some of
> them committed, and fell in one day three and
> twenty thousand.

Israel not only lusted after evil things and worshipped idols, but they also committed fornication. Fornication is an act of a married person committing sex with someone other than his/her spouse. Not controlling one's sexual passion leads to sexual immorality. Sexual immorality permeates our society. Anything goes nowadays. Wife swapping is a big occurrence now. Homosexuals and laubierinids have "come out of the closet." There are more sex crimes committed today than at any other time in history. It's not unusual to hear of a child being raped and babies as young as six months old, or younger, being molested.

First, Israel committed the sin of lust. Second, they committed the sin of idolatry. Third, they committed the sin of fornication, and next they committed the sin of tempting Christ.

Notice 1 Corinthians 10:9,

> Let us not tempt Christ as some of them also tempted Christ and were destroyed by the serpents.

Of course, this verse is referring to Numbers 21. They tempted Christ when they questioned God's good and perfect plan for their lives. Numbers 21:5 said,

> The people spoke against Moses and said: Wherefore [why] have you brought us up out of the land of Egypt to die in the wilderness? There is no bread, neither is there any water, and our souls loatheth [despise] this light bread [manna].

Their complaint about the manna was that they lusted for something to eat other than manna. They wanted a meat diet. God sent them meat to eat, and many died. Psalms 78:18 said,

> They [Israel] tempted God in their hearts by asking meat for their lust.

Psalms 106:23–24 states,

> They [Israel] soon forgot His works [God's works]; they waited not for His counsel: but

lusted exceedingly in the wilderness, and tempted
God in the desert.

Do people tempt Christ in our day? Yes! Both unbelievers and Christians tempt Christ. Unbelievers say in their hearts, "I'm going to do it my way, and that way is the devil's way." They say, "I don't want to believe what you want me to believe, but I want to do what I want to do." The reason they want to live their own life and do things their way is because they do not like God's way. They do not want to obey God's standards and requirements. People may not say it audibly, but they think doing it their way is the best way. Many say, "I would like to be a Christian, but I don't want the rules and standards that go with it." They want to live their lives the way the flesh dictates, not the way God leads. John 3:19 states,

This is the condemnation, that Light is come
into the world, and men love darkness rather
than Light, because their deeds are evil.

When unbelievers or Christians make their own decisions by their own standards, they are on the road to final destruction.

Christians tempt Christ by not following His plan for their lives. Our decisions are not inspired; God's Word is. Making our own choices is not inspired; God's Word is. Our decisions will lead us astray. God's Word will never lead us astray. We should never seek to do things our way, but allow God's Word to make decisions for us.

We commit the sin of tempting Christ when we disagree with His leadership. Sometimes we even get angry at God because He will not allow us to make our own choices. The bottom line is, we do things God's way or the devil's way. There are only two choices. Be careful to choose God's way. Israel sinned by rejecting Moses and God. Let's not do that!

Israel committed the sin of lust, the sin of idol worship, the sin of fornication, the sin of tempting Christ, and committed the sin of murmuring against God.

Fifth, Israel committed the sin of murmuring against God. Notice what 1 Corinthians 10:10 has to say,

> Neither mummer ye as some of them murmured, and were destroyed by the destroyer.

Of all the sins Israel committed against God, murmuring against God was perhaps the worst of sins. It's an extremely dangerous thing to murmur against God. Murmuring against God is to complain about the way God wants to lead. God wants to lead us His way which is the best way. If we murmur about that, it is a sin against God. Actually, murmuring is complaining against God. We as Christians don't complain against God and get away with it. Notice the phrase in verse 10, "were destroyed by the destroyer."

The destroyer was probably the same angel that killed every first born in Egypt. Exodus 12:23 says,

> For the Lord will pass through and smite the Egyptians.

Then again it could have been the angel that smote seven thousand men because of David's census. Second Samuel 24:15–16 states,

> The Lord sent pestilence upon Israel from morning even to the time appointed, and there died of the people from Dan even to Beersheba seventy thousand men. And when the angel stretched out His hand upon Jerusalem to destroy it, the Lord repented of the evil ["the Lord repented" means God decided to not punish Israel any longer], and said it is enough.

Murmuring against God means grumbling or complaining against God, and anytime anyone grumbles against God's purpose and plan for their life sins against God. That was not a very wise thing for Israel to do. People don't get away with complaining, murmuring, or grumbling against God. God is very patient and gives every possible chance for His people to do the right thing, but when they persist in murmuring against Him, they are walking on dangerous grounds. Second Peter 3:9 said,

> The Lord is longsuffering [patient], not willing
> that any should perish, but that all should come
> to repentance.

Sometimes we need to repent of what we want to do and then listen to what God wants us to do.

Even in our day, the world is filled with arrogant, self-confident, complaining, and grumbling people who murmur against God. People have a choice, you know. You and I have a choice. It's good if we make the choice that God wants us to make, but if we make a bad choice, we will suffer for it.

By the way, do you know why Adam and Eve wanted to do what they did? They wanted to do what they thought would make them happy. They left God's domain and chose the world's system which is controlled by Satan. Many people leave God and embrace the lies and lusts of Satan who is the power of darkness. They take their anger out on the pastor, the church, and even God himself. It's not very wise to follow our own fleshly desires and murmur against God. God will severely chasten us if we don't turn and repent. He chastened Israel. We need to determine whether or not we are really following God, or if we are following our own worldly desires.

Following are two steps of sound advice: First, we must know we have had a genuine salvation experience with Jesus Christ. Second, we must know we have dedicated ourselves to God for a life of service doing whatever He chooses for us to do.

Paul warned us to stay on guard against Satan's worldly and deceptive devices. He tells us the things that happened to Israel is a warning to us to not let it happen to us. Notice 1 Corinthians 10:11,

> Now all these things happened unto them [Israel]
> for examples: and they are written for our admo-

nition, upon whom the ends of the world are come.

Let's not think we can live like Israel and not receive discipline from God. First Corinthians 10:12 says,

> Wherefore, let him that thinketh he standeth take heed lest he fall.

We are tempted every day to sin like Israel sinned, and if we are not cautious, we will fall into Satan's trap like Israel did. Overconfidence about one's own spirituality has caused many to fall. We in our own strength cannot stand against Satan. We must depend on God's power to sustain us. Notice 1 Corinthians 10:13,

> There hath no temptation taken you, but such as is common to man: but God is faithful, who will not suffer [allow] you to be tempted above that you are able; but will with the temptation also make a way to escape, that you may be able to bear it.

If you hear someone say, I was overcome by temptation. That is a lie. Don't believe a word of it. That person had better come up with some other excuse because the Bible clearly states that God allows only temptations we can handle. It's by yielding to the lust and desires of the flesh that cause people to fall into sin.

Paul goes on to warn Christians to flee from sin. Notice what he said in 1 Corinthians 10:14–15,

> Wherefore, my dearly beloved, flee from idolatry.
> I speak as a wise man, judge ye what I say.

Idolatry is idol worship. It's worshipping something or someone that means more to you than God, and that makes you an idolater. Paul's advice is to "flee from idolatry." Second Corinthians 13:5 informs others to

> Examine yourself, whether you be in the faith; prove your own selves. Know you not your own selves, how that Christ is in you, except you be reprobates?

We should examine ourselves occasionally.

Paul knew what was best for the Corinthian Christians because he had gotten his instructions from God. God knew what was best for them, and He knows what is best for us. We get our instructions from God's Word. Let's ask ourselves, Is there something or someone more important to me than Jesus Christ? If so, let's change that and put God first.

The second subject in the outline is found in 1 Corinthians 10:16–22, and it is about fellowship at the Lord's Supper.

First, notice 10:16,

> The cup of blessing which we bless, is it not the communion of the blood of Christ? The bread which we brake, is it not the communion of the body of Christ?

The Lord's Supper (Communion) is to be observed in remembrance of the death, burial, resurrection, and coming again of Christ. Never forget, the Communion service is a holy ceremony. The Lord's Supper is a commemoration of Jesus Christ giving His body and blood on the cross to provide salvation for us. Jesus said in John 6:51,

> I am the living bread which came down from heaven: if any man eats of this bread, he shall live forever, and the bread I give is my flesh, which I give for the life of the world.

Therefore, we are to participate in the Lord's Supper with a clean heart.

A person is not worthy to take the Lord's Supper if he or she has an idol that comes before Jesus. Occasionally, we need to run a spiritual diagnosis on ourselves to see if there is anything, or anyone, who takes priority over Jesus.

By the way, Catholics, Eastern Orthodox, Lutherans, Anglican, Episcopalians, and some Methodists believe the bread and wine, when blessed, turns to the literal body and blood of Christ. If that is true, then at the first Lord's Supper, Christ had to cut off a piece of His flesh and give it to His disciples to eat, and He had to catch some blood in a cup and give it to His disciples to drink. That didn't happen! Furthermore, that is gross and doesn't make sense at all. The bread and wine represent the body and blood of Christ. Matthew 26:26 states,

> As they were eating, Jesus took BREAD, and blessed it and break it, and gave to His disciples, and said, "eat ye all of it." And He took the cup, and gave thanks, and gave it to them, saying, 'this is my blood [represents my blood] of the new testament which is shed for many for the remission of sins.

The blood and body of Christ does not change from bread and wine to the literal body and blood of Christ. It is a representation of the blood and body of Christ.

First Corinthians 10:16–17 tells us when we participate in the Communion service, we identify with Christ in His death, burial, resurrection, and coming again. Notice verses 16–17,

> The cup of blessings which we bless, is it not the communion of the blood of Christ? The bread which we break, is it not the communion of the body of Christ? For we being many are one

bread, and one body, for we are partakers of that
one bread.

It may interest you to know the word *communion* means "agree-
ment, closeness, or togetherness—thus communion." All of us who
have been born again are combined members of God's family, and we
are identifying ourselves with Christ in His death, burial, resurrection, and coming again when we take part in the communion service.
We agree with Christ. To be more precise, believing and receiving the
sacrificial death, burial, and resurrection of Christ makes it possible
for us to become members of God's family.

The above Scripture shows that all born-again Christians,
regardless of what denomination they belong to, can come together
and participate in the communion service. It's not designed for one
group only, but designed for every born-again Christian. Notice the
phrase "We being many are one bread." That means all born-again
Christians are one in Christ, and all members of the family of God
can participate in the communion service together.

First Corinthians 11:28 tells us what we must do before taking
part in the Lord's Supper.

Let a man examine himself, and so let him eat of
that bread, and drink of that cup.

We must be honest about sins in our life, confess all known sin,
and repent of any sin we don't know about before taking part in the
Lord's Supper. No man should partake at the Lord's Supper without
examining himself first. There is a reason for that. First Corinthians
11:27 issued a warning to those who takes part in the Communion
service unworthy.

Wherefore, whosoever shall eat of this bread, and
drink this cup of the Lord, unworthily, shall be
guilty of the body and blood of the Lord.

To be guilty of the body and blood of Christ is to side with those who beat, torched, mutilated, and crucified Christ. What a wicked sin. Taking part in the Lord's Supper is a very serious offense if we are unworthy.

Communion service is a time of spiritual worship in which Christians get together to observe the death, burial, resurrection, and coming again of Jesus Christ. First Corinthians 11:26 said,

> For as often as you eat this bread, and drink this
> cup ye do show the Lord's death till He comes.

Notice how 1 Corinthians 10:18 comments on Israel eating the sacrifice in relation to taking part in the Lord's Supper.

> Behold Israel after the flesh: are they that eat of
> the sacrifice not partakers of the altar?

Someone said it this way, "In the Old Testament, sacrificing the offering was in behalf of all who ate. By such action, the people were identifying with the offering, and affirming their devotion to God to whom it was offered." When we partake of the Lord's Supper, we are identifying ourselves with the one who offered His body as a sacrifice for our sins.

In the following verses, Paul turns his attention to the wickedness of idol worship as opposed to worshipping the Lord at the Communion service. Some were worshipping idols instead of worshipping the Lord. Notice 10:19–20,

> What say I then? That the idol is anything, or
> that which is offered to idols is anything?

Of course, the idol is nothing, and that which is offered to an idol is nothing. An idol is only worldly things people worship. They are put before Jesus. On the other hand, worshipping the Lord at the Communion service is something important to God. It is a serious ceremony because Jesus is alive and deserves our worship. Notice 10:20,

> But, I say the things which the gentiles sacrifice they sacrificed to devils, and not to God: and I would not that ye should have fellowship with devils. You cannot drink the cup of the Lord, and the cup of devils: you cannot be partakers of the Lord's Table, and the table of devils.

If we have an idol that comes before Jesus, we are worshipping devils while at the same time claiming to be worshipping the Lord. God is a jealous God, and He will not share His worship with devils. Notice 10:21,

> Ye cannot drink the cup of the Lord, and the cup of the devil. Ye cannot be partakers of the Lord's table, and of the table of the devil.

Paul is saying we cannot worship the Lord and worship the devil at the same time. If our life is not where it should be, we are worshipping devils, but pretending to worship the Lord. Notice what 10:22 says,

> Do we provoke the Lord to jealousy? Are we stronger than He?

Communion is a time in which we direct our thoughts and feelings toward Jesus Christ and what He has done for us. Therefore, if we take part in the Lord's Supper unworthily, we are in danger of being severely chastened by the Lord. We must make sure we have repented and removed any sin that comes before Jesus. If we don't, we are guilty of the body and blood of Christ. In other words, we are siding with those who beat, bruised, mutilated, tortured, and crucified Christ. How dare anyone that calls themselves a Christian side with those who crucified Christ.

The cup represents the blood that Jesus shed to pay our sin debt which we could not pay. The bread represents the body of Jesus Christ that was broken for us. No bones were broken, but His flesh was broken when they beat and mutualized His body. He endured the punishment we deserved. Now we can be reconciled to God because of Him. We must make sure we are born again and have repented of any sin in our lives before taking part in the Communion service.

First Corinthians 10:23–33 is the third subject in our outline, and it is about eating meat offered to idols.

In our day, we don't have problems with eating meat offered to idols, but we do have problems with doing questionable things. I am not necessarily talking about eating meat offered to idols but doing questionable things that might offend our weaker brother or sister in Christ.

Notice 10:23,

> All things are lawful for me, but all things are not expedient [not suitable, not appropriate, not right]; all things are lawful for me, but all things edify not.

That Scripture is saying when we do something that is not appropriate in God's eyes, it is a sin. Paul is not saying an outright blatant sin is lawful for him to do. He is saying some questionable things are lawful, but he is saying he will not get involved in them because he could lead his sister or brother to follow his lead and sin. Paul is saying, "I could get involved in eating meat offered to idols," or in today's applicable language, I could get involved in a questionable practice and not sin, but offending a weaker Christian is a sin.

Consider the consequences of offending a weaker brother or sister in Christ. We cannot edify weaker Christians by flaunting our liberties. Paul said eating meat offered to idols or having a questionable practice will not edify others. There are a lot of things we could do and not feel condemned over it, but let's determine not to do those things because they might offend our weaker brother or sister in Christ. Paul presents four points from the above Scripture and from 10:24.

First,

All things are lawful for me.

He is talking about questionable things such as eating meat that had been offered to an idol or participating in some questionable practice.

Second,

All things are not expedient.

Expedient means "not appropriate, not exactly the best thing to do." It does not promote the welfare of our Christian brothers or sister in Christ. It does not edify Christ or our weaker brother and sister in Christ.

Third,

All things do not edify.

The word *edify* means "to build up in Christian knowledge and in love." We are to edify each other by restricting ourselves in our liberty, which will build believers up instead of offending them. When we allow ourselves to get involved in questionable practices, we may lead other Christians to do the same, thus causing them to sin and break fellowship with Jesus. When they get involved in questionable things, it could make them feel guilty, and it would be our fault. Love for our Christian brothers and sisters will prevent us from doing that.

Fourth, notice 1 Corinthians 10:24,

Let no man seek his own, but another man's wealth.

That is saying, if we seek the well-being of others instead of our own well-being, we will restrain ourselves from questionable things.

In the context of offending other Christians, this verse is telling us to avoid questionable things because it may lead our weaker brother or sister into what they consider sin. We are not to seek our own liberty in such things as eating meat offered to idols, but seek to lead other Christian friends in the path of righteousness. It is saying put others first. Look at each situation from your Christian brothers' and sisters' perspective and do things that will build them up. Don't do things that might lead them astray and cause them to sin.

First Corinthians 10:25–26 seems to contradict what Paul just taught. Paul just taught about restricting himself in his liberties, but he is not contradicting himself. Notice 10:25,

> Whatsoever is sold in the shambles [meat markets], that eat, asking no questions for conscience sake. For the earth is the Lords, and the fullness thereof.

Even though Paul is referring to eating meat that has been offered to idols, he is not contradicting himself at all. He is simply turning his attention from those who have liberties to the legalist who feel everything is wrong. Some put so many religious restrictions on themselves that there is no way they can keep them. Those imposing those rules on others don't even keep them themselves, because they can't. When people add a list of dos and don'ts to their Christianity, it becomes legalism. Legalism means strict adherence to self-imposed laws, rules, and regulations. Usually, it is referring to those who are trying to "working their way to heaven" by keeping those rules. Some who have had a genuine salvation experience get caught up in a false religion from some sincere person that believes they must do something to keep their salvation. They believe one must keep the rules, laws, and regulations to keep themselves saved.

Paul is speaking to the legalists in the Scripture verse above. He is saying when you go to the meat market to buy meat, do not ask if the meat has been offered to an idol, but just buy it and eat it. Notice how 1 Corinthians 10:26–27 puts it,

> For the earth is the Lords, and the fullness thereof. If any of them that believe not invite you to a feast, and you be disposed [inclined] to go, whatever is set before you, eat, asking no questions for conscience sake.

Paul is saying to the legalist, "Whatever is set before you, eat it, asking no questions." But 1 Corinthians 10:28–29 (below) tells us if a liberated person mentions the fact that the meat was offered in sacrifice to an idol, don't eat it.

> But if any man say unto you, this is offered in sacrifice to idols, eat not for his sake that showed it, and for conscience sake: for the earth is the Lord's and the fullness thereof. Conscience, I say, not thine own, but of the other [weaker brother]: for, why is my liberty judged [controlled by] another man's conscience.

The answer is, my liberty is controlled by my weaker brother's conscience because I don't want to cause him to sin.

It's very important we remember Paul is not just talking about eating meat offered to idols, per se, but is talking about any questionable practice we may be involved in. Some Christians are offended by other Christians getting involved in questionable things. If you take advantage of your Christian liberties, or if you don't, there are those who will speak badly about you. However, it is better to not get involved in a questionable practice that might offend your Christian brother or sister.

Notice 1 Corinthians 10:30,

> If I by grace be partaker, why am I evil spoken of for that for which I give thanks?

If you feel you're in God's will, and can give thanks for what you do, then do it to glorify God. If you cannot give thanks and glorify God in what you do, it is a sin and you should not do it. First Corinthians 10:31 says,

> Whether therefore you eat, or drink, or whatso-
> ever you do, do all to the glory of God.

That is the key that will keep you from stepping over the line into sin. I say again, if you cannot give God thanks for what you do, it is a sin and you should not do it.

As much as possible, we are not to offend the legalist Christian, nor the liberated Christian, but if we make a choice, give God thanks and do what God would approve of. The bottom line is to keep others in mind when we do what we do.

First Corinthians 10:32–33 concludes this chapter,

> Give none offence, neither to the Jew, nor to
> the gentile, nor to the church of God: Even as
> I please all men in all things, not seeking my
> profit, but seeking the profit of many, that they
> may be saved.

Seeking to bring the lost to Christ should encourage us to make the right choices in doing what we do, and love must be our motivating force. Notice Romans 1:1–3 and verse 6,

> Him that is weak in the faith receive ye, but not
> to doubtful disputation [don't doubt his salva-
> tion] For one believeth that he may eat all things:
> another, who is weak, eateth herbs. Let him that
> eateth despise him that eateth not: and let not
> him that eateth not judge him that eateth: for
> God hath received him...He that eateth, eateth
> to the Lord; for he giveth God thanks: and he

that eateth not, to the Lord he eateth not, and
giveth God thanks.

Knowledge and love should be the controlling factor in everything we do for the Lord and others. Allow me to suggest you study
chapter 8 along with this section above.

Chapter 11
Has Three Subjects

Verses 1–2 deal with following Paul as he follows Christ.
Verses 3–16 deal with long and short hair.
Verses 17–34 deal with worship and the Communion service.

Verses 11:1–2 is the first subject, and it deals with following Paul as he follows Christ.

Paul said in 11:1,

Be ye follower of me, even as I also am of Christ.

He put emphasis on following him because he followed Christ. The results are those who will follow him will follow Christ because Paul's main purpose was to follow Christ and point people to Him. We are not to blindly follow some minister just because he is a pastor or preacher, but most certainly follow Paul who received his instructions from God. God's Word came to Paul, and Paul passed it down to us. So when we follow the Word of God, we are following Christ. If we follow any pastor who is following Christ we need to follow him. Paul's advice came from the words God inspired him to write.

When we follow God's Word, we are following Paul as he followed Christ. Paul said in 1 Corinthians 11:2,

> Now I praise [sincerely honor] you brethren, that you remember me in all things, and keep the ordinances, as I delivered them to you.

We must know the Word of God before we can keep the ordinances of God and follow the person who preaches the Word of God. A good rule to go by is to listen to your pastor to see if he is preaching God's plan of salvation correctly. If he adds something that you must do or not do to obtain salvation, he is not of God. There is no doubt Paul preached the Word of God, so we are to follow his inspired words to follow Christ.

First Corinthians 11:3–16 is the second subject in the outline, and it deals with long and short hair.

The Bible gives four lines of authority that should settle the issue of men wearing short hair and women wearing long hair.

Allow me to skip ahead and insert verses 14 and 15 from this chapter. It shows the Bible is referring to long or short hair when it teaches about being covered or uncovered. Verse 14 says,

> Doeth not nature itself teach you, that if a man has long hair, it is a shame unto him.

Verse 15 says,

> But if a woman has long hair it is a glory to her: for her hair is given her for a covering.

There is no doubt the Bible is teaching men are to wear short hair and women wear long hair. Someone may say, "What difference does it make how men and women wear their hair?" It matters because women wearing long hair and men wearing short hair show they honor and keep God's line of authority.

There are three levels of authority men and women must know before they can understand why it's important to wear their hair the way the Bible teaches. Once we understand the three levels of authority in 11:3, we can understand why the Lord put restrictions on how women and men are to wear their hair. Notice 11:3,

> But I would have you know, that the head of
> every man is Christ; and the head of the woman
> is man; and the head of Christ is God.

Did you get that? "The head of the woman is man. The head of man is Christ. And the head of Christ is God." These three levels of authority show that Christ is the head of man, man is the head of woman, and God is the head of Christ. God invented these three levels of authority and set them in motion; it's left up to us to obey them or reject them. Some woman may say, "No man is going to be over me." It's not for us to question why God chose to do it that way. We are to do it and ask no questions. Paul received his instructions from God on how men and women are to wear their hair. Men and women who wear their hair the way God directs them shows they fit into God's line of authority. It reveals the position and purpose in God's rules of authority. The purpose is to show obedience to God by following His rules of authority.

Paul strongly emphasized that women should wear long hair to show her position in God's line of authority, and men are to wear short hair to show his position in God's line of authority. I'm not saying wearing long or short hair is an ordinance like baptism. However, if men or women do not keep these rules, they are rebelling against God.

Keep in mind, it was not Paul's idea to write these rules; it was God who inspired him to write it. So they are God's commandments. If anyone disobeys these rules, they are dishonoring their head in God's line of authority, and that is displeasing to God. That is not a very wise thing to do.

We are identifying with Christ in His death, burial, and resurrection when we are baptized in water. It's true, baptism in water will not save you. Neither will the way you wear your hair save you, but we are to be baptized in water to show our commitment to God and present a message that we identify with the death, burial, and resurrection of Christ.

When we keep these rules about the way we wear our hair, we show others we are following God's line of authority. We identify with God by the way we wear our hair. Baptism in water has nothing to do with salvation, but we are to obey God by being baptized in water to show we believe the Gospel, which is the death, burial, and resurrection of Christ. Likewise, wearing long or short hair has nothing to do with salvation, but we are disobeying God if we do not wear our hair the way the Bible teaches.

Notice the test God gives in 1 Corinthians 11:4. This verse deals with men wearing short hair. Jesus Christ is the head of the man, and man dishonors Jesus—his authority—when he prays while wearing long hair. Notice 1 Corinthians 11:4,

> Every man praying or prophesying, having his
> own head covered, dishonors his head.

Jesus Christ is the head of man. God is saying men are not to wear long hair because it dishonors his head Jesus Christ. That test is saying men are disobeying God's plan of authority if he wears long hair.

I have seen Christian men who sing Christin songs wearing long hair, and I have seen preachers wearing long hair. They either don't know the Bible they sing about, or preach about, or they don't care. If they knew their Bible and did care, they would know it's not God's will for men to wear long hair.

First Corinthians 11:5 deals with women wearing short hair.

> Every woman that prayeth or prophesieth with
> her head uncovered dishonors her head [her
> husband].

Verse 6 goes on to say,

For that is even all as if she were shaven.

Verse 6 is saying if a woman does not wear long hair to cover her head, she may as well shave her head. The women at the pagan temples in Corinth shaved their heads to advertise their permissive lifestyle. If Christian women understood God's line of authority, I am sure they would not want to disobey His rules of authority.

Notice 1 Corinthians 11:6–10 that tells us why men are to wear short hair and women are to wear long hair,

> If a woman is not covered, let her be shorn [she may as well shave her head]: but if it be a shame for a woman to be shorn or shaven, let her be covered. For the man ought not to cover his head, forasmuch as he is in the image and glory of God: but the woman is the glory of the man. For a man is not of the woman; but the woman of the man. For this cause aught, the woman to have power on her head because of the angels.

Some say Paul was a narrow-minded bigot that degraded women by saying the head of the woman is the man. Some even go so far as to claim men are superior to women. Paul did not say men are superior to women, nor did he degrade women. He is simply stating that in the beginning, God created the three levels of authority. The levels of authority in the beginning were: God the head of Christ, Christ the head of man, and man the head of the woman. I believe God established His line of authority to show He is a God of authority. He established these three lines of authority so we can show we love Him by obeying these lines of authority.

God sets the rules. It's not our option to pick and choose which rules we are to obey and which not to obey. We are to obey all of God's rules. God made the rules for women and men. God's rules are right whether we agree with them or not.

Christian women wore long hair in Paul's days to show they fit into God's line of authority. That rule has never changed; it is the same for today. God established that rule and has never changed it. I have never read in the Bible where God changed any of His rules. Therefore, we must say God has not changed His mind about men wearing short hair and women wearing long hair.

By the way, what I am about to say is very important. Most pictures you see of Jesus, the artists paint Him as having long hair. Jesus did not have long hair. You may say, "How do you know?" Because He would not make a rule that men wear short hair and then break His own rule.

Allow me to qualify what I am about to say in relation to women wearing long hair and men wearing short hair. We must ask ourselves, "How long is long, and how short is short?" If God had said long hair is six inches and short hair is one inch, that would make it easy to understand short/long hair, but the Bible does not give the exact lengths. The following is my opinion: I believe a woman's hair should be long enough to cover her ears and neck, and a man's hair should be short enough to expose his ears and neck.

You can understand long/short hair by the following illustration. If I should say I have a friend who lives ten miles down the road, but my wife has a friend who lives twenty miles down the road, whose friend lives closest to us? You would immediately say your friend. Did you have a problem in understanding whose friend lives closest. Likewise, the rule that men are to wear short hair and women are to wear long hair should be easy understood. Long is long and short is short. That makes it easy to choose what is long and what is short. Is that hard to understand?

Keep in mind, we are talking about Christian men and Christian women. We are not talking about unbelievers. We are not to gage our beliefs by the unbeliever's standards, nor give unbelievers standards to live by. God's standards are for God's children.

We don't know why God chose women to wear long hair and men to wear short hair other than to show our submission to God's line of authority. Frankly, it doesn't matter why, but it does matter about obeying God's rule of authority. What matters is we should be willing to do what the Lord wants us to do whether we understand it or not. If the Lord would say we need to stand on our heads three times a day, someone may say that doesn't make sense. To be sure, that wouldn't make sense. However, it's not a matter of making sense, but doing it if God says to do it. Allow me to give an illustration from the Bible that did not make sense, yet the people of Israel did it. Chapter 7 of Judges records an army of thousands and thousands that consisted of the Midianites, Amalekites, and all the armies of the east. Notice what Judges chapter 7 says,

> The Midianites and the Amalekites and all the children of the east lay along in the valley like grasshoppers for multitude: and their camels were without number, as the sand by the seaside for multitude.

Gideon with three hundred men had only trumpets and pitchers with lights in them to defeat that enormous army. That didn't make sense. How could they defeat such a large army that way? Nevertheless they followed God's instructions and did it. They were victorious, and God got the glory.

We don't know why God chose women to wear long hair and men to wear short hair. Why not the reverse? However, we do know one thing, it is God's will for men and women to show their place in God's line of authority by the way they wear their hair. If anyone would like to argue about that rule, don't argue with Paul argue with God, because Paul only wrote what God told him to write.

Some say women wearing long hair and men wearing short hair only applied to the times in which Paul lived. They say it was a custom in those days. If that be the case, one may pick and choose other parts of the Bible and say it does not apply to us today, but it was only a custom in the early days of Christianity. You can't change God's rules because we live in a different age. If you change the rules, you cut things out of the Bible you don't like and keep things you do like. That is interpreting the Bible allegorically, and that is wrong.

Well, the bottom line is, God requires women to wear long hair and men to wear short hair to show their line of authority God established. That's it. Women and men are to read it, believe it, practice it, and obey it.

Corinth had a women's liberal movement. We do too. It's been that way all down through the ages. The city of Corinth had pagan temples with women prostitutes as leaders. Those who patronized the temples worshipped the female goddess Aphrodite who was a symbol of love, sex, and fertility. Prostitutes made themselves available to all who wished to take part in their religious worship ceremonies. The women exposed their liberal lifestyle by the way they dressed and wore their hair. Historical researchers show that they wore skimpy clothing, and some even shaved their heads. Sounds like some women of our day, doesn't it? They clearly identified themselves as prostitutes and members of the women's lib movement. The church of Corinth had thrown off all restraints and started dressing like the prostitute temple women and men.

Please don't misunderstand me or misinterpret me. I'm not saying all women who wear short hair and all men who wear long hair are perverts. They are not depraved, unprincipled, and wicked. It's just that they don't understand what the Bible teaches on this subject. Many are Christians but ignorant of what the Bible teaches about long and short hair.

Paul was not prompted to write that women are second to men, but he did write that women were made second to man in God's line of authority. First Timothy 2:13 says,

Adam was first formed, then Eve.

In fact, God made the woman for the man, not man for the woman. That's not to say woman are inferior to men. Women are men's companions. A man is incomplete without a good woman in his life. The fact is women are weaker vessels. They are subject to be led astray, more so than man because they are the weaker vessel. I didn't say that; God did through Peter. First Peter 3:7 states,

> Likewise, ye husbands dwell with them according
> to knowledge, as unto the WEAKER VESSEL…

Why is it offensive when Bible teachers say women wearing long hair show her dedication to her husband and men wearing short hair show his dedication to Christ? Men are not superior to women, nor are women superior to men. Women and men show their place in God's line of authority by the way they wear their hair, and that is honoring to God.

First Corinthians 11:13 says.

> Judge yourselves: is it comely [proper] for a
> woman to pray unto God uncovered?

Paul is saying, is it proper for a woman to wear short hair when she prays? Paul answered his own question in 11:15,

> If a woman has long hair, it is a glory to her, for
> her hair is given to her for a covering.

Paul wrote under the inspiration of God that a woman dishonors her husband if she does not wear long hair. Her long hair shows she honors her husband and God by staying in her line of authority. So 11:3 gives the line of authority, which is God, Christ, man, and then women. We would not say Christ is superior to God, or man is superior to Christ, neither can we say men are superior to women. Women and men must give evidences of submission to their line of authority by the way they wear their hair. God set it up that way to remind us of His original plan—a plan of order.

God didn't make Eve to wear short hair like Adam, nor did God make Adam to wear long hair like Eve. Someone may say, "How do you know they wore their hair that way?" Well, God would not have made a man and a woman and then made them to be different from His rules of authority about wearing long and short hair. God made women beautiful, tender, delicate, and with long hair to symbolize her place in God's line of authority. God made man rough, rugged, and tough, with short hair to show his place in God's line of authority.

Someone put it this way: The first time Adam looked at Eve, he said, "WOOOMAN!" I don't know about that, but I do know Genesis 2:21–22 tells us God made Eve to be a help mate for Adam.

> And the Lord caused a deep sleep to fall upon Adam, and he slept: and He [God] took one of his ribs and closed up the flesh instead thereof. And the rib, which the Lord God had taken from the man, He made a woman, and brought her to the man."

Notice 1 Corinthians 11:8–10 again,

> For man is not of the woman; but the woman of the man. Neither was the man created for the woman; but the woman for the man. For this cause ought the woman to have power [long hair] on her head because of the angels.

These verses are saying women are to wear long hair to show their submissiveness to their line of authority—their husbands. Wow! There I said it! Women are to show their submission to their husbands by wearing long hair.

First Corinthians 11:8–10 is about women having power on her head because of the angels. It is teaching that women wearing long hair will not offend the most holy angels that watch over the church.

Allow me to pause a moment and add a thought here. We know God watches over us, but according to the Scriptures above, angels are watching over us too. They not only watch over us to protect us, they watch over us to see if we are doing what God expects of us. Women project the right image when they submit themselves to their head authority. They wear long hair as a symbol of that submission. They live that lifestyle because angels are watching. I personally believe God and angels are not the only ones watching us, but also those who have gone on before us. Hebrews 12:1 says,

> Seeing we are also compassed [surrounded] about with so great <u>CLOUD OF WITNESSES,</u> let us lay aside every weight and the sin that doeth so easily beset us, and let us run with patience the race that is set before us.

The cloud of witnesses could be those in Hebrews 11, or those who have gone on before us, including those in Hebrews 11. I believe it is the latter. No doubt angels are watching us. Matthew 18:10 said,

> Take heed that you do not despise one of these little ones, for I [Jesus] say unto you that in heaven their angels [angels of God's children] always see the face of my Father who is in heaven.

That means angels are watching over God's children. We are God's children if we have put our faith and trust in Jesus Christ and are born again.

Notice 1 Corinthians 11:11–12,

> Nevertheless neither is the man without the woman, neither the woman without the man, in the Lord. For as the woman is of the man, so is the man also by the woman; but all things of God.

These verses are saying men and women are equal in God's eyes. The man is not more important than the woman, neither is the woman more important than the man. Galatians 3:28 said,

> There is neither Jew nor Greek, there is neither bond nor free, for ye are one in Christ Jesus.

Did you get that? We are all one in Christ, therefore equal in God's sight.

When the role of men and women reverses, sin reigns. Why is that? Reversing God's role of authority is in violation of God's plan. Eve violated God's plan by eating the forbidden fruit and by enticing Adam to eat. Adam's act plunged the world into sin. God has a plan, and we must not violate his plan. We may wonder why His plan is the way it is. Frankly, we should not be concerned with that. What we need to be concerned about is to never violate God's plan.

Notice 1 Corinthians 11:14,

> Does not nature itself teach you, that, if a man
> has long hair, it is a shame unto him.

Men are to wear their hair short like godly men. Notice 1 Corinthians 11:15,

> But if a woman has long hair, it is a glory to her,
> for it is given to her for a covering.

Women are to wear their hair long like godly women. To me (notice I said, *to me*), it is degrading to see a man who professes to be a Christian wearing long hair, and it's just as degrading (to me) to see a woman who professes to be a Christian wearing short hair. They degrade their place in God's line of authority.

I'm not getting legalistic when I say women are to wear long hair and men are to wear short hair. If that was the case, it would not matter how you wear your hair. You would have an option to wear it long or short. It would be a personal thing. But it is not a personal thing. It is falling in line with God's standard of authority. The way Christians wear their hair has nothing to do with their salvation. I'm just saying, God's original plan was for a woman to wear long hair and men to wear short hair to show their submission to their authority. That plan was passed down to us, and we are to abide by it whether we like it or not. The way men and women wear their hair is for Christians only. Galatians 3:27 says,

> For as many of you as have been baptized unto Christ [baptized by the Holy Spirit into Christ], have put on Christ.

So this rule is for Christians only.
Notice 1 Corinthians 11:16,

> But if any man seems to be contentious [want to argue about it] we have no such custom, neither in the church of God.

Paul is not nullifying all he taught about long and short hair. This verse is saying, if anyone wants to argue about these Scriptures, go ahead and do it, but the church God established will not change its mind.

First Corinthians 11:17–34 is the third subject in the outline, and it deals with worship and the Communion service.

I have already written on this subject in chapter 10, but allow me to give some additional thoughts. It may benefit you to go back to chapter 10 and refresh your memory on this subject.

Christ designed two ordinances for the New Testament church—baptism and the Communion service. Some claim foot-washing is a church ordinance, but it's not. Foot washing was practiced by Jesus and His disciples to teach a living lesson on serving others. When we do a service to others, it's symbolic of washing their feet. Foot-washing is a picture of serving others, and it's important we practice that.

First Corinthians 11:17 is about the Lord's Supper—the Communion service,

> Now in this [in the way they were observing the Communion service] I praise you not, that you come together for the better, but for the worse.

When the church of Corinth came together for the Communion service, they were not better for it but worse for it, because of the way they were observing it. The way they conducted the Communion service was a disgrace to God.

To understand the mistake they made, we first need to understand the "love feast." The New Testament church developed a special fellowship meal that came to be called the *"love feast."*

Jude (the one-chapter book) calls it *"feasts of charity"*—thus, love feast. After observing the love feast, the church of Corinth observed the Communion service. However, what supposed to have ended with a time of observing the Lord's death, burial, resurrection, and coming again turned out to be a glutton drunken party. The love feast was not designed to be a drunken party, but a time of fellowship, love, respect, and praise to Jesus for what He had accomplished through the church. It was to be observed totally apart from the Communion service. However, the church of Corinth combined the love feast with the Communion service, and it turned into an unrestrained party.

Modern churches of today observe the love feast, or what we now call a fellowship meal. We are not like the church in Corinth, but the mistake we make is that our conversations consist of everything but what it was first intended to include—love, respect, and praise to Jesus for what He has accomplished through the church. The fellowship meal is designed to celebrate Jesus Christ, but it has turned into a time of ordinary fellowship. Our fellowship meals are far removed from its original purpose. It has been my experience we don't celebrate Jesus Christ and talk about what He has done for the church. We talk about everything else. A fellowship meal is okay and talking about various things is okay, but wouldn't it be great to have a fellowship meal and talk about love, respect, and praise to Jesus for what He has done for the church? We have designed our fellowship meals just to fellowship with each other.

Paul is saying to the Corinthian church, "God is displeased in the way you conduct the love feasts and Communion service." He proceeded to point out their mistake and correct it. Notice 1 Corinthians 11:18–19,

> For first of all, when you come together in the church, I hear that there are divisions among you; and I partly believe it; for there must also be heresies among you, that they which are approved may be made manifest among you.

Paul is saying, "If there are divisions among you, that is an indication heresy is among you, and since there is heresy among you, it reveals the genuine Christians."

The Corinthian church was split over doctrinal issues. There were some members disconnected from the real purpose of Jesus Christ, the Communion service, and the love feast. They had joined the church for other reasons than to worship and fellowship with like believers. Jude calls them "spots in your feasts of charity" (Jude verse 3).

Paul points out that the love feast was not to be part of the Communion service. They evidently connected the love feast and Communion service together and turned it into a drunken unrestrained party. The love feast and the Communion service became so perverted it resulted in a sinful mockery of the Lord Jesus Christ.

Can you imagine observing the Communion service when it is turned into a drunken party? The Corinthian church was blaspheming the name of Christ. Paul severely rebukes them. First Corinthians 11:20–23 says,

> When you come together in one place that is not to eat the Lord's Supper. For in eating each one taketh before others his own supper: and one is

hungry, and another is drunk. What? Have you
not houses to eat and drink in? Or despise you
the church of God or shame them that have not.
What shall I say to you? Shall I praise you in this?
I praise you not.

Instead of waiting for all to arrive at the love feast and
Communion service, some selfishly indulged themselves with food
and drink before they came. A careful reading of 11:20–23 shows
that when the first-comers arrived, some were hungry and others were drunk. Some were intoxicated before they came to the
Communion service and love feast. I can't imagine a person taking
part in a Communion service or a church fellowship meal when he
is drunk. To say the least, it would be a disgusting mess and blasphemous to the cause of Christ.

This information Paul gave to the Corinthian church on the
order of the Communion service did not apply to them only but
applies to us as well. This information was not something new
Paul thought up, but information he had already mentioned in 1
Corinthians 10:16–17. You may want to go back and read that. Paul
filled them in on the purpose of the love feast and how to celebrate it
when they gathered together for the Communion service.

A Communion service is one of the most sacred, holy, and sol-
emn services one can participate in. It is done in commemoration of
the death, burial, resurrection, and return of Christ. It is ultimately
important we observe it in the way Paul instructed us to observe it.
Paul received his instructions from God, and when we obey Paul's
instructions, we obey God's instructions.

First Corinthians 11:23–25 tells us how Paul received his
instructions.

For I have received from the Lord that which I
also delivered unto you. That the Lord Jesus in
the same night in which He was betrayed took
bread, and when He had given thanks, He break
it, and said, Take, eat, this is my body, which is

broken for you: this do in remembrance of Me. After the same manner also He took the cup, when He had supped, said, this cup is the New Testament [new covenant] in my blood; this do you as often as you drink it, in remembrance of Me. For as often as you eat this bread, and drink this cup, you do show the Lord's death till He comes.

The instruction seen in these Scriptures describes the upper-room meeting where Jesus and His disciple met for the last time on this earth. First Corinthians 11:23 tells us this happened the same night in which He was betrayed by Judas.

This was the first Communion service and Christ's last meeting with his disciples. That Communion service was a performance of the Gospel—the death, burial, resurrection, and coming again of Christ. It presented a picture of the Gospel in its entirety. That is why it is so sacred.

The word *broken* in 11:24 (above) refers to Christ's body being broken, not His bones, just his body. It's referring to the lacerations, savage, barbaric, and brutal beating He suffered before His crucifixion. It refers to the blood Jesus shed for us in paying our sin debt. Revelation 5:9 said,

> Thou art worthy…for thou hast redeemed us by thy blood.

Revelation 1:5 said,

> Unto Him (Jesus) that loves us and washed us from our sins in His own blood.

First Peter 1:18–19 said,

> Ye were not redeemed with corruptible things, as silver and gold...but by the precious blood of Christ.

First John 1:7 says,

> The blood of Jesus Christ cleanseth us from all sins.

There is an old song authored by Elisha A. Hoffman (1878) that goes like this:

> Have you been to Jesus for the cleansing power, are you washed in the blood of the Lamb, are you fully trusting in His grace this hour, are you washed in the blood of the Lamb?

We who have received Jesus as or Saviour have been washed in the blood of the Lamb. The blood of Jesus Christ cleanses us from all sins. The above song reminds me that we are not only washed in the blood of the lamb, but we are looking forward to the coming again of the Lamb—the Lord Jesus Christ.

First Corinthians 11:27–34 presents the requirements one must meet before taking part in the Communion service. The Communion service is a wonderful time for the church to come together in singleness of mind, reflecting on Jesus and His coming again. However, that was not the case when the church of Corinth met. First Corinthians 11:27 says,

> Whosoever shall eat this bread, and drink this cup of the Lord, unworthily, shall be guilty of the body and blood of Christ.

The word *unworthily* means "those who live a life of sin like getting drunk and being indifferent to what the Communion service is all about." They are unworthy to take part in the Communion service.

Some churches of today have an "o-hum" attitude about the Communion service. It's as though they are saying, "Oh well, time for the Communion service again, so let's get this thing over with." If people cannot come to the Communion service without knowing they are saved, without knowing there is no sin in their lives, and without the "o-hum" attitude about the Communion service, they are not worthy to partake of the Communion service. In reality, they are guilty of the body and blood of Christ. The phrase *guilty of the body and blood of Christ* means "he/she is mocking the sacrificial death of Christ and siding with those who crucified Him." The Communion service is a sacred service to the Lord, and to profane or desecrate it is extremely dangerous. So it is imperative we examine ourselves first before we take part in the Communion service. Notice 11:28–30,

> But let a man examine himself, and so let him eat of that bread, and drink of that cup; for he that eats and drinks unworthy, eats and drinks damnation [judgment] to himself, not discerning the Lord's body. For this cause, many are weak and sickly, and many sleep [many are dead].

Paul said, examine yourself to see if there is anything in your life that is not right between you and God. It is time to take inventory of your life. It is a time to survey every aspect of your life to see if there is any hidden sin you're holding on to. If you're not sure, ask God to reveal any sin that you may repent of it. If there is ever a time pastors should give an invitation to confess sins, it is before participating in the Communion service. Therefore, *many sleep* means "whoever eats and drinks unworthy is in danger of death."

I believe the word *damnation* in the above Scripture is referring to God judging and chastening those who partakes of the

Communion service unworthily. It is not referring to eternal damnation in hell. A born-again Christian can never be damned into hell. Nevertheless, he or she who eats and drinks at the Communion service unworthy displeases God and God chastens them because they committed a wicked sin. Furthermore, those who eat and drink unworthy take sides with those who crucified Christ.

Notice 11:31–32,

> If we would judge ourselves, we should not be
> judged. But when we are judged we are chastened
> of the Lord, that we should not be condemned
> with the world.

When we let God reveal sins in our lives, He will lead us to repent and make us fit subjects to partake of the Communion service. We will not be judged like those of the world. However, if we refuse to repent, we will be judged by the Lord and, therefore, be chastened. Both *condemned* and *damnation* in the Scriptures above mean chastening. Those who have an indifferent attitude toward the Communion service God will severely chasten for desecrating and profaning the Communion service. In many cases some even die. Notice verse 30,

> For this cause, many are weak and sickly...and
> many sleep [many die].

First Corinthians 11:33–34 sum up our obedient requirements for taking part in the Communion service, and it finishes up chapter 11.

Wherefore, my brethren, when you come together to eat [to partake of the Communion service], tarry one for another. And, if any man is hungry, let him eat at home; that you do not come together unto condemnation [chastening of God]. And the rest will be set in order when I come.

Chapter 12
Has Four Subjects

Verses 1–3 deal with spiritual gifts and ministry.
Verses 4–7 are about using spiritual gifts.
Verses 8–11 give names of spiritual gifts.
Verses 12–32 show the church is one body in Christ.

Chapter 12 and chapter 14 deal with spiritual gifts, ministries, names of spiritual gifts, the church being one body in Christ, prophecy being the best gift, unfamiliar tongues, how gifts must be used, and how women must use their gifts in the church. However, chapter 13 (the love chapter) is tucked in between these two chapters—chapter 12 and 14. Why is that? We shall see when we get to chapter 13. Let's look at chapter 12 first.

First Corinthians 12:1–3 is the first subject in the outline, and it deals with spiritual gifts and ministries.

Verse 12:1 says,

> Now concerning spiritual gifts, brethren I would not have you ignorant.

The reason Paul wrote about spiritual gifts is that some in the Corinthian church misunderstood, misused, and some even counterfeited these gifts. Those who wrote to Paul had many questions. They wanted to understand the kinds of gift that was available to them and what purpose they had in ministry. Paul informed them, as he did to Christians in other places, that everyone does not have the same gifts. Romans 12:4 said,

> For as we have many members in the body [that is, in the body of Christ] but not all members have the same office [gifts].

There were diversities of gifts. Some had recognizable gifts and others did not.

All too often, in today's Christian circles, we place certain individuals in a higher echelon because they have observable gifts that appeals to the public. That often makes the person proud. Many Christians have observable gifts that others can see, admire, and desire. Pride could be the motivation force behind observable gifts. That is not always true, but it is true with some. Pride is one of Satan's most used tools. The Holy Spirit chose to introduce spiritual gifts to the body of Christ [all Christians] with a warning against pride. Proverbs 16:18 says,

> Pride goes before destruction, and haughty spirit before a fall.

No Christian should boast about their observable gift, for it's God who give gifts, and He can take them away.

The Corinthian church didn't understand God's purpose in spiritual gifts; neither do we fully understand God's purpose in spiritual gifts. Paul did not want the Corinthian church to be ignorant about spiritual gifts, nor does he want us to be ignorant about spiritual gifts. He wanted the Corinthian church to understand spiritual gifts from God's perspective, and he wants us to understand spiritual gifts from God's perspective. Gifts are for edifying Christ and promoting the cause of the church—the body of Christ. So at the beginning, let's get it right about spiritual gifts.

Notice 12:2,

> Ye know that ye were Gentiles, carried away unto
> dumb idols, even as you were led.

Paul is saying, there was a time you were ignorant about spiritual gifts. Most of the members in the church of Corinth consisted of Gentile converts. They were converted out of a paganism and knew very little about spiritual gifts. They were once non-Christian Gentiles carried away from God's truth to worship dumb idols. Paul is saying you are not to worship dumb idols after you are born again.

A preacher friend explained the Corinthian church situation in worshipping dumb idols like this:

> Incredibly, some church members in Corinth
> were mimicking certain demonic and bizarre
> practices of the mystic religions in which they
> had been formerly involved. They probably
> brought it into Corinth from the area they for-
> merly lived. The practice of ecstasy, considered to
> be the highest expression of religious experience,
> involving supposed supernatural interaction with
> deity, induced through frenzy hypnotic chants
> and ceremonies, made them subjects to the dev-
> il's invasion. The practice frequently included
> drunkenness and sexual orgies.

They worshipped dumb idols.
Exodus 32:5–6 gives an example of worshipping dumb idols.

> And when Aaron saw it [the golden calf he made],
> he built an altar before it: and Aaron made proc-
> lamation, and said, "Tomorrow is the feast of the
> Lord." And they rose up early on the morrow,
> and offered burnt offerings, and brought peace

offerings: and the people set down to eat and
drink and rose up to play.

They were worshipping dumb idols by participating in their
drunken, perverted, sexual orgies worshipping the golden calf—a
dumb idol. They must have thought, since they offered their burnt
offerings and peace offerings, their shenanigans were all right.
However, 1 Corinthians 10:7–8 said,

> Neither be you idolaters, as were some of them,
> as it is written. The people set down to eat and
> drink and rose up to play. Neither let us commit
> fornication, as some of them committed and fell
> in one day three and twenty thousand.

There had been at least 320,000 who died because they worshipped dumb idols like the golden calf.

The Corinthian church leaders faced a situation that demanded
attention. That is why someone wrote to Paul for his advice. They
wanted to know the truth about spiritual gifts and ministries. Notice
how Paul addressed their problem.

> Wherefore I give you to understand, that no man
> speaking by the Spirit of God calls Jesus accursed:
> and that no man can say Jesus is Lord, but by the
> Holy Spirit. (1 Corinthians 12:3)

Evidently, the Corinthian church had some new Gentile converts who had formerly patronized the pagan temples and worshipped dumb idols in their religious rituals. They introduced it into
the Corinthian church. As you may recall, the pagan temples had
all kinds of weird and bazar forms of worship. They had male and
female prostitutes that manned their temples, and these prostitutes
led people to take part in their sexual orgies. The Corinthian church
separatists would give themselves over to perverted demonic spirits

in practicing pagan temple radicalism. Their type of worship was blasphemous to Christ because they were worshipping idols.

Someone may say, "We don't have that problem today." Maybe not in that exact manner as the Corinthian church did, but many churches do have that problem, by the way they interpret the Bible and Christianity.

> Beloved, believe not every spirit, but try the spirits whether they are of God: because many false prophets are gone out into the world. (1 John 4:1)

> God is a Spirit: and they that worship Him must worship Him in spirit and in truth. (John 4:24)

There are many spirits in the world, but only one true Holy Spirit.

> Now the Spirit [that is the Holy Spirit] speaketh expressly [speaks very specifically, very clearly, very plain], that in the latter times some shall depart from the faith giving heed to seducing spirits and doctrines of devils. (1 Timothy 4:1)

Many religions and false teachers in our day have departed from God's Spirit. They worship and follow evil spirits while they pretend to be worshipping God. It has always been that way, but it is getting worse in these last days.

Many church members and church leaders of our day came out of ungodly lifestyles and hold the intuitive self-imposed belief that they have all knowledge about gifts. Therefore, they want to use their "spiritual gifts" to their advantage, to promote their cause and make money. They do not have the spiritual gifts that come from God, but claim to have the Spirit of God leading them. They claim to be preaching and teaching by the Spirit of God but all the while blaspheming the name of Jesus Christ. Some even hold to the traditional belief of Gnosticism, which is an intuitive belief that all things are evil, even Christ. They practiced what they believe and blasphemed Christ.

Gnostics in Paul's day were those of a select few who embraced the heresy that the world and everything in it was evil, including Jesus Christ. They claimed that people are evil, trees are evil, rocks are evil, dirt is evil, and everything and everybody are evil. They believed the spirit of Jesus left His body before He died, thereby leaving Him to die as a cursed evil man. That was the epitome of blaspheming Christ.

Whatever unbelievers or religious people have to say about Jesus Christ is the test of whether he is speaking by the Holy Spirit or by the spirit of Satan. Many speak evil of Jesus Christ, even in this day and time. Most cult religions are accepted by the world of unbelievers. Christianity and Christ are evil spoken of. The world and even most governments do not accept Jesus or Christianity.

Notice the phrase in 11:3,

> For no one can say Jesus is Lord but by the Holy
> Ghost.

When someone preaches, teaches, or speaks contrary to the Scriptures, they are not of God. The Holy Spirit is not ruling and reigning in their lives. They are of the devils. They do not have or understand God's spiritual gifts and ministries. Those who preach a half message of health, wealth, and prosperity are not preaching all of God's Word. Their preaching is done for profit and gratification. Those who preach that kind of messages are saying God wants to heal everybody, prosper everybody, and give everybody everything they ever wanted. They are not preaching God's Word. True preaching and true biblical teaching is validated by the Scriptures. The Scriptures say to "reprove," "rebuke," and then "exhort." There is a time for exhorting, but not all the time. If preaching glorifies Jesus Christ as Saviour, Lord, and Master, and if it is teaching Christians how to live, it is from God.

You can now see why the church of Corinth had so many questions about spiritual gifts and ministers.

First Corinthians 12:4–7 is the second subject in the outline, and it is about using spiritual gifts.

Allow me to comment on several things before I tackle this subject of the names of spiritual gifts.

Notice 12:4.

> Now there are diversities of gift, but the same
> Spirit.

Spiritual gifts differ, but there is only one Holy Spirit that distributes these gifts. It's the Holy Spirit who works through us to utilize gifts. Notice 12:5–6,

> There are diversities of administrations, but the
> same Lord; and there are diversities of operations,
> but it is the same God which worketh in all.

Whatever gifts we have, it is God who works in us to utilize these different gifts.

Spiritual gifts are not natural talents people are born with, but supernatural talents that can only be explained as a supernatural gift from God Almighty. God gives gifts that the body of Christ might profit. Notice 12:7,

> But the manifestation of the Spirit is given to
> every man to profit withal.

Gifts and ministries seem to fall into two categories—speaking and serving. They are given to edify the body of Christ.

I know a couple of preachers that do an excellent job in edifying the body of Christ by their preaching, yet they have no special talent that would help them preach. They have no educational training for the ministry, but they can edify God's church like no other. By the world's standards they should not be preaching, yet both have an amazing ability to point people to Jesus and edify the body of Christ. I heard one of them preach a message from Romans 8:17. He read his text verse like this:

Hairs of God and Joint hairs with Jesus Christ.

Wait a minute. I'm not putting a premium on ignorance. I'm just saying God can and does use the most unlikely candidates that are fully committed to Him. Some say D. L. Moody was such a preacher. He moved England and America toward Jesus. His wit and wisdom were astounding.

Moody stood one day to preach, and someone handed him a note that had only one word—*fool*. Moody held the note up and said, "This is the strangest note I have ever received. It has only one word—*fool*." He went on to say, "I have received many notes from people who forgot to sign their name when they wrote the note, but this is the first note I have ever received where a person signed his name, but forgot to write the note."

Some preachers have a shrewd ability to preach that can only be attributed to God who gave them the gift of preaching. Preaching is not a natural talent, but a gift from God.

The two preachers I mentioned above realize they could not preach without God's gift of preaching. Perhaps that is why they are successful in the ministry. In fact, to be a successful preacher for God, you must totally depend on Him.

The Bible recorded many people that God gave special abilities for speaking. Moses is a good example. The story of Moses is found in Exodus 4. God appeared to Moses in a burning bush and told him to go to Egypt and deliver his people from bondage. Here is what Moses said:

O! My Lord, I am not eloquent...but I am slow
of speech and slow of tongue. (Exodus 4:10)

Then God said,

> Is not Aaron the Levite thy brother? I know he
> can speak well...he shall be your spokesman to
> the people. (Exodus 4:14)

When you study the life of Moses, you will find he did all the speaking when he arrived in Egypt. His gift was not a natural talent, but a supernatural gift from God.

Do you know the devil can mimic God's preachers? Evangelist Walter Burrell preached nine years but did not know Jesus Christ as his Saviour. He graduated from Bob Jones University and preached what he heard Bob Jones preach. It really worked. He even witnessed people coming to Christ. He couldn't tell them how to be saved because he was not saved himself, so he asked others to talk with them.

One day Walter decided to throw his Bible in the trash and go his way. Before he did, a friend asked him to lead music in a revival campaign. Walter didn't want to but reluctantly agreed because he was asked by a friend. He made it through the week without being moved, so he said to himself, "Tomorrow I'm throwing my Bible in the trash and quitting the ministry." Upon leaving the meeting that last night, a lady met Walter and the evangelist in the parking lot. She was quite concerned about her disabled husband that was unsaved, and she asked the evangelist and Walter to follow her home and talk with him. Before Walter could say no, the evangelist said, "Yes, Walter and I will follow you home and talk with your husband."

When the evangelist told the lady's husband how to be saved, Walter was sitting in the corner of the house, but listened intently. Walter seemed to hear the Lord say, "Walter, it's now or never." That night as he heard the evangelist give the Gospel to the lady's husband, he repented and gave his life to Jesus Christ. He asked Jesus to come into his life and save him.

Walter didn't change his message because he was already preaching the Gospel. But from then on, he preached what the Holy Spirit gave him to preach instead of preaching what he heard Bob Jones preach. His preaching influenced thousands to come to Christ for salvation. In fact, my oldest daughter was saved under his ministry. God will bless His Word. Isaiah 55:11 says,

> So shall my word be that goeth forth out of my mouth: it shall not return unto me void, but it shall accomplish that which I please, and it shall prosper in the thing wherein I sent it.

Don't misunderstand me. I'm not saying unbelievers are called to preach, but if you have listened to TV preachers that are unsaved, but have large campaigns, you will agree with me that many people in their campaigns seem to give their life to Christ. I'm just saying unsaved people can mimic God's preachers. Almost all unsaved preachers preach a false message. It's the Word of God that leads people to Christ. Unsaved people do not have the Spirit of God to give them their messages. They must get it from some other source, like a true God-called preacher. False prophets can mimic God's preachers but almost always put a slant on their message that is not scripturally correct. First John 4:1 said,

> Beloved, believe not every spirit, but try the spirits whether they are of God: for many false prophets [preachers] are gone out into the world.

There is a great deal of difference between demonic preaching and someone who preaches a message from God. Those who get their messages from God preach the truth and God honors the truth.

There is a story in Acts 8 about a man named Simon who was a preacher, but was not a believer in Christ. Simon was a sorcerer. A sorcerer is one who practices black magic and wizardry. He had deceived the people of Samaria into believing he was a great man sent from God. He preached and even performed miracles by his demonic sorcery, and all of Samaria believed in him. Philip met Simon in Samaria, but when Philip performed miracles like casting out evil spirits, healing the lame, and other miracles, Simon made a false profession of faith. He wanted to perform those miracles for his own profit, so he offered the apostles money to give him that gift. But Peter who was with Philip said to him,

> Thy money perishes with thee, because thou hast thought the gift of God may be purchased with money. Thou hast neither part nor lot in this matter: for thy heart is not right in the sight of God. (Acts 8:20–21)

Then Simon begged the apostles to pray for him. Many Bible teachers believe Simon was truly sincere and eventually gave his heart and life to Jesus Christ. One thing we do know about Simon is, he performed miracles while being an unbeliever. The gift he used was not from God.

Verses 8–11 is the third subject in the outline, and it gives names of spiritual gifts.

Spiritual gifts are freely given to those whom God chooses, but not to unbelievers. There are many kinds of gifts God gives to His people. First Corinthians 12:8–10 comments on the different kinds of gifts and their purpose in ministry.

First, the first two gifts are wisdom and knowledge and are found in 12:8,

> For to one is given by the Spirit the word of wisdom: and to another the word of knowledge by the same Spirit.

The gift of "wisdom" is to know God's Word, and the gift of "*knowledge*" is to know how to tell others about God's gift of salvation. The Bible makes it clear that those who preach must speak the knowledge and wisdom of God with words. Notice what 1 Peter 4:11 has to say,

> If any man speaks let him speak as the oracles of God; [Oracles means God's Word]. If any man ministers, let him do it as of the ability God giveth: that God in all things may be glorified through Jesus Christ to who be praise and dominion forever ever and ever. Amen.

The best example I could find on this is about Jesus, and it is in Mark. Notice what Mark said,

> When the Sabbath day was come, He [Jesus] began to teach in the synagogue: and many [after] hearing Him were astonished, saying. From whence hath this man these things? And what wisdom is this which is given unto Him, that even mighty works are wrought by His hands? (Mark 6:2)

It was no accident that the word *wisdom* is placed in the Bible. God uniquely chose to show us that His wisdom cannot be understood until we come to know Jesus Christ as our Saviour. God's wisdom is exclusively hidden from unbelievers. In 1 Corinthian 2:7 Paul said,

> We speak the wisdom of God in a mystery, even the HIDDEN WISDOM, which God ordained before the world unto our glory.

It's no wonder Hollywood movies, sitcoms, and public communication sources get it wrong when it comes to scriptural accuracy. Most of them are unbelievers. They can't understand God's wisdom.

God's wisdom is foreign to them, and they cannot understand it. Second Corinthians 4:4 says,

> The god of this world [Satan] has blinded the
> minds of them that believe not.

Their minds are blind to God's wisdom. God's preachers hurl forth God's wisdom when they preach the Gospel, but the unbeliever who rejects God cannot understand it.

Notice again the phrase in 12:8,

> To another [is given] the word of knowledge by
> the same Spirit.

This Scripture is referring to the understanding of God's Word. Someone said to me, "I don't need any education to preach." Perhaps not, but it's very dangerous not to be knowledgeable of God's Word, because those who are uneducated in God's Word are the ones more likely to start religious cults. It is God's will we get a good education in His Word. There are many great Christian colleges and seminaries out there. Any fundamental preacher that has been to a fundamental Bible college or seminary can give you that information. It's important you get a good education before you embark on a ministry. In fact, 2 Peter 1:5 says,

> Add to your faith virtue, and to virtue knowledge.

How can we get knowledge if we do not go to where knowledge is found? I know we need to study God's Word on our own and apply it to our lives personally, but we need a formal education in God's Word in order to help others. Preachers whom God calls need the fundamentals of Christian doctrine from a good, reputable Christian high school, college, or seminary. Most importantly, when God calls you into some special ministry, such as pastoring, you most certainly need a seminary education. There are many problems arise which you will have no clue how to solve it if you do not have training in that area. You can get that training in a good reputable seminary.

Furthermore, preachers need a good library from those who spent their lives in studying God's Word and writing books and commentaries. The Bible makes it very clear that preachers are to preach God's Word, not his own opinions. To avoid preaching his own opinion, a preacher must be educated in God's Word. First Peter 4:11 said,

> If any man speaks let him speak the oracles [the words] of God.

Second Timothy 4:2 says,

> Preach the word; be instant in season and out of season; reprove, rebuke, and exhort with all long-suffering (with patience) and DOCTRINE.

Paul said in 1 Corinthians 9:16,

> Woe is me if I preach not the gospel.

Someone said to Dr. John R. Rice, "God doesn't need your education." Dr. Rice responded with, "Neither does God need your ignorance." The truth is, God doesn't need anyone. He can get along without any of us, but He can use those more effectually who have a good education in God's Word. In Ephesians 3:3 Paul said,

> He [God] hath made known unto me the mystery.

The mystery is about the death, burial, resurrection, and the coming again of Christ. You learn that by studying the Word of God.

Some preachers claim they get their messages directly from heaven. That's a lie. We get God's messages by studying His revealed words in the Bible and by using resources God provides. Anything short of preaching God's Word results in false doctrine.

Second, another gift called the gift of faith is found in Chapter 12:9,

> To another [is given] faith by the same Spirit.

Did you know you could not come to Jesus for salvation if God did not give you the faith to believe on Him? Paul said in Galatians 2:20,

> And the life which I now live in the flesh I live by the faith of the Son of God, who loved me, and gave Himself for me.

Notice Paul did not say, "I live by my faith," but said,

> I live by the faith of the Son of God.

Paul is saying he lives by the faith given to him by Jesus Christ. Therefore, a person cannot come to Jesus for salvation unless He gives him faith to believe. You might say, "How do I get that faith?" When you hear a God-called preacher preach God's Word, you receive faith to believe.

> Faith comes by hearing, and hearing by the word of God. (Romans 10:17)

God's Word brings faith that leads to salvation. So it is ultimate important preachers get their messages from the Word of God. When you hear the Word of God, you are given the faith that brings you to salvation.

Allow me to make a comment that might sound like a contradiction to what I have written. What about those who have never heard a Gospel message, have never seen a Bible, or have never heard the name of Jesus? Will they die and go to hell? They will if they don't respond to God's witnesses. Romans 1:20 says,

> For the invisible things of Him are clearly seen,
> being understood by the things that are made,
> even His eternal power, and Godhead; so that
> they are without excuse.

The answer is, people who have never heard a Gospel message have never seen a Bible, nor ever heard the name of Jesus are without excuse. Acts 1:8 says,

> You shall receive power when the Holy Spirit
> is come upon you and you shall be witnesses...
> unto the uttermost parts of the earth.

That is our job. But Acts 14:17 says,

> He [God] left *not* himself without a witness.

What or who is God's witness? His creation. God's eternal power and Godhead are clearly seen by the things that He made. The things God made are His witnesses. So the fact is, no one can say they did not know. God left them a witness in the things He made. You can see God in everything He made. So mankind is without excuse. God made His witnesses at the same time He created the earth and everything on it.

Now back to the gift of faith. If you are "saved by grace through faith" (Ephesians 2:8), then what must your faith be in? Does your faith have to be in good works to save you? Does your faith have to be in a religion to save you? Does your faith have to be in baptism to save you? Does your faith have to be in church membership to save you? Does your faith have to be in keeping the Sabbath to save you? Does your faith have to be in Mohammed to save you? Does your faith have to be in Buddhism, Hinduism, or any other religion to save you? None of the above will save you. If the object of your faith is not in Jesus Christ and His sacrificial death on the cross for your sins, you do not have saving faith. Ephesians 2:8 states,

> For by grace you are saved through faith [faith that Jesus Christ died for you]; and that not of yourself: it is a gift of God.

Acts 16:31 states,

> And they [Paul and Silas] said, believe on the Lord Jesus Christ, and thou shalt be saved.

Three, another gift called the gift of healing is found in chapter 12:9.

> To another [is given] the gift of healing by the same Spirit.

The gift of healing is grossly misunderstood. In fact, no preachers or individuals have the gift of healing in our day. In New Testament times the gift of healing was a temporary gift given to the Apostles to authenticate Christ as the Messiah. I know God can and does heal in our day, but the gift of healing by so-called healing preachers means they are fakes, frauds, scammers, and religious shysters. Men and women that choose the so-called ministry of healing do it for money. The gift of healing in Bible times came to special people to authenticate Christ as the Messiah. If anyone is healed today, it is God who does the healing. God does not give the gift of healing to so-called healing preachers.

Philip went to Samaria to preach and perform miracles, including healing. He was giving that gift of healing to authenticate Christ as the Messiah. Notice Acts 8:5–9,

> Then Philip went down to the city of Samaria, and preached Christ unto them. And the people with one accord gave heed unto those things

which Philip spoke, healing and seeing the miracles which he did. For unclean spirits crying out with loud voices, came out of many that were possessed with them: and many taken with palsies, and that were lame, were healed. And there was great joy in the city.

I realize some healing performances from some so-called healing preacher might seem genuine, but if God is not in it, it's not genuine. Do you know your mind can be convinced to believe things that are not true? Some so-called healing preachers might convince you that you are healed, but *when* God heals someone from a disease or sickness it is a permanent transaction, not just a temporary reprieve. Yes, God can and does heal, but there is no individual that has the gift of healing.

Fourth, another gift is found in chapter 12:10, and it is the gift of working miracles.

To another [was given] the working of miracles.

This is another gift that is grossly misunderstood. Miracles were used by Christ and by those Christ called for a specific purpose to manifest and authenticate Christ as the Messiah. John 2:11 says,

The beginning of miracles did Jesus in Cana of Galilee and manifested forth His glory.

Acts 2:22 said,

Ye men of Israel hear these words; Jesus of Nazareth, a man approved of God among you by miracles, and wonders, and signs, as ye yourselves also know.

John 20:30–31 said,

> And many other signs did Jesus... These are
> written that you might believe that Jesus is the
> Christ, the Son of God; and believing ye might
> have life through Him.

I say again, no preacher or individual in our day has the gift of working miracles or healing. Miracles were used by Christ and specific people that God chose to authenticate Christ as the Messiah. However, there is one miracle we can perform. We can lead the unsaved to Christ for Him to work the miracle of salvation in his heart. Leading a person to Christ is the greatest miracle one can perform.

Fifth, another gift is also found Chapter 12:10, and it is prophecy,

> To another [was given the gift of] prophecy.

Prophecy is hurling forth predictions in the Bible that have been fulfilled and those that will be fulfilled. Prophecy comes from God's Word, not by a special revelation from some so-called secret appearance of God. God has already given all the prophecies there is. And you can find them in His Word.

There are about 2,500 prophecies in the Bible, and many have been fulfilled to the minute detail with no errors. There are about 350 prophecies about Jesus, which were fulfilled between His birth and His death. The odds of those being fulfilled by chances are virtually impossible. Yet they all were fulfilled to the very minute detail as predicted.

Jesus said this about Himself,

> In the volume of the book [the Bible] it is written
> of me. (Psalms 40:7)

The Bible is all about Jesus. In fact, He said,

> Search the Scriptures, for in them you think you
> have eternal life: and they are they that testify of
> me. (John 5:39)

Since the last apostle died, there have been no new prophecies or revelations given. That completed the Scriptures. The Bible tells us there is a curse on those who add to the Scriptures. Quite often you hear someone say, "I got a new revelation from God." That is not true. That is a lie. It just did not happen. In fact, every cult and false religion in the world got started that way. Prophecy is explaining Bible predictions that happened in the past or predictions that will happen in the future. God's Word tells us what has occurred in the past and what will occur in the future. We learn that by studying God's Word.

The purpose of prophecy is given in 1 Corinthians 14:3,

> He that prophesies speaketh unto men to edifica-
> tion, and exhortation, and comfort.

This builds in us a deeper desire to prophesy, because we surely want to edify, exhort, and comfort our Christian brothers and sisters. First Corinthians 14:1 states,

> Follow after charity [love] and desire spiritual
> gifts, but rather you may prophesy.

Verse 14:39 states,

> Wherefore brethren, covet to prophecy.

That means, anyone can prophesy if they will take time to study the Word of God.

Sixth, another gift is also found in Chapter 12:10, and it tells us about discerning of spirits…"to another is given the discerning of spirits."

This gift enables us to distinguish the difference between evil spirits and God's Spirit.

> Beloved, believe not every spirit, but try the spirits whether they are of God… (1 John 4:1)

The devil and his followers are the main instigators of false spirits. You can recognize false spirits by their association with cults and false religions. John 8:44 records Jesus saying,

> Ye are of your father the devil, and the lust of your father ye will do. He was a murderer from the beginning, and abode not in the truth, because there is no truth in him. When he speaketh he speaks of his own: for he is a liar, and the father of it.

Demons and followers of Satan counterfeit God's message and work. The devil is religious. On this earth there is a great number of evil spirits which are controlled by Satan, but truth is controlled by God.

What does it take to qualify for the gift of discerning spirits? Christians who have the gift of discerning spirits can identify evil spirits and erroneous doctrine by knowing God's Word. God and His Word give the gift of discerning spirits. However, there is something we can do to make ourselves available for that gift. Study and know what God's Word reveals about the Spirit of God and the truth of God. To help you get started, I recommend a book by David Jeremiah that is called *The Spiritual Warfare Answer Book*.

> They [the Thessalonica Christians] search the Scriptures daily to see if these things were so. (Acts 17:11)

You don't necessarily have to study false spirits to recognize false spirits. Study God's Word that clearly identifies those who have false spirits. Any spirit that is not of God is a false spirit. Similarly, you don't have to study counterfeit money to recognize counterfeit money. You study real money, and you can easily recognize counterfeit money. If you know the real thing, you can recognize the false. If you know your Bible, you can recognize false spirits.

Acts 16:17 gave an example of false spirits. A woman followed Paul and Silas through the streets of Philippi, crying out saying,

> These men are the servants of the highest God,
> which show unto us the way of salvation.

That sounds good, noble, and righteous on the surface, but she had a false spirit—a spirit of divination—a spirit of fortune-telling. She did her shenanigans through the power of Satan. In other words, she was a fortune-teller with an evil spirit. She had an ulterior motive in mind. She knew the officials of Philippi would not stand for anyone promoting Christ, so Paul and Silas commanded the evil spirit to come out of her. They were thrown in jail because of that. How did they know she had an evil spirit? Romans 8:16 says,

> The Spirit itself bears witness with our spirit.

The woman's spirit did not bear witness with Paul's spirit.

You don't have to talk with someone very long who has an evil spirit to know he/she has an evil spirit. There spirit will not bear witness with your spirit.

To utilize the gift of discerning spirits, it takes knowing and understanding God's Word. When the gift of discerning spirits is not used in the church, false doctrine arises. It is important the church and pastor have the gift of discerning spirits. They can protect the church from satanic lies and false doctrine.

Seventh, another gift is found in 1 Corinthians 12:10, and it deals with different kinds of languages and the interpretation of languages.

> To another [was given] divers kinds of tongues [languages], and interpretation of tongues [languages].

On the day of Pentecost at Jerusalem, people from different parts of the world spoke different languages, yet they heard the apostles preach the Gospel in their own language. The apostles were preaching in their Galenian language, but the people from different parts of the world heard them preach in their language. Amazing indeed!

To understand or speak a foreign language today, one must study hard to gain that knowledge, and it takes months, sometimes it takes years to learn a different language. However, that was not the case on the day of Pentecost. The apostles were instantly given the ability to speak a foreign language whether they themselves understood it or not. That was an instant gift on the day of Pentecost. It was given to those who spoke it and heard it. Therefore, speaking in different languages was a temporary gift.

The gift of speaking in an unfamiliar language without learning it is no longer given. It is not needed now because it accomplished its purpose, which was to authenticate Jesus Christ as the Messiah. The apostles spoke a known language, a language they knew and used every day. Notice Acts 2:1–5 and 7–8.

> When the day of Pentecost was fully come, they [about 120 people] were in one accord in one place. And suddenly there came a sound from heaven of a rushing mighty wind, and it filled the house where they were setting. And there appeared unto them cloven tongues [split tongues, or different tongues] like as of fire, and it set upon each of them. And they were all filled

with the Holy Ghost, and began to speak with tongues [languages], as the Spirit gave them utterance. And there were dwelling at Jerusalem Jews, devout men, out of every nation under heaven… And they were all amazed and marveled, saying one to another, behold are not all these that speak Galilean? And how hear we every man in our own tongue [language]?

The apostles spoke in the language they learned from their parents, but others from different parts of the world heard the message in their language. That was an amazing event!

If tongue speakers in our day are genuine, then why do they not start with the sound of a rushing mighty wind and cloven tongues like fire setting upon each of them? Their jibber-jabber is not from God, but conjured up by some hypnotic spirit. Those who claim it is from God are nothing more than promoters of false spirits. It is their emotions out of control.

The apostles spoke a knowing language. The word *unknown* in 1 Corinthians 14:2, 4, 13, 14, 19, and 24 was not in the original manuscript but put there by translators of the KJV for clarification purposes. You will notice the word unknown is *italicized* in the KJV, which means it was not in the original letter Paul wrote. The language the apostles spoke at Pentecost was a known language. It would have been better if they had left the word *unknown* out and added the word *unfamiliar*.

First Corinthians 12:11 makes it very clear that spiritual gifts came from only one source, the Holy Spirit. Notice 12:11,

> But all these worketh that one and the self-same
> Spirit, dividing to every man severally as He will.

It is the Holy Spirit that works in the hearts of Christians to utilize the gifts God gives them. Without the Holy Spirit, any talent a person may have is a natural talent that he/she worked hard to develop or was born with it. Mankind cannot fake or manufactory spiritual gifts. Neither can they choose to use them by their own volition. Man cannot get these gifts by picking and choosing. All gifts come from the Holy Spirit. Some try to fake spiritual gifts through sorcery and deception, but that does not work. Examples of that are so-called miracle workers and healing preachers and those who speak jibber-jabber languages. Gifts are those given by God and are appropriate for people that have the God given ability to utilize them. In fact, it is God who equips you for certain gifts. God does not give us a choice of what gifts we want and what gifts we don't want. He chooses the ones He qualifies us to use. It's not wrong to seek a certain gift, but the final analysis is, it is God who qualifies you for a gift.

First Corinthians 12:12–31 is the fourth subject in the outline, and it shows the church is one body in Christ.

Chapter 12:12 states that every born-again Christian is a member of God's family regardless of what denomination or religious organization he or she may belong to. Notice 12:12,

> For as the body is one, and hath many members, and all the members of that one body, being many, is one body: so also, is Christ.

There are church denominations that claim one cannot go to heaven unless he/she is a member of their denomination. It's not a matter of belonging to a church denomination to be assured a place in heaven, but it's believing in Jesus, confessing sins, repenting, and receiving Jesus as Saviour. That is the way to heaven. When a person confesses his sins and receives Jesus as his Saviour he is baptized into the family of God by the Holy Spirit. That is the only way you can get into the family of God. Notice 12:13,

> For by ONE SPIRIT are we all baptized into one body, whether we be Jews or Gentiles, whether

we be bond or free; and have been all made to
drink of one Spirit.

In other words, we are not baptized into the family of God by
baptism in water, but by being baptized by the *Holy Spirit*.

On the day of Pentecost, the Holy Spirit came upon each individual believer who was assembled in the upper room. The 120
believers became one body in Christ, not two, but one body.

Each part of the body needs all other parts of the body to be a
complete body. For example, 1 Corinthians 12:21 says,

The eye cannot say to the hand, I have no need
of thee.

Every believer has a need for every other believer. We all are
part of each other. All who put their faith in Christ for salvation—
whether Baptist, Methodist, Presbyterians, Brethren, or any other
denomination—are members of the body of Christ. That means
Christ is the head of the body, and everyone who receives Him as
their Saviour are part of His body. Therefore, we cannot say to born-
again Christians in another denominational church, you are not a
member of the body of Christ because you are not a part of our
denomination. You cannot say,

We have no need of thee.

I like what a pastor said: "Can you imagine someone taking a
knife and stabbing his arm and saying 'I have no need of these'?" In
heaven there's not going to be a separate section for each denomination. I'm not saying compromise and embrace all religions, but I am
saying, if a person has put his faith and trust in Jesus for salvation,
regardless of what denomination he belongs to, he is one with us in
the family of God. He is a member of God's family.

The church, the body of Christ, was formed on the day of
Pentecost when believers were baptized into the body of Christ by
the Holy Spirit. The Holy Spirit is the baptizer, not man. When

some man baptizes someone in water, he then becomes their Saviour. The Holy Spirit is still baptizing repentant sinners into the family of God. When Paul wrote about baptism, he was not writing about water baptism bringing salvation, but writing about the Holy Spirit bringing salvation to all who put their faith in Jesus Christ. The Holy Spirit baptizes them into the family of God. Water baptism is a testimony of an inward change that is brought about by being baptized into the family of God by the Holy Spirit. Water baptism is identifying oneself with the death, burial, resurrection, and coming again of Christ.

> Know ye not, that so many of us were baptized unto Jesus Christ were baptized unto His death? Therefore, we are buried with Him by baptism unto death: that like as Christ was raised up from the dead by the glory of the Father, even so we also should walk in newness of life. (Romans 6:3–5)

We confess we have already been born again when we are baptized in water. It's an outward confession of an inward change. Therefore, "we also should walk in newness of Christ."

Paul emphasized all born-again believers are one body in Christ. Paul makes it very clear in chapter 12:14 that the body of Christ is only one body with many members.

> For the body is not one member, but many.

Paul is saying, regardless of what denomination a person may belong to, if he is born again, he is part of the body of Christ and a member of our family in Christ. That is a fact that no one who believes the Bible can deny. Of course, those that don't believe the Bible deny it.

Christ died once, so you become a member of Christ's body only once. Notice how Hebrews 10:10 puts it,

> By the which will we are sanctified [born again and set apart for a sacred use] through the offering of the body of Jesus Christ ONCE FOR ALL.

That is saying we are saved only once, and that is forever. If a person could lose his salvation, the only way he could get it back would be by Christ dying again, and that will not happen. All believers that have put their faith in Jesus Christ for salvation have been baptized by the Holy Spirit into the family of God once for all.

In the following verses, Paul gave three illustrations on how the body of Christ is one, but made up of many members. There were different groups in the Corinthian church that separated themselves from the main body of believers and claimed to be the only legitimate way. But Paul gave three illustrations to prove that they were all members of the body of Christ.

First, notice Paul's foot and hand illustration in 12:15,

> If the foot shall say, because I am not of the hand, I am not of the body is it therefore not of the body?

Of course, it is of the body.

Second, notice Paul's ear and hearing illustration in 12:16,

> If the ear should say, because I am not of the eye, I am not of the body, is it therefore not of the body?

It, too, is of the body.

Three, notice Paul's eye, hearing, and smelling illustration in 12:17,

> If the whole body were an eye, where were the
> hearing, If the whole body were hearing, where
> were the smelling?

Just as the human body is made up of many parts, the body of Christ, which is God's family, is made up of many members within different groups.

Chapter 12:18 Paul summarizes the proofs we are all of one body.

> But now hath God set the members every one of
> them in the body, as it hath pleased Him.

We cannot say, "You are not of our denomination, so you are not of the body of Christ." God places each member into His family, yet they all differ one from the another. Notice 12:19,

> And if they were all one member, where were the
> body?

This verse is saying, if all the members were one member like a finger, hand, eyes, or ear, where would the other parts of the body be? The simple answer is, if there were only one part of the body, there would be no body. It would be some kind of odd creature. If there is only one denomination through which one can be saved, there is no body but a freakish denomination. To be a complete body of believers there must be more than one member. Notice 12:20–21,

> But now there are many members, but only one
> body; and the eye cannot say unto the hand, I
> have no need of thee, nor again the head to the
> feet, I have no need of you.

We need each other because we are one family in Christ.

God puts just as much importance on a less usable member as He does on those who stand in the spotlight all the time. All parts of the body are necessary. Notice 12:22–25,

> Nay, much more those members of the body which seem to be more-feeble are necessary. And those members of the body which we think to be less honorable upon these we bestow abundant honor; and our uncomely parts have more abundant comeliness. For our comely parts have no need: but God hath tempered the body together, having given more abundant honor to that part that lacked, that there should be no schism in the body, but the members should have the same care for another.

Notice what 1 Corinthians 12:26–27 has to say,

> And whether one member suffers, all the members suffer with it; or one member be honored, all members rejoice with it. Now you are the body of Christ, and individual members.

God set everyone in the body according to the ability He gives them. It is God who gives us the ability to do what He calls us to do. Therefore, we are in the body of Christ to help each other. Notice 1 Corinthians 12:28–30,

> God hath set some in the church: first apostle, second prophets, third teachers, after that miracles, then gifts of healing, helps, governments, diversities of tongues. Are all apostles? Are all prophets? Are all teachers? Are all workers of miracles? Have all the gifts of healing? Do all speak with tongues? Do all interpret?

No single individual in the New Testament church had all the gifts. No member of any denomination has all the gifts. So it must be God's will that we work together to promote the cause of Christ instead of cause divisions by putting down those who are not members of our denomination.

First Corinthians 12:31 instructs us to desire the best gifts.

> But covet earnestly the best gifts, and yet show I unto you a more excellent way.

There is nothing wrong with desiring the best gifts, but the wrong comes in when jealousy is the ruling factor. There is a remedy for that problem. Notice what Paul said in the above Scripture,

And yet show I unto you a more excellent way.

What does the Bible mean by the phrase "a more excellent way?"

Allow me to explain that in the next chapter. It's important you remember that.

Chapter 13 is about love.

CHAPTER 13
HAS FOUR SUBJECTS

Verse 1 deals with representative love.
Verses 2–7 tell us how to recognize agape love.
Verses 8–9A tells us how we can have the fullness of agape love.
Verses 9B–13 show what will occur when that which is perfect is come.

Before I explain each subject, allow me to give a brief introduction to 1 Corinthians 13.

Some Bible teachers say chapter 13 is out of place. They say it does not continue with Paul's flow of thought on gifts. Well, that is true in one sense of the word, but love has a purpose in God's scheme of things. God had a purpose for Paul inserting chapter 13 between chapters 12 and 14. Chapter 13 is called the love chapter.

Dr. Henry Morris said, "Why did the KJV use the word *charity* instead of *love*?" He said, "Probably because 1 Corinthians 13 emphasizes what love does rather than what love is. Love acts with patience and kindness; it does not envy others or seek to impress others, neither does it exhibit arrogance or conceit. Love is never rude, does not seek its own way, is slow to take offence, and bears no malice or resentment. Love does not gloat over the sins of others and is delighted when truth prevails. Love will bear up under trials and will never lose faith; it is always hopeful and unlimited in its utterance."

Love, therefore, is a suitable word for *charity*. The dictionary definition of *charity* is an act of giving of self to help others. It is appropriate to say love never fails because love is the act of giving to help others. Verse 4 tells us *charity* is another word for *love*. Love "suffers [cruelty] long and is kind; love envieth not; love vaunteth [boast] *not itself, is not puffed up* [proud]."

Love controls our lives every day in one way or the other: love for sinful things or love for the Lord. You will see that as we progress through the thirteen verses that makes up 1 Corinthians.

The Bible uses different words to describe different levels of love. That is not true in the English language. We have only one word to describe love. The same word is used to express love for a spouse as well as love for a hamburger. Love is meaningless in our society when it comes to distinguishing different levels of love. Oh, I know! We can increase the intensity of love by using verbs or adverbs. But there is no single word that intensifies the level of love in our English language like it is in the ancient Greek language. When someone says, "I love you," we are not sure what they mean. Do they mean they love you like they love a slice of pizza, or is it a more intense love? We have no way of knowing unless they use another word to intensify it. Anything we are passionate about, we use the word love to describe it. Then again, the things we are most passionate about does not determine the level of its worth because we use the same word to describe both loves. We describe love for our country on the same level as love for a ham sandwich. We have no single word to describe the level of love's importance. Some things are more important to us than other things, yet we use the same love word to describe both. The word *love* in our society has no significant intensity or extreme degree. It has no level of importance or priorities in meaning. Love means the same for everything. We may have passionate love for our spouse but only have a slight affection for our dog, yet we use the same word to describe love for both. That is not true with the Greek definition of *love*.

The Bible uses many words to describe levels of love. I will use only four Greek words to describe four different levels of love. I start with a love that means a despicable love, and I end with God's love, which is the most passionate love possible.

The first word is *eros*, which refers to sexual, physical, or sensual love outside of marriage. This love is not referring to marital love between spouses, but adultery love. A good example is found in 2

Samuel 13:1–15, and it is about David's son, Amnon, who lured his virgin sister into his house pretending he was sick and needed help, but when she came to help him, he raped her. After satisfying his evil passion—his eros love—he kicked her out of his house.

The second word is *phileo*. This love refers to the love one has for a brother/sister or close friend. It's often called friendship love. Jesus had friends that loved Him like a brother. Many of them even laid down their lives for Him. In John 15:14 Jesus said,

> Ye are my friends [Phileo friends], if you do whatever I command.

The third word is *ohab* love. It refers to the affection people have for their spouse, or the affection a mother has for her child. A good example is found in 1 Kings chapter 3. Two women gave birth to babies. One mother, while sleeping, rolled over on her baby and smothered it to death. She placed her dead baby beside the mother that had a live baby, and she took the live baby and placed it on her side of the bed. They had a heated argument about whose baby it was. So both mothers were brought before King Solomon to find to whom the live baby belonged. Of course, Solomon didn't know, but he did come up with a solution. He ordered a soldier to bring him a sword. He said, I will cut the baby in two parts and give each mother a part. The mother of the living baby cried and begged Solomon to give the baby to the other woman. She had so much *ohab* love for her baby she was willing to give it up to keep it alive. By that Solomon knew the baby belonged to the woman who was willing to give her baby up to keep it alive. You may find this story intriguing and wish to read the complete story; you can find it in 1 Kings 3:16–27.

The fourth word is *agape* love—God's love. What is agape love? Someone put it this way: "Multiply God's agape love by infinity, take it to the depths of forever, and you will only get a glimpse of how much God loves you." This is the most important, intense, and compassionate love there is because it is God's love. It is the most intense and compassionate love known to mankind. Agape love is described in John 3:16.

> For God so love [agape] the world that He gave
> His only begotten Son, that whosoever believeth
> in Him should not perish, but has everlasting life.

Agape love is the highest and purest form of love.

It's not hard for an unsaved person to love someone who loves them back, but God's love is broader than that. God's love includes Christians, Muslims, Buddhists, Hindus, cultists, terrorists, atheists, and everyone else in the world. We love in order to satisfy our own desires, but God's love is unconditional. He loves everybody even if they never love Him back.

We sometimes wonder how a loving God could tolerate cruelty in the world. It's because we don't understand agape love. Second Peter 3:9 said,

> The Lord is not slack concerning His promises,
> as some men count slackness, but is longsuffering
> [extremely patient] to us-word, not willing that
> any should perish, but that all should come to
> repentance.

God loves people so much that He tolerates them. He loves them unconditionally.

The Bible gives several ways to explain *agape love*. First, let me mention the fact that chapter 13 has five applicable truths about God's love and how each one influences our lives.

First, agape love is a sacrificial love. To be more specific, it's the love Jesus Christ showed when he died on the cross to save us from an everlasting hell. Romans 5:8 states,

> God commendeth His love toward us, in that
> when we were yet sinners, Christ died for us.

Ephesians 5:2 tells us,

> Christ hath also loved us, and hath given Himself
> for us...

First John 3:16 informs us,

> Hereby perceive we the love of God, because He
> laid down His life for us.

First John 4:10 states,

> Herein is love, not that we love God, but that He
> loved us, and sent His Son to be the propitiation
> for our sins.

By the way, *propitiation* in 1 John 4:10 means God's agape love was the preparatory act of God in Christ who sacrificed Him on the cross for our sins so that we might live with Him forever. First John 3:16 states,

> Hereby we perceive the love of God that He
> [God] loved us and laid down His life for us.

That means God loved us so much that He sacrificed Himself for us. Those Scriptures show how much God really loves us.

Second, agape love is a wholehearted, unselfish, sacrificial love. God in Christ sacrificed Himself for us when He died on the cross to take our place, so we would not have to die.

Unbelievers do not have agape love because they do not have Jesus Christ residing in their hearts. Agape love is a trait that only God, Jesus Christ, and the Holy Spirit have—the Holy Spirit abides in us. Therefore, we have God, Jesus Christ, and the Holy Spirit abiding in us. So we who are born again have agape love in us. Since the Holy Spirit lives in our hearts, we can love others by allowing God that dwells in us to love them through us. Unbelievers will receive agape love only when they believe, confess their sins, and receive Jesus Christ as their Saviour.

Third, agape love is a giving love. It gives without expecting anything in return. The best way to describe agape love as a giving love is to understand the willingness of Jesus Christ to give his life on the cross for us. He expects nothing in return. The cross is an ultimate example of agape love.

Fourth, agape love is a commandment love. Matthew 22:37 and 39 tell us who are born again:

> You shall love the Lord your God with all your mind, with all your heart, with all your soul, and with all your strength...and love your neighbor as yourself.

We could not possibly love others the way we love ourselves without Jesus loving them through us. When considering unbelievers, it is impossible for them to totally love others, because they do not have agape love in their hearts. They do not have the ability to love others as they love themselves. Similarly, it's impossible for us to love unbelievers without agape love. Only Christians can demonstrate agape love and that by letting the Holy Spirit which lives in them demonstrate that love through them. We have God, Jesus Christ, and the Holy Spirit living in us; therefore, we can love others with our soul and spirit.

Allow me to sidetrack here for an important issue on a marriage that occurs between a believer and unbeliever in relation to love. Believers who are married to unbelievers will have a tough time making their marriage work, because one loves with their soul and spirit, and the other loves with human passionate love. One has God's love in his/her heart; the other one has human love in his/her heart, and that causes conflicts. That is why God allows divorce between a Christian and an unbeliever.

Fifth, agape love is a gift from God. Notice the last verse of 1 Corinthian 12:31,

And yet I show you a more excellent way.

The "more excellent way" is the love way—God's love. It is God's gift of love to us. Chapter 13 shows us the more excellent way is the agape love way.

First Corinthians 13 mainly refers to God's love. Agape love is the best and most intense love possible. Agape love is an exclusive love that originates and resides in the heart of God, and in our hearts if we have the Holy Trinity in our hearts. John tells us in 1 John 4:10,

Herein is love, not that we loved God, but that He loved us, and sent His Son to be a propitiation for our sins, and not for our sins only, but for the sins of the whole world.

Mankind cannot reach the level of God's love in their flesh. That level of love is designed for those who put their faith in Christ for salvation. The indwelling Holy Spirit reaches that level of love and use our bodies to display God's love. It is impossible to reach that level of love in the flesh. Colossians 3:14 says,

Above all things, PUT ON LOVE, which is the bond of perfection.

That means we must put on the Holy Spirit before we can put on agape love. We are baptized into the family of God by the Holy Spirit and at that moment we put on God's agape love. Therefore, if our souls and spirits sin, it means that the Holy Spirit sins. That will never happen.

First Corinthians 13:1–3 is the first subject, and it deals with representative love.

Paul said in verse 1,

> Though I speak with the tongues of men and angels, and have not love, I am become a sounding brass, and a tinkling cymbal.

The phrase *tongues of men* is clearly talking about languages. Sounding brass and tinkling cymbals are what stands out in a musical arrangement. It is out of tune with every other instrument. Preaching, speaking, or pastoring without love is out of tune with God, out of tune with Christians, and out of tune with mankind in general. Sounding brass and tinkling symbols represents nothing of importance, only confusion. However, God's agape love does.

Notice verses 2–3,

> And thou I have the gift of prophecy and understand all mysteries; and though I have all faith, so that I could move mountains, and have not love, I am nothing. And though I bestow all my goods to feed the poor, and though I give my body to be burned, and have not love it profiteth me nothing. And though I bestow all my goods to feed the poor, and though I give my body to be burned, and have not love it profiteth me nothing.

Paul draws a comparison between God's love and man's admiral traits. He is saying if a person's life is characterized by admirable traits and does not have God's love, he is out of tune with God, with Christians, and mankind in general. If a man has the gift of prophecy, understand mysteries, has all knowledge, and has faith to move mountains, but is not characterized by God's love, he is nothing. If a man gives everything to feed the poor, and gives his body to be burned, but is not characterized by God's love, he is nothing. Without love all those commendable traits profit nothing.

Love needs to be the controlling factor in everything we do and say. Without love we may as well quit trying to be Christians, go on our merry ways, and forget we are Christians for all the good it will do.

By the way, what motivates us to do what we do? We might name many things, but love must be the motivating factor in our Christian service to the Lord if we ever become successful for the Lord.

The second subject is found in 13:4–7, and it deals with recognizing agape love.

Theses verses points out fourteen characteristics of real true agape love that is easily recognized in people.

1. *"Charity suffers long."* That means those who have agape love endures hardship, persecution, suffering, and pain before defending themselves.
2. *"And is kind."* That means those with agape love are considerate of others. They put others first. They are not hostile but kind.
3. *"Envies not."* Envy is covetousness in regard to another person's possessions. It is a person being jealous toward someone because he/she has something they want. Those with agape love do not feel jealous because of another's possessions but are always grateful and happy because of the way God has blessed them.
4. *"Vaunts not itself."* *Vaunts* mean "to be boastful." Those with agape love do not brag about their self-worth, their righteousness, or what they have accomplished, but brag about the righteousness of Christ.
5. *"Is not puffed up."* *Puffed up* means "exalting oneself with pride." A person with agape loves is not characterized by pride but characterized by humility.

6. *"Does not behave itself unseemly."* The word *unseemly* means "living below moral standards that God expects from Christians." If a Christian is characterized by agape love, he/she will not live below God's expected moral standards, but will seek to live up to God's moral standards.

7. *"Seeks not her own."* Those with agape love do not seek to personify his/her own worth but personifies the greatness of Christ. They exalt Christ to the highest echelon possible. They talk about the goodness of God and others rather than themselves.

8. *"Is not easily provoked."* The word *provoke* means "to live or act in a way as to make someone angry." Those with agape love do not deliberately provoke people to anger, but are gentle, tolerant, understanding, and do not live in such a way as to make others angry.

9. *"Thinketh no evil."* Those with agape love are not hot-headed, continually thinking on evil things, but think on honesty, integrity, having a clear conscience, and love for others.

10. *"Rejoices not in iniquity but rejoices in the truth."* Jesus said, *"I am the way, the TRUTH, and the light."* Those who have the truth have Jesus and they rejoice in the truth. But those without truth do not have Jesus Christ as their Saviour, and they love iniquity more than they love God. But those with agape, love God supremely.

11. *"Bears all things."* Those with agape love are not on the edge all the time. They are not eager to lash out but as much as possible tolerate things. They are not obnoxious but gentle and pleasant to be around.

12. *"Believeth all things."* This is not saying Christians are so naive and gullible they will fall for anything. It means those who have agape love in their life believe everything God's Word teaches, and they do not doubt.

13. *"Hopeth all things."* Those with agape love have a sure and steadfast hope. They know they will see Jesus and their

loved ones again. They are not like those that have no hope of ever seeing their loved ones again.

14. *"Endureth all things."* Those with agape love endure everything that is possible to bear. They tolerate things the unbeliever would not tolerate. They see the end is near and can endure all things.

The third subject is found in verses 8–9a, and it shows us how we can have the fullness of agape love.

The joy of agape love brings joy that never ceases. People have tried many things with the hope that something will bring meaning, purpose, and joy to life. However, we as Christians realize everything on earth is headed toward an end, we *can* take heart in knowing agape love will continue forever. God is love, and so long as God lives, agape love lives. God will continue forever; therefore agape love will continue forever. It will never fail. Verse 8 tells us that prophecy, tongues, and knowledge shall fail.

> Whether there be prophecy they will fail: Whether there be tongues, they shall cease; whether there be knowledge it shall vanish away.

However, agape love will exist forever. We can enjoy agape here and in eternity as well. Think about that. Once we receive Jesus as our Saviour, we can no longer relate to those who have worldly love only, but absent of God's love.

Paul said in verse 13a,

> For we know in part, and we prophecy in part.

But what glory will occur when prophecy will cease, and we see Jesus face-to-face? What will it be like when we see Jesus? We can anticipate that meeting, but for now we will just have to wait and see. In the meantime, let's let God's agape love shine through us so the world can see what it is to be a Christian.

The fourth subject is found in 13:9b-13, and it shows us what will occur when that which is perfect comes.

Verse 9–10 says,

> But when that which is perfect is come, then that
> which is in part shall be taken away.

Many prophecies are yet to be fulfilled, but there is coming a time when prophecy will no longer be needed because all prophecies will be fulfilled.

Notice 13:11,

> When I was a child, I spoke as a child, I under-
> stood as a child, but when I became a man, I put
> away childish things.

This verse is saying we are all like children. There was a time we understood things like a child, but when we began to study God's Word, we see things from God's perspective, and we put away childish things and become mature Christians. To be sure, there is coming a time when we get to heaven, we shall put away what understanding we had on earth and be given perfect understanding. Born-again Christians will have the insight into things, not as they appeared here on this earth, but as they really appear from God's perspective.

Notice 13:12,

> For now we see through a glass, darkly, but then
> face to face: now I know in part; but then I shall
> know even as also I am known.

God shows His agape love toward us as His dear children, but in heaven we will be more like Him and will see and understand God's perfect love in a perfect way. We will not look at love in heaven as though we are looking through a dark glass, but then we shall see it in all of its purity and perfection.

Notice Paul said,

I shall know even as I am known.

Paul had friends on earth that loved him, but he also had ene-mies that wanted to kill him. In heaven it will not be that way. All shall love him because he shall be known as others knew him on earth. We, too, shall know our loved ones as we knew them here on earth.

When it comes to loving others, in many respects, we have not gone beyond the baby stage. That stage is like looking through a dirty window. We will never fully understand the depths of God's agape love until we come face-to-face with Him. But now we can enjoy His presence and love that resides in our hearts, but then with Him we can enjoy the fullness of agape love.

Notice 13:13,

And now abideth faith, hope, and love, these three; but the greatest of these is love.

There is nothing greater than God's agape love. The Scripture above says it is greater than faith and hope.

1. Why is agape love greater than faith? Faith is what we must have to be saved. If God did not give us faith to believe in Him, we would have no one to put our faith and trust in. If God did not show His love for us in dying on the cross, we would not have assurance of life after death. There would be no way we could get to heaven if God did not love us enough to give us faith to believe. He sacrificed Jesus Christ on the cross to provide us a way to heaven. We would have to fend for ourselves, hoping everything in this life would turn out all right. But thank God, God's love is greater than faith because God is love. God is greater than all. He showed His love for us by scarifying His Son on the cross for us. After all, we are saved by God's grace through faith.

God is love, and there is nothing or anything greater than God. God is the very embedment of love.

2. How can agape love be greater than hope? Hope is what we have when we take our loved ones to the cemetery and place them in a grave. We have hope of seeing them again and being together forever. How is love greater than hope? Agape love is greater than hope because God is love, and that love personifies His greatness.

A world without Christ has no hope. The hope mentioned in 13:13 is a hope we Christians know will happen. The hope we have is mentioned in Hebrews 6:19,

> Which hope we have as an anchor of the soul,
> both SURE and STEADFAST.

We will most defiantly see Jesus and our loved ones again because we have a hope that is sure and steadfast, which is the anchor of the soul.

Agape love is the greatest love because it is God's love, and it can be seen in us by the Holy Spirit living through us. It is a testimony to the world that we are followers of Christ. Many religions are based on hate, greed, or recognition, but the love we have is the love Christ gives us. In the upper room, as Jesus and His disciples were observing His last Passover, He issued a new commandment. He said,

> Love one another as I have loved you, that ye also
> love one another. (John 13:34)

Then He added,

> By this shall all men know ye are my disciples, if
> you have love one for another. (John 13:35)

We are not capable of fulfilling that commandment to love one another, but we can by letting the Holy Spirit display God's agape love through us.

If there is anything God's people need more than anything else in the world, it is love for others. I need it, you need it; it's a fact we all need it!

Agape love is a missing trait in the unbeliever's life, but sad to say, it is very seldom activated in the lives of many Christians. Jesus said,

> By this shall all men know you are my disciples, if
> you have love one for another. (John 13:35)

Let's face it, if a person does not show love for others, it is an indication that he/she is not a believer in Christ. How will people know we are believers if we don't show love toward them?

The world cannot understand God's love. God's love is not some soggy, senseless, mushy love we throw around like an overused phrase. God's love endures criticism and cruelty, yet loves. God's love is a pure love toward its offenders. Romans 5:8 stated,

> God commendeth His love toward us, in that
> while we were yet sinners, Christ died for us.

Love for others must become part of a Christian's life, and it does become a part of a Christian's life when the Holy Spirit moves in and takes His seat on the throne of our hearts. Ephesians 5:2 says,

> Walk in love, as Christ also hath loved us, and
> gave Himself for us.

As Christ loved others and gave Himself for others, we should love others and give ourselves for others.

Showing love for each other is not to be a doormat for them to walk on. That is not at all the way to love people. We show love to people because we want them to come to Christ for salvation and escape that eternal place of punishment. So in concluding this chapter, we need to be reminded that love is the better way. In fact, love must be the controlling factor in utilizing our gifts.

Chapter 14
Has Four Subjects

Verses 1–5 show prophecy is the greatest gift.
Verses 6–25 deal with unknown languages and interpreting languages.
Verses 26–33 show how gifts are to be used in the local church.
Verses 34–40 show how women are to use their gifts in the local church.

First Corinthians 14:1–5 is the first subject in our outline, and it shows prophecy is the greatest gift.

First Corinthians 14:1 says,

> Follow after charity [love], and desire spiritual gifts, but rather that you may prophecy.

Prophecy is the best gift, so we are encouraged to seek the best gift, but it must be done through love. Love must be the controlling force behind seeking the gift of prophecy. "Follow after love," the Scripture says.

Prophecy was the most desirable gift in Paul's day, and so it is for our day. We all want to know what will happen in the future. Prophecy is so intriguing it grabs our attention when someone is speaking on it. We can say prophecy is the greatest gift because it is so fascinating to us. Prophecy is still in use today.

Prophecy is revealing things that has happened in the past, and things that will happen in the future. The next verse tells us how prophecy should be obtained. Notice what 14:2 says,

> For he who speaketh in an unknown tongue [unfamiliar language] speaketh not unto men but unto God, for no one understandeth him; howbeit, in the spirit he speaketh mysteries.

When a prophet speaks, he edifies others; but when he speaks in an unfamiliar language, he is speaking to God only and not to man. When a prophet speaks in a language you can understand he reveals mysteries. Notice 1 Corinthians 14:3,

> But he that prophesies speaketh unto man to edification and exhortation, and comfort.

For example, if a Japanese minister preaches or prays in his language, he would edify himself because very few of us understand Japanese. We who do not understand Japanese would not have the slightest clue what he is saying. But if he preaches or prophesizes and someone interpreted it, the whole body of Christ would be edified. Notice 1 Corinthians 14:4.

> He who speaketh in an unknown [unfamiliar] tongue edifieth himself, but he who prophesieth edifieth the church.

Many Bible scholars say Paul spoke five different languages fluently, but it wasn't Paul's desire to display his intelligence. His desire was to speak prophecy so people could see things that were fulfilled in the past and things that are to be fulfilled in the future. Notice what 14:5 says,

> I would that you all spoke with tongues [in different languages], but rather that ye prophesied:

for greater is he who prophesieth than he who speaks in tongues, except he interprets, that the church may receive edification.

Paul is saying, speaking in an unfamiliar language does not edify the church, but if there is someone to interpret the message, it edifies the church.

First Corinthians 14:6–25 is the second subject in the outline, and it deals with unfamiliar languages and the interpretation of languages.

We need to understand there is a great deal of confusion about tongues. For example, some people in our day claim to speak in an unknown tongue that no one but God understands. However, there is no such thing as an "unknown" tongue. When the Bible speaks of tongues, it is referring to languages. The Bible makes it clear that the gift of speaking in unfamiliar languages ceased after Christ was proven to be the Messiah. Teaching about tongues must include the Bible's definition of tongues. The word *tongues* mean "languages." Notice Acts 2:7–8.

They were amazed and marveled saying one to another, Behold, are not all theses which speak Galileans? And how hear we every man speak in our own language, wherein we were born?

Theses verses tells us that people of different countries were in Jerusalem for the Passover, and they spoke different languages, yet those that were there could understand the apostles as though they were speaking in their language. To say the least, that was a phenomenal event. People in different sections of the world spoke different languages, yet they could understand the apostles as though they were speaking in their language. So tongues mean languages.

Let me emphasize this again: There is no such thing as an unknown tongue. Yes! I admit the KJV mentions the word *unknown tongue*. I favor the King James Bible and use it in my preaching, teaching, studying, and writing, but I think the King James translators made a mistake in 1 Corinthians 14 by including the word *unknown.* They should have included the word *unfamiliar.* That would have been a better translation. At least the KJV explains why they used the word *unknown.* The word *unknown* is italicized, meaning it was not in the original manuscript but added for clarification. Anytime you find an italicized word in the KJV, it is put there by translators for clarification. In some cases, it causes confusion, as is the case above. Since *unknown tongues* means *unknown languages,* a better translation would be "*unfamiliar* languages." On the day of Pentecost, the apostles spoke an unfamiliar language, not in an unknown tongue.

The gifts of speaking in unfamiliar languages were given to the apostles to authenticate Christ as the Messiah. The need to authenticate Christ as the Messiah is no longer needed. Christ has already been proven to be the Messiah. Therefore, the gift of speaking in a different language is not needed as it was on the day of Pentecost. Second Peter 1:20–21 states,

> Knowing this first, that no prophecy of Scripture is of any private interpretation, for prophecy did not come by the will of men, but holy men of God spoke as they were moved by the Holy Spirit.

Holy men of God were moved to speak on the day of Pentecost. After Christ was authenticated as the Messiah there was no need for a new revelation—a new Pentecost—a new tongue. No new revelation has been given, nor will be given in the future. The Scriptures are very clear on that.

Someone speaking in a language unfamiliar to us makes no sense at all unless it is interpreted. Paul gives an example of this in 1 Corinthians 14:6,

> Now brethren, if I come unto you, speaking with tongues [unfamiliar languages], what shall I profit

you, except I speak to you either by revelation, by knowledge, or by prophecy, or by doctrine?

First Corinthians 14:7–8 show how confusing unfamiliar languages are to us unless someone is there to interpret it. Notice 14:7–8,

> And even things without life giving sound, whether pipe or harp, except they give a distinction in the sounds, how shall it be known what is piped or harped? For if the trumpet gives an uncertain sound, who will prepare himself for the battle?

Speaking words not understandable is nothing more than jibber jabber to the person who does not understand it. It's nothing more than fanning the air. It doesn't prepare the person for anything because he does not know what is being said. In other words, a person would not know to avoid a rattlesnake if he did not understand the warning. First Corinthians 14:9 says,

> So likewise you, except you utter by the tongue words easy to understand, how shall it be known what is spoken, for you shall speak into the air.

There are many languages in the world, and all have distinct meanings and sounds. They make sense to those who understand that language. The words are not meaningless to them. To us it is an unfamiliar language because we don't understand what is being said. Therefore, it is of no value to us. First Corinthians 14:10 says,

> There are, it may be, so many kinds of voices [languages] in the world, and none of them without significance [to the people who understands them].

If an unknown tongue cannot be understood, it is barbaric to the listeners. It is without meaning. It has no significance. First Corinthians 14:11 says,

> Therefore, if I know not the meaning of the voice, I shall be a barbarian, and he that speaketh shall be a barbarian unto me.

The word *barbarian* means "a person is like a roaring beast without a understandable language." When a group of church members speak in an "unknown" tongue that nobody can understand, they are barbarians just fanning the wind.

The bottom line about tongues and prophecy is to desire the gift of prophecy so the church can be edified. First Corinthians 14:12 says,

> Even so ye, forasmuch as you are zealous of spiritual gifts, seek that you may excel to the edifying of the church.

If a person cannot interpret the unfamiliar language, he is not helping himself or anyone else. I cannot explain that any better than Paul did in the following Scriptures. Paul said in 1 Corinthians 14:13–17 (by the way, before you read this, I need to inform you, Paul is referring to himself),

> Wherefore let him who speaketh in an unknown [unfamiliar] tongue pray that he may interpret. For if I pray in an unknown [unfamiliar] tongue, my spirit prayeth, but my understanding is unfruitful. What is it then? I will pray with the spirit, and I will pray with the understanding also. I will sing with the spirit, and I will sing with the understanding also. Else when thou shalt bless with the spirit, how shall he that occupies the room of the unlearned say amen at the

giving of thanks, seeing he understands not what thou sayeth? For thou verily give thanks well, but the other is not edified.

Paul spoke in languages more than they all, but he preferred speaking in a familiar language to those whom he was speaking. Notice 1 Corinthians 14:18,

I thank my God I speak with tongues [different languages] more than ye all.

Paul was not bragging, but stating a fact. He spoke five different languages fluently. His desire was to speak in the language of the people to whom he was ministering. If a person in public prays or speaks in an unknown language how can the people know what they are indorsing when they say amen? Paul said he would pray with understanding, speak with understanding, sing with understanding, and give thanks with understanding so people would know what they indorsed when they say amen.

Paul had a command on different languages more than most of his equals, and he used that to edify the people to whom he spoke. He had a desire to teach God's Word with understanding rather than speaking in an unknown language that people did not understand. Notice what Paul said in 1 Corinthians 14:19,

Yet in the church I had rather speak five words with my understanding, that by my mouth I might teach others also, than ten thousand words in an unknown [unfamiliar] tongue.

Paul's desire was to know the language of the people to whom he spoke. Speaking words easily understood is what Paul wanted, and that should be what we want.

Paul said in 1 Corinthians 14:20,

> Brethren, do not be children in understanding:
> howbeit, in malice be ye children, but in under-
> standing be as men.

Paul urged the Corinthian church members to major on understanding rather than speaking in tongues which people were not
familiar with. Children are lacking in understanding because they
have not been taught or lived long enough to experience things. As
they mature, they gain knowledge. Similarly, the Corinthian church
members were well educated in evil things, but lacking in spiritual
understanding. Paul said he would rather they be like a child in malice rather than being babes in Christ. Notice the phrase

> In malice be like a child.

A child does not hold grudges, but are quick to forgive and be
friends again. Paul is saying, "Be like children in malice, but be like
adults in understanding."

Understanding what tongues are for eliminates confusion. It is
essential to comprehend Paul's teaching about tongues. Tongues were
not jibber jabber but languages. Paul stressed the fact that there must
be an interpreter when a person speaks in an unfamiliar language
so the church can be edified and people be saved. First Corinthians
14:21 said,

> In the law it is written: With men of other
> tongues and other lips I will speak to this people;
> and yet, for all that, they will not hear me, sayeth
> the Lord.

Paul is quoting from Isaiah 28:11–12, which says,

> For with stammering lips and other tongues He
> will speak to the people, to whom He said, this is

the rest wherewith ye may cause the weary to rest;
and this is the refreshing: yet they will not hear.

The purpose of tongues was gifts of speaking in other languages
to authenticate Christ as the Messiah and to lead others to Christ. It
was used in bringing unbelievers to a saving knowledge of Christ. It
was Paul's desire to lead people to Christ, so he used understandable
languages when he witnessed to them about Jesus. Nevertheless, people refuse to hear it as verse 21 puts it,

They will not hear me, sayeth the Lord.

Prophesy was for edifying believers, but languages was for
authenticating Christ to those who did not believe. Notice 1
Corinthians 14:22,

Wherefore tongues are for a sign, not for them
that believe but to them that believe not: but
prophesying serveth not for them that believe
not, but to them that believe.

Different languages have no purpose at all in a local church
where people speak only one language. Speaking in a foreign language is not for unbelieving strangers who do not understand the
language. Furthermore, believers in a local church who speak an
unfamiliar language in the company of other believers accomplish
nothing if the church does not understand the language.

The gift of speaking in a foreign language is to benefit unbelievers, or strangers who can understand it. Notice 1 Corinthians 14:23,

If therefore the whole church comes together
into one place and all speak with tongues [differ-
ent languages], and there come in those who are
unlearned, or unbelievers, will they not say that
ye are mad?

Unbelievers would say, "Those people at that church are out of their minds." The Bible tells us we are to speak for God's glory and speak to edify believers. If a group of people come together in church, and each one speaks a different language, it would be madding. On the other hand, prophesying with understandable words will bring encouragement and blessings to believers and conviction to unbelievers.

One thing we must keep in mind is that prophesy is to be done in an orderly manner and with interpreters. Notice 1 Corinthians 14:24–25,

> But if all prophesy [remember prophesy is for edification], and there come in one that believeth not, or one unlearned, he is convinced of all, he is judged of all (by the preaching), and thus, are the secrets of his heart made manifest; and so, falling down on his face he will worship God, and report that God is in you, of a truth.

These Scriptures present the powerful results of prophetic preaching. A good example of prophesy preaching is found in Micha 5:2. Micha, a prophet who lived seven hundred years before Jesus was born, prophesied that Jesus would be born in Bethlehem. That prophesy was fulfilled to the most minute detail. The record of that fulfilment is found in Luke 2:1–7. I urge you to read these two passages of Scripture together; they will bless you.

First Corinthians 14:26–33 is the third subject in the outline, and it shows how gifts must be used in the local church.

Confusion will follow in ministering gifts in a local church if Paul's advice is not received. Notice Paul's advice in 1 Corinthians 14:26,

> How is it then, brethren? When ye come together, every one of you hath a psalm, hath a doctrine,

hath a tongue, hath a revelation, and hath an interpretation. LET ALL THINGS BE DONE FOR EDIFICATION.

Carolyn and I visited a church because someone we knew invited us. On the first song they began speaking in a gibberish language. Soon they were rolling in the floor. It was a vulgar scene, to say the least, when women exposed themselves as they rolled on the floor. By the way, they call themselves "holy rollers." That was the first time, and I must say, the last time we will ever attend that kind of church service.

Carolyn and I slipped out the back door, but couldn't get out of the parking lot. Our car was blocked in by other cars. Finally, they ended their tongue-speaking holy roller service around ten and started leaving. We finally left the parking lot. I can most defiantly say that service was not done for edifying saints. It certainly did not edify Carolyn and me.

The church named in 1 Corinthians 14:26 made no mention of a leader. Each person did his/her own thing. It was confusing to say the least. Can you imagine what a crazy confused mess it was? Paul said, "Let everything be done for edification and be done in order." He gave the remedy for a confused tongue speaking church service. This was Paul's way of calling a halt to the chaos that arose in the church of Corinth.

Tongue speakers were to interpret what they were saying or else have someone interpret it for them. If they could not do that, they were to keep silent. Notice chapter 14:27–28,

> If any man speaks in an unknown tongue, let it be by two, or at the most by three, and that by course, and let one interpret. But if there be no interpreter, let him keep silent in the church, and let him speak to himself and to God.

Allow me to give an example of how interpreting should be done. Just recently my daughter, her husband, and their two children went to Thailand to help in a missionary endeavor and to lead Thai people to Christ. They had to use three languages: English, Japanese, and Thai language to communicate with the Thai people. My son-in-law was born in Japan and has a total command of the Japanese language as well as the Thai language. My daughter was born in America and knows English. A lady who is a missionary in Thailand knows English as well as the Thai language. They interpreted from Japanese to English to the Thai language to get the message across to them.

In the above Scriptures Paul said,

> Let it be by two, or at the most part by three, and
> that by course [one after the other].

In other words, one person at a time is to speak to interpret the language.

Speaking different languages in a church service is permitted, but there must be an interpreter. Let's say a person from America was invited by a foreign country to speak in a church, but he could not speak in their language. In that case he would need an interpreter. Someone must be an interpreter for the church to be edified. The bottom line is, it would be better not to speak in an unfamiliar language if there is no one to interpret.

First Corinthians 14:29–33 gives the order in which a prophet should speak in a church service where the church members do not understand his language.

> Let the prophets speak by two or three, and let the
> others judge. If anything is revealed to another
> [prophet] that setteth by, let the first [prophet]
> hold his peace.

The first prophet is to relay his message to another prophet and then remain silent until the second prophet relays the message to those they are trying to reach. Paul was strictly against tongue and prophetic confusion. They were to take turn in prophetic speaking as well as speaking in tongues (languages). Anything except taking turns in speaking cause confusion and chaos. For some to prophesy and others speak in tongues at the same time would cause confusion for sure. God is a God of order, not of confusion. Second Thessalonians 3:16 states,

> Now may the Lord of peace Himself give you
> peace always by all means.

Prophesying is to be done to encourage people, not to confuse people.

First Corinthians 14:31–33 tells us the gift of prophetic preaching should be done in order.

> For ye all are permitted to prophesy one by one,
> that all may learn, and all be comforted. And the
> spirits of the prophets are subject to the prophets,
> for God is not the author of confusion, but of
> peace, as in all churches of the saints.

Even though prophesy is preferred over tongues, confusion can occur if prophesy is not done in order. It will not make sense or edify others if all prophesy at the same time without an interpreter. So this section is saying speaking in tongues or prophesying should be done in order.

First Corinthians 14:34–40 is the fourth subject in the outline, and it shows how women are to use their gifts in the local church.

Notice 14:34,

> Let your women keep silent in the church, for
> it is not permitted unto them to speak; but they
> are commanded to be under obedience [to their
> husbands], as also sayeth the law.

So to what extent are women allowed to use their gifts in the local church services? There is much misunderstanding about this. I intend to be very careful in explaining this because we should never condemn women for taking part in a local church service.

I realize there are some things women are not permitted to do in a local church. They are not allowed to pastor a local church. Paul speaking under the inspiration of God said in 1 Timothy 2:12,

> But I suffer [instruct] a woman not to teach, nor
> to usurp [take authority] over the man, but to be
> in silence.

Taking authority over men is to take the position of pastoring. For a woman to pastor is to take authority over the church and lead it the way she wants it to go. That position is reserved for men. Why? Because God said so. God is saying through Paul, "I do not allow women to pastor and take authority over men." The Bible is very clear on that issue. We must admit there are women that takes the position of pastor in many local churches. That is wrong and should not be permitted. God does not approve of that.

Women are to follow the pastors' leadership, as do the rest of the congregation. If she has any questions about the pastor's decisions or sermons, she is to ask her husband at home, not vent her feelings in the church. Chapter 14 verse 35 says,

> And if they will learn anything, let them ask their
> husband at home; for it is a shame for women to
> speak [vent her feelings] in the church.

This means women are not to pastor and dominate the conversation in the church, nor vent her feelings in church. I'm not saying men have a right to vent their feelings in the church. Men are to discuss their issues in a controlled manner led by the pastor.

Men are called to pastor, and they are to make the decisions in leading the church. Let's read 14:34 again.

> Let your women keep silent in the church: for it is not permitted unto them to speak [vent their feelings]; but they are commanded to be under obedience, as also sayeth the law.

This implies that men only are to pastor, and the church is to be obedient to his leadership.

Following are two opinions of what women are allowed to do and not do in the local church. I will approach these two opinions as though I endorse both of them. Even good fundamental ministers disagree on these two opinions. I will with God's help attempt to explain each position and clear away the cobwebs about women participating in a church service.

Are women allowed to lead music, giving her personal testimony, teach a class, interpret a message, preach prophetic messages, and so on? That is the issue and the place where many disagree.

To begin, I must remind you that the theme of chapter 14 is about the gift of speaking in tongues (different languages) and prophesying. Therefore, let's keep this Scripture in context,

> I suffer [suggest] that a woman not to teach, or usurp [take authority] over man but be silent in the church. (1 Timothy 2:12)

According to this verse, women are not to pastor, yet women can lead music, give her personal testimony, interpret a message, and preach prophetic messages. In that case, there is a difference between pastoring and preaching.

Is a woman allowed to preach prophetic messages? That is the prevailing issue. The Bible states that Philip had four daughters who were prophetic preachers. Notice what Acts 21:8–9 says,

> The next day we that were of Paul's company departed and came unto Caesarea: and we entered the house of Philip the evangelist, which was one of the seven; and abade [stayed] with him. And the same man had four daughters, virgins who prophesied.

That occurred after the beginning of the church, not in the transitional period. According to that belief, God does allow women to preach prophetic messages in these last days. We all know the last days started when the Holy Spirit was poured out on the disciples on the day of Pentecost. The coming of the Holy Spirit ushered in what is called the last days. The day of Pentecost most defiantly describes the last days. Acts 2:13–17 records a sermon Peter preached on the day of Pentecost. The disciples of Christ were speaking in an unfamiliar language, and the Jews accused them of being drunk, but Peter said,

> These are not drunk as you suppose…but this is that which was spoken by the prophet Joel: "And it shall come to pass IN THE LAST DAYS, sayeth God [notice it was God who said 'last days'], I will pour my Spirit upon all flesh: and your SONS AND YOUR DAUGHTERS shall prophesy…"

According to this position, women can preach prophetic messages. Remember, prophetic preaching reveals events that will happen in the future and reveals prophecies that have already been fulfilled in the past. According to this position, women cannot take the roll of a pastor, but they can preach prophetic messages to men, women, children, and whoever the Lord puts before them.

The second opinion about women is that they are not permitted to preach at all under this grace dispensation. The coming of the Holy Spirit occurred during the transitional period from the law to grace, and the preaching of prophetic messages that Philip's daughters did was only a temporary gift.

God will pour out the Holy Spirit at the beginning of the millennial reign on earth like He did on the day of Pentecost, and then the prophecy of Joel shall be fulfilled.

And your sons and daughters shall prophesy...

Therefore, women are not permitted to preach at all in this grace dispensation but will during the millennial reign of Christ on earth. Opponents say those two views above are absurd because women will be preaching whether in this dispensation or in the millennial. So the bottom line is, women will preach.

Whatever view you choose on Joel's prophesy is okay because neither is essential to salvation. Salvation comes without any strings attached. It's free and requires nothing in return. It's a gift from God. So whatever view you hold on Joel's prophecy is okay! Don't rebuke me and tell me I can't say that because I just did. I'm not going to tell you what view I hold.

Women's opinions are no less important than men's opinions. It's just that God calls men to pastor and dominate the conversation in the church. Women are permitted to do many other things in the church, but not pastor or dominate the conversation in the church. Maybe God chose to do it that way because He made man first. The woman was deceived, not the man. Could this mean woman can be easily led astray? Just asking a question! First Timothy 2:3–4 says,

> For Adam was first formed, then Eve. And Adam
> was not deceived, but the woman being deceived
> was in the transgression.

This implies that women are more vulnerable and can be deceived easier because she is the weaker vessel. It's not the author of this book saying women are weaker vessels. It is God saying that. Notice 1 Peter 3:7,

> Ye husbands, dwell with them according to knowledge, giving honor unto the wife, as unto the weaker vessel.

Adam was not deceived, but Eve was deceived because she was the weaker vessel. When Adam ate the forbidden fruit, he knew what he was doing and knew what the consequences would be, yet he willingly chose to eat and sin. Romans 5:12 says,

> For by one-man [Adam] sin entered in the world.

Sin did not inter into the world by Eve but by Adam.

A man should not treat his wife as inferior to himself but exalt her to a higher degree than himself in their marital relationship. In fact, 1 Peter 3:8 says,

> Giving honor unto the wife, as unto the weaker vessel, and as being heirs together of the grace of life.

Ephesians 5:25 says,

> Husbands love your wives, as Christ loved the church and gave Himself for it.

Can you say you love your wife like Christ loved the church and gave Himself for it?

On the average, women are physically weaker than men, but not weaker intellectually. They are up there on the same level, and many times above their husband's intelligence. I know many women that are more intelligent than their husbands. It would be wise for the man to heed his wife's advice before making a serious decision. Her advice may be from God.

Paul states that his advice was from God. Notice 1 Corinthians 14:35–37.

> What? Came the word of God out form you, or came it unto you only? If any man thinketh himself to be a prophet, or spiritual, let him acknowledge that the things I write unto you are the commandments of the Lord.

Paul is saying the Corinthian church should receive the Word of God from him as did the church in Thessalonica. Notice 1 Thessalonians 2:13,

> For this cause thank we God without ceasing, because, when you received the word of God which ye heard from us, you received it, not as the word of man, but as it is in truth, the word of God.

Paul is saying, the Word of God did not come from him but from God. A wife's advice could possibly (notice I said, *possibly*) be from God.

Atheist, infidels, and unbelievers are deliberately ignorant of where the Word of God came from, who the author is, and to what purpose it was given. They think the Bible is just another book of fables and stories concocted by man, and especially by a man named Jesus Christ. Paul confronts people like that. His advice to that sort of people is found in 1 Corinthians 14:38.

> If any man be ignorant, let him be ignorant.

That is, "Let him remain ignorant," Paul is saying. If atheists, infidels, and unbelievers want to be ignorant about Scriptures, let them be ignorant. After all, if people reject God's Word, they reject God. Jesus said in John 3:18,

> He that believeth on Him is not condemned: but
> he that believeth not is condemned ALREADY,
> because he hath not believed in the name of the
> only begotten Son of God.

There are many ignorant people trying to prove there is no God. However, Psalms 40:1 said,

> The fool hath said in his heart, there is no God.

They are fools. They with their infinitesimal brains try to prove the nonexistence of God who has unlimited knowledge of all things. Atheist and infidels challenge the superiority of our intelligent God. It's like me claiming my intelligence is superior to Albert Einstein's intelligence. One day everyone will bow and confess the superiority of God.

Paul summed up chapter 14 by giving the Corinthian church three final words of advice on gifts. Notice 1 Corinthians 14:39–40,

> Wherefore, brethren covet to prophesy, and for-
> bid not to speak in tongues. Let all things be
> done decently and in order.

His first advice is to covet (desire) to prophesy. That is, prophesy is to be put first in gift priorities. His second word of advice is to speak in a foreign language when necessary, but only to edify saints and lead others to Jesus Christ. His third word of advice is to do everything decently and in order. So this section is saying women in the church do have a role in utilizing her gifts.

CHAPTER 15
HAS TEN SUBJECTS

Verses 1–4 deal with the resurrection of Christ.
Verses 5–11 present a list of those who witnessed the resurrection of Christ.
Verses 12–19 present the necessity of the resurrection of Christ.
Verses 20–23 give the order of the resurrection of Christ.
Verses 24–28 deal with the millennial reign of Christ on this earth.
Verses 29–34 are about the resurrection of believers.
Verses 35–50 major on the certainty of the resurrection of believers.
Verse 51–53 deal with the marriage supper of the Lamb.
Verses 54–58 show how the rapture of the church shall occur.
Verse 59 emphasizes steadfastness.

First Corinthians 15 consists of ten sections (listed above), but the overall theme of this chapter deals with the resurrection of Christ and resurrection of believers. The following pages will introduce 1 Corinthians 15.

God inspired Paul to write about the resurrection of Christ and resurrection of believers; therefore, Paul stressed the importance of the resurrection in relation to Christ and our salvation. The resurrection of Christ is an essential part of God's plan of salvation.

So in writing to the church of Corinth, Paul reminded them of the importance of the resurrection. While Paul was at the church in Corinth, he preached about the resurrection of Christ every time he preached. In fact, Paul preached about the resurrection of Christ everywhere he went.

The resurrection is so important that people must put their faith and trust in the resurrection of Christ to become members of God's family. You cannot be saved otherwise. This was the message Paul preached from the beginning. He hurled forth the Gospel, which is the death, burial, and resurrection of Christ. Paul was called to preach the Gospel. After all, Romans 1:16 tells us the Gospel "is the power of God unto salvation."

A person is saved by believing and receiving the Gospel. The Gospel is the death, burial, and resurrection of Jesus Christ. Paul said in 1 Corinthians 15:13,

> If Christ be not risen, then is our preaching vain,
> and your faith is also vain.

If we are saved by believing the resurrection of Christ, it's very important we learn all we can about it.

Christ died, was buried, and rose again to provide salvation for anyone who would believe and receive Him as Saviour. First Peter 2:24 shows that we accumulated an enormous debt of sin, but Jesus "bare OUR sins in His own body on the tree, that we being dead to sin, should live unto righteousness, by whose stripes ye were healed."

Second Corinthians 5:21 goes on to say, God "hath made Him to be sin for us, who knew no sin; that we might be made the righteousness of God in Him."

Christ died in our place, He paid our sin debt in full, and He rose again for our justification. In John 10:18, Jesus said this about Himself:

> No man taketh it [my life] from me, but I lay it
> down of myself. I have power to take it up again.
> This commandment have I received from my
> father.

Christ laid His life down for us and then took it up again.

The first subject in the outline is found in 1 Corinthians 15:1–4, and it deals with the resurrection of Christ.

Paul emphasized that the resurrection of Christ is part of the Gospel. Notice 1 Corinthians 15:1–2,

> Moreover, brethren, I declare unto you the gospel which I preached unto you, which also you have received, and wherein you stand, by which also ye are saved, if you keep in memory what I preached unto you, unless ye have believed in vain.

Therefore, the resurrection of Christ is an essential fundamental of the Gospel. If Christ did not rise, there is no Gospel. Paul frequently used the words,

> If there be no resurrection.

Notice 1 Corinthians 15:12–19,

> Now if Christ is preached that He rose from the dead, then how say some among you that there is no resurrection of the dead? But if there is no resurrection of the dead, then is Christ not risen: and if Christ be not risen, then our preaching is vain. Yea, and we are found false witnesses of God; because we have testified of God that He raised up Christ whom He raised not. For if the dead rise not, then Christ is not raised. And if Christ be not raised, your faith is vain; ye are yet in your sins. Then they that have fallen asleep in Christ are perished. If in this life only we have hope in Christ, we are of all men most miserable.

A person is saved by believing and receiving the Gospel. You cannot be saved without believing the resurrection of Christ, and the resurrection is an essential part of the Gospel. Romans 10:17 states,

> Faith cometh by hearing, and hearing by the word of God.

In chapter 15:1–2 (above), Paul clears up the confusion anyone may have about the death, burial, resurrection, and the coming again of Christ as being the Gospel. He emphasizes that one must believe and receive the Gospel to become a member of God's family. However, some believe in vain. Notice the last part of verse 2,

> Unless you have believed in vain.

What is it to believe in vain? The word *vain* means "without real meaning and purpose, without significance." For example, Pharisees had no real significant purpose other than popularity and recognition. They were hypocrites in their private life but presented themselves to be genuine in public. Jesus said,

> When you pray, you shalt not be as the hypocrites are. For they like to pray in the synagogues, and in the corner of the streets, that they may be seen of men. (Matthew 6:5)

They believed in vain.

Many church people of our day believe in vain. They do not receive the Gospel inwardly but present themselves in public as though they did. That is called believing in vain. All religions who do not believe in Christ believe in vain. They believe in something that will not get them to heaven. Those who do not receive Christ or have no desire to receive Christ or have no intention of making Christ ruler of their lives believe in vain. Some profess to be Christians, but anyone who does not believe inwardly what they pretend to believe outwardly believes in vain.

A true believer not only believes the Gospel, but he accepts the Gospel. He holds fast to the Gospel; he embraces the Gospel; and he lives by the Gospel. Believers make Christ part of their lives, and their lives show it. They manifest outwardly what they profess inwardly. James 2:20 says,

> Will you know, O vain man, that faith without works is dead?

We are not saved by works, but if we have never experienced a change in our life, that gives us a desire to produce good works we believe in vain. James 2:20 is saying true salvation will manifest itself in good works like measles manifests itself in the body. If a person professes faith in Jesus, but does not produce good works to show he is saved, he has dead faith; he believes in vain. Dead faith has no desire to produce good works. So many in Paul's day, and many in our day, "believe in vain."

Paul received the Gospel, preached the Gospel, and urged us to receive the Gospel which is the death, burial, and resurrection of Christ. Notice 1 Corinthians 15:3–4,

> For I delivered unto you first-of-all that which I also received, how that Christ died for our sins according to the Scriptures, and that He was buried, and that He rose again according to the Scriptures.

These Scriptures make the Gospel clear and easy to understand. It's most urgent we get the message across to unbelievers that they may believe Christ died for their sins, that He was buried, that He rose from the dead for their justification, and that He is coming again.

The second subject in the outline is found in 1 Corinthians 15:5–11, and it gives a lists of those who witnessed the resurrection of Christ.

The Bible presents many truths that prove Christ rose from the dead, but living witnesses were the most important proof. When Paul wrote 1 Corinthians, it was about twenty years after the resurrection of Christ. Many who saw Christ crucified and killed were still alive. They gave a true-life witness to the resurrection of Christ.

Paul gave us a list of the witnesses who were still alive. Notice 1 Corinthians 15:5–8.

> And that He was seen of Cephas [Peter], then of the twelve: after that He was seen of about five hundred brethren at once; of whom the greater part [most of them] remains unto this present, but some are fallen asleep [some are dead]. And that, He was seen of James, then of all the apostles: and last of all He was seen of me [Paul] also, as of one born out of season."

When the Scriptures stated that Jesus was seen by Peter, it is not saying Peter was the first to see Him after His resurrection. Paul is saying Peter was the first apostle to see Jesus after His resurrection. Therefore, Peter (Cephas) was not the first to see Jesus after His resurrection; Mary Magdalene was the first. Peter was the first apostle to see Jesus after His resurrection.

The event of the resurrection of Christ unfolds as follows. A message from angels was given to them as they stood at the tomb where Christ was buried. There was more than one woman and more than one angel affirming the resurrection of Christ. Notice Luke 24:22–26,

> Yea, and Certain women also of our company made us astonished [astonished us] which were early at the sepulcher; when they found not His body, they came, saying, that they had also seen

a vision of angels, which said that He was alive. And certain of them which were with us [in the upper room], went to the sepulcher and found even so as the women had said; but Him they saw not. He [one of the angels] said unto them.

O fools, and slow of heart to believe all that the prophets have spoken: Ought not Christ to have suffered these things and entered into His glory?

The resurrection of Christ is what makes Christianity different from all other religions. If Christ did not rise from the grave, Christianity is nothing more than all other religions whose founders died and are still dead. Our hope is anchored in the resurrection of Christ because we have proof He arose, and many eyewitnesses who saw Him crucified gave witness to His resurrection. Notice the order of His resurrection.

First, Jesus appeared to Mary Magdalene. Several ladies—including Mary Magdalene and Mary, the mother of Jesus, who was also the mother of James and Salome—were with the group that came to the sepulchre early in the morning. They witnessed an empty tomb. As they entered the tomb, they saw two angels, one at the head and one at the feet, where Jesus had lain. They ran and told the disciples what they saw. Peter and John ran to the tomb. Peter went in, then John went in. They marveled at what they saw, but they did not see Jesus. Peter and John went away, but Mary Magdalene remained at the tomb. Let me read what happened after Peter and John left. John 20:11–17,

But Mary [Magdalene] stood without at the sepulcher weeping: and as she wept she stooped down, and looked into the sepulcher, and seeing two angels in white setting, one at the head, and the other at the feet, where the body of Jesus had lain. And they say unto Mary, Woman why weepiest thou? She sayeth unto them, because they

have taken away my Lord, and I know not where
they have taken Him. When she had thus said,
she turned herself back, and saw it was Jesus...

Second, Jesus appeared to Cleopas and Simon on the road to
Emmaus. This is an intriguing story. You can read about that proof
in Luke 24:13–35.

Third, Jesus appeared to Peter and the disciples (Thomas not
being present). You can read about that proof in John 20:19–24.

Fourth, Jesus appeared to His apostles with Thomas present.
You can read about this amazing proof in John 20:24–28.

Fifth, Jesus appeared to more than five hundred at one time.
Notice 1 Corinthians 15:6,

After that, He was seen of about 500 brethren at
once...

Sixth, Jesus appeared to James and all the apostles a third time.
Notice 1 Corinthians 15:7,

After that, He was seen of James; then all the
apostles.

Thomas was present also.

Seventh, the disciples and many others watched Him as He
ascended into heaven. Notice Acts 1:11. An angel said,

Ye men of Galilee why stand ye gazing up into
heaven? This same Jesus that is taken up from
you into heaven shall so come in like manner as
you have seen Him go into heaven.

Eighth, Jesus was seen by Paul. Notice 1 Corinthians 15:8.

And last of all He was seen of me [Paul], as of one
born out of season.

Perhaps a thousand or more people saw Jesus after His resurrection. That should be proof enough for the most skeptical unbeliever to become a believer. However, some say they were having illusions. An illusion is a misleading visual image of something. Isn't it strange that a thousand or more people had the same illusion, at the same time, at the same place, about the same person? They saw the real Lord Jesus Christ after He arose from the dead and saw Him ascend into heaven. And they were willing to lay down their lives rather than deny the truth of Christ's resurrection. The evidence of the post-resurrection appearance of Christ didn't develop gradually over the years as a mythology distorted memory of his life. No, it happened just the way the Bible says it did. We have proof of that. Many saw the risen Christ, and even Paul, a first-century doubter, personally talked with these eyewitnesses to prove the truth of the resurrection of Christ.

If someone had talked with these witnesses and they denied seeing Jesus, Christianity would have stopped there. But none denied seeing the resurrected Christ. In fact, they were willing to lay down their lives rather than deny the truth of the resurrection.

Paul preached the resurrection of Christ in Corinth about twenty years after His resurrection. If Christ did not rise, anyone could have gotten to the root of the matter by talking to any of the witnesses, and if they would have denied it, Christianity would have ceased. But they were willing to lay down their lives for the truth of the resurrection of Christ. If Christ did not arise from the dead, why would people risk their lives and even give their lives by saying He did? That does not make sense, unless, of course, He did arise.

Paul's life was changed because of his encounter with the resurrected Christ. That confirms the certainty that Christ did arise from the dead. Paul's own conversion from skepticism to faith is unexplainable apart from the resurrection of Christ. Also, the lives of those who witnessed His resurrection were changed, and their lives unexplainable apart from the resurrection of Christ. Notice what Paul said in 1 Corinthians 15:9–11,

> For, I am the least of the apostles, and am not
> meet [worthy] to be called an apostle, because I

persecuted the church of God. But by the mercy
of God I am what I am: and the grace which was
bestowed upon me was not in vain; but I labored
more abundantly than they all: yet not I, but the
grace of God which was with me.

Paul's life was changed when he was confronted by Jesus Christ
on the road to Damascus, and he served Christ and Christ only the
rest of his life.

After weighing the evidence of Christ's resurrection, any logical
mind can only come to one conclusion: "Christ came back from the
dead."

*The third subject in the outline is found in 1 Corinthians 15:12–19,
and it presents the necessity of the resurrection of Christ.*

Notice 1 Corinthians 15:12,

Now if Christ be preached that He rose from the
dead, how say some that there is no resurrection?

This verse presents the necessity of the resurrection of Christ.
Paul is saying, if Christ did not come back from the dead, life is not
worth living, and we have no hope of ever going to heaven. The resurrection of Christ was absolutely necessary for us to be saved. Christ had
to be resurrected from the dead. He had to be raised from the dead to
complete God's plan of salvation and to assure us a resurrection.

Evidently, some Corinthian church members had adopted the
belief that was held by the Epicureans and Stoic philosophers that
Christ did not come back from the dead. They taught that everything physical was intuitively evil—that is, they taught that man was
evil inside and out. So the idea of a resurrection was repulsive to
them. Notice what they taught as recorded in Acts 17:32,

When they [philosophers of Athens] heard [Paul
preach] of the resurrection, some mocked: and

others said, "We will hear you again of this matter."

They ridiculed Paul's preaching because they did not believe in the resurrection. Little did they realize, believing in the resurrection was absolutely essential in getting them into the family of God. Some Corinthian church members adopted that philosophical belief because they were influenced by the Sadducees. The Sadducees didn't believe in the resurrection of Christ. I heard someone describe the Sadducees this way: "They were sad-u-see because they did not believe in the resurrection."

Both Sadducees and philosophers taught that the soul and spirit experience a resurrection but not the body. However, believing in the bodily resurrection of Christ is essential to salvation. Without believing that Christ arose, none of the Corinthian church members would have been saved, nor would any of us be saved. The death, burial, and resurrection of Jesus Christ is the main theme of the Bible. Without the resurrection of Christ, the death of Jesus makes no sense at all, nor does the Bible make sense.

Paul believed and preached the truth of the resurrection of Christ everywhere he went because he knew it was necessary to believe in the resurrection to be saved. Notice 1 Corinthians 15:13–19,

> But if there be no resurrection of the dead, then Christ is not raised. And if Christ be not risen, then is our preaching vain, and your faith is also vain. Yea and we are found false witnesses of God; because we have testified of God that He raised up Christ: whom He raised not up if the dead rise not. For, if the dead rise not then Christ is not raised. If Christ be not raised, your faith is vain, ye are yet in your sins. Then those also which have fallen asleep in Christ are perished. If in this life we have hope only in Christ, we of all men most miserable.

If Christ did not personally experience a resurrection, our lives are meaningless and not worth living. We have no hope of eternal life or ever seeing Jesus or our loved ones again. That would make life miserable, meaningless. Paul's statement about the resurrection of Christ in the above Scriptures describes our existence without Christ. But we do believe in the resurrection of Christ and have a steadfast and sure hope of seeing Him when we die. Our hope is in our resurrected Christ. He is alive, and that's what gives meaning to life. Our hope is real, and in a real person—Jesus Christ.

The fourth subject in the outline is found in 1 Corinthians 15:20–23, and it gives the order of the resurrection of Christ and believers.

Notice 1 Corinthians 15:20,

> But now Christ has risen from the grave and became the first fruits of them [all believers] that sleep [that died and are buried].

This verse gives the order of the resurrection of Christ and believers. Notice 1 Thessalonians 4:15–17 says,

> For the Lord himself shall descend from heaven, with the voice of the archangel, and the trump of God: and the dead in Christ shall rise first: then we which are alive and remain shall be caught up together with them in the clouds, to meet the Lord in the air and so shall we ever be with the Lord.

The order of the resurrection is: Christ first, those who are dead in Christ second, then those who are alive at His coming. All born-again Christians will be resurrected to be with the Lord forever.

Christ was the first to experience a resurrection, and we will experience a resurrection Just like Christ did. Death came because of Adam's sin, but salvation came because of what Christ did. The resurrection of Christ came because He had to complete God's plan of salvation, and His resurrection is an essential part of the Gospel.

First Corinthians 15:21 tells us Christ, the second Adam, will bring those who are dead in Christ to life again

> For since by one man [Adam] came death, by man [Jesus] came also the resurrection of the dead.

We will all die because Adam set death in motion. If the Lord doesn't come back soon, our generation will die, and another generation will come along. They too will die, and then another will come along, and then another, and so on until the rapture of the church. Hebrews 9:27 states,

> It is once appointed unto man to die.

No one will escape death except those who are alive at the rapture of believers. They will be caught up to be with the Lord. Therefore, we need not worry about death because 1 Thessalonians 4:13 says,

> I would not have you ignorant, brethren, concerning them which are asleep [who are dead] that ye sorrow not, even as others which have no hope.

The bodies of those who died will be raised from the dead when Jesus raptures the church! Notice 1 Corinthians 15:22 that says,

> For as in Adam all die, even so in Christ shall all be made alive.

Our hope is in the resurrection of Christ. He lives, so shall we live.

Notice the order of the resurrection as recorded in 1 Corinthians 15:23,

> But every man in his own order; Christ the first fruits; afterward they that are Christ's at His coming.

The resurrection began with Christ and will end with all born-again Christians that put their faith and trust in Him for salvation. Notice the continuation of 1 Thessalonians 4:13–17,

> I would not have you to be ignorant, brethren, concerning them which are asleep [in the grave], that you sorrow not even as those who have no hope. For if we believe Jesus died and rose again, even so also them who sleep [whose bodies sleep in the grave] in Jesus will God bring [their souls] with Him. For this we say unto you by the word of the Lord that we which are alive and remain unto the coming of the Lord shall not prevent [go before] them which are asleep. For the Lord Himself shall descend from heaven with a shout, with the voice of the archangel, and with the trumpet of God: and the dead in Christ shall rise first: then we which are alive and remain shall be caught up together to be with them in the clouds, to meet the Lord in the air: and so shall we ever be with the Lord. Wherefore, comfort one another with these words.

It's imperative we understand the difference between the rapture and the Second Coming of Christ. The rapture takes place before the Second Coming of Christ. In fact, the rapture occurs when Jesus comes in the clouds only. He will not come back to earth at that time. We will be resurrected from the earth to go up "in the clouds, to meet the Lord in the air" (1 Thessalonians 4:17).

The bodies (notice, I said *the bodies*) of believers sleep in the ground until Jesus comes to resurrect them. Their soul and spirit go to be with God at death. The Christians' bodies who died will be raised first; then we which are alive will be caught up to be with them to meet the Lord in the air and shall be with the Lord.

There are three Scripture verses that prove beyond a doubt that the *souls* of the born-again Christian go to be with Jesus at death, but the body sleeps in the grave until the resurrection.

First, Luke 16:19–22,

> There was a certain rich man which was clothed in purple and fine linen, and faired sumptuously ever day: and there was a beggar named Lazarus which was laid at the gate, full of sores, and desiring to be fed with the crumbs which fell from the rich man's table: moreover the dogs came and licked his sores. And it came to pass that the beggar died AND WAS CARRIED BY THE ANGELS INTO ABRAHAM'S BUSOM [heaven]. THE RICH MAN DIED...AND IN HELL HE LIFTED UP HIS EYES.

These Scriptures tells us that both the saved and unsaved *soul* instantly go to their eternal destination at death. The saved person's *soul* goes to heaven, and the unsaved person's *soul* goes to hell. They go to their eternal destination the very moment breath goes out of their bodies.

Second, Luke 23:42 and 43 record a conversation Jesus had with one of the criminals that was hanged on a cross beside Him. The criminal said,

> Lord remember me when thou comest into thy kingdom. (Luke 23:42)

> Jesus said unto him, TODAY shalt thy be with Me in paradise. (Mark 23:43)

Notice, Jesus did not say "Your soul and body must sleep for a while then you will be with Me in paradise," nor did he say "A thousand years from now you will be with me in paradise," but He said,

TODAY thou shalt be with me in paradise.

The soul of a Christian does not sleep in the grave to await the resurrection, but goes to heaven the very moment he/she dies.

Third, Paul said in 2 Corinthians 5:6 and 8,

> Therefore we are always confident, knowing this, while we [our souls] are at home in the body we are absent from the Lord. We are confident, I say, and willing rather to be absent from the body, and to be present with the Lord.

Paul is simply saying, "When I die my soul will be separated from my body, and it will instantly be present with the Lord."

The resurrection of Christ sets the Bible and Christianity apart from all other religions of the world. Jesus, the founder of Christianity, is the only leader of any religion who arose from the dead. The resurrection of Christ makes Christianity superior to any other religion. Without the hope of a resurrection, we would have no Gospel and no hope of every seeing Jesus or our loved ones again.

All unbelievers who die and those that are living at the second coming of Christ will be taken before the Great White Throne Judgment to be judged.

The fifth subject in the outline is found in 1 Corinthians 15:24–28, and it deals with the millennial reign of Christ on this earth.

Paul presents many Scriptures to show that Christ will put this earth under His control for a thousand years.

Before you can understand the millennial reign of Christ on this earth, you must understand the kingdom of heaven is not inside of you. The kingdom of heaven is the place where God dwells. In fact, the word *kingdom* means "a place where God rules." If the kingdom of heaven is inside of you, then God is doing a poor job of ruling. Most Christians I know, including myself, are unruly at times. Therefore, the kingdom of heaven is not inside of you, but it is where God dwells. The thief on the cross that was crucified beside Jesus said,

> Lord, remember me when THOU COMEST INTO THY KINGDOM...

Jesus said,

> TODAY THOU SHALT BE WITH ME IN PARADISE. (Luke 23:42)

In John 18:36, Jesus said,

> My kingdom is NOT OF THIS WORLD.

God's kingdom is in heaven, not inside of you. Yes, we do God's kingdom work, but the kingdom of heaven is where God dwells. It is in the third heaven. You become a member of God's family and part of His kingdom when you repent and ask Jesus to come into your heart and save you. You don't receive God's kingdom to become a member of His family; you become a member of God's family by believing, repenting, and receiving the Gospel—which is the death, burial, and resurrection of Christ. Notice what 1 Corinthians 15:24 says,

> Then cometh the end, when He shall have delivered up the kingdom of God; [the Kingdom of GOD makes up the church—all born-again Christians] even the Father when He shall have put down all rule and all authority and all power.

First, Christ must rule on this earth until He puts all world powers under His control. Read again 1 Corinthians 15:24 above. The kingdom of God and the kingdom of heaven differs. The kingdom of God consists of all who have repented and received Christ as Saviour, but the kingdom of heaven is where God dwells. Has Jesus ever put all rules, all authority, and all power under His control here on earth. No, but there is coming a time when He will. That will occur when He takes over the earth during His millennial reign.

Second, Revelation 12:5 says, Mary "brought forth a man child, who was to rule all nations with a rod of iron: and her child was caught up unto God, and to His throne."

There is no doubt this Scripture is referring to Jesus. It can only apply to Jesus because who else would be caught up unto God and to His throne? Notice the phrase "who was to rule all nations with a rod of iron."

What does the "rod of iron" mean? It means the lack of strength to withstand His power and His mighty angels when he comes. The ruling power of Jesus cannot be equaled. He will rule here on earth for a thousand years and put all nations under His control. No country or people will have the power or ability to resist Him.

Has Christ ever ruled the earth with a rod of iron and put all enemies under Him? No! But He will during His thousand-year reign on this earth.

Third, notice what John said in Revelation 20:1–3,

> I saw an angel come down from heaven, having the key to the bottomless pit [the bottomless pit is the center of the earth—it has no bottom] and a great chain in his hand. And he laid hold of the dragon, that old serpent, which is the Devil, and Satan, and bound him a thousand years. And cast him into the bottomless pit, and shut him up, and set a seal upon him, that he should deceive the nations no more, till the thousand years should be fulfilled: and after that he must be loosed for a little season.

Some say this verse is referring to Jesus being bound in the hearts of believers, and it makes Satan incapable of controlling and ruling their lives. Therefore, they say they can live a perfect and sinless life because Jesus bound Satan from their lives. They back up their theory by using 1 John 3:9,

> He that is born of God doeth not sin: because His
> seed remains in him and he cannot sin, because
> he is born of God.

The real truth of that verse is, when a person receives Christ as his Saviour, his soul never sins again, but it's his body that sins. His body is not saved; only the soul is saved. Therefore, it is the body that sins, not the soul.

Notice the length of time Satan will be bound. According to Revelation 1:3, he will be bound a thousand years. Will those who receive Christ as their Saviour live with Jesus a thousand years here on earth? Yes! We who were taken up in the rapture will come back with Jesus and live a thousand years with Him here on earth.

> For He [Christ] must reign, till He hath put all
> enemies under His feet.

Jesus will rule and reign on this earth and put all enemies under His feet. Satan will be defeated and prevented from deceiving the nations any longer until the one-thousand-year reign of Christ is over. Then Satan will be loosed for a short season. He will go upon earth to gather his army to fight with God. Revelation 16:16 says,

> And he [Satan] gathered together [the leaders of
> every nation of the world] into a place called in
> the Hebrew tongue Armageddon.

That will be Satan's last stand against God. He and his followers will be defeated and cast into the lake of fire.

Fifth, after Satan's last attempt to kill Christ, God will destroy death. Notice 1 Corinthians 15:26,

The last enemy that shall be destroyed is death.

Death is our enemy. It has caused more tears and heartbreaks than anything you can imagine. Thank God, death will experience death itself. God will destroy death. There will never be another death in heaven, and sad to say, no one in hell will ever die either.

Sixth, Jesus will restore His power over the earth and restore life existence as it was before Adam sinned and brought death. First Corinthians 15:27–28 says,

> For He hath put all things under His feet, but when He sayeth, all things are put under Him, it is manifest that He is accepted, which did put all things under Him. And when all things shall be subdued unto Him, then shall the Son also be subject unto Him that put all things under Him that God may be in all.

Has Christ ever gained control of this earth and put all things under His control? No! But He will during His thousand-year reign on this earth.

Seventh, John the Baptist came on the scene preaching

Repent for THE KINGDOM OF HEAVEN IS
AT HAND. (Matthew 3:23)

Notice John the Baptist did not say the kingdom of God is at hand, but the kingdom of heaven is. The kingdom of heaven means the place where God lives. The kingdom of God is His church. Has God's kingdom of heaven ever come to this earth? No, but it will during His one-thousand-year reign on earth. Anyone who believes the kingdom of heaven is on this earth now is ignorant to what the Bible teaches. Israel rejected her king. The world has always rejected

Jesus. In fact, we have a law in America that is called "Separation of Church and State." The world wants to remove Jesus Christ from society and kill those who receive Him.

God is not ruling and reigning on earth now. The kingdom of heaven is not upon this earth, nor is it inside Christians. God's kingdom is in heaven where God is. People reject God, but they will have no choice but to receive Him during His thousand-year reign on this earth.

Eighth, Jesus taught His disciples to pray.

> Our Father which art in heaven, hollowed be thy name. THY KINGDOM COME THY WILL BE DONE ON EARTH as it is in heaven. (Matthew 6:10)

Has there ever been a time when the kingdom of heaven came to this earth and His will was done on earth as it is in heaven? No, but it will be done during the thousand-year reign of Christ on this earth. Israel rejected her King, but there is coming a day when Jesus shall have His say, and all people on this earth shall bow before Him.

Ninth, Acts 2:29–31 tells us Jesus will sit upon David's throne in Jerusalem and rule for one thousand years.

> Men and brethren let me speak to you of the patriarch [David], that he is both dead and buried, and his sepulcher is with us unto this day [in the day when this verse was written]. Therefore, being a prophet, and knowing that God has sworn with an oath to him, that of the fruit of his loins, according to the flesh, He would raise up Jesus Christ to set on his throne.

Has Jesus ever sat on David's throne to rule this earth since God raised Him from the dead? No, He has not, but He will during His thousand-year reign on this earth.

Tenth, Revelation 11:15 tells us,

> And the seventh angel sounded; and there was a great voice, saying: THE KINGDOMS OF THIS WORLD ARE BECOME THE KINGDOMS OF THE LORD, AND OF HIS CHRIST, and he shall reign forever.

This verse is teaching that there shall be no end to the Lord's reign in eternity. When the thousand-year reign of Christ ends here on earth, we will step off into eternity and live with Him forever in that new city called New Jerusalem. Someone might say if that be true, why should He have thousand-year reign on earth? God's purpose is to put down all rule and all authority and restore this earth to Jesus Christ who was and still is rejected.

Eleventh, notice 1 Corinthians 15:28,

> And when all things shall be subdued under Him, then the Son also himself be subdued unto Him (God) that put all things under Him, that God may be all in all."

Those who deny the thousand-year millennial reign of Christ and try to disapprove the eleven observations above, will understand the truth of the matter when Jesus comes back to set up His kingdom here on earth.

The sixth subject in the outline is found in 1 Corinthians 15:29–34, and it is about the resurrection of believers.

I must first clear up the misunderstanding people have about 1 Corinthians 15:29.

> Else what shall they do who are baptized for the dead, if the dead rise not at all? Why then are they baptized for the dead?

There are four interpretations to this verse of Scripture that I know of. One group use this verse to promote their doctrine of baptismal regeneration. Another group interprets this verse by saying someone can be baptized for dead loved ones to get them into heaven. The third group say this verse is teaching believers are baptized to witnessing to those who are dead in trespasses and sins. The fourth group teaches that baptism is senseless if the dead rise not.

The above verse is not teaching baptismal regeneration, nor being baptized for a dead loved one to bring him/her to salvation, nor witnessing to those who are dead in trespasses and sins. The above Scripture is teaching that baptism is senseless if the dead rise not. Paul is saying, if there is no resurrection and no life after death, then why do people come to Christ and follow Him in baptism? He is saying people are being baptized because they believe the dead will come back with Christ when He comes to rule this earth for a thousand years. He is saying, if the dead do not rise like Christ arose, why get baptized like those who died believing in the resurrection?

According to the *Analytical Greek Lexicon*, the word *for* came from the Greek word *huper*.

It has many meanings, such as "above," "over," "for the hope of," "instead of," "on behalf of." For example, *huper* is used in Philippians 2:13 that says,

> *For* [on behalf of God] *it is God who works in you to will and to do for His good pleasure.*

The Greek word *huper* used here cannot mean "instead of." If it did, it would read, "For it is God who works inside of you instead of His good pleasure." That would not make sense. Neither does 1 Corinthians 15:29 make sense if the words *instead of* or *on behalf of* are used. You must interpret a Scripture according to its contents. Paul is not talking about being baptized instead of but on behalf of.

Keep in mind, baptism is an outward act of an inward change in a person's life. It is a testimony that Christ died, was buried, and rose again. It is an act of identifying oneself with Christ. If one could get salvation by being baptized in water, then being baptized for the dead would make sense. But it does not work that way. The reason Paul mentioned being baptized for the dead is that dead people will be raised to life, and if there is no resurrection, why get baptized to start with?

First Corinthians 15:30 tells us we are in jeopardy [in danger of losing] if we do not believe Christians will be raised.

And why stand we in jeopardy every hour?

Paul suffered many things from his enemies because of his stand for Christ and his belief in the resurrection. Why would he risk his life daily if there was no resurrection from the dead? Paul wanted us to know his hope was anchored in Christ who rose from the grave. That is where our hope is anchored.

Notice 1 Corinthians 15:31,

> I protest [protest here means to declare some-
> thing to be true] by your rejoicing which I have
> in Christ Jesus our Lord, I die daily.

Paul continually sacrificed his life in the arena of persecution. His life was always in danger. His objective was to serve his Lord regardless of his circumstances. He declared in Philippines 1:21.

> For me to live is Christ, and to die is gain.

That is a good attitude to have, isn't it? Paul is saying, "If I live, I win. If I die, I win." Whether Paul lived or died, he is saying "I win." His objective was to serve his Lord. In 2 Timothy 4:8, Paul said,

> Henceforth there is laid up for me a crown of
> righteous, which the Lord, the righteous judge
> shall give me...

Paul adds an illustration to show how hopeless life would be if there is no resurrection for believers,

> If after the manner of man, I have fought with
> beasts at Ephesus, what advantageth it me, if the
> dead rise not? Let us eat and drink for tomorrow
> we die. (1 Corinthians 15:32)

Paul is saying, "The way I have suffered for the cause of Christ leaves me empty and void of meaning if there is no resurrection." We can relate to that, can't we? If there is no hope of a resurrection of our bodies, we may as well live life to its fullness and spend everything to satisfy the flesh. If we have no hope of being resurrected, we may as well get all the gusto we can, because tomorrow we all die, and that will be the end of life. After all, what else is there to life if there is no resurrection? It's empty, void, and meaningless. Reminds me of the sad but true poem "Ring-a-round the Roses." The great plague of London, caused by flea bites from infected rats, lasted eighteen months and killed more than one hundred thousand people. Someone suggested people carry a pocket full of dead roses, and if they sniff the ashes, it would create an immunity to the plague. That didn't work, as you very well know. Ironically, someone wrote a poem that described the foolishness of such an idea. The poem goes like this: "Ring-a-round the roses, pocket full of posies. Ashes! Ashes! We all fall down."

If there is no resurrection for us, the only thing we can anticipate "we all fall down." But thank God, there will be a resurrection. We shall rejoice on that resurrection day when our souls return from heaven to reunite with our bodies that sleep in the grave. We will then go to be with our Heavenly Father and live with Him forever. That is our hope—a hope that is "steadfast and sure!"

Think about the unsaved. Anyone who rejects Jesus Christ and does not receive Jesus Christ as Saviour will be lost forever. The reason people believed that there is no resurrection of believers is because they heard someone teach it. However, 1 Corinthians 15:33 tells us the wise avoids evil communications.

> Be not deceived, evil communications corrupt
> good manners.

This verse is saying, "If you want to get on the wrong track, start listening to worldly advice, it will cause you to act like morons and corrupt you and lead you astray."

In 1 Corinthians 15:34, Paul gave some good advice to those in the Corinthian church, who did not believe in the resurrection of believers.

> Awake to righteousness and sin not: for some
> have not the knowledge of God: I speak this to
> your shame.

Of course, Paul is not only referring to the Corinthian church but people of today as well.

The seventh subject in the outline is found in 1 Corinthians 15:35–50, and it majors on the certainty of the resurrection of believers.

None of the creators of false religions arose from the dead. Mohammed, Buddha, and all other creators of false religions who died did not come back to life. Only Christ arose from the dead. It's politically correct to embrace all religions because, they say, all religions lead to God. No, all religions do not lead to God. Christ is the only way to get to God. Some know and accept that, but others do not. Some in the Corinthian church did not believe in the resurrection, nor had they accepted Christ as their Saviour. Paul chided them for their deliberate ignorance. In fact, he said in 1 Corinthians 6:5,

> I speak to your shame. Is it so, that there is not a
> wise man among you?

Paul is saying, it's sad you believe in entropy (decay of the body) and yet do not believe in the resurrection. We see entropy happening every day, all around us. In fact, Genesis 3:19 tells us,

> From dust thou art and unto dust shalt thou return.

Only God can reverse the law of entropy and make the earth return to the way it was before Adam sinned. That will happen during the thousand-year reign of Christ upon this earth.

Some questioned the certainty of the resurrection because they do not understand the difference between the heavenly body and the earthly body. Notice 1 Corinthians 15:35,

> But some man will say, how are the dead raised up, and with what bodies do they come?

Paul answers this question in 1 Corinthians 15:36–38,

> Thou fool [don't be foolish], that which thou sowest is not quickened, unless it dies. And that which thou sowest, thou sowest not the body that shall be, but bear grain, it may chance of wheat, or of some other grain. But God gives it a body as it has pleased Him and every seed his own body.

Paul is saying, don't be foolish by listing to those who do not believe in the resurrection. He used the wheat illustration to show how wheat comes to life again after it is planted in the ground. Decomposition sets in, and it ceases to exist in its formal state. But new life of the seed comes from inside the dead shell. It will be the same as the one that was planted, yet different. God gives new life to a grain of wheat, just like God gives new life to those who are raised from the dead at the rapture. Jesus said in John 12:24,

> Verily, verily, I say unto you, except a corn of wheat falls into the ground and dies, it abideth alone: but if it dies it brings forth much fruit.

Here Paul compared a seed to the certainty of the believer's resurrection. The new body that comes forth will be the same body that was buried in the ground, only it will be a glorified body. The seed Paul refers to will be the same seed, so will our bodies except we will arise with a glorified body.

Every seed is different from each other, but once a specific seed is planted, the new seeds remains the same as the ones that were planted but different because they are new seeds. They bring forth new seeds which spring forth from the dead seed that was planted. Wheat will not change to corn. Neither will the body change to something else. Notice how Paul explained it in 1 Corinthians 15:39,

> All flesh is not of the same flesh, but there is one kind of flesh of man, another flesh of beast, another of fish and another of birds.

This Scriptures make it clear that different seeds are not from the same seed, so is it with the flesh of man and animals. Paul states that there is a difference between species.

The atheists and evolutionists believe all flesh is of the same flesh. Their argument is, since all flesh came into existence from only one kind of life source at the beginning, all flesh is of the same flesh. The above Scripture disagrees with that, and rightly so, because species cannot cross. For example, a horse cannot crossbred with a cow. A dog cannot cross bread with a cat, and so on. That is very obvious. Have you ever seen a half horse and half cow? Neither have I. If they did cross, there would be at least one fossil out of billions of fossils that have been excavated over the years to prove transitional changes did occur, but there is not one—no, not one. That proves species do not cross. They do not cross because they are not of the same flesh. They do not cross because God made them different. Read 1 Corinthians 15:39 again.

If you plant a grain of corn, the outward part dies, but it has a life source inside that brings forth a new grain of corn—not wheat, not mustard, not peas, but corn only. Evolutionists imply that when a person's body dies it does not bring forth the likeness of the body that was buried, but a different kind of body. For example, they say the dust of a deceased person may come back as an animal. Just think, if they are right, they could come back as a bug, a skunk, a snake, a zebra, a milkweed, or something else, or something worse. Yuck!

They say man came from chimpanzees. They claim humans and chimps have the same DNA; therefore, they are from the same species. That has been proven untrue by Creation Science Research. They do not have the same DNA. That's good to know, isn't it? A belief like they have is stupid!

Evolutionists say things got started from nothing, then life came into existence, and millions of years later through many species changes, man came along. That is simply not true. That's implying things get better, not worse. Things do not get better; they get worse. The law of entropy (decay) states that everything gets old, dies, decays, and falls apart. We know that by observation and by experience. Atheists know that also, yet they believe everything gets better.

Not only does the law of entropy prove species do not cross, but the laws of nature prove species do not cross. wheat brings forth wheat, corn brings forth corn, and so on. That is the law of nature, and that is the way it works. Therefore, atheistic evolution cannot be true because it contradicts all three laws: the law of nature, the law of entropy, and the law of God.

Paul emphasizes the fact that the flesh of mankind will be raised at the rapture. Only it will change from corruptible flesh to incorruptible flesh. First Corinthians 15:40–41 show that there is only one difference in the resurrected body and the earthly body.

> There are also celestial [heavenly] bodies and bodies terrestrial [earthly]: but the glory of the

celestial is one, and the glory of the terrestrial is another. There is one glory of the sun, and another glory of the moon, and another glory of the stars: for one star differs from another star in glory.

These verses simply state that things are different in man when I changed from a terrestrial to a celestial body. Paul wanted his readers to understand that the body is like a grain of corn when planted. It brings forth a vibrant stalk of corn. It does not bring forth something different. Paul also compares the glory of the sun, the glory of the moon, and the glory of stars to show they are different just like the celestial body and the terrestrial body.

Notice 1 Corinthians 15:42–44,

So also is the resurrection of the dead, it is sown in corruption; it is raised in incorruption. It is sown in dishonor: it is raised in glory. It is sown in weakness; it is raised in power. It is sown a natural body; it is raised a spiritual body. There is a natural body, and there is a spiritual body.

First Corinthians 15:45–48 goes on to say,

And so it is written, the first man Adam was made a living soul; the last Adam [Jesus] was made a quickening [life-giving] spirit. Howbeit, that was not first which is spiritual, but that which is natural; and afterward that which is spiritual. The first man [Adam] is of the earth, earthly: the second man is the Lord from heaven. And as the earthly, such are they that are earthly, and as the heavenly, such are they that are heavenly. And as we have borne the image of the earthly, we shall also bear the image of the heavenly.

When we are resurrected from the grave and changed, we will bear a heavenly image. We will have a glorified body that will resemble the glorified body of Christ but look like ourselves. We may resemble His fleshly body He had upon earth. We will not be raised as something different, but like Christ. Notice how 1 Corinthians 15:49 reads:

> As we have borne the image of the earthly, we shall bear the image of the heavenly.

Christ is our only hope, and that makes life worth living.

First Corinthians 15:53 is the eighth subject in the outline, and it deals with the marriage supper of the Lamb.

Notice what 1 Corinthians 15:50–53 says,

> Now this I say, brethren, flesh and blood cannot inherit the kingdom of God; neither doeth corruption inherit incorruption. Behold, I shew you a mystery; we shall not all sleep, but we shall be changed, in a moment, in the twinkling of an eye, at the last trump, for the trump shall sound, and the dead shall be raised incorruptible, and we shall be changed. For this corruptible must put on incorruption, and this mortal must put on immorality.

Immediately after this change, we shall be ushered into the banquet of the marriage supper of the Lamb.

Those who have died believing in Jesus are those the Bible refers to as sleeping in Jesus. The body of believers will sleep in death to await the rapture—the change mentioned above. When a born-again

Christian dies, his body goes in the grave to sleep and his soul goes to be with Jesus. Paul said,

> To be absent from the body is to be present with
> the Lord. (2 Corinthians 5:8)

The believer's soul is released from the body at death and goes to be with Jesus. There is coming a time when this corruptible body shall put on incorruptible. At that time, the soul and body will be reunited again. Notice First Thessalonians 4:16–17,

> For the Lord, Himself, shall descend from heaven
> with a shout, with the voice of archangels, and
> with the trump of God: and the dead [those who
> are asleep in Jesus] shall rise first. Then we which
> are alive and remain shall be caught up together
> with them in the clouds to meet the Lord in the
> air: and shall ever be with the Lord.

Therefore, immediately after the rapture, all born-again Christians of all ages are taken up to heaven to enjoy the marriage supper of the Lamb.

> Blessed are those which are called to the marriage
> supper of the Lamb. (Revelation 19:9).

Paul says,

Comfort one another with these words.

What is the marriage supper of the Lamb, and how will it occur? First, after the rapture, the bride (the church of the born again) will meet her bridegroom (Jesus) to be personally united together forever. Therefore, the bride is the church—you and me, and the Groom is Jesus.

During the ceremony of the marriage supper of the Lamb, unbelievers will go through the seven-year tribulation period here on earth. Their final destination will be in hell to suffer forever for missing the marriage supper of the Lamb. Missing the marriage supper of the Lamb will be the most horrific experience in one's life, and that horrid feeling will last forever.

I have taken some of the information about the marriage supper of the Lamb from a sermon by Charles Spurgeon and edited it and included some things to fit modern day English.

The marriage supper of the Lamb is God's personified art piece of the Bible. It is remarkably described in detail. The apostle John, who was deposed to the isle of Patmos, was commanded by God to write Revelation 19:9.

> Blessed are they which are called to the marriage supper of the Lamb.

Even though these words were written by John, there is no doubt they were spoken by God Himself, because verse 9 continues with, "these are the true sayings of God." God spoke these words.

Revelation 19:9 proves the Word of God is inspired by God. God spoke it, and John wrote it on parchments. If the Scriptures are not inspired, there would be no marriage supper of the Lamb, nor help in a book called the Bible. The Bible would be like all other useless books. We would be without hope, meaning, and purpose in life. But God put Revelation 19:9 in the Bible to show the Scriptures are inspired. Revelation 19:9 was written to give us courage and to prove the Scriptures are inspired by God. It was written to show all Christians will be called to the marriage supper of the Lamb. It was written to give us something to look forward to.

Revelation 19:9 is not to be mulled over like the Athenians and strangers did in Athens. Acts 17:21 said,

> The Athenians and strangers spent their time in nothing else, but either to tell, or hear some new thing.

It's ultimately important we believe the inspired, inerrant, infallible Word of God. There will be a marriage supper of the Lamb. Believe that, because it will happen.

First, Christians who are born again will be called to the marriage supper of the Lamb. Notice 1 Thessalonians 4:16–17,

> For the LORD HIMSELF shall descend from heaven with a shout, with the voice of the archangels and with the trump of God: and the dead in Christ shall rise first: then we which are alive and remain shall be caught up together to be with them in the cloud, to meet the Lord in the air, and so shall we ever be with the Lord.

Immediately after the rapture, the marriage supper of the Lamb will occur.

A. There is no marriage if there is no Groom. Who then is the Groom? John 1:26 gives us insight into the identity of the Groom. John the Baptist said,

    Behold the LAMB which taketh away the sins of the world.
    The word *lamb* is referring to Jesus. Jesus is the Lamb, the Groom, at the marriage supper of the Lamb.

B. Who then is the *bride*? Revelation 22:17 says,

    The Spirit and the BRIDE say come. And let him that hears, say come; and whosoever will, let him take of the water of life freely.
    This Scripture refers only to all born-again Christians. Therefore, all born-again Christians are the *bride*. Jesus is engaged to be married to the

bride, the church of the born again. Revelation 19:7 says,

The marriage of the Lamb is come, and His wife has made herself ready.
That is, His wife has made herself ready by putting her faith in Jesus for salvation.

C. What is the meaning of the marriage supper of the Lamb? It means Christians who are dead in Christ and those who are alive in Christ will be caught up to be with the Lord Jesus Christ at the rapture.

Blessed are they which are called to the marriage supper of the Lamb. (Revelation 19:9)

This marriage shall occur after the rapture, and the ceremony will last for seven years. The earth will be going through the seven-year tribulation period.

Second, there is a tremendous blessing for those who are called to the marriage supper of the Lamb. Revelation 19:9 states,

BLESSED ARE THEY which are called to the marriage supper of the Lamb.

You have promises from the Word of God that blesses you right now, yet the blessing at the marriage supper of the Lamb is the ultimate blessing of all. If you were promised a gift that consisted of a mansion and promised you could move in tomorrow, you could say, "I go home today to a run-down, decaying house, but tomorrow I move into a mansion." That would be a blessing indeed! Think about it! We will have the greatest blessing ever when we are united forever at the marriage supper of the Lamb. We have the promise of something so great it is almost unimaginable. God's blessing is a promise God made to us, and it cannot be broken.

Third, I feel it will not be long until we go to the marriage supper of the Lamb. It may be today, or tomorrow, or next month, or a thousand years from now, but what is a thousand years compared to eternity. We shall share the glory that awaits us. We will live in comfort and happiness forever with our groom, the Lord Jesus Christ.

We can be certain we shall stand with our Groom at the marriage supper of the Lamb to be united with Him forever. Then after the seven years of tribulation here on earth pass, and after the thousand-year reign with Christ on earth is passed, we will move into our new mansion—New Jerusalem with Jesus—to never be separated from Him again.

In that new city there will be no need for the sun or moon, for Jesus our Groom shall be the light of that city; and there shall be one eternal day, for there shall be no night there.

> Blessed are they that are called to the marriage
> supper of the Lamb. (Revelation 19:9)

We will be there with our Groom, never to be separated again. We will be there as the bride of Christ that is married to Jesus. Thank God, that will lead to our forever honeymoon, a honeymoon that shall never cease.

Fourth, Jesus, our Bridegroom, will be delighted and satisfied with us, and we shall be delighted and satisfied with Him.

> Blessed are they that are called to the marriage
> supper of the Lamb. (Revelation 19:9)

The best of marriages in this life are not always full of joy and happiness. Couples are not content with each other all the time. There is no greater joy to know Jesus will be eternally delighted and content with us, and we shall be eternally delighted and content with Him. What a marriage! What a blessing!

There will be no need for hospitals, funerals homes, police force, locks on doors, or security systems. Every sickness, every heartache, every pain will be gone. We will live in perfect peace, perfect health, perfect safety, and be perfectly content forever. Think about that!

> Blessed are thy that are called to the marriage supper of the Lamb. (Revelation 19:9)

Now comes the sad part, and it is about missing the marriage supper of the Lamb. There are dire consequences for missing the marriage supper of the Lamb. I must say again that there are dire consequences for missing the marriage supper of the Lamb. The Scriptures reminds us time and time again that God's mercy and tolerance will not last forever.

> Behold, the day of the Lord cometh, cruel and with fierce anger. (Isaiah 13:9)

> The sun shall be turned into darkness, and the moon into blood, before the great and terrible day of the Lord. (Joel 2:31)

> The great day of the Lord…is a day of wrath, a day of trouble and destress, a day of vastness and desolation a day of darkness and gloominess, a day of clouds and thick darkness. (Zephaniah 1:14–15)

> The day of the Lord will come as a thief in the night; in the which the heavens shall pass away with a great noise, and the elements shall melt with fervent heat. (2 Peter 3:10)

Notice some other Scripture verses that describe the horrific consequences of missing the marriage supper of the Lamb. James 3:6 says,

> The tongue shall be set on fire of hell.

Luke 16:23–24 says this about the rich man who died without accepting Jesus as his Saviour,

> And in hell he lifted up his eyes, and sees Abraham afar off, and Lazarus in his bosom [heaven]. And he cried and said, "Father Abraham, have mercy on me and send Lazarus, that he may dip his finger in water, and cool my tongue, for I am tormented in these flames."

Hell is a place of everlasting fire. Revelation 21:8 gives a partial list of those who will go there.

> The fearful, and unbelievers, and the abominable, and murders, and whoremongers and sorcerers, and idolaters, and all liars, shall have their part in the lake which burns with fire and brimstone...
> Then shall He say to them on the left hand, depart from Me, you cursed, into everlasting fire. (Matthew 25:41)

> And the beast (Satan) and with him the false prophets...was cast alive into the lake of fire burning with brimstone. (Revelation 19:20)

> And whosoever was not found written in the book of life was cast into the lake of fire. (Revelation 20:15)

Those who die here on earth who are unsaved will live forever in a place characterized by evil and fire. Every lost soul shall be sent there. What a terrifying ghastly scene.

If there was no hell, missing the marriage supper of the Lamb would be hell. If there was no torment, missing the marriage supper of the Lamb would be torment. If there was no everlasting punishment, missing the marriage supper of the Lamb would be punishment beyond description. But those who miss the marriage supper of the Lamb will suffer the eternal consequences of hell fire.

A preacher I know who turned from believing in God to atheism said, "I don't believe in God any longer. He said, if it turns out that there is a God, and I meet Him, I will tell him to go to hell." (Those are his exact words.) No, he won't say that. He will fall on his face and cry out for mercy and the rocks to fall on him and hide him from the face of the Lamb.

Missing the marriage supper of the Lamb means a forever existence in the flames of hell. Oh, what sorrow. Oh, what remorse. Oh, what eternal regret. Oh, what agony to face eternity without hope, without heaven, without seeing your friends or family again. Please don't miss the marriage supper of the Lamb! Repent and receive Jesus as your Saviour now.

Every unbeliever's body will be raised from the dead to stand before God at the Great White Throne Judgment, and they will be judged and cast into the lake of fire. They will suffer eternal consequences for rejecting Jesus as their Saviour. There will be terrifying pain, horrific sullen groans, and shrieks of torture. Don't fool yourself, unbeliever, you will be damned in the same body that was placed in the grave. Your soul, your spirit, and your body will be cast into the lake of fire. However, your body will be a new body in one respect. It will be a body unable to be consumed by fire. Your soul and body will suffer forever. Your soul, body, and spirit will suffer with unceasing pain.

As saints of God, we will be like Jesus and raised with our glorified bodies, but you, unbeliever, shall be like your father the devil and raised to suffer hell in your torched bodies. You shall be judged and then cast into the lake of fire to burn in agony forever. You shall suffer the powers of death, yet you shall live. You shall be crushed by the stern powers of death, but you shall never die. You will endure an eternity of unutterable agony and woe. That should make you tremble in fear unbeliever, and it should make you cry out to God for mercy and salvation.

Believers shall stand before the Bema Seat of God, and the unbelievers shall stand before the Great White Throne Judgment seat of God, and both shall give an account for their deeds done in the body.

Daniel 12:2 prophesied,

> That many of them that sleep in the dust of the earth shall awake, some to everlasting life, and some to everlasting shame and contempt.

Contempt means "one who disobeys or despises the court's decisions." In the case of the Scripture above, *contempt* means those who reject Jesus while here on earth will be confined to a place of everlasting punishment. Many have rejected, laughed at, and ridiculed God's decisions, but in hell they are faced with the punishment for their decisions.

The same body in which a person sins and rejects Christ will be the same body that will be raised to stand before the Great White Throne Judgment to be condemned and cast into hell. Nowhere in the Bible does it say unbelievers will get a new body. John said in Revelation 20:12,

> I saw the dead [unbelievers who died without Christ] small and great, stand before God; and the books were open: and another book was opened, which is the book of life, and the dead were judged out of those things which were written in the book, according to their works.

Revelation 20:15 states,

> Whosoever was not found in the book of life was
> cast into the lake of fire.

If a person rejects Christ and dies in his sins, he will be judged and confined to hell forever. He will not get a new body, but will be cast into hell with the body he had here upon earth.

If unbelievers had to spend a thousand years in hell and then get out, they would have something to look forward to. If they had to stay in hell a million years, or ten billion years, or a trillion years and then get out, they would have something to look forward to, but they will never have anything to look forward to, because they will never get out of hell. They will spend eternity in the fires of hell without hope, without friends, without family, and without a chance of every getting out. That sounds horrid, cruel, and underserving, but consider the cruel and painful hell Jesus endured to keep unbelievers out of hell, and you will agree unbelievers deserve hell. It is sad people reject the sacrificial love Jesus had for them and choose hell over Him. All who reject Him choose hell over receiving Him as their Saviour. When an unbeliever dies, his body is placed in the grave to await the resurrection when his soul will be united with his body that died without Christ. But the very moment his soul dies, it lifts up its eyes in hell. Luke 16:22–23 tells us,

> The rich man died and lifted up his eyes in hell.

This is a morbid picture, but it's an event that will really happen to those who do not receive Jesus as their Saviour.

Someone said, "If there is a loving God, He would not send anyone to hell." God does not send people to hell. Regardless of what Jesus did for unbelievers, they reject Him, and they themselves choose to go to hell. They reject Him and choose hell over His love and forgiveness.

The same resurrected bodies of unbelievers will be the same decrepit bodies that were placed in the grave. The resurrected body of unbelievers will never have a new body like born-again Christians.

It may be that not many people know you here on earth, but you will be known in hell. For example, if you were a sex pervert here on earth, you will be known as a sex pervert in hell. You will be known by what you were here on earth. Your identity will not change. It will not be like that in heaven. Revelation 21:27 states,

> There shall in no wise enter into the city of God anything that defiles, neither whatever worketh abomination, or maketh a lie; but they that are written in the book of life.

Unbeliever, as you were here on earth, so shall you be in hell. The same hideous gaze that characterized your face when you first learned of your destiny in hell will remain with you forever. It's like the feelings, and looks, you get by being attacked by a pack of wolves, but worse. Oh, what regret! Oh, what remorse! Oh, what pain you will suffer. Oh, the darkness you will experience in hell. Oh, the condemnation that holds you in hell. Oh, what pain to know you made the worst mistake in your life by not preparing for the marriage supper of the Lamb. Unbeliever, please don't miss the marriage supper of the Lamb. Don't miss heaven. You only have one chance to make it right with God, and that must be done on this side of the grave when the Holy Spirit is dealing with you.

Perhaps you have heard many sermons that warned you of hell, but you laughed. There is no time to laugh after you die. You can only blame yourself because you rejected Christ and plunged yourself into the flames of hell. You cannot blame God. God did everything possible to keep you out of hell. If you go to hell you go as an intruder, and against God's will, it's not God's will that any go to hell. Second Peter 3:9 states,

> The Lord is not slack concerning His promises, as some men call slackness, but is long suffering

[extremely patient] toward us, not willing that any should perish, but that all should come to repentance.

Confess to God that you are a sinner deserving hell. Repent and surrender your life to Jesus Christ. Surrender all. Commit your life to Jesus and serve Him and Him only. In desperation, like a drowning man, cry out to Jesus Christ for mercy and forgiveness and receive Him as your only rescuer from hell.

The following song, "The Great Judgment Morning," by Bertram H. Shaddock (1894), describes the eternal horrid existence without Christ.

I dreamed that the great judgment morning had dawned, and the trumpet had blown;

I dreamed that the nations had gathered to judgment before the White Throne.

From the throne came a bright shining angel, and stood on land and on sea, and swore with His hands raised to heaven that time was no longer to be. (Revelation 10:6)

The rich man was there, but his riches had melted and vanished away; a pauper he stood at the judgment, his debt was too heavy to pay.

The great men were there, but their greatness, when death came, was left far behind. The angel that opened the records, not a trace of their greatness could find.

The moral man and woman came to the judgment, but their self-righteous rags would not do, the people who crucified Jesus passed off as moral men too.

The soul that put off salvation, "Not tonight," he said, "I'll get saved by and by." No time now to think of salvation. At last he found time to die.

And oh, what weeping and wailing as the lost were told of their fate, they prayed to the rocks and mountains to fall on them, they prayed but their prayers were too late.

Don't put off salvation. Don't miss the marriage supper of the Lamb! Repent and receive Jesus Christ as your own personal Saviour. Receive Jesus now. Do it now! Do it now! Do it now! You may never get another chance.

When you repent and receive Jesus as your Saviour, you will become a member of God's family and be assured a place at the marriage supper of the Lamb. Come to Jesus now, and you too can become a member of God's family.

I must say this in closing this section: You don't just decide one day to become a member of God's family; you must experience the conviction power of the Holy Spirit. Do you feel that conviction power now, right now? Repent and receive Jesus Christ as your Saviour right now. Do it for God's sake and for the sake of your eternal soul, spirit, and body. Don't put off salvation. If the Holy Spirit is dealing with you now, don't miss the marriage supper of the Lamb by ignoring Him. If you're experiencing the convicting power of God, it's not too late to be saved. Surrender to Him now because you may never get another chance. Give your life to Jesus right now before it's too late! Don't be left behind. The rapture is about to take place.

First Corinthians 15:51–58 is the ninth subject in the outline, and it shows us how the rapture of the church will occur.

Paul explains the rapture in verses 51–58. Let's read it.

Behold I show you a mystery; we shall not all sleep, but shall all be changed in a moment, in a twinkling of an eye, at the last trump: for the trump shall sound and the dead shall be raised incorruptible, and we shall be changed. For this corruptible must put on incorruptible, and this

mortal shall put on immortality. Then shall be
brought to pass the saying that is written. Death
is swallowed up in victory.

The phrase *we shall not all sleep* refers to those living when the
rapture takes place. Those who sleep in Jesus refers to those who died
from Adam down to this present day who died trusting in Jesus for
salvation. The body sleeps until the rapture, but the soul and spirit
go to be with Jesus at death.

When I refer to those who "sleep" in Jesus, I must emphasize
there is no such thing as soul-sleep. Sometime back I went to a grave-
side funeral of someone I knew. The officiating minister said, "Our
dear friend's soul, body, and spirit will sleep until the Lord comes to
get him." That is not true—that is not true! Second Corinthians 5:6
and 8 tell us why that is not true. Paul said,

> Therefore, we are always confident, knowing
> that, while we are at home in the body [that is,
> our souls and spirits are at home in our fleshly
> bodies], we are absent from the Lord.

When we die, our souls and spirits go to be with Jesus in heaven.
Paul said in 2 Corinthians 5:8,

> We are confident, I say, and willing rather to be
> absent from the body, and to be present with the
> Lord.

Paul is saying at death the believer's soul and spirit goes to be
with Jesus. The body is just a shell in which the soul and spirit lives.
The body is placed in the grave to sleep until the rapture takes place,
then the soul and spirit reunite. Notice 1 Thessalonians 4:13–14,

> I would not have you be ignorant, brethren, con-
> cerning them which are asleep [dead], that you
> sorrow not, even as others which have no hope.

> For if we believe Jesus died and rose again, even
> so also them which sleep in Jesus will God bring
> back with Him.

What does Paul mean by saying, "Jesus will bring them back with Him"?

If it is not the soul and spirits of saints who have been raptured, who then is it? The fact is, God's saints will come back to be united with their body at the rapture and then rule and reign with Christ for a thousand years on this earth. Paul is stating the fact that Jesus will bring them back with Him. This can only mean the souls and spirits of believers who go to be with Jesus at death. The souls and spirits of believers do not sleep; they go to be with Jesus at death. Then at the rapture, Jesus brings them back to be united with their glorified bodies. That glorified body will be raised from the grave.

Also notice the word *mystery* in verses 51–58. What is the mystery? The mystery is that the souls and spirits of believers go to be with Jesus at death because of what Jesus did to provide salvation for them. First Corinthians 15:52–58 explains the mystery because it was never explained in the Old Testament like it is in the New Testament by Jesus Christ. Notice 1 Corinthians 15:52 how it states that Jesus will come.

> In a moment, in the twinkling of an eye, at the
> last trump: for the trumpet shall sound, and the
> dead shall be raised incorruptible, and we shall
> be changed.

The rapture could take place at any moment. It will happen in a twinkling of an eye. We shall be changed, not in a blink of the eye, but in a twinkle of the eye. Someone said a twinkle is a millionth of a second.

People think they can wait until they see Christians go up then they will get saved. No, they won't. They won't have time. If they wait until then, it will be too late. Second Thessalonians 2:11 states that those who put off salvation and miss the rapture, God will give them a strong delusion that they will believe a lie and be damned.

> For this cause [because they were exposed to the Truth, but did not receive the Truth.] God shall send them strong delusions, that they shall believe a lie: that they all may be damned who believed not the truth.

One must believe and be saved before the rapture.

First Corinthians 15:53–54 tells us what kind of bodies we will have after the rapture. Our bodies will be changed. Notice verses 53–54,

> For this corruptible must put on incorruptible, and this mortal must put on immorality. So, when this corruptible shall have put on incorruption, and this mortal shall have put on immorality then shall be brought to pass the saying that is written, Death is swallowed up in victory.

The very moment the rapture takes place we shall get a new body and go to the marriage supper of the Lamb.

The above Scriptures list three changes that will occur at the rapture: corruptible must put on incorruptible, mortal must put on immorality, and death will be swallowed up in victory. First Corinthians 15:55–57 promises us victory over death, victory over the grave, victory over the sting of sin, and victory over strength of sin. All these promises come to us from our Lord Jesus Christ.

> O death, where is thy sting? O grave, where is thy victory? The sting of death is sin; [means sin brings death] and the strength of sin is the law [the strength of the law shows us how wicked sin is], but thanks be to God which giveth us the victory through our Lord Jesus Christ.

First Corinthians 15:58 is the tenth subject in the outline, and it emphasizes the important of steadfastness.

Paul concludes this chapter by urging us to be steadfast, unmovable, and always abounding in the work of the Lord. If we do these, we can rest assured our labor is not in vain in the Lord. We can know we are accomplishing something.

> Therefore, my beloved brethren, be ye steadfast, unmovable, always abounding in the work of the Lord, forasmuch as you know that your labor is not in vain in the Lord.

CHAPTER 16

HAS THREE SUBJECTS

Verses 1–12 are about Christians supporting saints in Jerusalem. Verses 13–18 teach that Christians should do everything with love. Verses 19–24 present Paul's benediction and farewell.

The first subject of the outline is found in 16:1–12, and it is about supporting God's saints in Jerusalem.

Paul encouraged the Corinthian church to following his lead in raising money for needy saints in Jerusalem. Notice 16:1,

> Now concerning the collection for the saints, as I have given orders to the church of Galatia, even so do you.

Funds were previously solicited by Paul in Galatia as well as Macedonia, and churches in Achaia. Paul mentioned the church of Galatia as an example of giving.

> In a great trial of affliction, the abundance of their joy and their deep poverty abounded in the riches of their liberality. (2 Corinthians 8:2)

Paul encouraged the Corinthian church to give like the Galatia church.

Paul tells us how important it is for churches of today to support God's work. That is why God chose Paul to set a good example of giving. God blesses us by allowing us to give to His cause. We give because it is God's desire. Not only should we give to support our home church, but we should give to churches of like faith that needs our help. Our church must have a strong mission program in our community, but support, assist, and help other churches and other ministries in other places of the world as well. One church cannot reach the world by itself, but it can financially help other churches get the Gospel to other areas of the world by giving to support missionary outreach programs.

Some churches contribute to their denomination, and a portion goes to support missionaries and mission programs. Other churches support their mission programs through "faith promise giving." They promise to give so much each week as God gives to them. There are other methods churches use to support their church and outreach ministries, but Paul instructs us in the best way to give. Notice 1 Corinthians 16:2,

> Upon the first day of the week [Sunday] let every one of you lay by him in store, as God has prospered him, that there be no gathering when I come.

Regardless of how you give, or the method you use, you are to plan ahead in your giving. Give as God has prospered you. Paul urged the Corinthian church to follow suit and give generously.

Allow me to sidetrack a moment and comment on the above Scripture that uses the phrase "upon the first day of the week."

The question arises: On what day should the church meet? The above Scripture implies that the early church met on Sunday. They met on Sunday at the church in Corinth as Paul instructed them to do. We meet on Sunday because we worship Jesus who arose on Sunday. We worship Jesus, not the Sabbath.

The above Scripture does not specify giving a certain percentage, but giving as God has "prospered" you to give. Giving the way the New Testament teaches is to give freely. In Luke 6:38, Jesus said,

> Give and it shall be given unto you…for with the same measure you meet withal it shall be measured to you again.

Some look at this verse as an investment that returns double back to them. We are to give expecting nothing in return. This verse is teaching God will bless us in proportion to our giving, but He does not specify a certain amount, nor does He say we will get back double what we give.

We should first plan on how we should give and then give as we planned to give. Someone said, "What you are destined to become is what you have decided to become." I think we should apply that principle to our giving. The amount we are destined to give is the amount we have decided to give.

When we plan our giving, we should keep 2 Corinthians 9:6–7 in mind,

> But this I say, He which soweth sparingly shall also reap sparingly, and he which soweth bountifully shall also reap bountifully. Every man according as he purposeth in his heart, so let him give, not grudgingly, or of necessity, for God loveth a cheerful giver.

A certain percentage amount of giving is not required in the New Testament dispensation because our giving should not be given out of constraint, neither of necessity, but what we have purposed in our hearts to give, we are to give. Therefore, we should give as we have decided to give.

Paul was willing to take the offering he collected to the saints in Jerusalem if it was necessary. Notice 1 Corinthians 16:3–4,

> And when I come whomsoever you shall approve by your letter, them will I send to bring you liberality unto Jerusalem. And if it be meet [necessary] then I go also.

Paul is saying, "Whomsoever you appoint to take your gift to Jerusalem, you have my approval in sending them with a letter, and if it be fitting for me to go with them, I will go."

At the end of Paul's third-year stay in Ephesus, his intention was to visit Corinth once again. Notice 1 Corinthians 16:5–7,

> Now I shall come to you when I pass through Macedonia: for I do pass through Macedonia. It may be that I will abide, yea, and winter with you, that you may bring me on my journey whithersoever I go. I will not see you by the way, but I trust to tarry a while with you if the Lord permits.

Paul's itinerary was to pass through Macedonia, and perhaps visit some of the cities there, but he first stopped at Ephesus in Asia. He probably wrote his second letter to the Corinthian church from Ephesus and gave it to Timothy to deliver. Paul had the opportunity of establishing a great ministry at Ephesus; however, he met immense opposition and persecution. Notice 1 Corinthians 16:8–9,

> But I will tarry at Ephesus until Pentecost. For a great door, and effectual is open unto me, and there are many adversaries.

Paul is saying, "This door of opportunity has the potential of bringing great results and many to Christ, but there are many apposing me." It has always been that way. When you start something for the Lord, there will be opposition. Those who oppose you will offer many reasons you should not do it. If opposition does not work, the devil will use persecution in various forms to stop God's work. His objective is to stop God's work in any way he can and take as many to hell as he can. Regardless of the oppositions we face, we are to take advantage of the opportunities we have.

Paul had a desire to visit the Corinthian church earlier, but had to delay his visit because there was a door of opportunity in Ephesus. Therefore, he sent Timothy and wanted to send Apollos also but Apollos refused to go. Notice 1 Corinthians 16:10–12,

> Now if Timothy comes, see that he may be with you without fear: for he worketh the work of the Lord as I also do. Let no man, therefore despise him, but conduct him forth in peace that he may come unto me: for I look for him with the brethren. As touching our brother Apollos, I greatly desired him to come unto you with the brethren: but his will was not at all to come unto you at this time, but he will come when he has convenient time.

First Corinthians 16:13–18 is the second subject in the outline, and it teaches Christians should do everything with love.

Paul urged the church in Corinth to do what they do with love. Notice 1 Corinthians 16:13–14,

> Watch ye [and] stand fast in the faith, quite ye like men, be strong. Let all things be done with charity [love].

There are five important thoughts we need to get hold of in these two verses. They are put here to help us face difficult circumstances that lurk along our paths.

First, "watch ye." Paul had just concluded chapter 15 about the coming again of Christ; therefore, he is reminding the Corinthian church and us to watch for the coming of the Lord. Matthew 24:42 says,

> Watch therefore: for you knoweth not what hour
> our Lord doth come.

Second, *"stand fast in the faith."* Paul admonishes us to never give up—never quit, never turn our backs on God. God is faithful to strengthen us and help us in difficult time. Psalms 123:3 says,

> He will not allow thy foot to be removed, He that
> keepeth thee shall not slumber.

Third, *"quite ye like men."* This means to avoid heated arguments that end up discouraging others instead of helping others. An argument has never strengthened anyone in the Lord, nor won a soul to Christ. We may win an argument, but will never win a soul to Christ by arguing with someone. On the other hand, charity (love) turns a person from resentment to acceptance.

Fourth, *"be strong."* Paul is admonishing the Corinthian Christians, and us, to be strong in the Lord. Therefore, we must fortify ourselves against the devil. How can we best do that? Proverbs 18:10 tells us:

> The name of the Lord is a strong tower. The righ-
> teous runneth into it and is safe.

We run to Jesus who gives us strength to overcome our weaknesses.

Fifth, *"let all things be done with love."* There are a lot of great gifts one can have as a Christian, especially faith and hope, and love, but the greatest is love. Love is the greatest because God is love, and when we love, we are being like God. It takes God's love to overcome resentment and bitterness toward someone else. We can experience that love when we learn what God's Word says about love. I don't know of anything that will turn a person from bitterness to love quicker than God's Word.

Notice 1 Corinthians 16:15,

> I beseech you, brethren, ye know the house of Stephanas, that is the first fruits of Achaia, and they have addicted themselves to the ministry of the saints.

The word *addicted* means "to be dependent on something or hooked on something." The Stephanas family was addicted to ministering to saints and promoting the cause of Christ. Paul writes about the family of Stephanas as a family standing faithful in the faith. His family was among Paul's first converts in Corinth. They were part of the believers Paul himself baptized. Notice 1 Corinthians 1:16,

> And I baptize the household of Stephanas: besides, I know not whether I baptized any other.

Just think about that—being baptized by Paul.

Stephanas visited Paul in Ephesus and was probably the one who delivered the letter mentioned in 1 Corinthians 7:1. Paul said,

> Now concerning the thing you wrote unto me.

We don't have that particular letter, but we have 1 and 2 Corinthians Paul wrote to the Corinthian church, which answered the questions that was in the letter sent to him. Paul is saying the household of Stephanas was so dedicated to God and His service they became addicted to it. I don't know of anything that would please God more than being addicted to serving Him and ministering to others.

Paul urged the church of Corinth to follow the example of Stephanas. Notice 1 Corinthians 16:16–18,

> That you submit yourself to such, and everyone that helps with us, and laboureth.

I am glad of the coming of Stephanas and Fortunatus and Achaicus: for that which was lacking on your part they have supplied. For they have refreshed my spirit and yours, therefore acknowledge ye them that are such.

First Corinthians 16:19–24 is the third and final subject in the outline, and it deals with Paul's benediction and farewell.

First, Aquila and Priscilla and the church in their house sent greetings. Aquila and Priscilla were Paul's closest friends. Think about that! How would you liked to have been Paul's best friend? Paul met Aquila and Pricilla in Corinth because they were deported from Rome. Aquila and Pricilla were tentmakers. Because of them Paul became a tentmaker. That brought a mutual friendship with them. They became friends forever. In fact, wherever you find Paul in his missionary journeys, it's very likely you will find Aquila and Priscilla. When Aquila and Priscilla moved to a different place, they almost always established a church in their home. They remembered they were once homeless without a church because Claudius drove them out of Rome. To say they were tremendous missionaries is an understatement. Notice 1 Corinthians 16:19,

> Aquila and Priscilla salute you much in the Lord, with the church in their house.

Secondly, Paul sent greetings from all his Christian companions. Notice 1 Corinthians 16:20,

> All the brethren greet you. Greet you one another with a holy kiss.

Greeting one another with a holy kiss was a custom for believers in Paul's day. Obviously, and for good reasons, that form of greeting is no longer used today. Hugging is not even appropriate in our day because of the possibility of sexual intent. There is nothing wrong with hugging, but you don't know what the other person is hugging you for. So it's better not to hug the opposite sex.

Notice what Paul said in 16:21,

> The salutation of me Paul with mine own hand. If any man loves not the Lord Jesus Christ, let him be Anathema Maranatha. The grace of our Lord Jesus Christ be with you. My love be with you in Jesus Christ. Amen.

From these Scripture verses, I will mention three things:

Firstly, this Scripture deals with Paul finishing this Corinthian letter and signing it himself. Obviously, Paul had his friend Timothy write this section. Sosthenes wrote the first part of the previous chapters, but Timothy wrote this section, and Paul signed it himself, making it more personal. Notice the phrase,

> The salutation of me Paul with my own hand.

Secondly, Paul gives his final warning in 1 Corinthians 16:22.

> If any man loves not the Lord Jesus Christ, let him be Anathema, Maranatha.

Anathema means "accursed," and *Maranatha* means "O Lord come." Paul said, "If any man loves not the Lord Jesus, let him be accursed." Evidently, Paul was weary and tired, and he wanted the Lord to come. He not only gave this warning to those who do not love Jesus, but emphasized the consequences if anyone did not heed it. First Corinthians 16:22 above can be explained by reading Revelation 22:11,

> He that is unjust, let him be unjust still: he that is filthy, let him be filthy still, and he that is righteous, let him be righteous still, and he that is holy, let him be holy still.

Thirdly, Paul made two comments before completing his letter to the Corinthian church.

First, he prayed for the Lord's grace (unmerited favor) to be upon the Corinthian church (and us). Paul said in 16:23,

> The grace of the Lord Jesus Christ be with you.

Second, he expressed his deep abiding love for them (and us). Notice 16:24,

> My love be with you all in Christ Jesus, Amen.

This concludes the study of 1 Corinthians.

About the Author

Walter became a believer in Christ at the age of 14. A few months later, he convinced the Army Draft Board he was eighteen years old and wanted to join the army. He was accepted, and after spending five years in the army, he moved back to Tennessee where he met the love of his life—Carolyn Davis. They were married on May 15, 1965. After marriage Walter went back to school and finished his High School Education, earning his high school diploma. He then entered Tennessee Temple College and Bible School in 1970. He graduated in 1975 with a BA degree, majoring in psychology and Bible.

After graduation Walter Pastored several Churches, worked on secular jobs and wrote his first book in 2014. First Corinthians is his second book. His prayer is that First Corinthians will change your life as it did his.

Walter passed away Feb. 28, 2020.

CPSIA information can be obtained
at www.ICGtesting.com
Printed in the USA
BVHW072203070621
608952BV00001B/18

9 781098 069759